DANGEROUS HERO

Also by Tom Bower

*Blind Eye to Murder: Britain, America and the Purging of
Nazi Germany – A Pledge Betrayed*

Klaus Barbie: Butcher of Lyon

*The Paperclip Conspiracy: The Battle for the Spoils
and Secrets of Nazi Germany*

Red Web: MI6 and the KGB Master Coup

Maxwell: The Outsider

Tiny Rowland: A Rebel Tycoon

*The Perfect English Spy: Sir Dick White
and the Secret War, 1935–90*

Heroes of World War II

Maxwell: The Final Verdict

*Nazi Gold: The Full Story of the Fifty-Year Swiss–Nazi
Conspiracy to Steal Billions from Europe's Jews and
Holocaust Survivors*

Blood Money: The Swiss, the Nazis and the Looted Billions

Fayed: The Unauthorized Biography

Branson

The Paymaster: Geoffrey Robinson, Maxwell and New Labour

*Broken Dreams: Vanity, Greed and the
Souring of British Football*

Gordon Brown: Prime Minister

Conrad and Lady Black: Dancing on the Edge

The Squeeze: Oil, Money and Greed in the Twenty-First Century

No Angel: The Secret Life of Bernie Ecclestone

Sweet Revenge: The Intimate Life of Simon Cowell

Branson: Behind the Mask

Broken Vows: Tony Blair – The Tragedy of Power

Rebel Prince: The Power, Passion and Defiance of Prince Charles

TOM BOWER

DANGEROUS HERO

CORBYN'S RUTHLESS PLOT FOR POWER

WILLIAM
COLLINS

William Collins
An imprint of HarperCollins*Publishers*
1 London Bridge Street
London SE1 9GF
WilliamCollinsBooks.com

First published in Great Britain by William Collins in 2019

1

A catalogue record for this book is
available from the British Library

HB ISBN 978-0-00-829957-6
TPB ISBN 978-0-00-829958-3

Printed and bound in Great Britain by
CPI Group (UK) Ltd, Croydon, CR0 4YY

MIX
Paper from
responsible sources
FSC
www.fsc.org FSC® C007454

This book is produced from independently certified FSC
paper to ensure responsible forest management.

For more information visit: www.harpercollins.co.uk/green

To Veronica

Contents

Illustrations

The eighteen-year-old Corbyn in Kingston, Jamaica.

Corbyn and his first wife, Jane Chapman. Their marriage would end in divorce. *(Hornsey Journal)*

Keith and Val Veness formed a close political relationship with Corbyn after his return from Jamaica and have remained trusted friends. *(Keith Veness)*

Alec Smith, for whom Corbyn worked at the National Union of Tailors and Garment Workers. *(Allstar Picture Library/ Alamy Stock Photo)*

Protesting NUTGW workers. *(Mary Evans/Marx Memorial Library)*

Corbyn with Ted Knight, the Labour candidate for Hornsey, and other party workers during the 1979 general election campaign. *(Hornsey Journal)*

Tariq Ali's Labour membership application was rejected three times, and Ted Knight was unsuccessful in the 1997 election. *(Hornsey Journal)*

Tony Benn, Corbyn's political mentor. *(Steve Eason/Hulton Archive/Getty Images)*

Corbyn with Ken Livingstone and Sinn Féin leader Gerry Adams. *(Paul Fievez/Daily Mail/REX/Shutterstock)*

Corbyn regularly joined demonstrations and trade union picket lines. *(The Times/News Licensing)*

Corbyn being arrested during a Trotsykist-organised picket against apartheid in 1984. *(Rob Scott Photography)*

Elected to the Commons in 1983, Corbyn forged close relationships with Tony Banks, Diane Abbott and Bernie Grant. *(PA/PA/Archive/PA Photos)*

In 1997 John McDonnell, an established Trotskyist who had struggled to get elected as an MP, was finally elected to the House of Commons. *(Tim Ireland/Xinhua News Agency/PA Images)*

Corbyn's second wife, Claudia Bracchitta. *(Daily Mail)*

Claudia asked former MP Reg Race, a mutual friend of the Corbyns, to advise them about their financial plight. *(Central Press/Getty Images)*

The announcement on 12 September 2015 of Corbyn's victory in the Labour leadership election. *(Jeff J. Mitchell/Getty Images; Lee Thomas/Alamy Stock Photo)*

Corbyn with his third wife, Laura Alvarez. *(Ian Forsyth/Getty Images)*

Corbyn's close political advisers Seumas Milne and Andrew Fisher. *(Ben Cawthra/LNP)*

Corbyn in Gaza with Hamas supporter Ibrahim Hewitt.

Corbyn laying a wreath at the 'Cemetery of the Martyrs of Palestine' in Tunis in 2014. *(Palestine Embassy, Tunis)*

Corbyn at a feast jointly hosted by the Muslim Association of Britain.

In 2009 Corbyn invited Muslim extremist Dyab Abou Jahjah to Britain to publicly denounce Israel, America and Britain.

Although Corbyn attended several meetings with Holocaust denier and anti-Zionist Paul Eisen, after his election as Labour leader he would deny knowing him.

Len McCluskey, the leader of the Unite trade union. *(The Times/News Licensing)*

Karie Murphy, Corbyn's office manager. *(Daniel Leal-Olivas/AFP/Getty Images)*

Labour general secretary Jennie Formby. *(Leon Neal/AFP/Getty Images)*

Corbyn addresses a Stop the War Coalition rally. *(Nigel R. Barklie/REX/Shutterstock)*

Corbyn with exiled Kurdish activist Ihsan Qaesr. *(Keith Veness)*

'Freedom for Humanity', the mural by American artist Kalen Ockerman ('Mear One') that was removed by Tower Hamlets council.

2018 protest in Parliament Square against anti-Semitism. *(Wiktor Szymanowicz/Barcroft Media via Getty Images)*

Luciana Berger receives police protection at the 2018 Labour conference. *(Leon Neal/Getty Images)*

Louise Ellman's campaign against the far left's anti-Semitism exposed her to gross intimidation. *(Rena Pearl/Alamy Stock Photo)*

Ian Austin, a vociferous Westminster critic of Corbyn's ostensible anti-Semitism. *(Jeff Morgan 03/Alamy Stock Photo)*

Corbyn's strategy in 2019 is to await the Tory party's self-destruction over Europe and enter Downing Street as Britain's saviour. *(James Noble)*

The publishers have made every effort to credit the copyright holders of the material used in this book. If we have incorrectly credited your copyright material please contact us for correction in future editions.

Preface

The genesis of this book started exactly fifty years ago.

At the end of January 1969, a group of Marxist and Trotskyist students at the London School of Economics led a stormy protest against the school's director, an authoritarian from Southern Rhodesia. He had ordered the staff to close a series of gates inside the building in Aldwych to prevent a students' meeting in the school's Old Theatre. In the mêlée, at about 5 p.m., a caretaker guarding the gates died from a heart attack and the students instantly started a month-long occupation, igniting similar sit-ins across Britain's universities.

Throughout that first night of occupation, hundreds of LSE students crowded into the Old Theatre to debate the prospects of a Marxist revolution in Britain. Led by American graduates from Berkeley, California, where the student revolt against the Vietnam War had started five years before, and with speeches from French and German students, battle-scarred from 1968 street fights in Paris and Berlin, LSE's Marxists and Trotskyists (there were many) told us we were the vanguard of a worldwide revolution – which would begin with the students, and the workers would follow. We believed it.

Aged twenty-three and from a conservative background, I had completed my law degree at the LSE (the country's best law faculty at the time), and while studying for the Bar exams was employed on legal research projects at the college. Long before that dramatic night I had concluded that English law protected property rights at the expense of the rights of individuals and real democracy. Surrounded by articulate Marxists studying sociology and government, and going to lectures by Ralph Miliband and other Marxist teachers, I became attracted to their analysis of society. In that era, for anyone interested in politics that was not surprising.

In the wake of the Sharpeville massacre in South Africa in 1960 (I had marched in protest through London with my school friends against apartheid during the early years of that decade) and the anti-Vietnam protests outside the American embassy in Grosvenor Square in 1968 (along with others, I escaped with just some nasty blows from the police), I shared the horror at the dishonesty and disarray of Harold Wilson's Labour government. Added to that, for family reasons I was influenced by events in Germany. In particular I became fascinated by Rudi Dutschke, an erudite Marxist who spoke in graphic terms in Berlin about 'the long march through the institutions of power' to remove the Nazis and their capitalist supporters from ruling post-war Germany. In April 1968 an attempted assassination of Dutschke illustrated the raw battle for power between good and evil raging across Europe and America. (I would meet Dutschke later in Oxford.)

Those days and nights of long debates about politics, the economy and society were decisive for many of us involved in the LSE occupation. After a month it all petered out, but that 1968 generation was marked for life. None of us attained high office in politics, industry or education. Instead, that seminal moment in Britain's social history created cynics: men and women who were dissatisfied, curious, nonconformist and determined to expose evil in the world, of whatever type and wherever it might be found.

As 'Tommy the Red' (I became a students' spokesman), that month I learned many vital lessons for the journalistic career I embarked on soon after, travelling for a week on a special train with Willy Brandt during his successful election campaign to become Germany's chancellor. I emerged from that train with a unique insight about politicians and statecraft. Not least, that every politician is best judged by his or her closest advisers. Thereafter I spent many years producing BBC TV documentaries in Germany (about the Allied failure to prosecute Nazi war criminals and to de-Nazify post-war Germany) and across the world. Witnessing a myriad of wars, elections, corrupt politicians and shady businessmen cured me of Marxism, but not of my curiosity and innate scepticism.

LSE's Marxist student leaders did not join the conventional world. Some died tragically young, often from suicide, while others committed their whole lives to the struggle for revolution. In researching this book I was reunited with several of them. After fifty years they had changed a good deal physically, but not in their core beliefs. Pertinently, they all genuinely sensed that their Marxist dream would finally come true, delivered by Jeremy Corbyn.

Despite being excited by that prospect, they have no illusions about Corbyn himself. None of those illustrious Marxists who have survived since the 1960s – all intelligent, well-educated, engaged and engaging – recall Corbyn as a major player over any of the four decades before his ascension as leader of the Labour Party in September 2015. On the contrary, although they did not doubt his sincerity, they were underwhelmed by his intellect. In any event, for them, winning power was all that mattered, and like many across Britain's political spectrum, they were certain that Corbyn would be Britain's next prime minister.

That possible outcome was the reason I wrote this book. With Corbyn having a good chance of victory, the public deserves to know more about him. Surprisingly for a politician, but not for a hard-left conspirator, he has done his best to conceal his personal life from the media – which he loathes.

My main criterion for writing previous biographies has been to identify those at the top of the greasy pole, ambitious to influence our lives but unwilling to reveal their pasts with a reasonable measure of truth. Often they have falsified their biographies to protect themselves from public criticism. Corbyn is no different. Despite his repeatedly stated commitment to improve the lives of the impoverished, fight injustice, champion equality and destroy greed, he has hidden away much about himself that is relevant to judge his character and Britain's likely fate under the Marxist-Trotskyist government he has always promoted.

There can be no doubt about his passion to improve conditions for his constituents and the less advantaged in Britain and across the world. Frugal in his clothes and his food, he poses as the 'good idealist' engaged in a lifelong fight for justice and equality. In varying degrees, that aspiration is common to every politician: even tyrants don't openly promise injustice and inequality. The difference between politicians is in their methods. Corbyn's credo reflects his abstemious lifestyle. He disapproves of ambition and success. Equating both with greed, he strives not for equality of opportunity, but equality of poverty. In his ideal world, recognising the guilt of its shameful empire, Britain would abolish immigration controls and allow the needy to enter the country to share its wealth. For the rest, by taxation and confiscation of property, Corbyn would irreversibly transform Britain. Inevitably, there would be winners and losers; and until recently he did not conceal his contempt for his quarry. However, in his efforts to win the next general election he has starkly modified his language, and his senior colleagues have followed his lead.

Just how Corbyn became a communist has never been revealed. Before he was elected Labour's leader he was not seen as a figure of consequence, and thereafter he did all he could to protect the mystery. Since he now offers himself as Britain's next leader, his background story has become relevant. Is he a danger to the country? How genuine are his beliefs or his public character? Is he as benign as Labour's spin doctors now insist?

Ever since the collapse of the Soviet empire in 1989, the number of those who advocate Marxism as a system of government has rapidly diminished. No one much under the age of forty-five is a credible witness of the oppressive dictatorships imposed by Russia on Eastern Europe. No one much under sixty can recall the industrial anarchy orchestrated by communist conspirators in Britain during the 1960s and 1970s. Only the far left looks back on that era with any nostalgia. The rest blame the widespread strikes of those years, often orchestrated by Marxists or Trotskyists, for permanent damage to Britain's economy.

Corbyn disagrees with that assessment. For him, his election as prime minister would be the curtain-raiser to completing the unfinished business halted by Labour's election defeat in 1979. His admirers, for whom he is a hero, agree. The older ones are resolute socialists; his younger supporters are idealists, ignorant of history. Across that spectrum, few understand the society that Corbyn and his fellow Trotskyists, including John McDonnell, Len McCluskey, Diane Abbott and Seumas Milne, intend to build.

I understand the Corbyn Utopia better than most, because I have spent my life and career among the hard left. At school and in my block of flats in north-west London, I grew up surrounded by the children of communists, and often visited their homes. In the late 1950s I began travelling to communist Czechoslovakia, and as a journalist, between 1969 and the fall of the Berlin Wall in 1990 I frequently travelled across communist East Germany to interview senior officials and study the government archives about the Nazi era. As a BBC TV reporter I spent a lot of time during the 1970s with British strikers, especially the miners led by Arthur Scargill and his fellow Marxist trade union leaders. In 1989 I began three years of work in Russia, interviewing high-ranking Soviet intelligence officers who played the spy game against the West. While filming wars in Vietnam, the Middle East and South America, I constantly encountered hard-left idealists and latterday commissars. As a result I am no stranger to the manoeuvres of Corbyn and his group to seize power, nor to their ambitions once in Downing Street.

This book, told with the help of eyewitness accounts by people who have known Corbyn throughout his life, reveals the nature of the man who, if the Conservatives successfully rip themselves apart over Europe, is set to become prime minister.

The question is whether a Labour government led by Corbyn would transform the country for the better. Has capitalism, as he argues, run its course, and would our lives be improved by socialism? If so, is Corbyn's socialism the same brand that we have experienced under successive Labour governments since 1945, or something more radical, like a Marxist miracle? Is he a reformer or a revolutionary? And what sort of socialist is Corbyn? His supporters damn every opponent, especially Blairites, castigating each critic, even sympathetic ones, as 'traitors' or worse. Does that aggression, and the accusations that paint Corbyn as an entrenched anti-Semite, override his image as an authentic 'good bloke' blessed with everlasting politeness. As described in this book, I have found another side of the man. Would his election have a happy ending for Britain? For some, he would be a dangerous hero.

Islington, Late 1996

'I've got all these debts,' Jeremy Corbyn told his long-time friend Reg Race. 'Can you work out why?'

'I don't need to be a genius to tell him what's wrong,' Race thought. 'He's in danger of bankruptcy.' But at first he said nothing. Sitting in the Spartan living room of Corbyn's semi-detached house in north London, Race picked up a single sheet of paper and read out the politician's financial death warrant. Across from him sat his host and Claudia Bracchitta, Corbyn's formidable Chilean wife. They had positioned themselves unnaturally far apart from each other.

Claudia had summoned Race as a mutual friend to solve their differences. Blending his expertise in both Marx and Mammon had won him the trust of the Corbyns. As Corbyn's close political ally on the far left for many years, Race, a former MP, had transformed himself in recent times from a political agitator into a successful financial consultant in Britain's health business.

The papers in front of him showed that the Corbyns owed their bank £30,000, the equivalent today of twice that figure. Several personal loans had been guaranteed by Corbyn's income as an MP. He was also burdened by high mortgage repayments. As a last resort, the bank could threaten to recover its money by seizing his home. 'You've run out of loans,' said Race. Unchecked, within five years the debts would amount to £100,000. Corbyn's annual salary was £43,000.

Claudia interrupted. This was entirely the result of her husband's folly, she said. She and their three sons had little money even to buy food and clothes. 'We can't afford a decent life.'

The principal cause of the debts was the Red Rose Community Centre on the Seven Sisters Road in Holloway, north London. Situated in the heart of Corbyn's constituency, the Red Rose was a bar and dance area on the ground floor of the building that fulfilled his commitment to open his party office in the constituency. Corbyn was paying its rent and some of its staff's salaries out of his own pocket. Simultaneously, he owed a large sum to the Inland Revenue for his employees' unpaid National Insurance and pension contributions. The financial chaos was matched by his style of management. His employees complained about being both undervalued and underpaid. Among the casualties was Liz Phillipson, his battle-scarred assistant, who had resigned rather than continue to tolerate Corbyn's fecklessness.

'You haven't got enough money for what you're doing,' Race said bluntly. 'You should close your office in Holloway and move to the Commons. That would cut your costs by 80 per cent.'

'I won't,' replied Corbyn.

'Oh, come on, Jeremy, you know he's right,' Claudia said, her voice rising. 'Why don't you believe him?'

Corbyn mumbled, then fell silent. His body language showed that he felt no inclination to follow Race's recommendations. Claudia was becoming noticeably agitated. 'It was clear a breakdown was coming,' thought Race.

He was not surprised by the tension. Corbyn had first met his 'utterly lovely' wife (she had an athletic figure and a characterful face) in 1987, and soon after they decided to marry. An intellectual with a deep understanding of South America, Claudia had bonded with him at a protest meeting against Chile's military dictatorship, addressed by Ken Livingstone. 'She wanted to get off with me,' Livingstone would recall, 'but I had to go off to meet Kate, my partner, so she went for Jeremy.' In the flush of romance and clearly infatuated, Claudia had not grasped that while her future husband's enthusiasm for making jam or turning wood on a lathe was appealing, his lack of interest in material things meant that he ignored her need for comfort. At one stage she had planned for them and their young sons to move from Islington to leafy Kingston-upon-Thames, but was quickly disabused of the idea. 'He has to live in his constituency,' Keith Veness, another close political friend, informed her. 'No one told me,' she sighed.

Long before the onset of their financial problems, life with Corbyn had proved difficult. Tony Banks, the Labour MP for Newham North-West, witnessed just how difficult as one day he walked into Westminster's central lobby and spotted Claudia standing by the wall, tearfully holding her children. Jeremy, she explained, had promised to meet her two hours earlier. He had not turned up. Banks took the four Corbyns to the Commons family room and went off in search. Eventually he found Corbyn in a committee room. 'You'd better come out and look after your children,' he suggested. Corbyn did not seem fazed for a moment. Banks was not surprised. 'When pushed to have a day off,' he recalled, 'Jeremy's idea was to take his partner to Highgate Cemetery and study the grave of Karl Marx.'

Reg Race had experienced something similar when he had invited the Corbyn family for a week's holiday at his country home in Derbyshire. On the day, Claudia arrived with the children.

'Where's Jeremy?' asked Mandy, Reg's wife.

'I don't know,' replied Claudia with sadness. 'He just told me "I've got to go to a meeting," and I haven't seen him since.'

Over the following thirty-six hours, Claudia called several numbers searching for her husband. Two days later he turned up, explaining his absence as a necessary sacrifice for 'the movement'. At the time, Race decided that Corbyn was absent-minded rather than neglectful. But a huge question about his attitude towards his responsibilities remained unanswered.

Shortly after, Keith Veness and his wife Val confronted the same thoughtlessness. Claudia, who had come from a middle-class family used to a certain degree of comfort, was always complaining about the shortage of money.

'I've told Jeremy that he should stop being an MP and get a well-paid job,' she confided.

'What can Jeremy do to earn more money?' Veness asked.

Val added, 'The miners get much less than Jeremy.' But Claudia, she realised, did not appreciate her husband's hair-shirt lifestyle. She had even wanted a cleaner, but Corbyn had vetoed that. Did Claudia have bourgeois tendencies, Val wondered.

None of Corbyn's constituents could have imagined the tension when he arrived at meetings with his family to speak about Ireland, a subject of no interest to Claudia. By contrast, he had a self-proclaimed (if questionable) passion for Arsenal Football Club. Claudia was worried about hooliganism at the team's home matches at Highbury, while Corbyn, according to Keith Veness, regarded the game as 'crude and awful', and much preferred not to go. So Veness took Corbyn's sons to matches, while their father went to political meetings.

'Jeremy wasn't interested in football,' recalled Veness, contradicting Corbyn's boast of passionate support for Arsenal. 'Except, that was, on Cup final day.'

By late 1996 the marriage was all but over, and with nothing left in common, the two had drifted apart. To Corbyn, Claudia's list of complaints was familiar. Ever since 1967, when he had met Andrea Davies, his first girlfriend, at the Telford Young Socialists, a succession of women had made the same observations: he never changed his ways, and he rarely thought about them. Throughout the years he wore the same shabby clothes, ate the same bland food and stuck to the same political convictions he had begun to absorb in Jamaica, where he had spent fifteen months as a teenager in the 1960s. Admirers hailed his inflexibility as proof of his uncompromising principles, and to some the purity of his other-worldliness was endearing. Detractors blamed his limited intelligence and lack of education for his failure to appreciate others. On his own account, amid a constant round of demonstrations, speeches and political manoeuvres, he claimed to avoid causing any personal insult. Further, to avoid criticising any of his partners, he would insist that politics was about ideas, not personalities.

Reg Race had helped him realise his first political dreams in the early 1970s. Ever since, Corbyn had trusted his advice, especially once his friend became the financial supremo at the

Greater London Council (GLC) during Ken Livingstone's turbulent reign in the 1980s. But as they forged a bond on the left of the Labour Party, Race had discovered Corbyn's ignorance about the bureaucratic requirements of government, and his simple-mindedness about finances. While the committed revolutionary strove to challenge powerbrokers across the world on behalf of the oppressed, he seethed about any personal criticism in his own home. With so much to hide, he condemned any revelations about himself as abhorrent.

However, on the day in 1996 on which Race described Corbyn's financial crisis, the focus was entirely on him. Even if a rich benefactor had volunteered to pay off all the debts (and that was improbable), he would soon have fallen behind again. He had little choice, Race told him, but to sell the family home. Claudia agreed. Reluctantly, so did Corbyn – and thereafter broke off his relations with Race. The messenger was to blame. After this experience, Race questioned Corbyn's character and his propriety to influence the direction of the Labour movement.

In early 1999 the Corbyns' home was sold for £365,000 (£730,000 today), and they downsized to a house in Mercers Road, a shabby street in Tufnell Park, off the Holloway Road. On the day of the move, Corbyn was told by Claudia to empty the fridge. He forgot. He also forgot to clear the garage. Late in the afternoon, while their former home's new owner, dressed in a camelhair coat, fumed on the pavement, the garage door was opened to reveal rubbish crammed to the ceiling. Corbyn had regularly picked wood from neighbourhood skips, and also collected railway junk as he criss-crossed the country on trains. Boxes of safety lamps, metal signs, track signals and other paraphernalia had been stuffed in any old how. Late in the day, everything was finally shuttled across to the basement of Mercers Road, creating a new world of clutter.

The move brought one advantage. The building had been converted into bedsits, making the estrangement between Claudia and Corbyn easier. She and their three sons took the top floors, where she lived with a young South American

dubbed 'the toy boy', while Corbyn, in the basement, had relationships with a series of younger women.

The couple's estrangement was kept secret for almost two
years. Late in 1999, while Corbyn was at a peace conference in
The Hague, a journalist contacted Claudia and asked whether
the two had separated. Instead of telling the complete truth, she
explained that their twelve-year marriage had ended in 1997.
She said that she had wanted their eleven-year-old son Ben to go
to Queen Elizabeth's grammar school in Barnet, but that Corbyn
had stipulated that he should go instead to Holloway School, a
local comprehensive notorious for achieving, for three successive years, the worst GCSE results in the country, and listed as
'failing' by Ofsted, the office for standards in education.

From The Hague, Corbyn confirmed Claudia's account.
Defending his ideological purity against selective schools, he
implied, was more important than his son's education – or his
marriage. To avoid being branded a hypocrite, he said he
preferred his son to be badly educated than to be given an unfair
advantage. Labour's Islington council, he knew, despite receiving additional government funds, had failed to improve
Holloway. The school was plagued with discipline problems and
classes in which up to twenty languages were spoken, the white
pupils being especially disadvantaged.

In a series of interviews, Claudia reinforced the same message.
'My children's education is my absolute priority, and this situation left me with no alternative but to accept a place at Queen
Elizabeth Boys' School. I had to make the decision as a mother
and a parent … It isn't a story about making a choice, but about
having no choice. I couldn't send Ben to a school where I knew
he wouldn't be happy.' To the public Corbyn appeared to have
acquiesced in his wife's wishes, but, like so many communists,
he had put his political principles first, and ended the marriage:
he could not live with a woman who did not accept his beliefs.
The only dent to that image of ideological purity was Claudia's
revelation that Corbyn had agreed for another of their sons to
spend two years at the local Montessori nursery, at £600 per
term.

If that had been the last word on the subject, the notion that the marriage had broken up over Corbyn's principles might have been plausible. He favoured, he said, France's strict laws on the privacy of public figures' family lives – laws which have been exploited to conceal rampant corruption among French politicians, including former presidents. But Claudia, possibly with Corbyn's encouragement, went further. 'He is first the politician and second the parent,' she said. 'He definitely felt it would have compromised his career if he had made the same choice that I did. It's very difficult when your ideals get in the way of family life … It has been a horrendous decision.'

Sixteen years later, the whole tale was expanded. Rosa Prince, Corbyn's semi-authorised biographer, described, with Bracchitta's help, a tormented family: 'Corbyn and Bracchitta went round and round in circles for months. She would not send Ben to Holloway School and Corbyn could not bear for him to go to Queen Elizabeth's … In choosing Queen Elizabeth's, Bracchitta was aware that she was ending her marriage … Once again, Corbyn had put politics above his relationship.' That version is clearly incorrect. The marriage ended because of Corbyn's behaviour – his financial incompetence, his thoughtless absences, his neglect of his family and his apparent misogyny. 'He told me that the marriage had ended long before the school bit,' Ken Livingstone recalled. 'We had a chat at the time and he said his marriage had fallen apart over other things, not the school.' Like Reg Race, Livingstone had discovered that Corbyn's 'authenticity' was fictitious – a confection for political appearances. He had posed as a man who refused to sell out, albeit he was never heard to advocate higher standards of teaching.

The posturing became even more apparent in July 2016, one year after Corbyn became Labour's leader. He appeared in a televised interview with the novelist and poet Ben Okri. The premise was Corbyn's love of literature, but this was totally fabricated. He had only ever read very little. Equally misleading was his declaration: 'You have to be honest with people. You have to say what you believe to be the truth. If you hide the truth you are very dishonest.'

Up to the present day, Corbyn has concealed or distorted the nature of his close relationships, his personal life and his prejudices. The communists understood the value of those Lenin called 'useful idiots' – the well-intentioned idealists in the West who blindly supported the Soviet agenda. Lenin also mastered one critical ruse to grab public support. 'A lie told often enough,' he said, 'becomes the truth.' He had gone on to adopt Dostoyevsky's wise observation in *Crime and Punishment*: 'They lie and then worship their own lies.' Considering his long involvement with Corbyn before his ambition to lead Britain materialised, in 2018 Reg Race made a measured judgement about his former friend. Realising that Corbyn was guilty of that same deception, he concluded, 'He's not fit to be leader of the Labour Party, and not fit to be Britain's prime minister.'

Rebel With a Cause

The Corbyns could trace their roots in England back to the eighteenth century and beyond. Farmers, priests, a tailor, a chemist and a solicitor conformed to a traditional middle-class background which in 1915 produced David Corbyn. David met his future wife Naomi Josling in 1936, at a meeting about the Spanish Civil War, when both were twenty-one-year-old students at London University. Naomi was studying science.

On 4 October that year Oswald Mosley, the leader of the British Union of Fascists, organised a march through London's East End to assert his power. Met with fierce opposition by socialists and local inhabitants, the ensuing 'Battle of Cable Street' entered folklore, especially among British Jews, as an example of their resilience. According to Jeremy Corbyn, David and Naomi's fourth son, both his parents were present at the famous confrontation, in which 175 people were injured. Those who later met his parents have cast considerable doubt on this claim. Similarly, Corbyn would boast that his father considered volunteering to fight in Spain, but that is also unlikely. Neither parent was an adventurer: rather they were hard-working, intelligent professionals. Their son, it appears, added Cable Street and the Spanish Civil War to their life stories to camouflage his comfortable middle-class roots.

David Corbyn, a skilled engineer, was employed by Westinghouse Brake & Signal Co., a British manufacturer of electrical devices used by the railways. Following the outbreak of the Second World War, his then employers, English Electric, moved their factory to the West Country, to avoid German bombs. The family settled in Chippenham, a historic market town between Bristol and Swindon. David's income increased, and he was able to buy a large stone house surrounded by a garden, fields and woods in Kington St Michael, a village three miles north of the town. In that pleasant environment, Corbyn's three older brothers were born – David, Andrew and Piers. All of them were clearly intelligent: David would become an electrical engineer and Andrew a mining engineer, while Piers pursued his childhood hobby to become an acknowledged weather expert.

By the time Jeremy was born, on 26 May 1949, the Corbyns owned a car, an unusual luxury in the immediate post-war years, but the whole family dressed scruffily, and were renowned for their unconventional lifestyle, not least because in a Tory area both parents were members of the local Labour Party. In that era there was nothing unusual in socialists sending their children to private primary schools to guarantee a good education and success at the 11-Plus exam. Indeed, most of the ministers in Clement Attlee's Labour government had been either privately educated or sent to grammar schools. Nor was it unusual that the Corbyns moved to another area after their second son, Andrew, failed his 11-Plus. He successfully re-sat the exam and entered Haberdashers' Adams grammar school in Newport, Shropshire. Jeremy would follow him there four years later. The family's new home, Yew Tree Manor, a five-bedroom seventeenth-century farmhouse, was exceptionally luxurious compared to that of most families, who struggled through post-war austerity with shortages of food and fuel and urban winter smog. Living an unconventional, slightly chaotic lifestyle, Naomi Corbyn, a grammar-school maths teacher, maintained a vegetable garden, while her husband converted their garage into a workshop where he would turn wood and build toys and carts.

The four sons were not detached from political or literary life. Naomi read modern fiction and contemporary history, and gave her youngest son a collection of George Orwell's essays for his sixteenth birthday. Jeremy never claimed to have read them, although in 2016, he said he had been influenced by *The Ragged-*

Trousered Philanthropists, a novel written in 1910 by Robert Tressell, the pseudonym of Robert Noonan, a house painter. The book describes the politically powerless underclass in Edwardian England, and its ruthless exploitation by employers and by the civic and religious authorities. Corbyn's reference to the novel fitted his narrative after he became Labour's leader, but in truth, as a teenager he did not read any literature. Rather, he sat in his bedroom poring over Ordnance Survey maps of the surrounding countryside and gazing at a world atlas, dreaming of future journeys. In the corner was a hand-operated Gestetner duplicator, used to produce leaflets for the local Labour Party. By that time he was already a political animal.

At school, he was regarded as an outsider. Unlike his three elder brothers, he was a poor student, uninterested in sport, insouciant and gauche. 'He was not noticeably clever,' recalled Lynton Seymour-Whiteley, his finely-named Latin teacher. Striking out against the school's mainstream, Corbyn joined the Campaign for Nuclear Disarmament, the Young Socialists at Wrekin's Labour Party, and the League Against Cruel Sports, the last an unusual show of contrariness in a Tory shire famous for hunting and shooting. Considering that the school motto was 'Serve and Obey', his refusal to join the Combined Cadet Force, and instead to hoe a vegetable plot, was principled defiance, and a singular reason for being remembered. In 1967 he sat his A-Levels, passing two exams with a grade E, and failing the third. With no chance of following his three brothers to university, he risked being marooned in Shropshire. On his last day at school, John Roberts, the headmaster, harshly predicted that fate: 'You'll never make anything of your life.' In embarrassment, his mother would later tell people that it was her youngest son's poor handwriting that had prevented his getting to university. Without any status, he was a downstart. He came to loathe achievers, especially undergraduates with ambitions to get to the top, disdained those who enjoyed material wealth, and showed little respect for religion. Most of all he hated the rich and successful, and identified with losers. In his self-protection he became conspicuously stubborn.

He drifted into odd jobs for nearby farmers and a local news-paper, but his main focus was to organise the Wrekin Young Socialists. May Day in 1967 was marked by taking a home-made red banner to the top of the nearby Wrekin hill, tying it to the trig point and singing 'The Red Flag'. Soon after, the Young Socialists held their annual dinner at the Charlton Hotel in Wellington. Clean-shaven, Corbyn arrived in a dark suit, white shirt and tie, looking like a typical middle-class teenager. Except that he faced an uncertain future.

His salvation was his parents' suggestion that he apply to join Voluntary Service Overseas (VSO), a Foreign Office initiative funded since 1958 to send young male volunteers to work in Britain's former colonies for £12 pocket money per month and free board and lodging. Most recruits were graduates, not eighteen-year-olds with poor A-Levels. Corbyn's luck was to be sent as a 'cadet teacher' to Kingston, Jamaica. He was contracted by VSO to stay on the island for two years. On 28 August 1967 he boarded a BOAC Boeing 707 with about thirty other volunteers for the twelve-hour flight.

The contrast between Shropshire and Kingston was dramatic. Jamaica had become independent in 1962, but that had done little to change the extreme divisions between rich and poor. 'It was impossible not to be influenced by the gulf between the iconic haves and the have-nots,' recalled Michael Humfrey, the head of the island's Special Branch. 'That would certainly have affected Corbyn deeply.' The 'haves', especially the twenty-one families who dominated the island, lived in luxury, while the 'have-nots', who inhabited three areas about a mile from Corbyn's school – known as Dunkirk, Tel Aviv and McGregor Gully – survived on a subsistence diet, without mains water or electricity, under zinc roofs resting on cardboard walls. The gap was aggravated by racism – whites at the top, followed by the Lebanese and those with light-brown skin, known as the 'high browns', then the Chinese, with blacks at the bottom. Jamaicans, quipped the locals, had 'an eye for shade'.

Corbyn was based at Kingston College, an elite grammar school for 1,600 fee-paying and scholarship pupils. Contrary to his version, the college was not in a 'deprived' area, nor in this period did he, despite his assertion that he was known throughout the school as 'Mr Beardman', grow a beard. Contemporary photographs show him mop-haired and clean-shaven, and none of his pupils or fellow teachers recalls him with a beard.

His one task was to teach Caribbean geography four times a week to third-form boys, all of whom had passed the 11-Plus, in classes of about thirty-five. Later, he would exaggerate that there were seventy pupils in his class. 'It was a really defining moment of my life,' he would say, 'because I was thrown in at the deep end as an eighteen-year-old.' He kept ahead by the time-honoured ruse for beginner teachers of reading the textbook in advance of the lesson, then reciting it. In years to come, he would not admit to the school's elite status. Dissembling further, in January 2018 he told *GQ* magazine that he had been 'working at schools and theatres and taught polio-stricken children in camps for the victims'. In truth, he worked at just the one school, helped with a single production in one theatre, and only briefly appeared at one camp for polio victims. There was a charity for such children attached to the town's university, and a local organiser recalls 'one white man helping', but did not identify him as Corbyn. His only job was to teach. Years on, he would boast that his experiences taught him to control a crowd and to deal with a crisis. His students recall the opposite.

Standing out with his pale skin, strange 'bouncy walk' and unusually long hair, and always wearing the same clothes – later dubbed 'Oxfam-reject style' – he faced a class which, Robert Buddan, one of his pupils, recalls, 'teased him. We were a bit troublesome and didn't make things easy for him. He was a good target.' Asking his charges to explain Jamaican swearwords did not improve Corbyn's standing. Faced with boys who spoke out in class and directly challenged any poor mark, he regularly exploded in anger. 'He would shout at us and turn red,' says Buddan. The apprentice teacher was also unable to add up the marks he awarded for classwork accurately, and the boys frequently complained that his final totals were wrong. He was soon mocked across the school as 'Fire Red', especially after one particularly humiliating incident. While Corbyn's attention was distracted, a boy called Michael ('Mad') Reid crept up behind the seated teacher and clipped a lock of his long hair. Corbyn leapt to his feet, lunged at the laughing boy and chased him through the school, at one point squeezing through a window on the first floor, keeping up the chase until he lost the trail. Sheepish and red-faced, he returned to the classroom. No one was punished by a detention or a caning.

At weekends the VSO volunteers would join up with Peace Corps aid workers from Canada and the USA, and meet local girls to drink Old Charlie's rum and dance to rock music. Corbyn never took part. 'He didn't mix with us,' recalled Dennis Dawes, another VSO cadet and later a Hampshire police officer. 'He was serious-looking.' Corbyn even avoided the Christmas Day party at the British High Commission. The unsociable teenager came to notice just once, in November 1967, when he was working as a lighting technician at The Barn, the island's first professional theatre, which was staging a production called *It's Not My Fault, Baby*. Otherwise, he spent weekends with groups of ten Kingston College pupils hiking across the hills above the town and towards the 7,402-foot peak of the Blue Mountain. On one trip to the north coast they watched refugees from nearby Cuba landing on the beach. One hundred miles to the north, a heroic figure dressed in military fatigues was fighting American imperialists.

During Corbyn's first year in Jamaica, the island was on the edge of turmoil. Fascination with Fidel Castro's Cuban republic, and the recent death of Che Guevara in Bolivia, had spread unrest across the region – although, unlike those in South America, Fidel's few disciples in Jamaica were cautioned against violence. Castro had judged Jamaica to be unsuitable for guerrilla warfare, and his intelligence service made only limited contact with the island's young Marxists. These were led by Hugh Small, Trevor Munroe and D.K. Duncan, each inspired to overthrow the white colonial legacy by America's Black Power movement, especially Martin Luther King, Stokely Carmichael and, most importantly, Malcolm X's anti-Semitic Nation of

Islam, which condemned 'Zionist dollars' bankrolling colonial oppression. 'We were young, black agitators looking for answers,' recalled Small. Ever since two British soldiers had been killed by black nationalists inspired by an American Trotskyist in 1965, Small had led the fight against Washington's influence, but his group, dispirited and fragmented, was failing to throw off the shackles of British rule.

Towards the end of 1967, the socialist People's National Party (PNP) unexpectedly lost a second successive general election to the centrist Labour Party. Many suspected electoral fraud. Following that defeat, Leroy Cooke, a Marxist, was appointed as the PNP's youth organiser to agitate in schools. Peter Croft, a VSO cadet teacher who arrived at the same time as Corbyn, recalls their 'endless discussions about Jamaican politics and the personalities involved'. Both young men read reports of the local socialists' tirades against colonialism, imperialism, racism and the capitalists' exploitation of Third World countries, and witnessed from the periphery the raw struggle between Jamaica's rich whites and impoverished blacks. In conversations over a beer in a bar on Friday after school with four other teachers, Corbyn would discuss the unrest. 'He asked about the difference between Labour and the PNP,' recalled Victor Chang, one of his drinking companions, 'and was interested in socialism. He was curious about Jamaican Marxism.'

Unknown to Chang, Corbyn was unsettled by Kingston College. His classroom overlooked the school's large chapel, where once a week Bishop Gibson, the Anglican cleric who had founded the school back in 1925, still preached. The pupils were focused on academic excellence, and were proud of the school's reputation as a powerhouse of sport. The grounds were located close to the island's famous Sabina Park cricket ground, and England played the West Indies there in February 1968, but Corbyn was uninterested in that intense contest, or in the endless track competitions outside his classroom. The school's motto – *Fortis Cadere Cedere Non Potest* (The Brave May Fall But Never Yield) – was painted in large letters on a wall over-looking the sports field. Equally irritating to him were the boys' well-pressed khaki uniforms and ties, the compulsory combined cadet force, and the choir. Lest he forget religion's importance, he could see Holy Trinity Catholic Cathedral across the road and, a little further down, St George's school, a rival private college rigorously overseen by Jesuit priests. Taken together – education, sport, tradition, the army, organised religion and the quest for achievement – Kingston College epitomised nearly everything Corbyn loathed.

As 1968 began, the mood in Kingston became tense. Walter Rodney, a twenty-six-year-old Guyanese, arrived from Havana to forge an anti-capitalist alliance between radicals, Black Power supporters and what were called 'the discontented'. Rodney was already well known to the island's Special Branch. In 1962, while studying at University College of the West Indies in Kingston, he had travelled to Havana, where he met Fidel Castro, and returned to Jamaica with a plan to spread Marxism across the West Indies. Later that year he flew to a so-called peace congress in Leningrad, earning the CIA classification of 'convinced Communist with pro-Castro ideals and an interest in Black Power'. Back in Jamaica, he took a small group of young Marxist graduates to 'Reasonings' – meetings across the island with the dispossessed and Rastafarians. Encouraged by Armando Velazquez, the Cuban consul on the island, he spoke about revolution at secondary schools, churches and youth centres. Although Rodney was banned by the school's administrators from speaking at Kingston College, Corbyn heard about his lectures, and about CIA plots to overthrow governments in Cuba and across Latin America. He learned about the importance of the Soviet Union's contribution to Castro's revolution. Without Moscow's assistance, the left's ambitions across South America would have been snuffed out by America. And ever since the failed CIA-inspired invasion of Cuba at the Bay of Pigs in 1961, Jamaica had been treated as Washington's appendage, and hated for that.

In the summer of 1968 Corbyn was joined at Kingston College by Paul Wimpory, a physics graduate from Birmingham, also on a VSO contract, and the two became friends. By that time Corbyn had moved into a rented room in a house on Easton Avenue, a residential area in New Kingston, owned by the aunt of Dawn Tapper, one of the school's English teachers. On the eve of her marriage, Tapper asked Corbyn to be the chief usher in the church. He agreed, only to forget his principal chore – he left all the wedding programmes in the house, and there was no time to return to collect them. As a result, the ceremony was confused, the minister omitted parts of the service, and the congregation did not say the responses. 'He felt very bad about it,' Tapper recalled.

Walter Rodney lived in an adjoining road to Corbyn. Wimpory believed that Corbyn, no longer under the direct supervision of the High Commission, was 'rebelling against his affluent background' and his links with traditional Britain. None of the VSO students who attended a drinks reception at the High Commission in early September recall seeing Corbyn. By then, about to start his second year of teaching, Corbyn frequently expressed to Wimpory his dismay about the 'vast inequalities' on the island, 137 years after slavery in Jamaica was abolished. He became convinced that the British Empire had not benefited Jamaicans, and that it had left behind a legacy of guilt for the gross exploitation of innocent, impoverished people.

On 15 October, Walter Rodney attempted to return to Jamaica via Canada. By then his trips to Cuba and Moscow, combined with reports of student revolts in Europe and guerrilla warfare financed by Moscow in Asia, Africa and Latin America, had aroused fear among pro-Western Jamaicans. In that mood, the government banned his entry. Three days later, the university campus in Kingston erupted. For two days, left-wing students rioted, burning buildings and cars in what became known as the Rodney Riots. The unrest was put down, but the government failed to recover its authority. Remarkably, none of the young Marxists recalls seeing Corbyn during the rioting, and neither Wimpory nor Chang ever discussed those tumultuous events with him. He has never mentioned witnessing the uprising, and has never since met the Marxist students who subsequently became prominent Jamaicans. Yet their influence on him would seem to have been profound. Within eight weeks of the riots, Corbyn decided he could no longer tolerate Kingston College. To his good fortune, the school had been underpaying him by £1 per week, so he received a lump sum of £52 (about £900 today), and planned in secret how to escape.

The first casualty of his leaving was one of the college's pupils, Derrick Aarons, a fourteen-year-old weekend hiker and a participant in the Duke of Edinburgh Award. Aarons had completed all the requirements for the award's Bronze Medal, and had been assured by Corbyn that the necessary forms had been sent to London, and that in January 1969 he would receive his medal from Jamaica's governor general. The excited boy frequently asked Corbyn if he had received a reply yet from London. The answer was always no. In January Aarons returned from his holidays, and was told that Corbyn had decamped back to Britain. The medal never materialised. 'I was,' recalled Aarons, 'a very disappointed teenager.' Had Corbyn even submitted the forms? During a recent trip to London, Aarons, today a prominent Caribbean doctor, contacted Corbyn's office to arrange a reunion. 'I was convinced,' he said, 'that he would remember me as the keenest of his hikers, but I never received any acknowledgement.'

The more important casualties of Corbyn's decision to quit early were the pupils in his four geography classes. No replacement could be found. 'I always thought how curious to leave part of the way through the school year,' observed Paul Wimpory. 'It was not very professional.' Corbyn left Jamaica, Dawn Tapper recalled, just days after her wedding on 14 December. 'Jeremy told us that he was returning to Britain,' she said. 'I gave him a piece of my wedding cake to eat on his journey.'

Corbyn has always concealed what he did after leaving Kingston. 'I spent my youth in Jamaica,' he told Channel 4 News in 2015, but did not elaborate. According to his account, he left Jamaica in July 1969, having fulfilled his two-year contract. Not only is that untrue, but he has never honestly revealed what happened during the missing seven months. His description of the journey from Jamaica is vague: 'I took a sailing boat around the Caribbean, and then a fishing boat to Guyana.' The only local passenger ship leaving Kingston and going as far as Trinidad was a small island-hopping freighter. That left 430 miles along the coast to Georgetown, Guyana's capital – hardly the route for a 'fishing boat'.

Corbyn says that he 'spent some time in Guyana', a pertinent revelation. The former British colony was then Walter Rodney's home. Until 1964, Cheddi Jagan, a Marxist, had been the country's leader, but with the connivance of the British and the CIA he had been replaced by a pro-Western prime minister. Nevertheless, in 1968 the strong Cuban presence in Guyana, Castro's base for guerrilla warfare in South America, remained undiminished, and with Rodney's help Corbyn could have flown to Cuba via Mexico. He has never said when he first visited Cuba, and the extent of his Marxist education in Guyana remains unknown. Like so much of his account of his life until he left Guyana, it is partly romanticised, and possibly an invention.

According to Corbyn's version, he travelled from Guyana to Brazil, and on to Uruguay, Argentina, Chile, Bolivia, Paraguay, Peru, back to Buenos Aires, and then sailed to France in 1970. He has said that during the year he spent travelling he had been impressed by the culture of South America's indigenous tribes, the history of the European settlers' revolts against the colonial powers, and the countries' battles during the 1950s against rapacious American corporations and CIA subversion. The journey confirmed his socialist ideals. Here was a cause that suited his 'loser' personality – he would fight for the downtrodden against their oppressors.

More recently, Corbyn has claimed that he was influenced by *Open Veins of Latin America*, by the Uruguayan journalist, writer and poet Eduardo Galeano, a critique of the exploitation of the continent's Indians by monarchs, the Catholic Church and multinational American corporations. That is doubtful. The book was first published in 1971, a year after Corbyn returned to Britain, and he could not read Spanish. Pertinently, shortly before his death in 2015 Galeano repudiated the book as a distortion of the continent's economic history, and confessed that he was embarrassed by his youthful prejudice in favour of South America's left-wing dictators. In his enthusiasm for the book, Corbyn ignored Galeano's disclaimer. He was enchanted, he said, by the indigenous customs and languages of South American civilisations – Incas, Quechua and Aymara – all smothered by Spanish colonialism.

He would also claim to have been influenced by Walter Rodney's *How Europe Underdeveloped Africa*, published in 1972, which described the Caribbean search for identity after the end of colonialism. Rodney's and Galeano's ideas, picked up after his year in Jamaica, thereafter became the foundation of Corbyn's principles and way of looking at the world. He loathed imperialism – Spanish, American or British. He never sought to understand how Greek, Roman and successive European empires were the foundation of Western civilisation, but stuck resolutely to his belief in the unalleviated evil of white colonial oppression. In 2015 he demanded that the then prime minister David Cameron apologise to Jamaica for Britain's 'brutal' involvement in the slave trade. 'It's a history of the most gross exploitation of people,' he said. He would never condemn Russian, Chinese or Arab oppression in similar terms. Nor, as a self-proclaimed pacifist, could he explain how the victims of imperialism – either the local Indians in Latin America or Europeans as the prey of the French, Soviet and German empires – could have regained their liberty without fighting.

In 1970, three years after leaving Britain, Corbyn returned to his family's Shropshire home. He had not once spoken with his parents during his time away. On the single occasion he telephoned his home, there was no reply.

He returned to a seemingly empty future. Not only did he have no prospects, but he had missed the best of the swinging sixties. Although he would later claim to have joined his brother Piers on an anti-Vietnam war demonstration in London, that famous clash between the children of the counter-culture and the police had erupted during his absence, back in 1968. He also missed the big anti-apartheid marches of the 1960s, only joining their mini-successors two decades later, such as the Trotskyist

'Non-Stop Picket' breakaway group championing illegal protests in London, during which he was arrested. In speeches or interviews he never mentioned the outbreak of urban terrorism – Baader Meinhof in Germany, the Red Brigade in Italy, the Red Army in Japan, the Weathermen in America, the Quebec separatists in Canada, the Angry Brigade in Britain. Unlike every other leftist, he did not march with CND from Aldermaston to London every Easter. The politics of the sixties philosophers who had so influenced young undergraduates had no relevance to someone filled with Walter Rodney's protests against colonial oppression. Perhaps a particular loss, he had missed the election in November 1970 of Salvador Allende, Chile's Marxist president. His only contemporaneous eyewitness experience was the resurgence of the IRA's war against colonialism.

On his return to Britain, now twenty years old, he had good reason to be apprehensive. Minimally educated, unqualified and unable to engage in hard work, he was isolated in Shropshire, forced to take a series of local jobs. In May 1972, after rejoining the Wrekin Labour Party, he arrived at the Young Socialists' annual congress in Skegness with Andrea Davies, a nurse from Telford, his first British girlfriend. Although ostensibly a Labour Party function, the camp for five hundred members was run by Liverpool's Militant Tendency, a group of revolutionary socialists formed in Liverpool in 1955 with the express purpose after the mid-1960s of infiltrating Labour to make the theories of Trotsky, Marx, Lenin and Engels official party policy.

Among those Corbyn met at the camp were Keith and Val Veness, two activists from Islington, then a rundown area of north London. Keith, a salt-of-the-earth, self-educated employee of NUPE (a trade union for public sector workers), was on the verge of joining the Workers Revolutionary Party, another group of Trotskyites, more intellectual but less well organised than Militant. 'I was on the right wing of the delegates,' he recalled. He regarded Clement Attlee's post-war government as 'social democrats, not the real Labour Party'.

Over the weekend, the four bonded. 'I'm from Telford New Town,' said Corbyn, suggesting that he lived in a working-class area. Keith Veness found his new companion's intense commitment instantly charismatic. He told him that Labour membership had been much reduced during Harold Wilson's government. 'We're an empty shell in London,' he said, explaining that Labour's branches were open to far leftists like himself. He urged Corbyn to join the cause, and as an introduction 'to read the classics – Marx, Trotsky and other philosophers'. Corbyn nodded enthusiastically. To get him started, Veness handed him a copy of Trotsky's *History of the Russian Revolution*, which he had just won at the camp's raffle. Six months later Corbyn returned the book, still in its wrapping. 'He wasn't interested in reading anything,' Veness concluded. 'Not even Lenin on imperialism. It was a waste of time talking to him about books.' Veness could not decide whether Corbyn was unintellectual or just lazy. There was no disagreement about politics, however. Over that weekend Corbyn immersed himself in a group dedicated to highlighting class conflict. By raising people's consciousness about the horrors of capitalism, his instructors explained, the masses would be mobilised for revolution. To achieve equality and justice, capitalist wealth would be confiscated and aggressively redistributed to the poor.

Corbyn and the Venesses came together at a decisive moment in British politics. The Tories under Ted Heath were in turmoil. The unexpected defeat of Harold Wilson's Labour government in the 1970 election and the Conservatives' victory had followed a decade of industrial strife. Trade union shop stewards continually called for strikes. Repeated walkouts by seamen, dockers, railway workers and employees of all the country's major industries – shipbuilding, car manufacturing and engineering – had crippled the economy. Continental Europe was thriving while Britain tottered on amid shortages of food and fuel. Exports drained away, and foreign competitors grabbed Britain's traditional markets. After devaluing the pound in 1967, the Labour government was accused of creating 'the British disease' – a growing trade deficit, low productivity, high unemployment, a ballooning national debt, an exodus of talented professionals and, above all, industrial anarchy. Under Wilson, eleven million working days were lost to strikes in 1970 (compared to 900,000 in 2017). Once Wilson abandoned his attempts to control trade union militancy, the electorate had turned to Heath to prevent left-wing union leaders from destroying the country.

Heath, however, fudged his party's manifesto pledge to unravel the socialist economy imposed by Labour governments since 1945. Airlines, the telephone network, road haulage, the steel industry, utilities, coalmines and the railways were all state-owned. Whitehall's civil servants not only managed the economy but also, through joint committees with trade unionists and employers, industrial production, the regulation of incomes and prices in shops. Privatisation would eventually show that the public-owned industries were largely run for the benefit of their employees. Nationalised industries were 40 per cent over-manned, and costs were inflated by about 20 per cent; but after two years in government Heath lacked the conviction and the courage to destroy the consensus accepted by both Tories and Labour since the war. Besieged by strikes, Heath faced in particular Arthur Scargill, a Marxist miners' trade union leader who had called out his members to strike for a 40 per cent pay rise. 'We took the view we were in a class war,' said Scargill. 'We were out to defeat Heath.' Thousands of miners confronted and outnumbered police. 'This conflict,' wrote Heath, 'was the most vivid, direct and terrifying challenge to the rule of law that I could ever remember.' Knowing that the miners held the country to ransom because its electricity supplies depended on coal, Heath panicked. In his search for a way to escape, he appointed Lord Wilberforce, a senior judge, to review the miners' pay. Wilberforce decided in just three days that the 16.5 per cent pay rise they had been offered was insufficient, and that they should receive 20 per cent. Heath instantly capitulated, despite knowing full well that every other union would demand similar pay rises. In 1972, twenty-three million working days were lost to strikes.

Corbyn and his new friends rejoiced in Heath's surrender. It was a tumultuous moment in the Labour Party. Britain's trade union leaders, some of them on Russia's payroll, were sabotaging the economy in order to topple the government. The outrage among the Tories only increased the pleasure among the Young Socialists gathered at Skegness.

The infiltration of Labour had been advocated by Lenin. 'Support the Labour Party as the rope supports the hanged man,' he had told Sylvia Pankhurst, who had hosted the first meeting of the British Communist Party. Lenin taught that the far left should gain political power in Britain by taking control of the Labour Party. Once the communists commanded the party, and then became elected to government, they could destroy capitalism. Thus battle was joined. In the early days, democratic socialists expelled communists and Trotskyites from Labour, but during the 1960s Harold Wilson inexplicably relaxed the controls, and 'entryists', as they were known, were allowed to join the party. Constituency parties were infiltrated by Trotskyites, who then deselected any social democrats. Effectively, a separate hostile party was flourishing within Labour, and more and more communists were elected as Labour MPs. Their object was to use the democratic machinery of Labour to undermine democracy. The result was toxic. In February 1973, in the wake of Heath's surrender to the miners, Wilson succumbed to left-wing pressure to sign a 'compact' for the party's next election manifesto. To win workers' support, Labour pledged to extend nationalisation, prevent Britons taking money abroad, impose a rent freeze, enforce price controls on private business, finance widespread food subsidies, and push through a 'large-scale redistribution of Britain's income and wealth' – precisely the programme that Corbyn and the Venesses saw as the first step towards their Marxist ideal.

In that era, the distinction between Marxists and Trotskyites was important. Refashioned as the 'new left' to separate themselves from Stalin's crimes, the Marxists viewed history through the lens of the class struggle. Britain's evolution into a truly socialist society, they believed, would start with a communist state under the dictatorship of the proletariat. British Marxists like Keith Veness spoke about a 'revolution' to assert the proletariat's control, but without the bloodshed that had marked events in Russia in 1917.

Trotskyites were more aggressive. Leon Trotsky had led the Red Army after 1917 to defeat the counter-revolutionary tsarist White Army supported by Winston Churchill and the British government. Thereafter, ignoring the mass starvation caused by the Bolsheviks' forced collectivisation of agriculture, he campaigned to spread the communist revolution across Europe and then the whole world. His militarist internationalism and belief in fostering a permanent international revolution were opposed by Stalin, who wanted first to consolidate his takeover of power in Russia. In turn, Trotsky accused Stalin of obstructing the proper course towards global communism by refusing to encourage the working class to agitate and cause unrest in every country. In 1929 Trotsky, fearing for his life, fled Russia. He settled in Mexico, from where he urged his followers to engage in a permanent struggle. Unwilling to be threatened by an ideological foe, Stalin arranged for Trotsky's assassination in August 1940. His death galvanised his disciples to recruit members, organise meetings, constantly debate, and to secure power wherever and however possible. Organisation, Corbyn was told by Veness, was paramount. Salvador Allende's election in Chile was a crucial lesson for Marxists: it showed that they could win elections even in capitalist democracies. The vital ingredient was to have an effective political machine.

Soon after that weekend, Corbyn prepared to move to London. At his mother's suggestion he had enrolled at the Polytechnic of North London in Holloway to study trade unionism. He barely entered the building before he abandoned the course. 'I was utterly bored,' he would say later, but he knew that academic work was beyond his abilities. To conceal his failure, he and his brother Piers would in later years craft a story of defiance: how he had walked out of the polytechnic after an argument with a lecturer about his course. Others knew the truth. Val Veness was working at the left-wing newspaper *Tribune* when Corbyn appeared in her office along with a friend, John Pickering. He had just arrived in London, he said, and having rented a bedsit in Islington was looking for work. 'He never mentioned the poly,' she recalled.

2

The First Rung

In his search for employment, Corbyn aimed low. An advertisement placed by the National Union of Tailors and Garment Workers for an assistant in its research department attracted just one reply – Corbyn's – and he got the job. Based first at the union's headquarters in Kensington, then at Hoxton in the East End, he worked directly for Alec Smith, who was the national officer for the union from 1959 until he became its general secretary in 1974. In 1973 Smith was negotiating with employers at the Retail Bespoke Tailoring Wages Council, at a time when the industry in Britain was declining as production moved to Asia. Out of 112,901 union members, just 7,220 lived in London, the majority of them women. Working under Smith was Mick Mindel, a Jewish communist and the union's representative at the World Jewish Congress. Mindel articulated his members' passionate support for Israel, reflecting the fact that most of their employers were also left-wing Jews. Like Mindel, they looked to communism to abolish injustice and prejudice, including anti-Semitism. Mindel and many of the union's members became Corbyn's first encounter with Jews.

In Corbyn's version, although only an assistant in the research department, he personally challenged the employers to recover members' unpaid wages after their bosses 'had mysteriously gone bankrupt just before Christmas, owing their workers a lot of wages and not paying National Insurance and all this kind of thing. Scumbags, actually. Crooks. My job was to try and chase these people through Companies House and so on.' According to Corbyn, he forensically examined the companies' accounts in order to verify phoney bankruptcies. That notion is contradicted by Alec Smith, and also by the trade union's well-catalogued records, which do not reveal any issues about 'unscrupulous employers', or refer to any member complaining about being unpaid, especially after Christmas. On the contrary, Jack MacGougan, the union's general secretary, who recruited Corbyn, proudly announced in his annual report for 1972 that the union had won a trailblazing four weeks' paid holidays for its members, and had established a forty-hour week. Smith is certain that Corbyn 'never had any contact with our members. He just sat in at meetings passing me information.' Further, added Smith, 'He was OK, but he didn't have the chance to shine.' Smith also recalled: 'The clothing industry is a tough business. If an employer went broke it was because of trading conditions – not to fiddle their employees.' Corbyn, not for the first time reshaping the truth to improve his self-image, conjured a tale of a brave personal fight against exploitative Jewish employers of sweatshop labour. Parochialism and fantasy fed the original source of his anti-Semitism – namely, as he saw it, the malign collective power of Jews.

Corbyn was immersed in an unfamiliar world. The union was dealing with struggling, overworked, self-employed Jews. Tailoring was a fragmented, insecure industry, and bad luck could turn an employer into an employee overnight. In that alien culture, Corbyn had no time for those seeking self-improvement – to fulfil the dream of moving from East End slums to north London's suburbs. Thirty years later he boasted that at the end of one Wages Council meeting, a Jewish tailor had offered to make him a suit if he provided the cloth. Corbyn had spurned the offer. 'Imagine trying to bribe a union official,' he laughed about the generous gesture.

Since he disdained materialism, culture and anything spiritual, Corbyn was an empty vessel, uneasy with a race complicated by its history of survival over two thousand years of persecution. While Jamaica was black against white, and South America's indigenous Indians fought against the Spanish, Jews in London were the victims of discrimination by all classes of Europeans, including the working class. That truth did not quite fit the Marxist theory of history that Corbyn had imbibed in Jamaica and Skegness: workers exploited by employers, who needed his protection as the first stage before eventually seizing power to govern the country.

Those nuances eluded him even as he found his metier. Here was a cause that secured him both an office and status, so that his sense of inferiority was partially alleviated. With a regular income, he could afford a better home: he left Islington and rented a flat in neighbouring Hornsey. There he joined the local Labour Party, a moribund group split between the extreme left – communists, Marxists and Trotskyites – and conventional social democrats. At meetings held in a dilapidated headquarters on Middle Lane in Crouch End, Corbyn deftly gave the appearance of not belonging to any faction. But Barbara Simon, the branch's long-serving secretary, was not fooled. 'He was a natural Marxist,' she noted, seeing him as a sly, diligent agitator seeking political advantage at every turn to secure control of his small domain.

Corbyn was transformed, and politics became his life. Soon he was appointed chairman of the branch's Young Socialists, and he would regularly cycle around the constituency, chatting to potential voters in every public venue and council estate, and offering application forms to join the party. His energy transformed Labour's status in Hornsey. Through jumble sales and collections, he also helped to raise enough money to repair the local party headquarters. Toby Harris, a member of the branch from the age of sixteen, was struck when in the summer of 1972 he returned from Cambridge University and saw the newcomer tirelessly undertaking the thankless chores hated by everyone else.

The one odd note was Corbyn's parsimony. Ever since he had witnessed the treatment of farm animals in Shropshire, he had been a vegetarian. In addition, he rarely drank, and did not smoke, go to the cinema, watch any sport or enjoy any social activity, so he had little in common with most members. His one concession to frivolity was to sing Irish protest songs in an

Irish pub. Commitment to the reunification of Ireland was not wholly outlandish at the time. In March 1971 Harold Wilson had flown to Dublin to speak to the IRA's leaders about peace and a planned transition to a united Ireland, and he later welcomed them to his home in Buckinghamshire. The former prime minister, however, received no credit for that initiative from Corbyn, who shared his fellow members' anger at what he saw as Wilson's betrayal of socialism during his last government. Unlike Corbyn, Wilson was not dedicated to hastening the imminent collapse of capitalism. Rather, as 'the principal apostle of cynicism', he was blamed for 'too great a number of tawdry compromises [which] pollutes the atmosphere of politics'.

Like others on the left, Corbyn was not taken in by Wilson's compact with the trade unions, and in 1973 he joined the new Campaign for Labour Party Democracy, an organisation that reflected his own commitment to establish a communist society. Thereafter his ideals never changed. To secure victory in the class war, he embraced the mantra of Tony Benn, at that time the rising star of Labour's parliamentary radicals, to encourage direct action by workers on the streets and in workplaces to establish what the left called 'industrial democracy'. Benn had just read *The Communist Manifesto*, and had become passionate about the overthrow of capitalism and its replacement by a Utopian, classless society, a mystical world. In this vision, the economy would be nationalised without compensation. That would include all the major industries, banks and property corporations. To turn Labour into the agent of that revolution, Corbyn adopted Benn's rallying cry: 'There are no enemies on the left.' Their only adversaries were capitalists.

Douglas Eden, a polytechnic lecturer and a member of the Hornsey Labour Party, watched as Corbyn manoeuvred patiently to secure control over the branch. 'In his carefully self-controlled way,' said Eden with bitter admiration, 'he presented himself to the lower orders of society, the vulnerable and inadequate people who felt indebted to him, as working-class. Once he got power, he dominated the branch and got their votes.' One of the early casualties was the branch's moderate chairman Andrew

McIntosh, who Corbyn eased out. 'Andrew didn't learn his lesson,' recalled Eden, who openly described Corbyn to the Labour Party's headquarters as 'a patrician from a wealthy background'. In revenge, Corbyn marked Eden for similar treatment – an official complaint to force his expulsion.

By late 1973, Corbyn felt emboldened. The tailors' union moved its headquarters out of London, so he resigned and moved on to become a researcher for Tony Banks (later MP for Newham North-West) at the Amalgamated Engineering Union (AUEW), one of Britain's most powerful associations, with nearly 1.5 million members. Banks apparently assumed that the well-spoken ex-grammar schoolboy could produce the required research. Corbyn's self-esteem and confidence rose, as did his salary. He would later boast that he even organised a picket of striking AUEW workers outside their own headquarters against the union's moderate leadership.

In September 1973 Salvador Allende was killed by the Chilean military, supported by the CIA. Washington's involvement aroused worldwide outrage. Naturally, Corbyn demonstrated against the CIA's conspiracies. His antagonism would be justified after Senator Frank Church delivered volumes of evidence to Congress in Washington in 1976 about the CIA's undercover operations. That, combined with the earlier revelations in what became known as the Pentagon Papers of the lies told by President Johnson and others about American involvement in Vietnam, and the collapse of Richard Nixon's presidency after Watergate, strengthened Corbyn's loathing of American influence. And then British intelligence, frustrated by a ferocious IRA bombing campaign, was exposed for torturing the innocent as well as the guilty in its attempts to identify murderers in Ulster. The eventual consequences of those sensational disclosures were unpredictable.

On 6 October, while Israelis were observing Yom Kippur, the three neighbouring Arab states, Egypt, Syria, and Jordan, launched a surprise invasion intended to drive the Jews into the sea. After a fierce nineteen-day war, the intruders were routed. Any chance for a peace settlement between Israel and the Arabs was lost. Days later, Opec, the cartel representing the world's dominant oil producers, quadrupled its prices. Global mayhem followed. Emboldened by the financial squeeze on Britain, the country's miners sensed another opportunity to overthrow Heath. The government's latest 16.5 per cent pay offer was rejected, and an overtime ban imposed. As 'flying pickets' dispatched by Scargill prevented coal deliveries to the power stations, Britain's economy suffered, and by year's end the miners were out on strike. With electricity supplies cut, Heath ordered industry to work a three-day week. Just as in wartime, streets were dark, offices were unheated and unlit, and ration books were needed to buy petrol. TV broadcasts finished early, and unemployment soared. A Tory government was overseeing a nightmare. In Scotland, shipbuilders on the Upper Clyde occupied their yards, and a wave of strikes immobilised the car industry. Left-wingers gleefully anticipated the collapse of capitalism. Tariq Ali of the International Marxist Group (IMG), Gerry Healy, a Trotskyist who would head the Workers Revolutionary Party (WRP), and other far-left groups demonstrated to advance the revolution. Predictions were made that, just as anti-Marxists had overthrown Allende, so Heath would be toppled by the masses.

To save his government, Heath called an election for February 1974, posing the question 'Who Governs Britain?' The Tories were expected to win a landslide against a Labour election manifesto that promised 'a fundamental and irreversible shift of wealth and power'. Corbyn's role in that campaign was to prove decisive for his own future. Ignoring his obligations at the AUEW, he worked indefatigably as the agent for Irving Kuczynski, Labour's candidate in Hornsey, described by the Tories as 'communist-backed', against the sitting Tory MP Hugh Rossi, a staunch Roman Catholic who was to be a junior minister under both Heath and Margaret Thatcher. Corbyn flooded the constituency with party workers, knocking on every door and posting leaflets for a candidate he did not particularly like. In the process, he himself was transformed. The unsocial outsider formerly employed by the tailors' union had become an energetic, effective and popular organiser, utterly committed to scoring an electoral triumph.

In the midst of the campaign, officials employed by a government pay board, a socialist quango, ruled that the miners' pay claim was justified by Lord Wilberforce's inquiry in 1972. As a result of the chaos that ensued, the electorate turned. Angered that the deprivations caused by the three-day week – including shortages of petrol, sugar and bread, and hospitals without clean bed sheets – was all apparently pointless, the electorate became incensed with Heath. It was not only his cack-handed management of the economy: asked by a journalist to name his favourite dish, he had tactlessly replied, 'Lobster Thermidor with two wine sauces.' Harold Wilson, asked the same question, chose Cornish pasties with brown sauce.

Unexpectedly, although the Tories won a quarter of a million more votes, Labour emerged on election day as the largest party. Heath was ousted and Wilson returned as prime minister, knowing that he would have to call another election soon as he lacked an overall majority. However, for his supporters it was an important victory. The organised working class had overthrown a Tory government. Tony Benn would acclaim the result as a decisive moment. Rejoicing on the far left was met elsewhere with apprehension and dismay. The middle classes were visibly terrified by the prospect of widespread unrest, manifested by an outbreak of Marxists and anarchists squatting in empty houses, and the trade unions, led by Jack Jones of the Transport and General Workers' Union, celebrating their return to power.

In Hornsey, Hugh Rossi survived Corbyn's best efforts, albeit with a much-reduced majority. During the endless hours leafleting, canvassing and cajoling Labour's supporters to the polls, Corbyn had met the woman who would become his first wife. Jane Chapman was twenty-three, an attractive university graduate researching the French textile industry in the 1920s for a doctorate at the London School of Economics. Soon after they met, Corbyn declared his feelings. 'He professed love early on,' she recalled, 'and said that I was "the best of the best", so I thought this must be the thing.' Consumed by what she described as a 'whirlwind romance' over three months – 'he constantly urged us to marry' – she agreed, because 'he was friendly and lively and seemed bright and not bad-looking'. Most important, both of them were devoted to changing Britain in a fundamental way. They would celebrate together at any sign that events were running in their favour: in April 1974 they were excited by the overthrow of Portugal's fascist regime, and they rejoiced in the continuing defiance of left-wing organisations to government *diktats*: socialist councillors in Clay Cross in Derbyshire had been declared bankrupt after refusing to set low rates dictated by the Tory government, but their action made them martyrs to the left.

Corbyn and Chapman's enthusiasm for their cause made an impression: their respective local Labour branches selected each of them to stand in the May 1974 council elections for Haringey, a north London borough that included Hornsey and that embraced both affluent areas in Muswell Hill and Highgate and severely deprived sections in the east, around the Tottenham football stadium. They were both elected. Two days later, on 4 May, they were married at Haringey Town Hall.

Neither set of parents was impressed by their child's choice. Chapman's mother, a lifetime Tory, was not pleased that her daughter, ambitious to be an MP, was marrying a poorly-off, uneducated trade union official. On her side, Naomi Corbyn disliked her new 'alpha female' daughter-in-law. It was wrong, she thought, to have such an obvious competitive element in a marriage. However, since the Corbyns avoided confrontation, nothing was said. Chapman became fond of her husband's generous father, although she remained wary of his uncommunicative mother. From the outset the tensions were aggravated when Piers Corbyn arrived at the town hall looking even more scruffy than normal. Embarrassed by her son, Naomi swept him off to buy a shirt and a suit. They did not return until after the ceremony was over. Everyone then headed for the reception at Chapman's father's bowling club in Weston-super-Mare, 140 miles from London, before the newlyweds headed off for a brief honeymoon in southern Ireland.

They returned to a tiny ground-floor studio room in Etherley Road in Haringey, which they had bought with a mortgage from the Greater London Council. One year later, they moved to a bigger ground-floor flat in Lausanne Road, near Turnpike Lane. Several chickens, a cat christened Harold Wilson and a dog named Mango ran around the garden. Married life became a succession of meetings, demonstrations and campaigns. At 5.30 on some mornings they would head for a picket line to support strikers, then meet up again at the end of the day. Their social life was confined to meetings of the Labour Party, functions to support Troops Out and Cuba Solidarity, council meetings and demonstrations, while Chapman intermittently researched her doctorate in Paris and Corbyn ostensibly worked for the AUEW.

To Corbyn's delight, as a councillor he represented mostly immigrants: Greek Cypriots, Asians and Afro-Caribbeans. He genuinely enjoyed mixing and socialising with the rainbow of communities in Haringey, assiduously attending their main social events and promising to look after their needs. However, that did not include the inhabitants of Chapman's ward in Stamford Hill, in the south of the borough, where the Orthodox Jews were the backbone of local Labour. To Chapman's regret, while she showed interest in her husband's constituents, he was indifferent to those in her ward, including her fellow councillor Aaron Weischelbaum, who was Jewish. 'Jeremy,' she explained, 'was conflicted because he supported Palestine and the abolition of Israel so that Palestinians could recover their homes.' Corbyn spoke of Israel as the worst example of American imperialism. Occupying land, in his opinion, was an obvious form of colonialism. This made Zionists racist, and therefore he opposed Israel's existence. He condemned the Balfour Declaration, the British government's promise in 1917 of a homeland for the Jews, and dismissed the effect of the Holocaust as explaining the Jewish people's longing for their own country after 1945 to avoid future persecution. In Corbyn's hierarchy of oppression, the descendants of slaves were the most victimised, while Holocaust survivors were at the bottom of the list. He did not distinguish between Jews in London and Zionists in Tel Aviv. To him, they were all guilty.

Among the surprises for Chapman was the absence of books in her husband's life. Throughout the four years of their marriage, he never read a single book. He did not think deeply about ideology or political philosophy. Her initial judgement that he was 'bright' was mistaken. As an agitator, he relied on his wife for political friendship. 'He didn't get depressed. He was driven by his motivation to change society,' she recalled. His handicap, he was acutely aware, was his lack of a working-class pedigree. By then his parents had moved to a new home in Wiltshire – chosen to enable them to pursue their burgeoning interest in archaeology. During Corbyn and Chapman's visits for Sunday lunch, politics were politely discussed, but Corbyn's parents never mentioned that they had been present at the Battle of Cable Street, or that David had ever considered going to fight in the Spanish Civil War. Their son's introduction of those key events into the biographies of his parents would come much later. Both smacked of fiction.

To compensate for the limitations of his background and education, Corbyn played on his status as a councillor, trade union official and energetic activist. He became expert at working out how to win new votes, and would spend hours calculating where and how Labour could maximise its strength in Hornsey. Although he never read Trotsky's writings, he adopted his ideas of process, and mastered the political skills to produce what Trotsky had called 'a permanent state of unrest' for eventual victory.

With both Corbyns' support, Haringey's ruling Labour group increased the rates by 23 per cent, making them the highest in the country. Shortly after, the borough's housing workers went on strike for more pay. Consistent with socialist policy against any dismissals, Corbyn successfully urged his fellow councillors to award the hefty increase. In recognition of his commitment he was made a vice chair of the subcommittee on development, and would boast that the 42 per cent increase in the council's overall budget, financed by local ratepayers, had allowed Labour to double the number of its staff. Annoying Haringey's middle classes gave him particular delight. Faced with a huge housing problem after the arrival of thousands of Cypriot refugees in London, Corbyn proposed building homes on green parkland. Local residents were outraged. The rich, he scoffed, clearly disliked living alongside immigrants – but they would have no choice.

In October 1974, Harold Wilson called another election. With Irving Kuczynski standing once again as Labour's candidate, Corbyn's energetic campaigning, supported by the prime minister visiting the constituency, reduced Hugh Rossi's Tory majority to 782 votes, both a success and a disappointment for Corbyn. Wilson returned to office with a narrow parliamentary majority of three.

Although electioneering was over, Corbyn remained in perpetual motion. Leaving home early in the morning, he would bounce between council meetings, Labour Party gatherings, demonstrations, leafleting and occasional trips to the AUEW's office to justify his salary. His pride and joy was Hornsey Labour Party. Nominally only the 'assistant/minutes secretary', he had swelled the local party's membership, making it, he asserted, the second largest in the country. The huge influx was divided between moderates and committed hard leftists, who attracted the attention of MI5, the domestic security agency. The branch's agenda reflected Corbyn's priorities. Shortly after the general election, three resolutions were passed: to condemn the exploitation of tea-pickers by British companies; to deplore the imprisonment of twenty-one Iranian students after a sit-in at the Iranian embassy in London; and to support the boycott by the Labour leader of Hornsey of a visit by Prince Philip to open a new housing development. 'I believe you've got to stand by your principles,' Corbyn told the local newspaper. He also put forward motions in Haringey council meetings to impose import controls, restrict individuals spending money abroad, and to oppose Britain's continued membership of the Common Market. There were no motions to deplore Haringey's poverty, low rates of income, or the council's failure to build more homes.

The inspiration for many of Corbyn's ideas was Tony Benn, the new industry minister. Born in 1925 to an aristocratic family, Benn had been elected an MP in 1950, and was a social democrat as a minister during Wilson's first term. By 1974, he was moving far to the left. One of a number of Labour Members disillusioned with Wilson's excessive caution in promoting a socialist agenda, he became popular among Marxists, regularly visiting militant shop stewards at shipyards and factories to encourage class consciousness. At those meetings he railed against Britain's membership of the European Common Market as a threat to parliamentary sovereignty. European socialists were condemned as revisionists, while East European communists were praised. To build socialism, in 1975 Benn created the National Enterprise Board (NEB) to take over Britain's biggest twenty-five corporations and nationalise the City's financial institutions. NEB officials, Benn believed, could manage industry in the public interest. To demonstrate the success of socialism, he diverted taxpayers' money to support unprofitable corporations.

Among the beneficiaries was British Leyland in Birmingham, one of Britain's biggest car producers. Neither Benn nor Corbyn understood Leyland's plight. The company had been managed for years by Donald Stokes, a corrupt salesman, while its managers had ignored their foreign competitors' technical improvements. Their attention was too often focused on surviving the anarchy on the production lines. Leyland's Longbridge plant was blighted not only by ruinous restrictive practices imposed by competing trade unions, but also by daily strikes. These were organised by Derek 'Red Robbo' Robinson, a towering Marxist shop steward who apparently delighted in furthering the ruin of Britain's motor industry. Neither Corbyn nor Benn ever criticised Robinson. In their world, trade unions were sacred. To that end, on the AUEW's behalf Corbyn presented Benn with a blueprint to reconstruct the motor industry by increasing shop stewards' powers. Benn was delighted with Corbyn's work, an accurate reflection of its limitations. Neither considered the consequence of the constant strikes: defective products. For the

first time since 1945, Germany and France produced more cars
than Britain, and the country's vehicle imports rose from 14 to
57 per cent of the market. Neither Benn nor Corbyn was
alarmed. 'He immatured with age,' was one of Wilson's less
offensive comments about Benn.

As Jane Chapman discovered, her husband's grasp of economics at the national level was no better than his understanding of
their domestic finances. His lack of interest in money was
reflected by his complete silence about improving their standard of living. He never talked about buying a bigger home, a car
or increasing his income. He had few material requirements. To
her surprise, since they had married so soon after meeting,
when he returned home at night he would happily open a can
of beans, swallow them cold and declare himself satisfied.
Occasionally he returned late from a meeting of the Hornsey
Labour Party with friends to sing IRA songs while they all got
drunk on beer. He would sit on the floor in his greasy, unwashed
pea-green jacket, bought at an army surplus shop in Euston,
oblivious to her irritation. They rarely went out together.
Invitations to dinner with the Venesses were refused. Corbyn,
they were told, did not socialise.

Chapman spent lonely evenings in their small flat with
Mango, the dog, and Harold Wilson, the cat, as her only
companions while Corbyn went about extending his circle of
political contacts. Among them was Tariq Ali, a Marxist intellectual originally from Pakistan, and Bernie Grant, a bombastic
Black Power Marxist from Guyana and a Haringey councillor.
'It's racism to control immigration,' Grant told Corbyn, adding
that it was discriminatory to prevent anyone from the West
Indies from settling in Britain. Corbyn adopted that opinion.
Similarly, he did not openly protest about Grant's view that boys
and girls should be segregated in school, and that girls should
be sent home when they were menstruating. Grant's interest in
questions of race was inconsistent, however: asked by Reg Race
about the cultural oppression of immigrant women in
Tottenham, he replied: 'I don't know and I don't care.' In their
conversations, Grant and Corbyn rarely mentioned economic

or social policies. They focused on community and ethnicity, subjects that were not only congenial to Corbyn, but at the heart of his political ideology. Anti-capitalist and disdainful of markets, he wanted citizens to live together in Soviet-style communes or self-supporting districts, as he had seen in Jamaica and South America. Joining in the black-and-white battle of morality against immorality, of good versus bad, underpinned his feelings of self-worth. Thanks to Grant, he was appointed chairman of the council's new Community Development Sub-Committee, with responsibility for using public money to build community centres for immigrant groups. Within a year he was accused of 'reckless spending' by his fellow councillors, and of recruiting 'community workers' without giving them specific jobs. To Haringey's Tory councillors, permanently in opposition but nevertheless vocal critics, Corbyn appeared to be signalling that he was left-wing on all issues, despite his lack of any coherent programme.

Mirroring Tony Benn, he agreed with the government's response to rocketing oil prices. To avoid inflation, the American and German governments had cut spending, but Denis Healey, the British chancellor, did the opposite, increasing public spending by 31 per cent in his first year, and by 29 per cent the following year. Most of the money went to state employees, whose wages rose by 32 per cent. To Corbyn's glee, Healey simultaneously raised income taxes for top earners to 83 per cent, and added an extra 15 per cent tax on unearned income. Some individuals were paying between 92 and 101 per cent in taxation. Healey's mantra, 'Squeeze the rich until the pips squeak,' matched Corbyn's nostrums. Both men seemed oblivious to the consequences. While inflation in Germany was 7 per cent, in Britain the figure soared to 27 per cent. Rather than face Labour's punitive taxes and lose their savings to hyperinflation, thousands of the country's most talented professionals, scientists and engineers emigrated to America and the Far East in what was called 'the brain drain', a phrase coined in 1960. The loss to Britain was little short of catastrophic. By the end of 1975, Wilson's schemes to control capitalism had crippled private investment and Britain was on the brink of bankruptcy. Joe Haines, his media spokesman, later summed up Labour's policies as 'trying to make water run uphill – against the facts, against events, against common sense and against human nature'.

Corbyn was deaf to such complaints. Taxing the rich was right; he disputed the possibility of any permanent damage. In the cause of building socialism, he also opposed modernisation, including widening a main road that ran through his borough. During a delegation's visit to Bill Rodgers, the new junior minister at the department of the environment, he had gone into a long harangue. Rodgers had retorted, 'You are tiresome, Councillor Corbyn.' Far worse humiliations followed. He was fired by the AUEW: his research was judged unacceptable. Corbyn would explain his sacking by saying that he had been a target in the clearout of leftists. His boss, he claimed, had decided that his celebrating the American withdrawal from Vietnam, continually attending political meetings or standing on picket lines across the country, was unwelcome. In reality, without an academic background, he lacked the skills to present a cogent analysis of political and economic issues. 'He never told me he was sacked,' recalled Chapman, whose own career was advancing: she had been selected as Labour's parliamentary candidate for Dover and Deal, a Tory marginal.

Once again, fortune intervened. NUPE, the trade union for public employees led by Alan Fisher, an ambitious left-wing firebrand, was recruiting officials to increase its membership among the underpaid. Replying to an advertisement, Corbyn arrived in Charing Cross for an interview. Reg Race, at that time the NUPE official in charge of the process, looked at the bedraggled applicant, whom he had never seen before. The Brylcreemed panel of men conducting the interviews, Race knew, would never consider someone wearing unpolished shoes, no jacket, and an un-ironed grey shirt, open at the collar. 'Go down The Strand, buy a tie and smarten up, or else you've got no chance,' he advised.

On this occasion Corbyn did as he was told, and in truth the union had every reason to employ him. He was tirelessly active and a committed socialist, respected by both the Hornsey Labour Party and the Haringey Labour group. He was duly hired as the organiser for two London boroughs, Barnet and Bromley, a job that gave him responsibility for the area's low-paid Inner London Education Authority (ILEA) workers, mostly school dinner ladies and caretakers. Given an old green car, he toured his domain in what Keith Veness, also a NUPE official, called 'a sinecure job'. Corbyn was in seventh heaven. He had status and a good income. As an outstanding recruiter – the union's membership would increase from 50,000 to 250,000 over the following seven years – and a keen organiser of strikes, he quickly won popularity with the union's five hundred dinner ladies. However, he had nothing in common with the macho Cockney dustmen swearing over their pints down the local. In an attempt to win their acceptance he renamed himself 'Jerry' – no dustman would bond with a Jeremy – and, to avoid their hard-drinking sessions, would make his excuses and go off early to join another picket line.

During his endless discussions with like-minded allies, Corbyn saw Britain's industrial turmoil, rising interest rates and the collapse of the value of the pound as an opportunity to destroy capitalism. Ranged against Labour were the enfeebled Conservatives, led since February 1975 by Margaret Thatcher, who held that Britain was ruled by the unions, the majority of which were controlled by committed Marxists and agents of Moscow. In that febrile atmosphere, right-wing elements in the military, the City and the media plotted to stage a coup against Wilson, whom they suspected of being a KGB agent because of his regular trips to Moscow in the years immediately after 1945. Corbyn would not have been surprised if the plot had been implemented. Reports from America described the White House orchestrating military coups, assassinations and invasions across Africa, Asia and Latin America. The oppression and torture carried out by the military dictatorship in Chile particularly appalled him. The atmosphere of paranoia and persecution was agitated by leaks from committees in Washington investigating the Nixon government's secret operations. Adding to the hysteria, 'experts' forecast that by 2000 the world would be convulsed by widespread famine, followed by total destruction. The uncertainty excited the left.

In March 1976, Harold Wilson resigned as prime minister because of ill health. In the first round of voting among the 313 Labour MPs to choose Wilson's successor, Tony Benn and Michael Foot, both left-wing unilateralist disarmers, together outscored James Callaghan, the right-wing candidate, with 40 per cent of the vote. In the final ballot, Callaghan got just thirty-nine more votes than Foot. The left did not feel defeated. Corbyn and his allies interpreted the loss as a temporary blip, and an incentive to redouble their efforts.

Callaghan proposed to cut public spending in an effort to halt the country's slide towards bankruptcy. Benn disagreed, offering as an alternative a siege economy that limited imports and confiscated even more money from the wealthy. The government was split. Many middle-class Britons feared that proletarian hordes, led by a Bennite commissar, would be incited to seize their property. In Haringey, Corbyn and his brother Piers, himself by now a Trotskyite candidate in a local election, led squatters into unoccupied houses across London. Piers's group even picketed the home of Hornsey Labour Party member and GLC councillor Douglas Eden near Muswell Hill to protest against the GLC seeking to have unauthorised occupiers expelled from empty properties. Alarmed, Eden telephoned Corbyn to ask him to intervene. It did no good. 'Corbyn waffled because he supported the squatters,' said Eden, who realised too late that Corbyn equated his own ambitions in Haringey to those of Salvador Allende's Marxist government in Chile.

In that febrile atmosphere, Corbyn and Chapman set off on his 250cc Czech motorbike in the summer of 1976 for a camping holiday across Europe. 'Jeremy always chose to go on holiday in August,' explained Chapman, 'because there were no political meetings.' To her distress, her husband showed no interest in her political duty to nurse her constituency in Dover in preparation for the next general election, nor in her academic work. She also feared that the holiday would be as uncomfortable as the previous year's in France, Spain and Portugal. The ordeal was not just riding pillion on Corbyn's bumpy bike, but his passion for abstinence. While Chapman wanted to sleep in a proper bed at night and eat in interesting restaurants, Corbyn insisted on a small tent and cooking tins of beans on a single-ring Calor gas stove. The nearest Chapman got to comfort was after a rainstorm flooded their tent outside Prague. Begrudgingly, Corbyn agreed to spend the night under cover – not in a hotel, but in a student hostel. He became furious when his motorbike broke down in Czechoslovakia, assuming that because it had been manufactured there it would be easy to have it repaired. Instead, he was introduced to the realities of a communist economy. The bike had been made exclusively for export, and no Czech garage mechanic knew how to fix it, or where to obtain spare parts. For two days he fumed until it was finally repaired.

During their journey, Chapman discovered that her husband was not interested in equality within marriage, or in sharing any domestic chores: 'Women living out their sex lives as a personal statement was ignored by him,' she recalled. 'He never spoke about sex, music, fashion or books. He put class first.' Equally distressing was his indifference to Europe's most beautiful cities. In Vienna, he refused to enter the palace of Schönbrunn, the Kaiser's summer retreat, because it was 'royal'. 'You go in,' he told her. 'I'll stay outside.' European culture offended him. Oblivious of his surroundings, he stood in Vienna's beautiful Ringstrasse and pronounced it 'capitalist'. He walked past all the museums and art galleries, and found no pleasure in medieval towns. In villages, he was interested to watch the peasants going about their lives. In Prague, soaking wet from torrential rain, he did not lament a missed visit to Hradčany castle, and turned down a walk through the old town. Nor did he comment on the dilapidation of the city's old buildings, all neglected by its communist overlords. 'Preservation of architecture and heritage,' recalled Chapman, 'didn't appear to be on his agenda.' For similar reasons he had always refused to accompany her to Paris, where she did occasional research, or to Los Angeles to visit her aunt. He spoke only about elections, campaigns and demonstrations, although his knowledge even of these was incomplete. Strangely, considering his claims forty years later of his profound sympathy for South America's indigenous people, he never mentioned that supposed fascination to her. By contrast, he expressed a deep interest in Britain's manhole covers, especially their dates of manufacture: 'My mother always said there's history in drain covers. So most people think I'm completely mad if they see me taking a picture of a drain cover, but there we are.'

Most travellers who crossed into Czechoslovakia from Austria during the Cold War were shocked by the experience. Running just behind the customs buildings were two rows of electrified barbed wire. Between them was a wide, sandy strip of ground concealing a minefield. Looking out over the eerie silence were armed soldiers in guard towers, with orders to shoot on sight anyone approaching from the Czech side. Those caught within five miles of the border without police permission could expect imprisonment. Any Western visitor riding a motorbike through those fortifications would be left in no doubt that Eastern Europe was a prison. Czechs were badly dressed, had limited food, and lived in decaying buildings. Czechoslovakia, a rich democracy before 1939, was a police state. But Corbyn uttered not a single word of criticism, and expressed no sympathy for the country's 1968 attempt at liberation from the Soviet Union. He simply dismissed what he was seeing as a delusion, just as he dismissed the victims' accounts of the horrors of Soviet Russia. He wilfully ignored the despair suffered in the name of 'social justice' not only by Czechs, but by hundreds of millions of people in Russia, China and the other countries in 'liberated' Eastern Europe. He said nothing about the thousands of skilled and scholarly Czechs forced to take menial employment as street cleaners or worse, as punishment for opposing the Soviet occupation. 'He was a Tankie,' said Keith Veness, meaning that Corbyn had supported the Soviet suppression of the Hungarian revolt in 1956 and the Prague uprising twelve years later. When in conversation Veness mentioned Stalin's cruelties, 'Jeremy walked away. He couldn't do political arguments. He was a communist fellow-traveller. The bastard never apologised for the Moscow trials.' In that Cold War era, Corbyn's sympathies were stark. 'NATO's object', he said, and that of 'the war machine of the United States is to maintain a world order dominated by the banks and multi-national companies of Europe and North America'. Only the South Americans deserved to be liberated – from American imperialism. Both during that European holiday and through-out their relationship, Corbyn never mentioned to Chapman his time in Jamaica, nor his interest in Guyana or Cuba. Considering the profound influence those places supposedly exerted on his world view, his silence was remarkable.

The Corbyns returned to London with Jeremy unaware that their marriage was cracking up. 'Jeremy never thought there was anything wrong,' recalled Chapman. 'He assumed that, because our politics were compatible, that amounted to a proper relationship.' 'She tried to make it work,' said Keith Veness, 'but he was uninterested. He never came home, and the relationship just slowly broke up.' Chapman's requests for more than just a political life – cinemas, restaurants, clubs, children – were ignored. 'He didn't acknowledge my emotional side,' said Chapman. 'He doesn't recognise a woman's feelings.'

Despite their disagreements, early on 20 August 1976 the two set off to Willesden in north London to join the picket line outside Grunwick, a film-processing plant where female Asian workers were on strike and unsuccessfully trying to prevent strike-breakers taking their places. During that long but forlorn struggle, Corbyn became a familiar face as a footsoldier against employers. 'Jeremy was a Trotskyist,' recalled Chapman. 'No doubt about it.'

A hammer blow to the left fell in September 1976. The pound's value sank still further, and the markets were in turmoil. Britain once again became the 'the sick man of Europe'. While some spoke of humiliation, Tony Benn and Corbyn saw an opportu-nity to introduce draconian controls to create a socialist econ-omy. Jim Callaghan took the opposite view. The government appealed to the International Monetary Fund for a loan – the biggest in the IMF's history – and agreed to reduce inflation by cutting public expenditure and imposing pay limits. The left was outraged. If taxpayers' money and huge loans were not spent by the government, they believed, unemployment would soar. Labour was irreconcilably split. In the ideological battle chancellor Denis Healey was on one side, Benn and Corbyn on the other, shouting slogans on marches in support of Benn's 'alternative economic strategy'. It was a dialogue of the deaf.

On his own patch, Corbyn worked towards a breakthrough. In the 1978 council elections, contrary to predictions that Labour would do badly because of the huge rates increases, his vigorous organisation produced a high turnout, and Corbyn turned the tide by using his links with the immigrant community, who agreed to come out to vote. The count was held in the cavernous Alexandra Palace, an exhibition hall built in the nineteenth century overlooking London and fittingly called 'The People's Palace'. Seeing the piles of Labour votes outnumbering the opposition's, Corbyn felt rewarded. Compared to the national 8 per cent swing to the Conservatives, there was a 2.5 per cent swing to Labour. Excitedly he awaited the formal announcement of victory and then, with a clenched-fist salute, led the singing of 'The Red Flag'. The Tories had been trounced. Under the headline 'Hornsey Defies National Picture', the local newspaper described Labour supporters as 'ecstatic', while Tories 'wandered around dumbfounded'. Keith Veness judged that Corbyn's skill was to pose as 'everyone's mate and not a faction-fighter'. Others, including Sheila Berkery Smith, a former Labour mayor of Haringey who had served twenty-four years as a councillor, saw a different figure. On Corbyn's orders, she had been deselected from the party's slate. Where others saw the friend to all, she saw 'intolerant Marxist extremism'.

The Corbyns were duly rewarded for their hard work. Chapman became chairman of housing, while Corbyn was made head of the Public Works Committee. Houses had up to that point been given to families in need; Chapman instead allocated homes to gays and single mothers. Moderate Labour councillors became alarmed. 'She was a classy but poisonous lady,' recalled Robin Young, the party whip in Haringey. 'Cold, extreme left and not capable as a chairman.' Others noticed the competition between Corbyn and his wife, and judged Chapman the superior talent. Mark Killingworth, a left-wing committee chairman and an ally of the Corbyns, recalls Jeremy as 'hungry for power'. Already at that early stage, Killingworth observed, 'his ambition was to be an MP'.

As the chairman responsible for the council's services to the community, Corbyn once again set about hiring more workers, doubling the size of the direct labour workforce and increasing their wages. No one mentioned that as a NUPE official representing those council employees, he had a clear conflict of interest. In his mind, that notion was a capitalist ruse. Rewarding the workers was his duty. As a man devoted to causes rather than to the hard graft of implementing decisions and managing their consequences, he had no difficulty spending money to enrich his members. Here he imitated Keith Veness, who as a councillor negotiated on behalf of the ILEA, with Corbyn representing the NUPE workers. 'I gave NUPE as much as possible,' recalled Veness, who preferred dealing with Corbyn than with Bernie Grant, who, he complained, would threaten employers with physical violence. By contrast, Corbyn allowed his shop stewards to do the intimidating. The result was the same. Tony Franchi, a wood craftsman and Tory councillor, accused Corbyn of the 'misuse of our money'. On one occasion he watched five council workers arrive outside his workshop in Crouch End to sweep the road. 'Only one man did any work. The other four stood smoking cigarettes.' This was not just a Haringey problem: the waste, repeated across the country by Labour councils, became unaffordable.

In the country as a whole, to prevent an economic collapse Callaghan had imposed a 5 per cent limit on pay increases, but it was not long before the bulwark was crumbling. Trade union leaders warned that high inflation was eroding their members' wages, and that they were unable to hold back pay demands. In October 1978 Labour was still ahead in the opinion polls, but despite expectations Callaghan refused to call an election. Soon after, the dam broke. When their demand for a 20 per cent pay increase was rebuffed, road haulage and oil tanker drivers went out on strike; some rail workers followed. Then Liverpool's dockers walked out, crippling not only Britain's biggest port but devastating local industries and eventually the city itself. Against this background, NUPE demanded a more than 40 per cent wage increase for council workers. The government refused, and Corbyn called on his members to vote for a strike.

Leading the militancy was Jack Jones, general secretary of the Transport and General Workers' Union, Britain's largest trade union. Callaghan was stymied. He relied on Jones to support his economic policy, even though MI5 had warned Harold Wilson that a raft of British trade union leaders were being paid by Moscow to advance communism in Britain. Among them was Jones, identified as a paid Soviet agent since the mid-1930s. Wilson had repeated that intelligence to his successor, but Callaghan chose to ignore the danger. That Christmas, the country sensed the lull before the storm. Corbyn stood and waited.

3

The Deadly Duo

Jane Chapman was torn. Politically and as an academic, she was a rising star, but her personal life made her miserable. For Christmas lunch she prepared a special five-course vegetarian meal for Corbyn and Piers. 'They stuffed it down their gullets and never said thanks,' she recalled in an even tone. Her husband, she knew, would have been happy with a can of beans: 'Usually Tesco, not Heinz, but he wouldn't know the difference. It was all just fuel to keep him going.' Their conversation was, as ever, about politics, mainly the inevitability of widespread strikes after the holiday.

Within Haringey council, everyone knew about Corbyn's conflict of interest. He was in charge of the employment of NUPE members, and at the same time he was their trade union representative organising a strike against the council. He was also responsible for the housing maintenance department, from which £2 million had gone missing annually for several years in succession. Council employees were both stealing money and inflating their claims for overtime. The consequence was a two-year backlog of repairs to council homes. Because workers had failed to do the necessary repairs, Haringey's housing was in a bad state, not least on the Broadwater Farm estate, the Tottenham home of over four thousand people that was ostensibly managed by Chapman in her role as chairman of housing. She would claim that the estate's day-to-day management had been delegated to a local association, but, along with her husband, she was doing little to remedy the borough's appalling housing shortage. In her defence she could

rely on the support of Bernie Grant, who tagged the accusations of corruption as 'absolutely ridiculous'. The Tories called
for an independent investigation, but Corbyn refused to countenance it. 'We will conduct the inquiry,' he said, despite a
previous internal inquiry ending, according to the Tories, in 'a
whitewash exercise'. No one expressed any confidence in
Corbyn's investigation, especially as his solution was to increase
the number of council workers without their either carrying
out any identifiable tasks or producing any benefits to the local
community.

In late December 1978, Haringey's employees' demands for a
40 per cent pay increase were rejected – at the time that private
sector employees were accepting 7 per cent rises – and they
went on strike. Corbyn, even though he was their employer,
joined them as a NUPE official on their picket line outside the
council's premises. Rapidly, Haringey's streets filled with bags of
uncollected rubbish, children could not enter their schools (the
caretakers prevented them), and repairs to council homes were
abandoned. 'Volvos are sliding on the ice on Muswell Hill,'
Corbyn gaily told Toby Harris, the local party chairman and a
fellow councillor. The sight of suffering middle classes, Harris
noticed, evidently pleased Corbyn. Identical strikes hit many
parts of Britain. The lurch towards national panic was highlighted by council workers refusing to bury the dead. Newspaper
photographs of Haringey's plight showed the irate parents of
some of the 37,000 children denied their education. 'The press
is just full of crisis, anarchy, chaos, disruption,' Tony Benn
recorded in his diary on 22 January 1979. 'I have never seen
anything like it in my life.'

With noticeable glee, Corbyn continued to support the strikers. On NUPE's behalf, he had skilfully organised the dustmen's
dispute. Only the drivers went on strike. The loaders stayed at
'work', and shared their wages with the drivers, while Corbyn
refused to hire private contractors to collect the rubbish. He
also sided with the school caretakers, who were forbidden to
hand over the door keys to headmasters to open the borough's
ninety-six schools. Teachers were ordered not to enter the

buildings, and those who agreed to help educate children outside their classrooms were threatened by a NUPE rent-a-mob, vocal agitators summoned by the union to assert its cause. Haringey's parents were furious that no other children in London were being denied their education, but Corbyn dismissed their protests as immaterial to the workers' rights, which he said came first. The parents staged several public demonstrations, protesting that Haringey had failed in its statutory duty to provide education, but Corbyn arranged for Trotskyites, holding banners that read 'Low pay, no way', to stand between them and the TV cameras. 'He wasn't a great one for education,' recalls Chapman, 'and as he didn't have kids he didn't care about opening the schools.'

Although lambasted by local newspapers, Corbyn was ignored by the national media – the chaos was universal, not just in Haringey. The strikes ended after six weeks. In that decisive moment, the post-war consensus between Labour and the Tories to accept the state's control of markets, industries and housing was over. Most Britons blamed the trade unions for crippling industries, and in particular their restrictive practices which prevented modernisation and lowered productivity. Conservative leader Margaret Thatcher was committed to unravelling the monopoly of state socialism. By contrast, the left was excited by the display of raw working-class power. Polls showed that the strikes were highly unpopular with the public, but Corbyn dismissed this, and ignored complaints by local NUPE members that his political agitation was coming at the expense of their private lives.

There were consequences. Corbyn had forbidden private construction workers to cross the picket lines, and eventually the council had to pay them £6,160 in compensation for loss of earnings, the equivalent today of £25,000. A committee was set up to award bonuses to council workers who had to clear the backlogs caused by the strike: Corbyn was its chairman. His conflict of interest was referred by the borough's chief executive to the director of public prosecutions. He would be acquitted of any wrongdoing, and was merely castigated for managerial incompetence. Around the same time, he forbade an animal circus to perform in the borough.

The strikes divided the forty-two Labour councillors in Haringey. The moderate majority, with the support of the seventeen Tory councillors, opposed Corbyn's ambitions to turn their borough into a mini-Marxist state. In his undisguised bid for power, he challenged council leader Colin Ware, a conventional social democrat. Although he was defeated, he had demonstrated that he had considerable backing. 'You could not out-left Corbyn,' recalled Robin Young, the Labour whip. 'He detested everyone who disagreed with him. And he always got others to do his dirty work.' Constantly calculating the numbers and the strategy to assert control, Corbyn quietly ordered junior councillors to propose motions to destabilise the moderates, encouraged activists to challenge his ideological enemies in the Labour branches, and energetically recruited far leftists as Labour Party members. As an organiser he was showing real political gifts. Young's biggest gripe was that 'Corbyn played no part in building Haringey's houses and social services. He just played politics.' Even Mark Killingworth, a fellow left-wing councillor, had grown to dislike Corbyn's conspiratorial ways. 'He wanted all the power and to be the one leader everyone should follow. Jeremy and Jane turned every meeting of the Labour group into a terrible argument.'

Corbyn's opponents would not go quietly. Raucous meetings of the Hornsey Labour Party were testing Toby Harris, its chairman. 'Corbyn was encouraging all the left groups to join. Some arrived with fake names, especially the hardliners. They were out-lefting each other, and he loved that, but he never identified with one group. He just distributed leaflets, announced the next demo, but never stood up as a leader to say what we should do.' A general election was imminent – the five-year parliamentary term expired that year – and Corbyn was certain that Labour would win, especially in Hornsey, which was a marginal seat. All that remained was to select a candidate.

Corbyn was well prepared. His support was based entirely on an individual's political beliefs, not on their personal relation-

ship with him. So in the final run-off to select the Labour candidate he made no distinction between Reg Race, the friend who
had secured his job at NUPE, and Ted Knight, a well-known
forty-five-year-old unmarried Trotskyite. Knight was leader of
Lambeth council, notorious for its debts, its corrupt workforce,
and for failing to prevent serious sexual abuses at a young children's home. Ostensibly, Corbyn supported Race's nomination
by introducing him to the members in every ward, but he
seemed untroubled when Knight won selection by a single vote.
With the support of the local party's far-left professionals,
recruited by Corbyn, he would be the Labour candidate.
Corbyn, however, had private reservations. Always dressed in a
dark suit, Knight addressed everyone as 'Comrade', delivered
with a distinct hint of menace, and in private screamed obscen-
ities. 'He scares me,' Corbyn admitted to Keith Veness. No genuine friendship was ever forged between the two, not least
because they supported opposing Trotskyist factions.

In a campaign leaflet issued by Corbyn, Knight pledged to
strengthen the legal protection of strikers, to 'weaken the capitalist police who are an enemy of the working class', pay 'not a
penny for defence', and repeal the Prevention of Terrorism Act,
which gave the police emergency powers to deal with suspected
terrorists. As IRA supporters, Corbyn and Knight opposed any
law specifically targeted at the Irish which empowered the
police to stop people entering or leaving Britain, and to control
the membership, activities and finances of proscribed organisations like the IRA. Going well beyond Labour's official policy,
the two men also advocated mass nationalisation of banks,
industry, major shops and newspapers – all without compensation. These promises were important, but in targeting the immigrant vote Corbyn made race an issue by recruiting Martha
Osamor of the United Black Women's Action Group to spread
the word that Labour would abolish immigration controls. In
his election speeches across Hornsey he accused Thatcher of
promoting 'racism and fascist forces'. To create a false image of
the National Front storming through the borough, he and
Knight constantly staged protests under the banner 'No Nazis

in Hornsey'. The far left and immigrant groups admired this side of his campaigning, but when he refused to pay homage on Remembrance Day to those who had died in the two world wars, he was criticised even by moderate Labour supporters for 'exploiting the anti-fascist platform for left-wing political ends'. Tories directly accused his canvassers of telling West Indian immigrants that they would be sent home if Labour lost the election. Haringey's one black councillor supported the Conservatives' protest – which was perhaps not surprising, because he was a Tory.

In his unquestioning allegiance to Knight's utterances – even supporting the extremist demand that all local shops be nationalised – Corbyn for the first time exposed his attitude towards Jews. In July 1976, Israeli special forces had carried out a raid at Entebbe airport in Uganda to rescue 102 hostages on board a hijacked aeroplane. It was a spectacular success, but during the election campaign, Knight publicly criticised the operation, and Corbyn agreed. 'His support for Knight,' said David Barlow, a middle-of-the-road Labour councillor in Haringey, 'an awful candidate who was destroying Lambeth council, showed that Corbyn was dubious.' Jews who were otherwise Labour supporters refused to vote for Knight. Some were also uncertain about Corbyn, by then a prominent local politician in Haringey and now identified as Knight's henchman.

Galvanised by the industrial unrest, Corbyn and Knight grasped the opportunity to lead a left-wing takeover of the entire London Labour Party (LLP), covering the capital's thirty-two boroughs, with over a thousand Labour councillors and fifty-one out of ninety-two MPs. They made no effort to conceal their Trotskyist agenda. Corbyn began writing regular articles for the *Socialist Organiser*, a weekly newspaper representing the Trotskyist Revolutionary Socialist League, and was frequently seen marching under the banner of the Socialist Campaign for a Labour Victory with Alan Thornett, a leader of the Workers Socialist League. Corbyn and Knight worked closely with Ken Livingstone, a forty-four-year-old GLC councillor well known for disrupting neighbouring Camden council's housing department (Livingstone was the department's chairman) with rent freezes, strikes and compulsory purchase orders. 'Jeremy's just like me,' Livingstone would say. 'You get what you see.' *Socialist Organiser* was Livingstone's mouthpiece for the ambitious Trotskyite group inside the Labour Party. While Livingstone was selected as the Labour general election candidate in Hampstead, and Knight in Hornsey, Reg Race became the candidate in Wood Green, the adjoining borough.

Corbyn's continuing embrace of Trotskyites alarmed several of his colleagues. In a plea to Jim Callaghan to stop the left's takeover of 'many of our inner city parties', Douglas Eden, a member of the Hornsey branch for fifteen years, identified Corbyn – along with forty-three Labour MPs and twenty-six parliamentary candidates, including Knight – as one of the ultra-leftists who 'overtly associated themselves with extreme Marxist activities'. Corbyn and the others, wrote Eden, were 'unrepresentative of Labour voters' and had 'no scruples about associating themselves with totalitarian organisations'. Naming the 'public-school-educated Cllr Jeremy Corbyn and his fellow-traveller' Chapman, Eden attacked the 'fascist left [who] manipulate any public office they hold to further their own undemocratic ends'.

Among his examples was Jane Chapman's removal of three moderate Labour governors of Creighton School, a Haringey comprehensive, which she carried out without notice or hearing. Allegedly, the governors had tried to open the school during the caretakers' strike, and were accused of 'not giving support at a critical time to the strikers'. Despite their denials, they were replaced by three ultra-leftists including Bernie Grant. 'Are there any moderates left,' asked many Labour voters in Haringey, 'to stop these empire-building fanatics, or have they been eliminated by the "deadly duo"?'

The reckoning was unexpectedly swift. In March 1979, Margaret Thatcher tabled a motion of no confidence in Callaghan's government, which was passed by just one vote (311 to 310), triggering a general election to be held in May, six months before the end of the five-year term. In April, just weeks before the election, Labour's ruling group in Haringey fired five left-wing chairmen, including Corbyn, Chapman and Mark Killingworth. In what the moderates called 'The Night of the Long Knives', their spokesman explained: 'We were fed up with these individuals. The elite was making a mess of certain jobs.' Corbyn was naturally outraged: 'The council leadership have given us a tremendous kick in the teeth despite all the good work we have done.' Killingworth blamed the departing chairman's self-interest: 'I didn't like his ambition and conspiracies. He created the "organiser" job so he could be powerful and then allowed the Trotskyites to infiltrate the constituency without us knowing.' Not surprisingly, the local Tories highlighted Labour's 'wild extravagance' and pronounced, 'The party is over.' That proved to be true on 3 May, the day Margaret Thatcher swept to power with an overall majority of forty-three. Labour lost a total of fifty seats.

Corbyn was shocked. He had even printed a leaflet announcing Hornsey as a Labour win. Every copy had to be dumped. Hugh Rossi, supported by traditional Labour voters changing their allegiance, secured by far his biggest majority – 4,037, up from 782 in October 1974. In endless post-mortems, Corbyn failed to draw the link between the strikes and how people had voted. Instead, he blamed Callaghan for refusing to destroy capitalism. By imposing a wage limit, the 'non-believer' had 'betrayed the working class'. As a result, the party's natural constituency had refused to vote Labour. 'You'll see,' Corbyn told his acolytes. 'The Tories will be out in four years after the people see the truth.' The only immediate consequence was a court summons for Corbyn and Knight for breaking electoral law by overspending in the campaign by £49.

Corbyn rightly saw Thatcher's pledge to reverse his community-style socialism and resurrect individualism and the market economy as a threat. Her instant dismissal of the government-appointed regulators of wages and prices, her introduction of laws to prevent trade unions organising wildcat strikes, the denationalisation of inter-city coaches, the abolition of exchange controls so that Britons were allowed to take more than £50 a year out of the country, and the sale of council homes all enraged him. Her promise to cut government expenditure despite inevitable unemployment was, in Corbyn's world view, a declaration of war. He demanded 'a massive campaign against the cuts'. Together with Ken Livingstone, Bernie Grant, Ted Knight and Keith Veness, the knights of the Socialist Campaign for Labour Victory, he plotted to reverse Labour's political fortunes.

Haringey was one of the Tory government's prime targets. Over the previous five years, the council had employed an additional thousand people and accumulated a £6 million deficit, yet its services were deteriorating. Now, Thatcher forbade all councils to increase their debts, and at the same time reduced their government grants. Most councils sought to improve their efficiency, but Corbyn protested that less money meant cuts in services. Without appreciating the irony, he told the Labour group, 'We must positively defend and protect services which have already been badly hit.' He took no responsibility for the uncollected rubbish, closed schools and unrepaired council homes. Instead, as the leader of the left, he launched a counter-attack, demanding that the Labour group defy the government by setting illegally high rates. 'We'll be personally surcharged,' the moderates retorted, fearing that their privately-owned homes would be seized to pay the fines. Corbyn continued to demand the sacrifice, without revealing that his own flat had been bought with a GLC mortgage, and was therefore safe from repossession.

Robin Young, Labour's new council leader, discovered that there was nothing gentle about Corbyn's politics. 'He was very ambitious but always careful not to get into trouble with the party,' Young observed, echoing Mark Killingworth's assessment, adding that 'he always disguised his grabs for power'. Toby Harris also noticed that while Corbyn presented his arguments in calm and considered terms, he deliberately generated hostility towards moderates, while managing the inevitable disputes among the left about demands and tactics to present a united front. His success, observed Barbara Simon, the Hornsey party's general secretary, owed much to his being 'good-tempered, patient and hard-working'. But despite his qualities, Corbyn still led only a minority of councillors. Undeterred, in 1980 he sought to topple Young by standing against him in the Labour group's leadership election. Once again, he employed a mild manner to disarm his opponents. 'He never had stand-up rows,' Killingworth noticed. 'He was more cunning than that.' Without being confrontational or physically threatening, Corbyn expressed his bitter intolerance of his ideological enemies in quiet tones. 'He would propose motions about housing, rates or council employees in party meetings,' recalled Killingworth, 'with extreme demands but worded as if only the Tories could oppose his ideas. And he cleverly presented himself as seemingly detached while encouraging his supporters to threaten his opponents with no-confidence motions. Those meetings were really nasty.' Nevertheless, on this occasion Young came out the victor.

The intensity of these political battles finally destroyed Corbyn's marriage. Just before Christmas 1979, Chapman walked out of the family home. 'He didn't see it coming,' said Toby Harris. Keith Veness agreed that Chapman 'just gave up on him'. Nothing about Corbyn was an enigma. The monochrome was reality. As she packed her belongings, Corbyn told his wife, 'You should read Simone de Beauvoir and never write your autobiography.' Clearly, ever the non-reader, he had heard about de Beauvoir from someone, and had failed to understand the author's philosophy. Women, de Beauvoir complained, were regarded as 'the second sex', and defined by their relationship to men. To rescue themselves, they should elevate themselves by exercising the same choice as men – precisely what Chapman had decided to do. Corbyn's reference to her autobiography also jarred, because the flat was filled with boxes of leaflets, minutes of party meetings and newspaper cuttings – all kept, he explained, for when he decided 'to write my memoirs'.

Corbyn was exhibiting all the contradictions of an unresolved personality, disconnected from the real world. His self-portrayal as a universal 'do-gooder' was at odds with his inability to care for his wife, or indeed any female companion. He was quite incapable of understanding why his marriage had collapsed. 'He thought I left him on a feminist kick,' recalled Chapman, 'but it was because I wanted some fun. His lack of emotional awareness didn't change. My emotional life as part of a relationship was forgotten.' Finally she realised that his judgement at the beginning of their relationship that she was 'the best of the best' was because 'I was the only woman who admired him and would put up with his political obsessions'. There was no parting gift. 'I got neither the dog nor the cat,' said Chapman, 'because I moved into a single room in a West Indian's flat. I had nowhere else to go.' Nearly twenty years later, Corbyn invited Chapman for tea in the Commons. 'You should lighten up,' he advised her, convinced as usual that he had been in the right. If anyone lacked a sense of humour, thought Chapman, it was her former husband.

Shortly after his wife's departure from Lausanne Road, Corbyn encouraged Keith Veness and Steve Hull, another political ally, to join him in posting leaflets around a council estate and starting to canvass for the next local elections. At about 11.30 in the morning he announced, 'We need to collect more leaflets,' and drove them back to his flat. The three of them walked in to discover a naked woman on the bed. Diane Abbott, Corbyn proudly announced, was his new girlfriend. 'He wanted us to see her in his bed,' recalled Veness. 'She was shocked when we entered.' She had quickly wrapped herself in a duvet.

Abbott was the antithesis of a white, middle-class English woman. Born to Jamaican immigrants in 1953 (her father was a welder, her mother a nurse), she went to a grammar school in London, then to Cambridge. As the first female black student from a state school at Newnham College, she enjoyed a hectic social life. Articulate and determined, she became firmly hard left, committed to the class struggle. She would always blame 'the system' for the educational failure of black British children, never their parents or her own community. After graduating with a lower second in history she was hired by the Home Office, but swiftly moved to the National Council for Civil

Liberties (NCCL) as a race relations officer. Belying the human rights group's name, her fellow employees rummaged through her desk and found her private diary. One entry recorded her sexual fantasy of being manhandled by her lover Corbyn, 'a bearded Fenian and NUPE national organiser', and also descriptions of a motorbike holiday with him around France and a passionate romp in a Cotswold field, which she described as her 'finest half-hour'.

Corbyn's passion for Abbott ended any hope Jane Chapman might have had that their relationship could be restored. He had found a political soulmate who shared his anger at Callaghan's treachery, regarded Britain as the country that 'invented racism', and echoed his praise for the IRA. 'Every defeat for the British state,' Abbott would say, 'is a victory for all of us.' Feisty and, in her early years, good-looking, Abbott persuaded Corbyn to change his habits to suit her, at least for a while: he enjoyed social evenings with her and friends at restaurants and dinner parties. 'We had a working supper in our living room one time,' recalls Barbara Simon. 'Jeremy brought Diane, who didn't come across as noisy and brash. She must have found the scene of two warring factions in Hornsey intimidating.' Simon had equal sympathy for Corbyn: 'Women were chasing him and he got trapped.'

Despite his and Abbott's sexual and political closeness, Corbyn spent Christmas Day 1979 alone. 'What will you do?' Toby Harris had asked him. 'I'm going to the Suffolk seaside and letting my dog run along the beach,' Corbyn replied. Others described his despair because there were no political meetings on Christmas Day, as he could not face his family.

He returned to London to pursue his vocation – politics. As leader of Haringey council's left-wing caucus, he could not be ignored. The safe option was to elect him chairman of the planning committee, a role without any budget. Unlike his predecessors, he did not attract even a suspicion of favouritism – he appeared wholly incorruptible. He refused all invitations for drinks with possible lobbyists, and would not even meet developers. His hatred of the middle class was as fervent as ever: he encouraged plans to build council blocks among private houses, and when people protested he dismissed them, scoffing: 'The arrogance of all those doctors and lawyers, talking about the environment when what they're scared of is black kids.' To further spite Muswell Hill's middle class, he allowed gypsy families to set up an encampment on local playing fields.

Corbyn's high profile locally was not mirrored across the capital. Only Ken Livingstone, a better speaker and a consummate networker, had the ability to take control of London's left. After his defeat in Hampstead in the 1979 general election, Livingstone recruited Corbyn, Keith Veness and Ted Knight for 'Target 82', a secret timetable he submitted to the Trotskyist Socialist Campaign for Labour Victory (SCLV) to take control of the GLC after its elections in May 1981. After long discussions, their fellow members in the SCLV dismissed the plan. The Trotskyites, Livingstone grumbled, were 'gross, grovelling toadies' – a slightly odd insult, as one of his hobbies was keeping newts.

'I'm pissed off with factional Trots,' agreed Keith Veness. Like the other three, he wanted to concentrate on gaining political power rather than engage in internecine warfare, the usual fate of most far-left groups. Breaking with the SCLV, some time in 1980 Veness invited Livingstone, Knight, Corbyn and Bernie Grant to his Highbury home, and together the group created a new cadre, London Labour Briefing. 'We're an open conspiracy to get rid of the right wing,' Corbyn declared. 'It's a two-stage insurgency,' added Veness. 'First grab control of the GLC, and then Thatcher's government.' The first step towards Target 82, they agreed, was to take over the London Labour Party and secure the nomination of fellow Trotskyists as Labour candidates in the GLC election. Acting to a strategy outlined by Trotsky, the minority would eventually make itself a majority. Trotsky himself, wrote the historian Robert Conquest, was 'a ruthless imposer of the party's will who firmly crushed the democratic opposition within the party and fully supported the rules which gave the ruling group total authority'. Abiding by those tactics, the Target 82 group agreed to remove their enemies as quickly as possible, consolidate their control, and never give it away.

The launch of London Labour Briefing was staged at the GLC's headquarters in County Hall. It attracted two hundred people, and was regarded by Livingstone, its prime organiser, as a 'great success'. Like all such groups, Briefing's credibility depended on publishing a newspaper. 'Even if it's not read,' said Veness, laughing, 'we've got to have one.' The editorial board of the weekly news-sheet included Corbyn as the group's general secretary, the reliable dogsbody prepared to undertake the unglamorous chores. Their aim was to deselect moderate Labour councillors and take over constituency parties, which would vote for Tony Benn as Labour leader when Jim Callaghan, as was expected, resigned. In the alphabet soup of initials of the rival left-wing groups, London Labour Briefing was affiliated to the London Representation Committee (LRC), a group chaired by John McDonnell, a member of Liverpool's Trotskyite Militant Tendency. The LRC urged 'mass extra-parliamentary action' to disrupt the economy, and published hit lists of Labour MPs it described as 'traitors'. McDonnell openly enthused about riots as the precursor to an uprising. That difference did not prevent him and Corbyn bonding during the endless meetings favoured by the left.

In their joint cause, Corbyn eagerly began to organise his supporters in Hornsey to force out his enemies. He particularly targeted Douglas Eden, not least for his having mocked him as 'public-school-educated'. 'It was a *grammar* school,' Corbyn told the *Hornsey Journal*, adding that it was 'now happily a comprehensive'. This was another small untruth. The school remained fee-paying for selected children. If it burnished his left-wing credentials, Corbyn was still willing to lie about trivialities.

Chairing the inquiry into Eden's loyalty, Corbyn allowed the social democrat to speak in his own defence for forty-five minutes – then promptly announced his expulsion. Eden protested to Reg Underhill, Labour's national agent at party headquarters, that he had been 'hounded out by Corbyn'. Underhill, who was leading the hunt against Trotskyist infiltration, notified Haringey's branch secretary that she had failed to follow the proper procedures, and the inquiry should be reheld. Unabashed, Corbyn started the expulsion process again, with the same result.

Eden's fate was replicated across London. As moderate members were forced out of the party, Corbyn, Knight, Livingstone and McDonnell were elected to the national executive of the London Labour Party, and immediately began the deselection process of moderate councillors who had been put forward as candidates for the May 1981 GLC elections. Under the banner of the Campaign for Labour Party Democracy, every candidacy was to be openly contested, ostensibly to allow greater democracy but in fact to allow the left to take over. This would, to use Tony Benn's catchwords, transform Labour into a 'pluralist grassroots party of the masses', one that would exclude dissenters, especially social democrats. In Brent East, where Livingstone hoped to snatch the parliamentary nomination from a moderate MP, he, like Corbyn, had forged close relations with immigrant groups by pledging to remove the restrictions on migrants settling in Britain. In return, over a hundred Asians – many of them unable to speak English – were enrolled as party members in the constituency and obediently voted against Livingstone's rivals. A similar pattern emerged in Islington. 'If voting changed anything,' sniped one moderate, 'they'd abolish it.'

Livingstone asked Corbyn if he planned to stand in Haringey for the GLC, and was surprised when Corbyn said he did not. As a full-time NUPE official, he explained, he would find it difficult to attend the GLC's daytime meetings. The truth was different. Corbyn was sceptical about joining an authority with limited powers, and was still harbouring his secret ambition to become an MP. His allies were unaware that because of his extremism he had already been rejected as the prospective parliamentary candidate in Enfield North. Next, he had unsuccessfully applied in Croydon, but a chance encounter in the Croydon party's headquarters with his old friend Val Veness, who was also applying for the seat, changed his life. 'I didn't realise you wanted to be an MP,' she said. 'I might be able to help you. But it's got to be kept secret.' Keeping secrets had never been a problem for Corbyn.

For years, Keith and Val Veness and their claque had been trying to remove Michael O'Halloran, the Labour MP for Islington North. Despite being accused of corruption and incompetence, O'Halloran had allegedly been installed, then protected, by 'the Murphia', the local Irish mafia. O'Halloran accused the Venesses of bombarding him and his family with personal abuse in their attempts to hound him out. In the standoff, the Venesses had agreed with their group that if O'Halloran were removed, none of them would seek the nomination to replace him. The left therefore needed a candidate to counter any moderate applicants. Secrecy, they decided, was essential if they were to outwit their opponents. When Livingstone persisted in his attempts to secure Corbyn's nomination to the GLC, he was told sharply by Val Veness, 'Keep your hands off our candidate.' He backed down, accepting Corbyn's promise that he would work tirelessly to execute the coup at the GLC and also act as the agent for Kate Hoey, a member of the Marxist IMG, to win the Labour GLC nomination for Haringey.

During that frantic period of plotting, Corbyn paid little attention to Diane Abbott, who by then was working as a TV producer in London. 'She was noisy, ambitious, lefty and overweight,' was Jonathan Aitken's impression during their encounters in the television world. In her excitable manner, Abbott fretted that Corbyn and Chapman were still meeting each other at Haringey council. Chapman recalled a 'nervous, tense and slightly hostile' Abbott knocking on her door one evening, and when Chapman answered making her demands clear.

'Get the hell out of here,' said Abbott. 'You're in the media and everywhere and I want you out of town.'

'I can't,' replied Chapman. 'I've been elected to office.'

Abbott was clearly disgruntled.

Later, Chapman explained, 'She wanted a clear run. I was in the media a lot then because of my political work and she wished I wasn't.' Abbott was also fed up with Corbyn's way of life; just as he had ignored Chapman, he was now ignoring her. Although she had enjoyed many relationships, none had led to as intense a friendship as she now had with Corbyn, but that too was failing. At twenty-seven, she wanted marriage and eventually children. Corbyn wanted neither.

One morning, Bernie Grant called Keith Veness. 'Diane's had enough of Jeremy. She's moving out. Come and give us a hand.' Veness arrived at Lausanne Road in a large van. The flat was strewn with papers and clothing. 'It's hard to have a relationship with someone who doesn't come home for two weeks,' said Abbott defensively. She, Grant, and Veness set about packing away her things. Suddenly the door opened, and in walked Corbyn. 'Hello, mate,' he said to Grant. Then he saw Veness carrying out Abbott's possessions. After hearing why the two men were there, he walked away without comment; he was off to a meeting, he said. Appalled by the way Abbott, a fellow child of the Caribbean, had been treated, Grant chased after Corbyn. 'Get real,' he said, knowing full well that Corbyn remained insult-proof, and would certainly feel no guilt. Later Corbyn would recall, 'Diane always says to me, "You learned everything you know in Shropshire, and unfortunately you've forgotten none of it."'

In his political life at least, Corbyn was feeling empowered. Inflation was still rising, and Tory cuts were causing high unemployment and widespread distress. Daily, he would rush off to join picketing strikers or anti-government marches through another city centre against cuts and apparent Tory heartlessness towards the sick and unemployed. In March 1980, convinced that Labour's 1979 election defeat could be reversed by direct action, Corbyn and twelve other left-wing Haringey councillors urged Robin Young not to bow to government pressure to limit rises in the rates in order to control inflation, then running at 14 per cent. Young refused to act illegally, and set a 36 per cent increase, a phenomenal hike, but insufficient for Corbyn, who wanted nearer 50 per cent, and refused to support the Labour council. Young had no illusions about the forthcoming encounter: 'Corbyn built his own Berlin Wall and stood on the other side. He introduced hatred and divisions between us. He got it so that the left would not speak to the right, and after that battle we barely spoke. He hated anyone who didn't subscribe to his view. He wanted them out.' In the vote over the rates increase, Corbyn led his group of thirteen fellow-travellers to side with the Tories. The Labour moderates won – just. 'They were pretty horrible people,' recalled Young, but he did not dare discipline his rival. Two months later the group made a renewed attempt to oust Young, and again failed.

By then Corbyn's relationship with Tony Benn had become unusually close. 'Benn would come to love Corbyn as his son,' reckoned George Galloway, a twenty-six-year-old Dundee-born Marxist and a rising star in the Scottish Labour Party. Corbyn was devoting much of his time to supporting the ambitions of Benn, who embodied the aspiration of many idealistic young socialists, for the party leadership. For Benn, corporate capitalism was incompatible with democracy, and formed the main threat to civilised life, a philosophy embraced by Corbyn. At Labour's Blackpool conference in September 1980, Benn won a vote in favour of unilateral disarmament and cowed Jim Callaghan into allowing the mandatory reselection of MPs, a critical part of the strategy of 'democratising' the party. The left was gaining power.

Popular discontent about early Thatcherism created fevered excitement among Corbyn's associates, who believed that the government was heading towards a cliff edge, with the cabinet divided over her abandonment of the post-war consensus. Losing public support, and even her customary self-confidence, Thatcher was expected by the left to capitulate to their demands. Instead, she turned defiant. At the Tory party conference she scolded: 'To those waiting with bated breath for that favourite media catchphrase, the U-turn, I have only one thing to say: You turn if you want to. The lady's not for turning.' That phrase had been written for her by Ronald Millar, her speechwriter and a well-known playwright.

Five days later, on 15 October, Callaghan resigned as Labour leader, hoping that Denis Healey would be elected as his successor. If Tony Benn were chosen, Callaghan feared, Labour would be transformed into a genuinely revolutionary and unelectable party. There were three candidates: Benn, Healey, and that veteran of the democratic left, Michael Foot. Convinced that enough moderates had been expelled in the constituencies, Corbyn assured Benn that he would win, but Benn decided not to divide the left's vote, and withdrew. As a result, Foot, who distrusted Benn as a disloyal, divisive and opportunist upstart, became leader. Healey's defeat plunged the party into turmoil after Bennites won a majority on Labour's National Executive Council (NEC). Led by European Commission president Roy Jenkins, a sophisticated former home secretary and chancellor, the moderates openly debated whether to quit Labour and set up a new political party. But for Corbyn and the left, Michael Foot was equally unacceptable, as a 'prisoner of the right'.

The growing likelihood of Benn challenging Foot encouraged Tariq Ali, a member of the IMG and the author of, among other publications, *Trotsky for Beginners*, to abandon Trotskyism (in public at least) and, with Corbyn's encouragement, apply to join his local Hornsey Labour Party. In practical terms, it made sense for Ali to jump aboard the Benn bandwagon and try to take over Labour from within. Although he condemned Benn's politics as 'bourgeois', he could see how popular he was among voters. In Hornsey, Corbyn's alignment with a well-known Trotskyite angered the moderates. What he called a 'rainbow coalition' was, in their opinion, outrightly subversive of the Labour Party. Even Toby Harris, a Corbyn ally and a leading member of the local branch, objected to Ali's membership. Within weeks, Corbyn manoeuvred for Harris to be voted off the General Management Committee. Max Morris, a former communist and the chairman of the ward Ali joined, denounced Corbyn as Ali's puppet. He too was threatened with expulsion by having his ward packed with new members, all Trotskyists. In response, a local party executive publicly condemned Corbyn for 'the most extraordinary manipulation of the rules'.

On 13 May 1981, the Queen opened a new shopping centre in Haringey. Corbyn made sure he was absent – another move calculated to drive moderates out of his local party. The resulting tumult persuaded party headquarters to veto Ali's membership application. Labour's leaders, complained Corbyn, were 'hell-bent on an unremitting war on the socialists in the party – they have no intention of disarming or taking power from the City'. In defiance, he accepted Ali's second application to join the party, and persuaded Barbara Simon to issue him with a membership card. After all, he said, Ted Grant and Peter Taaffe, both members of the Trotskyite Militant Tendency, were members of the party in neighbouring Islington: the discrimination against Ali reflected outright political prejudice. This was not Corbyn the obedient class warrior on a treadmill – he had become engaged in a frontal war.

Immersed in ideological battles in Hornsey and Haringey, he was simultaneously engaged with violent strikers – his own council employees, who were hurling abuse at Haringey's moderate councillors (such as remained). In the middle were the police – 'a barrier to the people's revolution', as Corbyn saw them. Inside the town hall, he plotted with local trade union chiefs to challenge his party leaders with a new demand for a 43 per cent rates increase. 'They object to rate rises,' he said of his Labour opponents, 'because they can't get over them like they can fiddle corporation tax and their profits.' The moderate Labour councillors retorted that he was pandering to the totalitarian left by 'speaking out unashamedly in favour of terrorism' and by leading the 'anti-patriotic, anti-police faction'. From the Tory side, he was dubbed a 'tinpot dictator' for protecting what they dubbed 'Jeremy's Angels' – Haringey's corrupt council workers. The indictment was irrefutable: the district auditor had discovered that Haringey's caretakers were submitting fraudulent overtime claims and the dustmen had stolen council property.

Corbyn's response was to approve a triple pay bonus for dustmen. 'While the Labour council remains in power,' he said, 'no trade unionist in its employ will want for anything.' Equally, he ignored the consequences of his demand for rates increases, which had caused two major employers, Gestetner and Thorn Electrical, to move away from the borough. Corbyn did not comment. Instead, he tried again to topple Robin Young, but again failed to get a majority of the forty-two Labour councillors. In revenge, the moderates voted Corbyn off the planning committee. Characterised as a spendthrift, he even lost the vice chairmanship of the allotments committee. Undeterred, he continued to plot Young's removal by deselecting more long-serving moderate councillors in favour of his own sympathisers. By early 1981, fourteen out of twenty-two new candidates in Haringey had been nominated by London Labour Briefing. Across the capital, at least twenty moderates had been deselected, and 130 Labour councillors had stepped down rather than face humiliation. Inevitably, Corbyn denied any part in orchestrating the purge. 'We don't draw up lists,' he told the *Hampstead & Highgate Express*. Instead, he explained, the councillors selected were 'politically experienced in community politics' – 'community' being his euphemism for using the Labour Party to spread revolutionary socialism.

In March 1981 the skirmishes in Haringey, replicated across the country, finally provoked senior moderates within Labour to split. Exasperated by the activities of the far left, the anti-Marxists led by Roy Jenkins resigned from Labour and created the Social Democratic Party. Few believed the SDP had any chance of electoral success, but within months it had won both parliamentary seats and council elections. Corbyn and Benn blamed Michael Foot. Although the Tories criticised the Labour leader as a dangerous leftie, to Corbyn he was a paternalistic parliamentarian obsessed with 'bureaucracy' rather than mobilising the masses for revolution. Even worse, Foot ignored Benn's protest against 'the thought police' in the party, and ordered the expulsion of Trotskyites, Marxists and other entryists. Among the first casualties were the editors of Liverpool's *Militant* newspaper, although their expulsion did not undermine Derek Hatton and his fellow Trotskyists on the city council intent, like Corbyn, to challenge the government.

In April 1981, anti-police riots erupted in Brixton – home of the largest police station in the capital outside Scotland Yard – sparked by disaffected black youths living in deprived areas. The riots spread to Liverpool and Manchester. After a mob outside a police station yelled 'Kill, kill', Corbyn condemned the 'capitalist police' and attacked the media's reporting of the riots as 'disgraceful'. He and John McDonnell welcomed the rise of revolutionary fervour against Thatcher, and were delighted when it spread to Northern Ireland. The world's attention was focused on Bobby Sands, a twenty-six-year-old IRA member leading a hunger strike in the Maze prison outside Belfast. Naked and near death, Sands had just won a by-election to become a Member of Parliament. For Corbyn and the far left, his defiant martyrdom symbolised the resonance of their struggle. The next stage was to deliver the Target 82 coup in the GLC elections in May.

Ken Livingstone believed that all his work over the previous two years to replace moderate Labour candidates would win his faction a marginal majority within the Labour group in the GLC. But every vote was important. To his irritation Kate Hoey, the candidate in Hornsey, unexpectedly resigned to stand for Parliament. Livingstone renewed his appeal to Corbyn to stand, but he again declined, not least because of the way he was approached. 'Politics is like biting lumps out of people,' Livingstone had told him. Biting people was a practice Corbyn resisted – both verbal attacks and violence. He preferred others to do the dirty work. If he engaged in front-line warfare alongside Livingstone he would be exposed, not least to journalists who might begin investigating his past. That would interfere with his parliamentary ambitions and more. Instead he found a new candidate, David Hart, the son of Judith Hart, a left-wing Labour MP, who was duly voted in. Hart celebrated his victory with Livingstone, one of fifty Labour councillors against forty-one Tories. Within twenty-four hours Andrew McIntosh, the party's moderate GLC leader, had fallen victim to the Target 82 plotters: just as planned, Livingstone marshalled a bare majority of the Labour councillors – many his hand-picked leftists – to usurp McIntosh and win election for himself as Labour's leader. McIntosh, who six years earlier had been ousted as a councillor in Hornsey by Corbyn, had failed to learn his lesson. 'He wasn't a proper politician,' scoffed Livingstone.

The new GLC leader had much in common with his loyal acolyte. Like Corbyn, he too was portrayed by the media as a ruthless revolutionary living for politics and happy to be separated from his wife. 'Ken's not interested in ordinary human relations,' said one Labour councillor, 'simply in getting to the top of the greasy pole.' He wasted no time in putting his agenda into action: remaining moderate Labour members of the GLC were appalled by his imposition of higher rates to pay for cheap transport fares and, after Bobby Sands' death had incited the IRA to burn a mother of three children to death, his instant declaration of support for the IRA. Corbyn, by contrast, cheered Livingstone's audacity. Phase One was completed: the GLC was theirs. Thatcher was next.

4

The Other Comrade

'Where's that member of Militant who just won in Hayes?' asked Livingstone jocularly about a trusted comrade in the headquarters of the Greater London Council opposite Parliament.

'That's me!' replied John McDonnell. 'And I've left Militant.'

Livingstone admired McDonnell's 'macho form of class-based politics'. The Trotskyite's fondness for a violent revolution to topple the capitalists, said Livingstone, had been learned during his training as a supporter of Militant Tendency. Emerging from the shadows to become Livingstone's deputy at County Hall, McDonnell was soon voicing his disgust that moderate Labour GLC councillors dared to criticise his boss. Their so-called colleagues, he sneered, were traitors for advocating 'middle-of-the-road policies'. 'Traitor' was a word he was to use often in the years to come.

Born in Liverpool in 1951, the son of a docker, McDonnell had moved with his family to Great Yarmouth in the late 1950s. His father became a bus driver and his mother worked at the local British Home Stores, for a time at the biscuit counter. Good at maths, the flame-haired ten-year-old sat next to a girl named Judith Daniels at St Mary's Roman Catholic primary school. In later years, McDonnell suggested that he had whispered a maths answer to her to save her from a severe caning, but in reply she ridiculed his exaggeration. His whisper, she said, 'saved me from a gentle tapsy from an inspirational nun'. The small lie was similar to Jeremy Corbyn's attempts to build up the story of his early years, but in other respects their narratives were very different.

After passing the 11-Plus, McDonnell went to Great Yarmouth Grammar School, but left early due to trouble at home and at school. After briefly considering the priesthood, he arrived in Burnley to be employed first as a manual worker at Silent Night Beds and then at Mullard's in Simonstone, making TV screens for Philips. Shortly before his twentieth birthday he met Marilyn Bateman, a local nursery nurse four years his senior, at a miners' club. They married and moved to a small terraced house in a cul de sac in nearby Nelson. At nights he resumed studying for History A-Level at Burnley Municipal College. Three years later the McDonnells moved with their two daughters to west London, to establish a business fostering up to ten children in their home. McDonnell enrolled in an evening course in politics and government at Brunel University. During the first year, his political beliefs hardened.

At the beginning, his militancy was ambiguous. Barbara Goodwin, his tutor on government, recalled him as the least extreme in a group of eight students. 'He was regarded as a class traitor for defending Labour against the Trotskyites,' she recalled. Later, David Shapiro, his personal tutor, declared him 'academically unteachable. He was already a Marxist and it was all water off a duck's back. But he was pragmatic and sensible.' After graduating in 1976, McDonnell was employed as a researcher at the National Union of Mineworkers. By then he had become well known at the Hayes and Harlington branch of the Labour Party for leading a campaign to oust Neville Sandelson, the sitting Labour MP. The public-school-educated, cigar-smoking Jewish barrister was pro-Europe. 'He can't understand the grassroots trade union activists,' claimed McDonnell, who forced a vote that Sandelson should retire or be deselected. The MP survived by three votes, to be re-elected in the 1979 Labour bloodbath.

During the following three years, McDonnell left the NUM to work in the TUC's welfare section. As secretary of the TUC's book club, he selected each month's read. 'It's *Das Kapital*,' he told the other staff at the TUC's headquarters in Bloomsbury. 'That's the only book we're going to study.' He found himself alone in the room. Before Labour's defeat in 1979, he had gravitated towards the Trotskyites. Sitting in a café in Lambeth with George Galloway and the Workers Revolutionary Party leader Gerry Healy, he discussed the creation of the *Labour Herald*, a glossy magazine to be financed by Saddam Hussein and Muammar Gaddafi. Although he was a thug, rapist, fraudster and anti-Semite, Healy attracted many idealists to the WRP, including Keith Veness. 'McDonnell was a proper Trot in a way that Corbyn was not,' observed Galloway. Veness confirmed the judgement. With a hatchet face and jutting chin, McDonnell was confrontational, spouting Marxist jargon about constant agitation in his advocacy of violent disruption. Appointed as the new magazine's editor, he regularly appeared at WRP meetings to promote revolution, after which would come the mass nationalisation of the British economy and the abolition of all private land ownership, without compensation. With his new role, his life changed. His Trotskyist sympathies qualified him to become head of policy at Camden council, and his marriage ended. While his estranged wife continued to run the fostering business, he lived with Julia Fitzgerald, a Camden councillor, in a flat in Kentish Town.

During the following year, McDonnell plotted with Corbyn, Knight, Grant and Livingstone to take over the country's government. After the victory in 1981, he focused on anything that would challenge the government. Disguise was one chosen weapon. 'Cut your hair, dress properly, wear a tie and act the part,' he advised Toby Harris. 'He was always professional to win power,' says Harris, a member of the London Government Assembly, an elected group representing the London boroughs. Corbyn was very much part of the group, alongside McDonnell, Livingstone and Veness, and was the 'organiser' of London Labour Briefing. After his election as Labour leader in 2015 he would deny any official role for London Labour Briefing, but he is listed in the group's literature as responsible for the sale of tickets to a social event that offered curries during a discotheque evening, and two years later was named as overseeing the group's mailing list. Labour moderates in Haringey were

appalled by Corbyn, but the local newspaper, noting the election of more far-left councillors and Corbyn's brazen resubmis-
sion of Tariq Ali's third application to become a Labour member
in the borough, tipped him to become the council's next leader.

By then, fearful of the Marxists' threat to Britain's social
fabric, Conservative Central Office had appointed a professional
investigator, Peter Shipley, to monitor relations between Labour
MPs and the far left. Ever since James Callaghan had ended the
listing of proscribed organisations, left-wing Labour MPs had
joined lobby groups that were outwardly reputable, including
the World Peace Organisation, but that were in fact secretly
financed by Moscow. Among the British associations Shipley
investigated was the Movement for Colonial Freedom (MCF),
established by Fenner Brockway, a veteran Labour MP and a
paid Soviet agent. In 1981 the MCF, managed by Tony Gilbert,
a communist agent also controlled by Moscow, counted Corbyn
a member. Corbyn met Gilbert frequently, but establishing his
political sympathies towards Moscow was beyond Shipley's
remit. All he recognised was the far left's flaws.

Zealous and serious, all those in the group around Corbyn
appeared to march under the same banner, but they disagreed
constantly about ideology. They were brothers-in-arms rather
than soulmates, and as individuals showed no particular warmth
towards each other. One exception was the relationship between
Tony Benn and Corbyn. Benn's radical socialism had polarised
Labour. His ascent gave many Marxists and Trotskyites hope that
the Labour Party they had abandoned during the 1960s was
worth rejoining. To establish their shared ambitions, Tariq Ali,
Reg Race and others met Benn in the Commons along with
Corbyn, who said little, although everyone knew he could be
relied upon to make the logistical arrangements for Benn's imminent battle against Denis Healey in the election for Labour's
deputy leadership, the result of which was to be announced at
the Labour Party conference in Brighton on 27 September 1981.

In the days before the vote, Corbyn assured Benn of victory.
Combined with the defection of many Labour councillors to the
SDP, the deselections and intimidation were certain, he

predicted, to deliver the bulk of the constituency votes to the left. Corbyn also reckoned that Benn was assured of trade union support, including NUPE's. He was right about the constituencies (81 per cent voted for Benn), but wrong about the unions. Although Benn could attract huge crowds – even during an unannounced stop at a motorway service station nearly a hundred people had gathered to hear him make an impromptu speech – he also inspired hatred. The *Times* columnist Bernard Levin titled him 'Mr Zigzag Loon', while Denis Healey dismissed him as 'an artificial lefty'. The majority of the unions, including Haringey's branch of NUPE, voted against Benn, whom they saw as an extremist, but to the moderates' shock Healey's overall victory was wafer-thin – 50.4 per cent against 49 per cent for Benn. Corbyn's disappointment was intense. In the days following, Conservative Central Office became so convinced that the hard left was broken that Shipley's contract was not renewed. The Tories were profoundly mistaken. On reflection, Benn's narrow loss gave the left hope. In the nature of Corbyn's long road, there was never defeat, just one more precursor to another start, another campaign.

'What next?' Corbyn asked. Wounded by his defeat but pleased by the party's imminent split, Benn decided to host a monthly discussion group with Britain's leading Marxists on Sunday evenings at his home in Holland Park, west London. Among those invited to what he later called the Independent Corresponding Society were Ralph Miliband (the father of David and Ed), university teachers of sociology Hilary Wainwright and Robin Blackburn, and Tariq Ali. In the hierarchy of the left, Benn and Ali had inherited the political skills of the ruling class. They were also intellectuals – self-disciplined agents of social engineering – which Corbyn was certainly not. While Corbyn sat meekly as their NCO, a team player rather than a manager, their ideological theorising passed over his head. But he found comfort in their descriptions of the best tactics against the capitalists.

In a series of debates, the group considered whether peaceful reform was possible through Parliament and what Tariq Ali

called 'class collaboration' (the old Marxist notion that the bour-
geoisie would eventually unite with the working class).
Parliament only became relevant, Ali argued, when subjected to
pressures from outside groups, and should eventually be abolished. Distrustful of elections, since the mid-1960s Miliband
had preached that Parliament should be totally ignored. The
masses, he argued, should disregard both the trade unions and
the Labour Party, because socialism could be built only by
armed struggle. 'The elite always sells out,' he told the gathering,
and urged Benn to support revolution followed by the creation
of democratic soviets, or communities.

This was not yet Corbyn's thinking. Although energised by
disdain for Parliament and impatient with liberal democracy, he
accepted Benn's philosophy that 'to change the world you need
to join the Labour Party and work from within'. By hard work,
Benn said, Labour's Methodist roots would eventually be
replaced by true socialism with no need for violence. While
Benn's programme for socialism lacked the historical and
cultural perspective of Michael Foot and other intellectual
worshippers of the great socialist heroes, he was obsessed by the
need for democracy within the party. Structures and machinery
were fundamental to his programme to transform Labour, and
then the country, into a Marxist idyll. Without studying either
economics or finance, Corbyn absorbed Benn's slogans about
'equality' and 'justice', and adopted the belief that 'The role of
private capital should be ended.' Beyond that, he was intellectually adrift. 'He didn't understand the relevance of Marxist theory
about markets or a planned economy,' said one of the participat-
ing academics. 'You can't be an unconscious Marxist.' Corbyn's
ignorance did not diminish his passion for Marxism: he was
totally committed to the confiscation and redistribution of
wealth to produce equality – but knowing the philosophical
explanation was beyond him. As he retold stories in praise of
Salvador Allende to the group – his principal contribution to
their discussions – he came across as the most committed of
Marxists. Strangely, he never mentioned his experiences in
Jamaica or Guyana.

In later years, the impassioned discussions about Marxist dialectics and modern capitalism would be described as substitutes for Corbyn's missed university education. They were hardly that. Nevertheless, he did learn from Benn and Miliband that socialism would be built by mobilising workers to take over the ownership and control of key industries, and the importance of organising people in their workplaces and housing estates to struggle against the capitalists. Thereafter, employees and their trade unions would negotiate government investment and production plans with the managers, rather than be subject to employers, bankers and Parliament. Tellingly, in 2017 Labour's election manifesto would reflect Benn's promise to give workers the statutory right to buy their own companies at discounted prices with taxpayers' money. Thirty-six years earlier, in February 1981, Benn and Corbyn imagined Labour sweeping the Tories aside to implement just those policies. Their dream was encouraged in late 1981 by the miners' threat to strike in protest at the government's decision to close uneconomic pits. Fearing the same defeat as Heath, Thatcher surrendered. Soon after, Arthur Scargill was elected as the leader of the National Union of Mineworkers. The left felt further emboldened. Across the country, other militants similar to Corbyn were seizing control of Labour associations, galvanising the trade unions to replicate the miners' industrial challenge to Thatcher, and giving the impression of engaging in subversion.

In 1982, Corbyn, now thirty-two, ranked among the leaders of the left in the capital. Recognised by the *Economist* as London Labour Briefing's 'general secretary figure' and by the *Hornsey Journal* as joint editor of its newspaper, he boasted that the organisation was 'moving the leadership of most London authorities well to the left'. Reflecting that influence, he was elected as Hornsey's representative to Labour's regional executive, appointed the chairman of its finance committee, and also sat on a number of the London party's subcommittees. For the next council elections, he had ensured that half the Labour candidates in Hornsey were associated with London

Labour Briefing. All of them echoed his call for 'a full-frontal attack on the government', and obeyed his directive that they would vote to 'defy the law and the unelected judges' to increase rates, cut bus fares and back a twenty-four-hour general strike. Even so, within Haringey's Labour caucus his supporters were still a minority. In a vote in February 1982, the majority blocked his attempt to break the law and act outside 'the constitutional mechanism of Parliament'. They feared, however, that their victory was temporary, and that the 'anarchists', led by Corbyn, would stage a coup. Their anxiety was noticed in Westminster. Acting on Foot's instructions, his lieutenants purged the far left from the NEC. Right-wing Labour MPs, led by Bob Mellish, the chief whip, dismissed Corbyn as a 'middle-class Trot' with little contact with the working class.The Bennites were forced to retreat.

All those criticisms bounced off Corbyn, as did the endless complaints of Haringey's residents. Their list was damning. Parents were angered when a go-slow by council bus drivers, supported by Corbyn, left their handicapped children stranded at home; the homeless protested that his refusal to accept government money for rebuilding houses meant that 1,500 council properties had been left unoccupied; a quarter of the council's street cleaners were permanently absent on 'sick leave'; buildings had been flooded after the rubbish on Haringey's unswept streets had blocked the drains; and a Labour group report had exposed a 'bonus racket' rewarding council employ-ees for not working. Haringey's councillors admitted that they had lost control of their employees, mostly members of NUPE. Corbyn expressed no regret. Management and detail were of no concern to him. Nor was he sympathetic to the anger of white applicants for council jobs that Bernie Grant's aggressive campaign against racism intentionally discriminated against them. In his world, immigrants' interests were paramount. They were the victims of oppression. Any who disagreed, including Haringey's disgruntled residents, were the enemy. Just as he was unable to deal with his own personal life, he was unable to resolve many causes of other people's misery. He was an activist, not a manager willing to immerse himself in detail to improve the lives of *all* Haringey's inhabitants.

In spring 1982, as part of his single-minded quest to seize power, Corbyn was elected chairman of the Hornsey Labour Party, and immediately reignited his battle against the moderates. On 24 March a party meeting erupted in physical violence as he once again attempted to ram through Tariq Ali's membership, despite the opposition of the national executive. Moderates erupted in anger that a notorious Trotskyist, contrary to the rules, was even notionally admitted to the party. Blows were exchanged, and eyewitnesses reported that 'bedlam spilled out on to the street'. In the midst of these and other fights, Corbyn theatrically presented Ali with a party membership card. His conduct, according to George Page, London's Labour Party leader, was 'the most extraordinary study of bias and manipulation of rule and customs I have ever witnessed'. Corbyn wore that criticism as a badge of pride. After the national council elections in May, he believed, Britain would be one step closer to Michael Foot's election as prime minister. Margaret Thatcher, he was convinced, could not recover from the deep unpopularity she had attracted during the previous months, following cabinet splits and an economic crisis – private polling by the Conservatives showed the Tories' support had fallen to just 20 per cent. 'The Tory vote will disappear,' Corbyn predicted, 'and I think we shall win.' In his manifesto for re-election in Haringey he pledged 'the smashing of the capitalist state' – not an unusual declaration in those fevered times. 'I don't have any personal ambitions,' he added. That was untrue, and struck his council colleagues as laughable.

Six weeks later, after Labour had won the council elections, Corbyn moved once again to topple Robin Young, his key enemy among the moderates. On the fourth attempt, having at last gathered sufficient support after a succession of purges and deselections, he was successful. 'I was persuaded to go,' Young admitted ruefully. 'They were a funny lot, the hard left.' Mindful of the impending nomination of Labour's parliamentary candidate in Islington North, Corbyn next marshalled Haringey's twenty hard-left Labour councillors against the remaining thirteen moderates, and appointed Angela Greatley, an aspiring quangoist, as the council's 'patsy' leader. He himself returned to chairing the uncontroversial planning committee, and awaited the next general election with confidence. The invasion of the Falkland Islands on 2 April dashed his hopes.

Military dictators had ruled Argentina since 1976. To crush the opposition, thousands of civilians had disappeared in the so-called 'dirty war'. Some victims, including socialists, had been pushed out of military helicopters over the Atlantic, their babies and young children then handed to childless supporters of the regime. By any measure, Corbyn should have opposed General Leopoldo Galtieri's dictatorship, and welcomed the opportunity to liberate oppressed Argentines. Instead, he opposed Margaret Thatcher's dispatch of a naval task force to recapture the islands as a Tory plot. In his hatred of America and Britain, he supported anyone who was their enemy – Stalin, Mao, Castro and now Galtieri. According to Corbyn's logic, while he did not condone the dictators' murders, they were not to blame for all the excesses that had occurred under their rule. That was the fault of the imperialists – America and Britain – for subjugating the poor. In Galtieri's case, his crimes could be excused as the price for liberating the Falklands from Britain.

Regardless of the islanders' overwhelming wishes to continue the legal settlement established in 1833 that the Falklands were part of the UK, Corbyn demanded that Thatcher 'pursue peace' and negotiate their surrender to the Argentinean dictator. 'We resent the waste of unemployed men who are being sent to the Falklands to die for Thatcher and Galtieri,' he stated in a motion tabled in Haringey council, and continued, 'A tide of jingoism is sweeping the country … It is a nauseating waste of money and lives.' The 'grotesque' war, he said, was conceived to keep the Tories' 'money-making friends in business'. To explain why he ignored the rights of both the Falklanders and the Argentines to live in freedom, he declared that Thatcher was 'exploiting the situation'. Allowing people to live under military tyranny, he said, was preferable to removing despots by force. The cost of the war would be better spent on housing, hospitals and wages in Britain, or to feed the starving in Africa. He saw no contradiction in his attack on the British armed forces rather than the Argentine dictator. 'He's always lived according to his principles,' explained Chris Mullin, a sympathetic Bennite MP. To Corbyn's dismay, in the Commons Michael Foot supported the government, and in a bravura speech blamed the 'guilty men' at the Foreign Office for the Falklanders suffering Argentinean oppression. Only a handful of Labour MPs voted against the dispatch of the task force.

In Haringey, the consequence of rule by Corbyn was an accelerated exodus of businesses and residents. The escapees feared yet another 40 per cent rates hike to fund another 50 per cent increase in administrative staff. Among the 4,500 additional employees were two 'anti-nuclear officers', charged with 'promoting peace' in the borough. On Corbyn's initiative, Haringey had been twinned with Grenada, then led by a Marxist government; and with his encouragement another large group of gypsies had moved onto the site of a pony club for handicapped children. The gypsies used the field as a dump for commercial waste. 'It's become a filthy rat-infested mess,' complained Robin Young, 'and the source of dysentery among schoolchildren.' A year later, the council paid over £45,000 (£90,000 today) to clear the site. Once again, Corbyn refused to apologise. 'The decision not to evict the people,' he told the council, 'was correct.'

Haringey had become Britain's highest-spending local authority, with the highest rates for residents and businesses. Its few remaining moderate Labour councillors, angry about the chaos, appeared powerless. Outraged by the discovery of another £1 million fraud executed by council employees who were supervised by the Public Works Committee formerly chaired by Corbyn, they were shocked by his reaction to a bomb explosion outside the local Labour Party headquarters which had severely damaged the door and outside wall. 'He blamed the police for not being more vigilant,' said a resident about the unsolved crime. 'That's the same Corbyn who criticised the police presence in Haringey as a threat to ethnic minorities.' The critic was referring to his condemnation of the 'increasingly repressive nature of London policing'. The blast exposed a familiar characteristic of Corbyn's management: there was no correlation between recruitment and efficiency. Although he had presided over a record number of new members joining the party, the constituency was mired in debt and there was no money to repair the bomb damage. The party was forced to close the building.

That December, Corbyn faced a moment of reckoning when Haringey's Labour moderates threatened to join with the Tory opposition to defeat his latest proposal to increase spending. 'You are like little Hitlers,' the *Hornsey Journal* accused Corbyn, Bernie Grant and their cabal. 'Like him, you will eventually be rejected by forces of democracy.' To Corbyn's good fortune, the newspaper lacked the resources to publish a muckraking exposé. Nor could the editor penetrate the wall of secrecy surrounding Corbyn, who always refused to speak to the 'capitalist press'.

The major obstacle to Corbyn's ambition to become a parliamentary candidate was his continued support of Tariq Ali's membership of the Hornsey branch – endorsed on Corbyn's insistence by the borough's general committee. After the NEC rejected Ali's third bid, Corbyn was warned that the branch would be disbanded if he issued him with another membership card. This was not the best time for Corbyn to oppose the party leadership, and at his request Ali withdrew his application. He would later describe Corbyn – quoting E.P. Thompson's judgement on the socialist poet and textile designer William Morris – as 'unsteady among generalisations, weak in analytic thought, his response to life was immediate and concrete'. And that was a friend talking. Corbyn was not a willing martyr, but he was vindictive. Max Morris (no relation), the chairman of the ward that was opposing Ali's membership, was ousted by an influx of thirty Trotskyists at an 'emergency meeting'.

There was good reason for Corbyn to hasten the end of the saga. Unexpectedly, the Labour MP for Islington North, Michael O'Halloran, switched his support to the SDP. In the next general election, he announced, he would stand as their candidate. Most of the constituency's moderates joined him in defecting, giving the left a sudden advantage. This was Corbyn's chance. He badly wanted the seat, but accepted the advice of Val Veness, for some time now a powerbroker in the local party, that his nomination would have to be handled discreetly if he was to secure the support of both the party and the constituency at large.

He approached Clive Boutle, a linguist and publisher, to organise his campaign for selection. Boutle left their initial two-hour discussion about strategy convinced that Corbyn was 'left-wing, experienced and not self-important like others'. In the selection process, Corbyn was introduced as Val Veness's preferred candidate. In exchange, she applied to be the Labour candidate in Hornsey, where his influence would be crucial.

Corbyn's emergence as a candidate surprised Toby Harris. Like others, he had not realised his ally's burning ambition for national recognition. To Harris and other enquirers, Val Veness claimed that Corbyn was a 'reluctant' candidate who she had had to persuade to apply for the seat. 'They seem certain to pick an extremist,' a Labour moderate predicted, 'who will be fully in step with the mad majority.' Others reckoned that 'left-wing revolutionaries' like Val Veness were 'unacceptable to Michael Foot'.

In the final race, a month before the June 1983 general election, the choice was between Corbyn and Paul Boateng, a barrister educated in Ghana. Corbyn won the contest by four votes. Aware that Michael O'Halloran for the SDP could expect substantial support, he promised in his campaign to prevent mass unemployment following the inevitable recession if the Tories were re-elected. The working class, he was convinced, would be attracted by higher taxes, more powers for trade unions, unilateral disarmament and the renationalisation of shipbuilding, aerospace and steel. George Cunningham, the SDP MP for Islington South, urged electors to consider the reality of socialism. He portrayed Islington's Labour council as resembling an East European communist authority. While council tenants waited 'months' for repairs to their homes,

Labour officials spent huge amounts of public money to promote their political ambitions, and wasted more on illegal projects. 'The Labour Party in Islington,' Cunningham told the Commons, 'has gone a long way down into the swamp of corruption.' While chasing around the constituency, Corbyn ignored such criticisms.

That year's Labour manifesto was famously dubbed 'the longest suicide note in history'; certainly the electorate was terrified by the party's extremist pledges and Militant Tendency's noisy demands for the draconian confiscation of wealth. Across the country, Labour secured its lowest percentage of the vote since 1918 – just 27.6 against the Tories' 42.4. Those working-class voters who owned cars and homes voted 47 per cent to 26 per cent for the Tories. As usual, the left interpreted their defeat as victory. Tony Benn, who lost his seat in Bristol South-East, welcomed the result, because 'for the first time since 1945 a political party with an openly socialist policy has received the support of over eight and a half million people. This is a remarkable development by any standards.' Corbyn himself avoided the rout. Despite the SDP winning 22 per cent of the vote in Islington North, and Labour's share falling by 12 per cent, his exhaustive campaign won him a majority of 5,607. Four miles to the north-west, John McDonnell was defeated in Hampstead by the sitting Tory MP, Geoffrey Finsberg. McDonnell had also contrived to lose Labour's seat in his own branch, Hayes and Harlington. Neville Sandelson blamed McDonnell's persecution when he was deselected after thirty-two years as the constituency's Labour MP. He stood as the SDP's candidate, splitting Labour's vote and allowing Terry Dicks to become the constituency's first Conservative MP since 1950.

Corbyn and McDonnell blamed Michael Foot for Labour's defeat. The party leader, said McDonnell, was a right-wing 'welfare capitalist'. Even the manifesto's promise to impose socialist protectionism and ban the import of foreign cars was too liberal. Labour would have won, both men believed, by promoting the complete renationalisation of the British economy, the ruthless confiscation and redistribution of wealth and the disbandment of the military to transform Britain into a pacifist, nuclear-free, non-aligned nation. Convinced of that error, Corbyn spoke at Marxist meetings about working through Labour to democratise Parliament out of existence. In public speeches he ridiculed the moderates' suggestion that the far left had failed to recognise the working class's appreciation of consumerism, of mortgages to buy their council homes and of the abandonment of restrictions on foreign travel. He told his allies in London Labour Briefing about his determination to reverse Thatcherism's plot to destroy 'class solidarity'. After all, he was now an MP, on a national stage that offered unlimited opportunities.

5

Four Legs Good, Two Legs Bad

Dressed in a dirty jacket, creased trousers and open-necked shirt, Jeremy Corbyn arrived in Westminster unmoved by the British electorate's rejection of Labour. He joined thirteen other far-left MPs who sympathised with East Europe's communist governments and supported trade union militancy to break Margaret Thatcher's government. He told the Venesses that he considered Parliament 'a waste of time'. Westminster's agenda bore no relevance to his Islington constituents, especially the immigrant communities. 'I don't like this place,' he told Keith Veness as they walked through the arched corridor from St Stephen's Entrance to the central lobby. As they passed the huge paintings depicting the glories of British history, Corbyn added, 'It's all phoney, set up to make you feel intimidated.' The advantages for him personally were a good income and a job for the foreseeable future, with the opportunity to indulge his interests, especially foreign travel.

Reflecting his self-imposed isolation, Corbyn's office in Dean's Yard was far from the centre of political activity of what he called 'a gentleman's club'. (The 1983 intake included just fourteen Conservative and nine Labour women MPs.) In the Commons chamber he preferred to sit on the back seats, away from other MPs. At the regular votes he walked alone through the lobby, and he made little contact with his fellow Labour MPs, other than to discuss the best cycle routes to and from Westminster. He also kept his distance from the party whips. When asked to remain in the House to release other Labour MPs to work in their marginal constituencies in the hope of saving their seats, Corbyn refused. 'I'm focused on my own constituency,' he replied, complaining about the power the whips tried to wield. 'I won't be at their mercy,' he told one party official. He was also somewhat isolated from his four London Labour Briefing allies, who were still struggling to find seats.

To meet his constituents, he set up offices in the Red Rose Centre at 129 Seven Sisters Road in Holloway. His promise at his selection meeting to open an office in the constituency had, he believed, won him decisive votes. The building was bought from the Co-op, with the aid of a loan provided by a brewing company that would finance the initial conversion works in exchange for the exclusive rights to supply the club's drinks. The caretaker's flat on the first floor became Corbyn's office. He was personally liable for the rent, since as a London MP he was required by parliamentary rules to use a room in his local party's headquarters to meet his constituents. Under those same rules, he could not reclaim his personal expenses at the Red Rose, or the cost of additional staff in the club. This was a wholly unreasonable arrangement for an MP to make. The poisoned chalice that would haunt him thirteen years later was his signed personal guarantee to repay any losses the club incurred.

Many people came to the large, cavernous building, which was soon filled with people discussing politics, enjoying the bar and the end-of-week cabaret. Upstairs, Corbyn's door was open to a tide of misery: Cypriots, Jamaicans, Indians, Pakistanis, South Africans, South Americans, Somalis, West Saharans and Kurds all sought his help. In his opinion, all immigrant communities were victims of white imperialists, and the British state owed them a financial obligation. To achieve a fair and equal society, they should be provided with their basic needs, rather than the state expecting them to take personal responsibility for their fate. Beyond that, the possession of any unnecessary wealth was greed. For Corbyn, those praised by Thatcher for creating wealth were exploiters of the working class. He despised her gospel of 'reward for success'. As an enemy of aspiration, he championed losers. Not being successful was a sign of moral probity.

To strengthen his cause, he welcomed into the Islington North branch a small group of Trotskyites calling themselves 'Socialist Action'. Among their number were Simon Fletcher, an ally for the next twenty-three years, and Kate Hudson, who had directed her fellow members to join Labour without revealing their allegiance (since Michael Foot's edict Trotskyites were again effectively banned from joining the party). 'We must move to a clandestine form of entry,' she wrote. 'Under the present circumstances a public-face organisation is a millstone around our neck. It must go.' Corbyn was sympathetic to her further strategy to target black Britons involved in the recent race riots in Brixton, Bristol and Toxteth as potential recruits. Anyone who challenged the British establishment – for whatever reason – was viewed as a likely supporter. Among Corbyn's other confederate organisations was the Militant Tendency, an important supporter over the coming years. But by far his most important ally was Ken Livingstone.

Corbyn would regularly see the GLC leader, along with his deputy John McDonnell and Keith Veness, at *Labour Herald* editorial meetings. Throughout 1983 the newspaper pursued a consistent far-left line, praising the North Korean dictatorship, for example, as a 'model of successful, self-reliant, socialist development', even though by then about a million North Koreans had been murdered by Kim Il-sung's regime. Among Corbyn's other allies were the anti-Semitic playwright Jim Allen, and Tony Greenstein, an anti-Zionist who ran the Labour Movement Campaign on Palestine (LMCP). LMCP regarded Israel as an 'apartheid state' without the right to exist, an opinion reflecting Corbyn's own antagonism towards Jews and Israel, feelings that had hardened since his employment by the tailors' union in 1972. Ever since Israel's defeat of the Arab invasion in 1973, the country's growing military and financial dominance over its Arab neighbours, and Israeli settlers building new permanent homes in Jordan's West Bank, had aroused anger among those sympathetic to the Palestinians.

Corbyn's antagonism towards Zionism is one of the most notable through lines of his entire career. During the 1980s he

sponsored the LMCP's campaign to 'eradicate Zionism' and
replace Israel with Palestine. In 1984 he chaired a conference
blaming the Labour Party for colonising Palestine. 'Zionism',
asserted the LMCP, 'is inherently racist', and that same year he
sponsored an LMCP newsletter calling for the disaffiliation of
the Poale Zion, the only Jewish group attached to the Labour
Party. He also supported the expulsion of Jewish societies by
student unions. At the time he was never asked to explain his
motives, but in the opinion of Harry Fletcher, a Labour
campaigner who would become an aide to Corbyn during his
bid for the leadership in 2015, he did not understand his own
anti-Semitism. For Fletcher, Corbyn was 'institutionally anti-
Semitic' – by which he meant that he unwittingly subscribed to
the left's inherent prejudice.

Showing similar dogmatism in favour of the IRA, soon after
his election Corbyn organised a rally in Finsbury town hall for
Gerry Adams, the leader of Sinn Féin, and Martin McGuinness,
then head of the IRA. At the time, Britons were dying as a result
of IRA terrorism. Corbyn opposed the government's anti-
terrorism legislation, arguing that the innocent sons and
daughters of many of his Irish constituents became alienated
after being wrongly banned from travelling to the UK, or had
been imprisoned without proper evidence. Ireland, he believed,
should be reunited without asking for the consent of all its
people. He had touched a popular nerve. A thousand people,
mostly Sinn Féin supporters, packed into the hall to give the
IRA leaders a standing ovation. In his introduction, Chris
Smith, the Labour MP for Islington South and the meeting's
host, because the hall was in his constituency, bravely told the
audience: 'I don't accept the use of violence for political reasons
…' Prolonged booing drowned the rest of his sentence.
Alongside him, Corbyn showed no sympathy for his trembling
neighbour. The following day, Corbyn called Smith: 'Gerry
thanks you for being there, and don't worry, he respects what
you say.' Corbyn had won notoriety, and this was the first of
countless occasions on which he would share a platform with
terrorists. By coincidence, he had stepped into the national

spotlight in the midst of the election of a new party leader after Michael Foot resigned in June 1983, and at the beginning of what Denis Healey later described as 'one long tribal battle for the soul of the Labour Party'.

In that toxic atmosphere, Eric Heffer, a bullying Trotskyite, was the left's candidate against Neil Kinnock, who was also left-wing but not so extreme. From his retirement, Harold Wilson, evidently alarmed by the continuing Trotskyite infiltration of the party, encouraged his supporters to oppose Heffer, who ended up with just 6.3 per cent of the vote. Kinnock was elected, with Healey as his deputy. Corbyn regarded Kinnock as a traitor for refusing to support Tony Benn's bid for the deputy leadership, and now saw no reason to be loyal to the party. His litmus test was Northern Ireland. He opposed Labour's policy of self-determination and constitutional change, and supported the IRA's policy of violence to end 'British imperialism'. He made no effort to establish a relationship with Kinnock, and rarely went to the weekly parliamentary Labour Party meetings. On the few occasions he entered the Commons tearoom, he sat with like-minded MPs such as Dennis Skinner and Tony Banks, and shunned the rest. For their part, the majority regarded him as someone not to be taken seriously – the source, as one Commons wag had it, of a 'single transferable speech'. In reality, he subscribed to Keith Veness's outburst against the non-believers: 'The difference between the traditional social administrators composing Labour Party policies and the revolutionary socialists at the GLC,' he said, 'left an acid taste.' Like Veness, Corbyn detested those not utterly loyal to the struggle.

Real life was outside Parliament. 'Smash the Tory state!' he would yell into his megaphone on endless marches through Islington, blaming American imperialism for his constituents' ills and, with clenched fist, praising Fidel Castro and Daniel Ortega, the leader of the Nicaraguan Sandinistas, for showing the road to socialism. The left's eventual victory in Britain, Corbyn proclaimed, depended on the people, not the politicians. Revolution, he promised, would end the Tory government's curse upon Islington of bad housing and unrelieved squalor.

Much of his constituency was made up of white English and Irish workers alongside immigrants. Most inhabited either unrepaired private houses or dilapidated council estates. They suffered bad schools, stretched health services and one of the worst Labour councils in the country: inefficient, expensive and corrupt – even worse than Haringey. Officials in the housing department bought whole streets of private houses by compulsory order, ostensibly for council tenants, used council labour to rebuild them, and occasionally moved themselves into the best. Corbyn never complained about that corruption or criticised the council's incompetence, not least because Val Veness was the chairman of the council's housing committee.

One key relationship for any MP at that time was with the editor of their local newspaper. After watching Corbyn for nearly a decade, Tony Allcock, the editor of the *Islington Gazette*, understood the new MP's politics, but was surprised by his approach. Unlike Chris Smith, Corbyn never issued press releases about local issues. His frequent publicity flyers were about Palestine, Ireland, the Western Sahara (occupied by Morocco since 1974) or Nicaragua. 'They went in the bin,' recalled Allcock. 'He said that he was aligned with the oppressed, but most of his releases were in favour of murderous dictators.' Equally surprisingly, Corbyn's dislike of the media prevented him from contacting Allcock, who concluded: 'He was a maverick outsider who did not care about his image and would not play the game.' For his part, Corbyn decided he did not need the paper's backing. In his concern for his ethnic constituents, especially their attempts to get council houses, welfare benefits and their families into Britain, Corbyn had become the go-to person. 'People thought he was a nice bloke,' conceded Allcock. 'He made them feel comfortable. He even charmed his adversaries.' In his constituency dealings at least, Corbyn had perfected a genial mask, despite not yet proving himself an effective MP.

His constant activity hid a new laziness. Rather than engaging in the detailed work necessary to organise the parliamentary left (his task as secretary of the Campaign Group), he preferred to board a plane heading for some far-off destination. He loved the intrigue of travelling in secret across the Sahara on a camel to meet Polisario guerrillas; or flying to Nicaragua just eight weeks after Britain's general election. Or, on his return to Westminster, protesting against the American invasion of Grenada after Marxists had murdered Maurice Bishop, the island's prime minister. As ever, he selected the issues he thought were important. In the Commons he blasted Geoffrey Howe, the foreign secretary, as 'pathetic' for supporting America rather than the Grenadian murderers, yet avoided mentioning the Cuban military base, targeted at the USA, on the island. 'The Member for Antarctica North', he was called by a Tory MP for sentimentally 'banging on' about parts of the world irrelevant to most Britons. Copying Tony Benn's style, he had become a 'platform man', delivering speeches while uninvolved in attempts to change or improve government policies. To some, his passion for protest lacked any strategy – he expressed wholehearted support by attending endless meetings, but offered no ideas about the route to reach any destination. In contrast to his years in Haringey, he made no attempt to seek real influence in Parliament. Unlike Ken Livingstone, he never considered how to forge alliances with moderates. To some, he appeared to find the task beyond his abilities, and instead plotted for the revolution. Beyond Parliament, in the shadows, he was active with London Labour Briefing, for which the next stage was a coup to oust Thatcher and take over Britain. To most, the idea was as fanciful as Palestinians adopting the last words of the traditional Jewish prayer at the beginning of Passover dinner, 'Next year in Jerusalem.'

To cut spending, a new law compelled councils to set rates below a defined limit. This remained anathema to Corbyn. In retaliation, he and the Labour Herald group at the GLC, especially Livingstone, McDonnell and Knight, planned to refuse to set any rates, or else to set them illegally high. At a series of meetings with an assortment of Trotskyites, Marxists and far-left councillors from across the country, especially the Militant Tendency in Liverpool, London Labour Briefing offered to orchestrate huge displays of disobedience. By law, the government had the power to fine individual councillors and ban them from office for five years for setting illegal rates. Mass disobedience and national resistance, the conspirators believed, would impair the government and cause local services to collapse; in the ensuing turmoil the government and the City would surrender to the left, and Thatcher would be forced to resign. McDonnell spoke about a mass movement of workers engaged in direct action to overthrow capitalism. To hasten that revolution, he, as chairman of GLC's finance committee, claimed that Thatcher's new law would force the GLC to cut services totalling £180 million (the equivalent today of £440 million). Corbyn spoke up too. Urging his former colleagues in Haringey to join him, he forecast with conviction that a pincer movement of defiance by councillors and miners would topple a second Tory prime minister, just as it had Heath. To the believers, their conspiracy was sane and timely.

Ever since 1980, when the Consett steelworks in County Durham had been closed down, costing 3,700 jobs, the left had accused Thatcher of plotting to destroy the steel industry, break the trade unions and damage working communities. Until 1984, the realities of British Steel, especially its declining fortunes, did not interest Corbyn. He was unaware that British steelworkers in 1978 were 40 per cent less productive than their German or Dutch counterparts: each British steelworker took fifteen man-hours to produce a tonne of steel, while the same tonnage in Germany took about six hours. Overmanning and under-investment were compounded by the British trade unions' refusal to allow the introduction of automated production methods that would improve efficiency and lower costs.

Protected by state ownership, the competing unions guarded their restrictive practices and resisted flexibility, with the result that in 1980 the industry was losing £1 billion a year, at taxpayers' expense. Yet that same year steelworkers went out on strike for a 20 per cent pay increase, and won. By the time they returned to work, victorious after a three-month battle, some customers had switched to permanent contracts with

Continental European suppliers. Then Thatcherism hit the steel industry. Corbyn was outraged when the steelworkers failed to force a surrender and Consett was closed. The left vowed revenge.

On 8 March 1984, Arthur Scargill declared a national miners' strike without calling a ballot. Ostensibly, miners in Yorkshire and Scotland were protesting against the threatened closure of seventy-five coalmines that the government considered uneconomic. Scargill, like Corbyn, was dismissive of the industry's annual £1.3 billion subsidy from taxpayers (in 2019 terms, nearly three times that figure). They were equally uninterested in the barbaric working conditions endured by the miners, most of whom ended their careers with painful injuries or chronic medical conditions, or died prematurely from incurable illnesses. Protecting so perilous an industry made no economic or altruistic sense; but that was not the left's concern.

To avoid the miners repeating their success against Heath, from as early as 1981 Thatcher had started to build her defences. In normal times the country stocked about six weeks' supply of coal. Thatcher paid the miners overtime to build up six months' worth of stocks. The coming battle would define her premiership, as she and Corbyn both knew.

Adopting John McDonnell's self-proclaimed 'fondness for violence', Scargill dispatched miners from Yorkshire and Scotland – so-called 'flying pickets' – first to the Nottinghamshire coalfields, then across the country. Tasked to stop miners entering the pits by intimidation and assaults, the pickets persuaded the police not to protect working miners, and many pits closed. Infuriated, Thatcher ordered the police to enforce the law. Scargill counter-attacked with a show of might. On 18 June 1984, ten thousand miners surrounded the Orgreave steel mill in Yorkshire to prevent the delivery of coke and compel the plant to close. After a fierce battle with five thousand police, Scargill's forces were defeated. With a renewed sense of purpose, union leaders called on dockers – the vanguard of the workers – to strike, reckoning that once all the ports were closed the country would be crippled. Alarmed, Thatcher demanded retribution against 'the enemy within'. By then, MI5 had penetrated Scargill's operations and discovered that he was receiving money from both the Soviet Union and the Libyan dictator Muammar Gaddafi. Scargill's dishonesty was not condemned by the left: the *Guardian* journalist Seumas Milne was to write a book praising the miners' leader despite Scargill's secret acceptance of those funds. Even Neil Kinnock, fearful of losing the left's support, refused to denounce Scargill outright. But the left misjudged the working class. The dockers refused to obey their leaders, and once again the Labour Party was split.

Corbyn naturally supported the striking miners, although, lacking any relationship with Scargill (a hardline pro-Soviet Marxist and not a floating Trotskyist), he did not stand on the picket lines or fight the police at Orgreave. Rather, he joined Livingstone and McDonnell in a show of solidarity by confronting the government over council rates. In late 1984 Livingstone led the way, unaware that McDonnell had meanwhile encountered a problem with Reg Race, whom he had employed after his defeat in the 1983 general election to oversee the GLC's budget. Observing McDonnell, Race was impressed by his 'Janus-faced' manner, his mask concealing the truth: 'He adopted a moderate position whenever necessary to smoothly reach out to bankers and say whatever was necessary regardless of his true intentions.'

Within months, Race discovered that the GLC was awash with cash. No less than 60 per cent of its budget of £325 million remained unspent, the consequence of incompetent bureaucrats failing to commission approved projects. The money lay in plain sight in the GLC's bank account. McDonnell, the chairman of the finance committee, had proved incapable of managing the council's finances.

Race calculated that, contrary to his superior's dire warning of the GLC being compelled to cut £180 million of services, there was no need for any cuts – or at most, the maximum reduction would be just £11 million. That fact did not suit McDonnell. When the two men met, Race recalled, McDonnell was 'very angry'. Ignoring his adviser, in early 1984 he announced that the GLC, because of the government's directive, would impose cuts of £140 million. To keep up the pretence, he went around County Hall telling staff, 'It's going to be Armageddon.' Even Livingstone was not told the truth. Instead, McDonnell urged the GLC leader to fight the cuts. 'The whole point of our administration,' he told Livingstone in a memo, 'is that we are a challenge to the central capitalist state.' Any surrender would 'undermine the confidence shown in us by hundreds of thousands of socialists throughout the country'. Local government, he continued, was a 'terrain of the class struggle'.

Unaware that McDonnell was fabricating the figures, Livingstone repeatedly declared that Thatcher's orders would endanger London's services. Many, including moderate GLC Labour councillors, disputed his warnings, and refused to break the law and face personal surcharges. Among those dissidents was John Carr, who publicly labelled McDonnell 'on the far edge of the hard left', with 'dodgy' political judgement.

The disagreement, carefully kept secret by Race and McDonnell, simmered as in October 1984 the Tories gathered for their annual conference in Brighton. Corbyn had good reason to feel uneasy. Despite the government's clumsy resistance, the NUM was being defeated by the coal stocks, which were being resupplied with new coal produced by strike-breaking miners. Simultaneously, Labour's championing of the white working class against exploitation was being eroded by Thatcher's sale of council homes, education reforms and the statutory limitation of trade union power, while many heavy industries were closing after the government refused to subsidise loss-makers.

The destruction of Britain's industrial heartlands made Corbyn's hatred of Thatcher personal. The proof was an early-morning phone call he received on 12 October from Val Veness. An IRA bomb, she reported, planted at Brighton's Grand Hotel, had killed five Conservatives and injured thirty-one others, narrowly missing its main target, Margaret Thatcher. Corbyn, a man who promoted himself as a compassionate paci-fist, made absolutely no comment to Veness, either of shock or

sympathy. He made no statement welcoming Thatcher's emergence from the rubble, or praising her subsequent defiance.
After rejecting police advice that she return to London, she
appeared on stage in the conference hall and linked the IRA
murderers to Scargill's 'organised revolutionary minority'. Her
boldness, pitching traditionalists against extremists just hours
after escaping death, inflamed Corbyn. Over the following days,
he appeared impressed by the IRA's daring. A *Labour Briefing*
editorial would announce, 'The British only sit up and take
notice [of Ireland] when they are bombed into it.' The following
month, the paper published a supplement admitting that these
words had 'produced an immediate and overwhelmingly hostile
response' from readers. The editorial board dissociated itself
from its own editorial. Corbyn denied any involvement in the
original glorification of the attack, although in a later issue the
paper praised its 'audacity' and, defying credibility, asked, 'What
do you call four dead Tories? A start.' It also mocked the trade
and industry secretary Norman Tebbit, who had been pulled
from the rubble with his badly injured wife – she would prove
to be permanently paralysed: 'Try riding your bike now,
Norman.' That degree of hatred characterised the far left.

Two weeks later, before all those who died in Brighton had
been buried, Corbyn invited two IRA terrorists to the Commons.
They would discuss, he said, the prison conditions of convicted
IRA murderers. In particular, he was concerned about the strip
searches of IRA suspects. He later defended himself by saying
that MPs had the right to meet anyone with a point of view,
although he never invited Ulster Protestants for discussions.
Soon after, he flew to Belfast, where, hosted by IRA sympathisers, he condemned the British Army's shooting of IRA bombers
as 'an act of terrorism', and demanded that the troops should
immediately leave Northern Ireland, regardless of the civil war
that would surely follow.

In Corbyn's lexicon, his support for the IRA, or for squatting
and strikes, was all part of his role as a revolutionary. His new
ideological lodestar was Mike Marqusee, a well-educated
American Marxist living in Hackney, who reinforced Corbyn's

conviction about the power of the left. As a Jewish anti-Zionist, Marqusee had abandoned his own country to build socialism in Britain, while he also campaigned for the rights of Palestinians – and enjoyed cricket. He and Corbyn had hoped that the national refusal to cut council rates would overthrow Thatcher. But then they had had to face reality.

In February 1985, Reg Race once again presented McDonnell with documentary proof that the government's rates cap was irrelevant to the GLC. 'You have no financial problem,' he said, handing him a memo presenting his calculations: his master's threat of £140 million of cuts was bogus. 'I hear what you say,' McDonnell replied in what Race would call an 'icily furious tone', then ordered, 'Shred the document. Destroy it.' Race refused. 'It was remarkable,' he observed, 'that McDonnell felt he could ask a civil servant to collude with him to falsify the council's financial options.' Yet he was not wholly surprised. As a member of three Trotskyite groups – the London Labour Party (LLP), London Labour Briefing and the WRP – McDonnell refused to allow the rates revolution to melt away. Shortly after, Race briefed Livingstone. 'If these figures are right,' Livingstone later told McDonnell in anger, 'we are going to look like the biggest fucking liars since Goebbels.' Nevertheless, for a brief time Livingstone chose to maintain the façade. On 6 March, at a rally in London for the last striking miners, he pledged to defy the law. Four days later he surrendered and agreed to the government's command to fix a legal rate. Corbyn sat in the public gallery with Ted Knight in the decisive GLC meeting as Livingstone told Labour councillors that McDonnell had 'deceived' him, blaming his subordinate's dishonesty on his 'training as a supporter of the Militant Tendency'. Visibly outraged, Corbyn watched as Livingstone voted for a legal budget. But while Corbyn endorsed McDonnell's defiance, he stepped back from illegality himself. He refused to break the rules.

Livingstone fired John McDonnell for his dishonesty. In the midst of divorcing his wife, McDonnell retorted that he would never forgive Livingstone because he had 'bottled out' to avoid disqualification from office, and had 'betrayed the Labour movement'. It was a strange preference of one ethic over another. Livingstone snapped back that McDonnell was always going to lose if he failed to adopt a 'more honest approach'. Later, the GLC leader would recall that Gerry Healy had approached him to try to save McDonnell from dismissal. In outright contradiction of the eyewitness evidence, McDonnell would subsequently deny having 'any relationship with the WRP or with Gerry Healy, whom I have never met'. Lying in his self-interest came easily to McDonnell. He would never change his opinions. 'A socialist society is my religion,' he would assert. Shocked by McDonnell's dishonesty, Livingstone reeled from the blowback. 'I had no idea,' he would later write, 'of the bitterness that was about to break around me, or that a decade would pass before John or I would get over it.' His publication of a long memo exposing McDonnell's perfidy that was circulated to all Labour GLC councillors, he would later admit, had been a 'tactical disaster'.

In Westminster, Corbyn acknowledged that the left was fractured. All London's revolutionary councils, including Ted Knight's Lambeth, also surrendered to the government's order that they set a legal rate. The one stand-out was in Liverpool, where forty-nine Militant Tendency councillors led by deputy council leader Derek Hatton continued to defy Thatcher. Their illegal budget edged the city towards formal bankruptcy. As the district auditor prepared to issue surcharge orders against the councillors for voting to fix an illegal rate, 31,000 council employees were dismissed. The political apocalypse anticipated by Corbyn had evaporated. In Thatcher's words, 'the winter of discontent' fuelled by 'the enemy within' had been routed.

By March 1985, despite arrests, injuries sustained in pitched battles with the police, and broken communities, nearly all the miners had drifted back to work. A victorious Thatcher initiated the abolition of the GLC. Under Livingstone, the authority had spent £8.87 billion in the previous three years, created many problems, and solved but a few. The main beneficiaries were minority groups – the Irish, peace groups and women's organisations – and the advertising industry, which was enriched by the GLC to promote its leader. Sensing the public's antagonism towards the left, Labour leader Neil Kinnock ignored Livingstone and, in a withering speech at Labour's party conference in Bournemouth, humiliated Derek Hatton for orchestrating 'the grotesque chaos of a Labour council, *a Labour council*, hiring taxis to scuttle round the city handing out redundancy notices to its own workers'. In anger, Corbyn joined Tony Benn and Eric Heffer in a revolt against Kinnock's perceived betrayal of Marxist councillors and his purge of over a hundred Trotskyites from the party, the three men walking out of the conference hall in full view of the television cameras. On the eve of a general election, even some on the left condemned their display as 'tactically idiotic'. In his defence, Corbyn complained to Keith Veness, 'Kinnock never even said "Hello" to me.' To some, he appeared out of his depth on the national stage. As a municipal politician he performed well, but in the party's factional battles he had drifted away from influencing events, even in Antarctica North.

Five days after Kinnock's speech, riots erupted in Broadwater Farm, the housing estate in Tottenham owned by Haringey council. Both the councillors and officials of the self-proclaimed 'People's Republic of Haringey', the debts of which had now soared to more than £700 million (£2.8 billion today), had failed to remedy the sordid, poorly maintained, and crime-ridden complex of buildings. Among the neglectful councillors had been Corbyn. The riots started after a black woman, a suspected illegal immigrant, died during a police raid. Bombs were thrown at firefighters and police. A police constable, Keith Blakelock, who was protecting the firemen, was hacked to death by a mob.

The horror divided politicians. Thatcher called it murder, adding: 'This new terrorism in our midst is like a cancer – and similarly it must be overcome.' Corbyn blamed police intolerance for creating the volcanic frustration of the rioting black youths, who, he pronounced again, were 'at the sharp edge of the class struggle'. Bernie Grant, by now Haringey leader, also blamed the police: 'What they got was a bloody good hiding.' Later he added, 'Maybe it was a policemen who stabbed another policeman.' Corbyn's proposed solution to the mayhem was to spend billions of taxpayers' pounds on the inner cities; but he never offered a detailed plan to improve Broadwater Farm. Thatcher opted for private initiatives, including the endorsement of a proposal by Canadian developers to transform London's derelict Canary Wharf docks into a new financial centre. Her championship of capitalism, not least building dockland office blocks rather than homes, offended Corbyn as much as her vow to destroy the trade unions after the miners' defeat. In early 1986 he witnessed all those strands come together in an audacious coup orchestrated by Rupert Murdoch. Acting with the prime minister's blessing, the Australian newspaper tycoon pitched himself into the front line against the left.

For decades, the printers and other employees of Fleet Street's national newspapers had threatened or sabotaged – financially and physically – most nights' production. Some printers registered for a second salary under fictitious names like 'Mickey Mouse', while others slashed the paper rolling into the presses until that night's demand for an additional payment was approved. Not only did the unions blackmail the owners for outrageously high wages; they prevented the introduction of computer technology embraced by virtually every other newspaper across the world, threatening strikes unless Fleet Street continued to use the nineteenth-century hot-metal process. To overcome the Luddites, Murdoch had secretly built a modern printing plant in Wapping, in east London, staffed by electricians who opposed the print union leaders. On 24 January 1986 the printers declared an immediate strike.

The next day, Murdoch's first computer-produced newspapers, using 90 per cent less labour, appeared on Britain's streets. Taken by surprise, the printers rushed to blockade Murdoch's plant. Jeremy Corbyn was roused to join the siege of 'Fortress Wapping'. Early every morning for nine months he stood for two hours outside the gates with the pickets, seeking to prevent trucks entering or leaving. Daily, the violent clashes – the pickets threw darts at the police horses – confirmed to Corbyn that the police were Thatcher's tool to destroy the working class. 'The

News International dispute,' he told the Commons in December 1986, 'was an example of an oppressive government which paid thousands of police officers to keep five thousand people out of work.' Corbyn was well aware that the printers had repeatedly rejected Murdoch's offer for them to operate a computerised printing plant; he simply opposed any modernisation. His anger at the establishment was aggravated by the conviction of three men for the murder of PC Blakelock, based on evidence concocted by the police. After a six-year campaign all three would be released. At the same time, he was also campaigning for the release of the Guildford Four and the Birmingham Six, both groups wrongly convicted of involvement in IRA bomb plots in the 1970s. All those miscarriages of justice reinforced his alliance with Thatcher's enemies.

Frequently, he spoke at meetings of the Troops Out Movement, often alongside its chairman Richard Stanton, who had described the IRA's Brighton bomb as a 'justifiable act of political warfare'. On 9 June 1986 he was arrested outside the Old Bailey, where he had been protesting to 'show solidarity' with Patrick Magee, prosecuted for the murder of five people in the Brighton bombing. Magee, claimed Corbyn, was the victim of a show trial. He chose to ignore the evidence of Magee's guilt, which the IRA bomber confirmed after his eventual release from prison, having served fourteen years. Over the following months Corbyn appeared repeatedly at IRA rallies to protest against the plight of convicted murderers. In 1987 he handed Margaret Thatcher a petition urging the release of Hugh Doherty, arrested in 1975 and convicted for sixteen murders, including that of Ross McWhirter, the co-founder of *The Guinness Book of Records*, during a fourteen-month campaign of violence across southern England. Corbyn described Doherty as a 'political prisoner' whose visiting conditions should be improved. He signed a Commons motion after an IRA bomb on Remembrance Day in 1987 killed eleven people in Enniskillen – 'the Poppy Day Massacre' – declaring that the violence 'stems primarily from the long-standing British occupation'. In May 1987, at a meeting in Conway Hall to honour an eight-man IRA hit squad shot dead in an SAS ambush at Loughgall in County Armagh, Corbyn took the microphone. His words were predictable. He exhorted the audience to stand in silence to show their respect for the dead terrorists. State execution, he said, defied the rule of law. No other British MP appeared so prominently in the spotlight alongside terrorists. Corbyn claimed that he was contributing to the peace process, but his participation as an MP at events supporting the armed republican cause legitimised the IRA's use of bullets and bombs in their struggle to unite Ireland.

In self-defence, Corbyn argued that earlier 'freedom fighters' opposing British colonial rule – for example EOKA in Cyprus and the Mau Mau in Kenya – were classified as 'terrorists', but after independence their leaders became internationally respected statesmen. Similarly, the resistance groups that fought the Nazis in Europe during World War II were regarded by the Germans as criminals, but admired as freedom fighters by the Allies and most of their fellow countrymen. The IRA, Corbyn said, was no different. But he was mistaken. The IRA disdained all governments, including Dublin's: its operations were outlawed by the Irish Republic, where Sinn Féin won few votes, and the majority of Irish people on both sides of the border opposed unification. The democratic vote showed that the IRA, unlike EOKA and the Mau Mau, represented a tiny number of people. That crucial distinction – the democratic deficit – entirely eluded Corbyn.

His continuing antagonism towards Britain aroused the interest of Ján Sarkocy, an intelligence officer at the Czech embassy in London. Operating from an unsightly building in Notting Hill Gate, Czech 'diplomats' had been aggressively spying in Britain since the communist state was established in 1948. Under the cover name 'Ján Dymic', the thirty-two-year-old Sarkocy, nominally responsible for 'peace issues', met Corbyn in the House of Commons on 25 November 1986. Although Corbyn would later claim that he encountered Sarkocy only once, the Czech's reports to his superior in London and to headquarters in Prague accurately documented four meetings over the following two years.

Sarkocy had been introduced to Corbyn by Tony Gilbert, the communist leader of Liberation, originally the Movement for Colonial Freedom. Gilbert, a paid Soviet agent, had been briefed by Cynthia Roberts, a Czech intelligence agent who concealed her true allegiance in order to gain employment with a Labour MP in the House of Commons. Using the codename 'Hammer', Roberts managed Labour Action for Peace (LAP), an anti-nuclear group financed by the Czech government. Among the Labour MPs linked to LAP were Tony Benn, Dennis Skinner and Corbyn, who eventually became the group's president. Corbyn's particular usefulness to Sarkocy was that while he openly sympathised with many of Britain's revolutionary leftist groups, he worked within the Labour Party. The Czech had every reason to expect a comradely relationship with a fellow-traveller – or, in Lenin's description 'a useful idiot'. Sarkocy knew that his presence at Westminster would not be a secret. Corbyn was obliged to register his visits with the parliamentary authorities, and he assumed that an MI5 officer shadowed him. During their first hour together, Corbyn warned him about intensified surveillance on East European diplomats, and bizarrely handed over a copy of the *Sunday People* which described the failed MI5 investigation of an East German spy in Britain.

After that first meeting, Sarkocy met Corbyn at the Red Rose, driving there by a circuitous forty-five-mile route in an attempt to 'lose' the MI5 surveillance team. By then Corbyn had been codenamed 'COB', and was described as 'positive' towards the 'Soviet peace movements', and a potential collaborator, Sarkocy reporting: 'He seems the right person for fulfilling the task and giving information.' They met again in the Commons on 22 October 1987, and on a fourth occasion, on 19 September 1988, in Holloway with the American Marxist Mike Marqusee. Corbyn was neither a paid agent nor a source of secrets, but he was a genuine sympathiser. His only criticisms of the Soviet system, he would write in the *Morning Star* in 1989, were its disregard for nationalism and its elitism; nothing else. The relationship between Corbyn and Sarkocy was only disrupted by

Sarkocy's expulsion from Britain after the collapse of communism. 'I have known Mr Jeremy Corbyn as a decent man,' he would say in 2018, 'who had a positive attitude towards the former Czechoslovakia. And he was not alone.'

Later that year, 1987, Corbyn tabled a motion in the Commons asking the government to demand that the Kremlin 'gives complete rehabilitation to Leon Trotsky'. Virtue-signalling was the highlight of his political activities as Labour headed for another electoral humiliation.

6

The Harmless Extremist

In the run-up to the 1987 general election, Keith Veness, by this time a NUPE official employed by neighbouring Hackney council, agreed to become Corbyn's constituency agent. As a close friend he anticipated the obstacles that would face the campaign. 'I had spent years screaming at Jeremy that he had no money,' he said. Corbyn could not even buy his own food. 'That was my hold over him. He had to come to me for breakfast, and then I could control him for the rest of the day.' Fortunately for Corbyn, Sogat, the printers' union, gave him £8,000 towards his election expenses in gratitude for his daily attendance on the Wapping picket line. Other small contributions came from admirers grateful that he had given a speech or attended a funeral. 'Jeremy was very good at funerals,' said Veness. 'He could always look solemn, miserable, and also speak to people.' Corbyn counted on his agent to produce a black tie.

During the previous election campaign he had frequently disappeared from his own constituency, taking a train to speak in Oxford, Plymouth and elsewhere. His unreliability was the result of his fondness for recognition. He would travel anywhere to hear an audience say, 'He's a good bloke.' But to Tariq Ali and serious left ideologues, he remained no more than 'a parochial figure who saw himself as a gadfly to irritate the government'. There was no substance to his socialism, Ali thought. 'I shared many platforms with Jeremy,' he recalled, 'but I can't remember what he said except that he was on the right side.' During the 1987 campaign, to make sure Corbyn arrived at meetings as scheduled, Veness arranged for two minders to be with him constantly. 'Don't listen to anything he says,' he ordered. 'Just pick him up and take him to the next place.'

Amid the flurry of campaigning, Corbyn found time just one month before the election to marry for the second time. His bride was Claudia Bracchitta, the daughter of Chilean exiles. The family had arrived in London in 1973, when Claudia was eleven, to escape from the Pinochet regime after Salvador Allende's overthrow, and had settled in Haringey. Thirteen years later, as leader of the 'Chilean Committee for Justice', Corbyn had met Claudia at a GLC meeting addressed by Ken Livingstone. She was good-looking and intelligent, and although she was already married, he was smitten. By the following year she was pregnant, and rushed through a divorce in order to marry her new admirer. Neither of Corbyn's parents was present at the wedding: his father had died the previous year, and his mother was not invited. In fact, he did not tell even his close friends about his marriage.

In the weeks immediately before the election, some opinion polls predicted a Tory collapse, although most predicted a Conservative majority of up to a hundred. Throughout the campaign Margaret Thatcher was the target of vituperation, but she profited from Neil Kinnock's support of unilateral disarmament, increased taxes and the removal of the requirement for trade unions to call strikes only after a secret ballot. Kinnock, humiliated in 1983 when he was filmed falling into the sea on Brighton beach during the party conference, was again embarrassed, this time by a dismissive press release when he paid a pre-election visit to Ronald Reagan at the White House, the result of sabotage by Thatcher's team, which portrayed the Labour leader as having been spurned during their conversation by the US president. On the other hand, his chances were improved by his appointment of a new director of communications, Peter Mandelson, who rebranded the party by replacing the red flag with a red rose. Unlike Corbyn, Mandelson understood Thatcher's appeal: low taxes, low inflation, fewer strikes, home ownership and opportunities for self-improvement free from state control. The unions' defeat at Wapping had damaged Labour, while the Tories' election poster showed a soldier with his arms raised in surrender, and the slogan 'Labour's policy on arms'. It all confirmed Corbyn's belief in Thatcher's malevolence. Dressed in power suits with padded shoulders, she inspired hatred as an evil fascist even among moderate leftists. Corbyn had no concern about his own re-election. Labour's appeal to the middle classes in newly gentrified parts of Islington guaranteed a comfortable victory.

In the run-up to polling day, Keith Veness expected the candidate to take a break from campaigning because Claudia was due to give birth to their first child. To his surprise, Corbyn telephoned from outside the delivery room at the Royal Free hospital in Hampstead. 'I'm really worried,' he complained. 'We haven't put out that leaflet about Northern Ireland.'

'Haven't you got something more serious to worry about?' asked Veness.

'What's that?'

'You're about to be a father. I've never heard of anyone who lost an election because they didn't get a leaflet out.'

The opinion polls proved more or less accurate. The Tories won a majority of 102 seats, the first time since 1918 that a party had secured a consecutive third term. Corbyn found Labour's electoral defeat even harder to understand than those of the two previous elections. He resented the fact that the national debate had ignored his support for immigration and his condemnation of Britain's behaviour towards the undeveloped world.

His detachment from mainstream Britain was reflected on the first day of the new Parliament. To celebrate a new era, Britain's first three black MPs – all Labour – marched into the Commons chamber together. Paul Boateng, Diane Abbott and Bernie Grant, together with the Asian Keith Vaz, each dressed in their parents' national costumes, created an unprecedented spectacle as they walked towards the speaker to take the oath. Acting as part-sepoy and part-valet, Corbyn walked immediately behind, pleased to have a place as the honorary white man for the black caucus. 'Look at Jeremy,' said Brian Wilson, a new

Scottish MP, to George Galloway, who had also been newly elected. 'He would black up if he could.'

In the four years since Corbyn had left Haringey council, his image had changed. Few at Westminster had witnessed his vituperative campaign against the moderate Labour councillors, and it was not widely known that Corbyn, regarded around the Houses of Parliament as a 'good guy' because unlike so many hard leftists he was pleasant to everyone, had masterminded deselections and the dismissal of political opponents. The 'hatred and divisions' recalled by Haringey councillors at 'nasty meetings' orchestrated by Corbyn were concealed by a smoke-screen of indifference. His calculated makeover was sealed by a shy confession: 'I'm not personally a combative person. It's not my style.' The image was of a harmless extremist peddling political nonsense from the fringe.

Four months after the election, in October 1987, the world's stock markets crashed, and property prices tumbled. For Corbyn and his allies, hope was once again rekindled. Capitalism's days seemed numbered. 'The world will never be the same again,' announced Ken Livingstone, another of those newly elected to Parliament. It was the end of Thatcher and Reagan's monetarism, he asserted, and the moment for the state to take control of Britain's economy. Corbyn echoed that opinion, and went even further, predicting an imminent people's revolt.

Tony Benn, re-elected to Parliament as the Member for Chesterfield in a 1984 by-election, was more realistic. Prompted by the party's third successive electoral defeat and the financial crash, he considered Labour's predicament. The decline of traditional industries had hit Labour's relationship with the working class, with many of its diminishing numbers voting Tory. He had little time for Kinnock's intention to make Labour electable by diluting its commitment to socialism, and asked Reg Race, a part-time adviser after Thatcher abolished the GLC, to organise a conference in his Chesterfield constituency to 'reaffirm and redefine the socialist project in Britain for the 1990s'. Naturally, Corbyn decided to go.

On the eve of his departure for the conference, his office took a call from his wife. She told him that his mother had died, and asked him to come home. But Corbyn decided against either going home or travelling to Wiltshire to see his mother's body. Instead, he went to Benn's convention in Chesterfield.

To the surprise of Benn and Race, the event on 24 October 1987 attracted about two thousand activists, representing a rainbow coalition of socialists, communists and Trotskyists. After twenty years on the fringe, many had decided that a revolution was more distant than ever. Benn offered his familiar alternative route, taking power through Parliament. 'I'm sure the conference is a turning point in British politics,' he said outside the hall. Inside, he urged those present to help bring about the reincarnation of their party. His optimism was echoed by Ralph Miliband, who declared that the Chesterfield congress was the British left's most important event since communists met in Leeds in 1918 to celebrate the Bolshevik revolution. Their manifesto, he declared, was for the state to dominate Britain's economy and industry. Corbyn gave a dour speech about equality, taxing the rich and abolishing war. Never a convincing orator, he failed to present a sophisticated analysis of society, or even to offer a coherent Marxist reading of Britain's woes. On the rare occasions when a speech of his was interrupted by applause, he would be so surprised that he would stop and start again from the beginning. 'His speeches were one mile wide and an inch deep,' said George Galloway. 'Was he speaking about equality of wealth, or equality of misery?' Unable to finely craft his beliefs, he sparked no imagination about the uncertain future. To Tariq Ali, who did not go to Chesterfield, the conference exposed the left's weakness. The comrades departed, he felt, without having redefined the left's philosophy or agenda. What did the party actually believe in? Corbyn was untroubled by any ideological vacuum. 'I have a point of view,' he said. 'I try to listen a lot and to be representative of those who don't feel represented.'

Among those he continued to support was the IRA. On 8 May 1988, at an official meeting to commemorate dead IRA terrorists, Corbyn knew his hosts were also celebrating the murder in

Holland the previous week of three British servicemen by an IRA squad. 'In this, the conclusive phase of the war to rid Ireland of the scourge of British imperialism,' the programme exalted, 'force of arms is the only method capable of bringing this about.' At that meeting, to demonstrate his unconditional loathing of any opponent of the IRA, Corbyn attacked the Anglo-Irish Agreement signed in 1985 to start the peace process. Pointedly, he criticised the Irish republic's elected Catholic politicians as 'cannon fodder' who prevented rather than hastened Irish reunification. He shared Diane Abbott's description of the Protestants in Northern Ireland as an 'enclave of white supremacist ideology' akin to Zimbabwe's white settlers. Ian Paisley, the firebrand Protestant leader, suspected that Corbyn supported the ethnic cleansing of the entire Protestant community from Ulster. His suspicion was shared by Gerry Adams and Martin McGuinness, although from a different perspective. For despite Corbyn's zealous commitment, the IRA leadership never trusted him with information about their contemporaneous secret negotiations with the Thatcher government. He was a useful megaphone, but nothing more. He faced the same mistrust among his fellow MPs. And then the slide into obscurity accelerated.

In 1988 Corbyn automatically supported Tony Benn's challenge to Neil Kinnock for the party leadership. As Benn's trusted footsoldier, he was the obvious person to organise the campaign. Ignominiously, Benn won only 11 per cent of the Parliamentary Labour Party's vote. 'Benn's madness destroyed the left's credibility,' fumed Livingstone. 'The left just fell apart.' The following year Kinnock embarrassed the parliamentary left still further by officially embracing the market economy, endorsing Britain's membership of the European Economic Community and abandoning nationalisation and nuclear disarmament. Then, to marginalise the Bennites even further, the party's rules were changed. Candidates for the leadership were required to be nominated by at least 20 per cent of Labour MPs.

The left's final mortification was the collapse of communism in Eastern Europe. Despite his self-promotion as a champion of the oppressed, Corbyn lacked any sympathy for East Europeans oppressed by the Soviet Union. During the bitter battle in Poland between the Solidarity movement and the pro-Soviet dictator General Wojciech Jaruzelski, many Labour MPs had occupied the Polish embassy in London. Corbyn refused to join the protest, with the excuse that he was 'staying out to go on holiday.' He did not celebrate the liberation of hundreds of millions of Europeans from Soviet control when in 1989 the Berlin Wall fell. Similarly, *Glasnost* in Russia, the first step towards abandoning communism, provoked his despair. Tens of thousands of people, he lamented, had lost their security of employment, their pensions and their community. He made no speeches about the people's victory over tyranny. On the contrary, he lamented that the Cold War had been won by the wrong side. NATO, he declared, should 'shut up shop, give up, go home and go away'. The alliance was nothing more than 'an engine for the delivery of oil to the oil companies and the major nations of the world'. Unlike the Soviet Union, he said, NATO had never been 'overly troubled by concepts of democracy or human rights'. Remarkably, he was baffled by communism's collapse. Unwilling to concede defeat, and as ever nostalgically clutching the red flag, he chose that moment to begin writing for the *Morning Star*, the newspaper financed by Moscow. By any reckoning, his personal commitment to Stalinism set him apart from most Labour Party members. Authoritarianism, his critics would say, was embedded within his soul.

His comfort was the performance of his trusted quartet – Ken Livingstone, Diane Abbott and Bernie Grant plus George Galloway – at Westminster. In the Commons chamber he could hear Livingstone praise the communist revolution in Afghanistan for having 'advanced the rights of workers and peasants', or Grant criticise Reagan's 'state-sponsored terrorism' to topple the Marxist government of Nicaragua. Corbyn himself eulogised Cuba as 'a beacon', and Fidel Castro as 'an inspiration ... a champion of social justice'. Castro's leadership, he enthused, 'emancipated the world's poorest people from slavery, hunger and the denial of human rights'. The Cuban leader's imprisonment of political opponents and the country's permanent food rationing were offset by free health-care. Corbyn ignored the fact that in 1962 Castro had urged Nikita Khrushchev to launch a nuclear attack on America. He also brushed aside the million Cubans who had fled to Florida, often on makeshift rafts. In his opinion, the cause of any suffering in Cuba was US imperialism. American presidents, he said, suffered 'paranoia' because the island was a 'threat by example'.

His beliefs were unshakable, as was his fixation on certain aspects of foreign affairs – the plight of the Kurds in Iraq and Turkey, the Chilean regime's acquisition of British arms, the fate of the Marxist rebels in Angola, and the Moroccan persecution of Polisario in the Western Sahara. All demanded his presence. He was soon heading off to Nicaragua to give his support to the Sandinistas. By chance, the Labour MP Brian Wilson and some Scottish doctors were helping to build a medical centre in the Nicaraguan countryside when Corbyn arrived. While Wilson's group was living in discomfort, Corbyn, well practised in the art of negotiating upgrades, moved into the capital's best hotel. 'What are you doing here?' Wilson asked when Corbyn turned up at the site. 'Showing solidarity,' came the reply. Corbyn's penchant for revolutionaries wearing military uniforms and killing off their opponents evoked cynicism among Foreign Office officials. 'Corbyn's being a pain in the arse,' complained Charles de Chassiron, head of the South American Department, about the MP's endless questions about Chile. De Chassiron and most Foreign Office officials viewed Corbyn's champion-ship of justice in that country with some contempt, considering his stark inconsistencies.

On 2 August 1990, Saddam Hussein's army invaded Kuwait. Amid considerable brutality, Kuwaitis were held hostage in their own country. Many British nationals were also detained. Only the Palestinians who had been given shelter and work by the Kuwaitis welcomed the Iraqi occupation. According to Corbyn's logic, since Saddam, an ally of Palestine, was pledged to destroy Israel, it was right to support the invasion. In his opinion, the Kuwaitis were allies of America and Britain, friends of Israel, and therefore his foes. At the United Nations, Resolution 678 condemned the invasion and sanctioned military intervention if Saddam refused to withdraw. Despite the build-up of American and British forces in neighbouring Saudi Arabia, Saddam rejected the ultimatum. Corbyn felt no qualms about the contradiction that, while he preached that conflicts should be resolved by the UN, he supported Saddam's invasion. Despite Kuwaitis being murdered, he voted in the Commons against the use of force. Sanctions, he argued, should be given more time. Days later, the allied armies stormed into Kuwait and also entered southern Iraq. Corbyn criticised that invasion, and damned President George Bush's 'occupation of all or part of Iraq and the imposition of a US puppet government'. In the Commons he asked for an assurance that nuclear weapons would not be used. 'The carnage of the bombing must be stopped,' he said, praising the Soviet Union's 'attempts to keep the hope of peace alive'.

He urged John Major, who had succeeded Margaret Thatcher in November 1990, to compare the hundreds of millions of pounds spent on the Gulf War, 'causing 150,000 casualties and deaths', with 'the miserly figure of £28 million spent on the African famine'. Major was not amused. Corbyn's account 'missed out one or two material facts', he said, including 'the liberation of Kuwait … the Iraqis were murdering Kuwaitis, dismantling Kuwait, damaging the environment and committing unpardonable sins. I very much regret that the Honourable Gentleman does not recall that.'

Unwilling to topple Saddam, Bush halted the invasion on 28 February 1991. The US Army withdrew, abandoning the Kurds, a stateless people squeezed into the fertile land between Iraq, Iran and Turkey. They had good reason to feel aggrieved. In response to Bush's appeal, they had risen up against Saddam – partly in revenge for his murder in 1988 of about three thousand Kurds in the city of Halabja by gas. Three years later, after America's withdrawal, vast numbers were massacred in reprisal by Saddam's army in further gas attacks. To prevent yet more deaths, Britain and America enforced a no-fly zone over a

Kurdish safe haven. In response, Corbyn condemned the US for killing 100,000 people during the war, then criticised them for failing to protect the Kurds. He uttered no criticism of Saddam.

Over the previous years Corbyn had developed a close relationship with Ihsan Qaesr, an exiled Kurdish activist living in Islington. In July 1991, at Qaesr's invitation, he travelled through Turkey to Iraqi Kurdistan. Escorted by a group of Peshmerga soldiers, he and Qaesr spent seven days touring an area hit by an Iraqi gas attack two months previously. The scenes of desperation, recalled Qaesr, were 'unforgettable'. In their efforts to protect the Kurds from more deaths, America planned to bomb the Iraqi factories that produced the gas. To Qaesr's surprise, Corbyn opposed any allied bombing of or attacks on Saddam's military bases. Standing in the site of one devastating Iraqi raid, he told Qaesr that the UN should initiate a peaceful dialogue to negotiate a solution. Although he was grateful for Corbyn's interest, Qaesr admitted, 'I was frustrated by Jeremy's refusal to support military retaliation and the military defence of safe havens for the Kurds.'

Corbyn occupied an unusual position. He had been sympathetic to East Europe's communist regimes, he supported Saddam Hussein's illegal occupation of Kuwait, he condemned Kuwait's liberation, and he endorsed Fidel Castro's dictatorship. Shortly after his visit to Iraq he travelled to Cuba with Claudia as official guests. The highlight was dinner with Castro, who in his welcoming speech hailed Corbyn as a trusted friend against American imperialism. The main course was meat. To Claudia's bemusement, rather than mentioning the fact that he was a vegetarian, her husband swallowed the beef with his principles.

Corbyn's lengthy absences from Britain had coincided with the political demise of Margaret Thatcher. Her flagship policy, the poll tax, had provoked disobedience in Scotland and riots in Trafalgar Square. Alongside his close allies, Corbyn publicly vowed not to pay the tax. Eventually, after some dithering, he did pay, but assuaged his conscience by making a well publicised visit to Terry Fields, a Trotskyite councillor who had been jailed for sixty days for refusing to pay £373 in council tax.

Corbyn's protests barely registered among the public. Wearing sandals and his usual rumpled clothes, and known for his unkempt beard, he continued to be dismissed in Westminster as a member of the loony left. Although he worked hard at the Red Rose to resolve his constituents' problems, and was especially helpful to immigrants and refugees, he seemed oblivious to Islington being ranked as London's worst borough for social services, housing, education and street maintenance. Under Margaret Hodge, the council leader between 1982 and 1992, the People's Republic of Islington boasted a red flag fluttering above the town hall, and a bust of Lenin proudly placed inside the building. Ideological battles took precedence over care for the residents. At every level, councillors and their officials were seeped in chaos. Dismissed as a 'barmy borough' by Thatcher, the council had outlawed use of the word 'immigrant' in its communications, banned Irish jokes and provided gym mats for lesbian self-defence courses. Despite levying London's highest council tax, the borough had debts that in 1998 would lead it to the brink of bankruptcy. Forty-seven per cent of its residents lived in 35,000 council homes notorious for infestation with crime, drugs, damp and dilapidation because Islington's unionised labour force refused to undertake repairs, despite threats of dismissal. NUPE, the workers knew, would protect their jobs. A recent auditor's report highlighted tax arrears of £23.7 million, with £4 million missing in uncollected fines. Foreign benefit cheats were pocketing thousands of pounds because council investigators had been ordered not to contact immigration officials. Despite that record, Margaret Hodge was surprised by Corbyn's silence. While she regularly received complaints from Chris Smith, the Labour MP for Islington South, she never heard from Corbyn. Nor did Smith, although he did recall hearing Corbyn complain in the Commons that all Islington's woes were entirely due to the limits on Whitehall's financial grants. 'The answer to our problem lies with the government,' Corbyn told a minister. Spending more money was his answer to every problem when he met his constituents. Frequently seen cycling around Islington on his way to some event, he never volunteered to challenge the council's performance, other than to stage a successful campaign to change a by-law to allow clothing factories owned by local Greek Cypriots to operate at high noise levels despite residents' complaints. Helping immigrants, especially those with visa problems, guaranteed him votes from entire communities. He was consistent in his inconsistencies.

Preoccupied by the needs of immigrants, Corbyn appeared uninterested in the systematic sexual abuse of vulnerable children in Islington's residential homes, all of which were staffed by council employees, members of NUPE. Over the previous five years, evidence of sex orgies run from a 'hot house' on the council's Elthorne estate had been exposed. Children had been rented out from a brothel to paedophiles. Among the many victims was Vivien Loki, a seventeen-year-old girl whose decomposed body was discovered on the estate six months after her murder by a paedophile. Further north, at Gisburne House, another Islington home, children were being abused on an industrial scale. 'All this,' Islington social worker Liz Davies discovered, 'was happening on Corbyn's doorstep. He knew all about it because it was raised by [Conservative MP] Geoffrey Dickens in the Commons.'

In October 1992, five Islington council social workers, led by Liz Davies, confronted Corbyn in his office at the Red Rose and revealed that dozens of drugged, hungry and distressed young people of both sexes living in twelve council homes were being routinely raped by council employees. Paedophile gangs were rampant across the borough, and at least thirty employees suspected of crimes had been allowed to quietly resign. Peter Righton, founder of the pro-paedophile group the Paedophile Information Exchange (PIE), had been given authority by the Home Office to brief council social workers to place vulnerable children with known sex offenders. Their criminality was known to the NCCL, run by Harriet Harman. In conjunction with PIE, the NCCL had agreed that known paedophiles could stay overnight in children's homes to avoid infringing their rights as gay adults. Having set out this appalling scenario, the social workers told Corbyn that their complaints to Margaret Hodge had been ignored. After the *Evening Standard* published a detailed exposé of Islington's employment of known paedophiles, and the officials' shredding of documents to cover up the crimes, the council accused the paper of 'gutter journalism'.

The council employees' meeting with Corbyn lasted ninety minutes, during which he pronounced, 'I've heard similar issues from other constituents,' and then said little else. As usual when confronted with complicated or unpalatable facts, he retreated into his shell, mumbling and smiling but offering no meaningful replies. At the end he promised to speak to Virginia Bottomley, the health minister, but she does not recall any such conversation having taken place. He had even protested when Geoffrey Dickens mentioned the abuse in the House of Commons. 'We heard nothing more from Corbyn,' Liz Davies recalled. 'We don't know whether he did anything to help us.' Later, John Mann, a moderate Labour MP, accused Corbyn of ignoring the reports, and blamed the 'trendy left' for a cover-up motivated by cowardice, self-interest or laziness. Corbyn, Mann wrote, had 'inadvertently helped the rubbishing of allegations'.

Later, several investigations would reveal that the 'establishment', with Whitehall's approval, had concealed the network of paedophiles abusing children in forty-two Islington council homes, precisely the sort of protection racket a left-wing MP would usually delight in exposing. Yet Corbyn was silent, except to denounce Mann's attack as a 'new low'. He had called, he claimed, for an independent inquiry. Nothing in the public record confirms such an assertion. 'Corbyn ignored the abuse,' Tony Allcock, the editor of the *Islington Gazette*, recalled, 'to show solidarity with the left-wing councillors and NUPE and the other trade unions.' The local MP, he observed, 'did not react well to criticism', especially the charge that he allowed 'dirty deeds to be done in his name'. To deflect the attacks, Corbyn presented himself as a good man whose behaviour was beyond reproach. Those who criticised him personally were accordingly bad people, and he refused to engage in personal abuse. At the time, he was not important enough for any national newspaper

to report his apparent indifference to the children's fate. Only
the *Islington Gazette* highlighted his disregard of the borough's
chaos in the months before the general election of April 1992.
Not that he cared about such coverage. According to the opinion polls, Labour would win.

Wilfully separating himself from Neil Kinnock and the main
party, Corbyn looked askance at the leadership's attempt to
produce a vote-winning manifesto based on the banishment of
socialism. 'It's soap-opera populism,' he scoffed about both
Labour's 'new agenda' and Peter Mandelson's demand for party
discipline. Particularly repugnant to him was the acceptance of
Thatcher's market economy, manifested in Canary Wharf, the
new financial centre which provided jobs for 100,000 people.
'We do our opinion polls,' he mocked, 'find out what people
want and say, "OK, you can have it," without asking what kind
of society we now have and what kind of society we want to
replace it.' Despite the improvements to services, he wanted all
Britain's privatised industries to be renationalised, especially the
telephone network. This was wilfully ideological. Since the
privatisation of British Telecom in 1984, the public no longer
faced a six-month wait to get a telephone line, and the utility's
appalling record for providing repairs had improved. BT now
provided telephones on demand, and no longer were British
visitors to America awestruck by the huge banks of pushbutton
phones and instant connections by credit card; but for Corbyn
better services were irrelevant. 'It is a negation of democracy,' he
complained, 'that we hand our services over to the private
sector' – or 'vultures', as he called entrepreneurs.

As Corbyn moved from council estate to demonstration,
meeting or picket line, he noted that others were also angry
about the 'betrayal of socialism'. Those he regarded as the
authentic voice of the party's rank and file were disillusioned.
Principles were being abandoned in the hope of winning power.
Many local parties were in a state of political exhaustion after
Labour's headquarters, taking its lead from Neil Kinnock's
speech at the party conference in Bournemouth in 1985, system-

atically forced any remaining Trotskyists and communists out of the party. 'The man who destroyed the Labour Party', wrote Benn of Kinnock. Corbyn shared that anger. 'The branches have had a hell of a battering with expulsions, candidates imposed on them by Machiavellian procedures and so on,' he complained, seemingly having forgotten his own conduct ten years earlier in Haringey. 'People are not coming to meetings and there's a low level of local activity.' The removal of Trotskyites, he observed, had left the party with 'a shallow, unhealthy base'.

The 1992 general election handed the Conservatives their fourth successive victory, albeit with a majority cut from 102 to twenty-one. Although opinion polls leading up to the vote had shown Labour consistently if narrowly ahead, this time the defeat did not surprise Corbyn. Only real socialism, he believed, would win a majority for Labour. Unlike him, the party's moderates were plunged into despair. They questioned why Labour won only 34 per cent of the vote, while the Tories got 42 per cent. Even diluted socialism had been rejected. An exception was Islington North. Winning 57 per cent of the ballot, Corbyn increased his majority to 12,784. As usual, he relied on the immigrant vote, solicitously attending their events while maintaining his calculated lack of interest in the council's misconduct.

After the election, Keith Veness resigned as his constituency agent. 'I've had enough,' he told Corbyn. 'You're an anarchic shambles, without any discipline.' In particular, he was fed up with the candidates's obsession with leaflets. 'There's so much paper around that no one can open the doors,' he carped about the offices at the Red Rose. Corbyn's financial indiscipline was another irritation. Whenever Veness protested that there was no money for another leaflet, Corbyn replied, 'We'll find it.' As his friend's tirade finished, Corbyn said amicably: 'Oh, don't worry, mate. Are you all right?'

The following year, while Corbyn was collecting the headquarters rubbish, a chore he undertook as a member of a 'democratic office', he came across a note about a surprise party planned to celebrate his tenth anniversary as local MP. At least he attended. Surrounded by Kurds, Chileans and Nicaraguans, he sang 'The Red Flag' and raised a glass of beer to his comrades. Prophetically, he admitted to a local journalist that the Red Rose was losing money. 'The problem is,' he admitted, 'I'm not into market economics.'

But it was the markets that changed Labour's fortunes. Black Wednesday, on 16 September 1992, just five months after the Tories had retained power, handed Labour a priceless advantage for the next election. John Major's government had mismanaged Britain's membership of a European currency agreement, the Exchange Rate Mechanism (ERM), and as sterling collapsed and interest rates soared, the panicking Conservatives lost their reputation for economic competence. Labour's support for the ERM was forgotten as the party's fortunes improved. They advanced further after the sudden death in May 1994 of John Smith, a traditional tax-and-spend socialist who had replaced Kinnock as leader after the election. In the immediate aftermath, Corbyn did not anticipate that Tony Blair would stand against Gordon Brown for the leadership. Nor did he foresee that in the choice between a social democrat and a Thatcherite marketeer, the parliamentary party would overwhelmingly reject the divisive Brown. As Blair's New Labour took over, Corbyn complained about a 'coup within the party', but the left was powerless to prevent Blair's abandonment of socialism. At a special conference in April 1995 the party voted to abolish Clause 4 of its constitution, the pledge to nationalise Britain's entire economy, described as 'the means of production'. Only three constituencies supported Corbyn's opposition to the motion, with 86 per cent of the membership supporting Blair. The party of towering intellectual MPs like Richard Crossman, Roy Jenkins and Tony Crosland was no more.

Propelled by the Tories' split over EU membership, New Labour's popularity as a middle-class party soared. Its seemingly unassailable lead in the opinion polls did not, however, please Corbyn. Angered by Blair's professed admiration for Margaret Thatcher, he opposed his new leader's tough line on inflation, his intention not to tax, borrow and spend, and his pledge to remove welfare dependency. Above all, he despised

Blair's love of wealth, celebrity and success. Even worse for the left was Blair's trip to Australia in July 1995 to woo Rupert Murdoch. Clare Short's criticism of the 'forces of darkness' surrounding Blair, especially Mandelson's obsession with the media, was shared by Corbyn. 'Clare is right to draw attention to the appalling power of the spin doctors and the way that modern politics is dominated by totally unrepresentative focus groups,' he said. 'There is a real danger of us risking upsetting our core support, which could lose [us] the general election.' One hundred Labour MPs, he continued, were unhappy about Blair's 'kitchen cabinet' – a coterie of like-minded advisers controlling everything. Blair's response, that New Labour had attracted 100,000 new members, made no impression on Corbyn, despite it being in line with his own early successes in Haringey. Labour MPs, he retorted, possibly tongue-in-cheek, deserved to be treated with respect, even those who repeatedly voted against the party. He supported a petition launched by the Trotskyite Socialist Workers Party attacking Labour's front bench for failing to 'reflect their class-based loyalty to the party'. That complaint resonated with Clive Boutle and other disillusioned leftists in Islington. 'Jeremy became our voice in the wilderness years,' recalled Boutle. 'He was the go-to guy.' Twenty years later, as leader, Corbyn would organise the management of the party from his own office in an identical manner to Blair and his close circle of insiders.

By 1996, however, his politics appealed only to the fringes. For them, royal weddings were unwelcome, Britain should accept unlimited numbers of economic migrants to alleviate world poverty, and Jane Brown, a lesbian head teacher in Hackney, should be applauded for refusing to take schoolchildren to a Royal Ballet performance of *Romeo and Juliet* because it was 'a blatantly heterosexual love story'. This last episode wasn't a one-off oddity: Corbyn agreed with Brown that Shakespeare's 'heterosexist' play reflected white society and was racist. Similarly, he supported Diane Abbott's criticism of staff at her local east London hospital as 'blonde, blue-eyed Finnish girls' who were not suitable to be nurses because they had 'never met a black person before'. Confused prejudice did not trouble Corbyn: while he had opposed sending his son to a grammar school, he did not criticise Abbott for sending her son to the private City of London school rather than a Hackney comprehensive. (She later described her decision as 'indefensible' and 'incoherent', but said she feared her child would fall in with 'black gangs' if he went to a state school.) He also remained silent when Abbott in turn criticised Tony Blair and Harriet Harman for choosing selective schools for their children.

Corbyn's attitude towards women was unusual. Ignoring his feminist colleagues, he would propose the decriminalisation of prostitution and, in 2016, support men who identified as women regardless of their physical state. His pronouncements, and also his silences, increasingly irked Tony Blair, particularly when after an IRA bomb on 15 June 1996 injured over two hundred people and devastated the centre of Manchester, Corbyn said nothing, just as he had remained silent three years earlier when an IRA bomb in Warrington killed two children and injured fifty-nine people. Val Veness, who was still employed by Corbyn at the Commons, says that there was 'delight in the office' when in April 1993 an IRA bomb had gone off in the City of London. 'The insurance companies told the British government to produce a solution in Ireland because the repairs would cost them £1 billion,' she recalled with satisfaction. During the most recent negotiations between Britain, Ireland and the two communities to end the killings, Corbyn's support for the IRA provoked the *Guardian* to comment, 'Mr Corbyn is a fool and a fool the Labour Party would be better off without … His actions do not advance the cause of peace in Northern Ireland and are not intended to do so.' The MP for Antarctica North could cause ripples, but never waves.

Three months after the Manchester bombing, Corbyn invited Gerry Adams to launch his new book, *Before the Dawn*, in the Jubilee Room at Westminster 'as part of the peace process'. The book glorified both the IRA's killing of eighteen British soldiers at Warrenpoint in August 1979, and the murder at Westminster of Airey Neave, the Tory MP close to Margaret Thatcher, in

March of the same year. Most Labour MPs condemned Corbyn, and Blair threatened him with expulsion from the PLP. Backtracking, the book launch was moved to a hall in Islington. There Corbyn intended to justify the murder of Protestants and British soldiers and condemn the death of any IRA man, but to his disappointment Adams cancelled his visit, supposedly because of the arrest of an IRA bombing unit and the death of an IRA bomber. Corbyn never knew what was really happening in Northern Ireland. With Adams's encouragement he continued to argue that only reunification would guarantee peace, but in his unworldliness Corbyn could not understand that the IRA was on the verge of defeat. Sinn Féin continued the peace negotiations only because the British intelligence services had completely penetrated the IRA's command. At the same time, Corbyn remained dismissive of Ulster's Protestant majority, merely tolerating a rare encounter with Ian Paisley in the corridors of Westminster.

His diffident manner and political irrelevance helped neutralise the irritation he caused. Yet he was not coy about his ambitions. To assert a separate identity from Tony Benn, he stood for election to Labour's National Executive Committee (NEC). His manifesto pledged to renationalise every industry privatised by the Tories, ban Britain's nuclear weapons, withdraw from the EU, increase pensions and all welfare benefits, hold a referendum to abolish the monarchy, agree for Britain to pay reparations to its former colonies, and submit the country to the International Court of Justice for the crimes committed during the empire. He also opposed the construction of an 'awful' new railway terminal at King's Cross (the result was a stunning success), described the London Eye opposite Westminster as 'an eyesore and totally inappropriate for that site' (four million people enjoy riding it every year), and advocated women-only railway carriages as a way of protecting them from sexual harassment. With time to spare, he travelled with Talal Karim, an Islington activist, for three weeks across India – from Mumbai to Calcutta – on steam trains at a snail's pace, either sitting on a carriage roof or on the footplate shovelling coal into the furnace. 'You're mad,' Claudia told him before he left. At least no one could accuse him of sitting on his hands.

His relationship with his wife was troubled. Claudia was a serious intellectual. Well-read and belonging to the mainstream of the left, she had become impatient with a husband who rarely read books and misunderstood South American politics. Corbyn's belief that the government of rabble-rousing revolutionaries in Nicaragua, Bolivia and other small states could be replicated by community politics in Britain reflected how superficial was his understanding. They were virtually living separate lives, and she played little part in his next election campaign.

Polling day was set for 1 May 1997, with forecasts of a huge Labour victory. Meeting in the Commons on the eve of the campaign, the thirty members of the Campaign Group were deflated. The anticipated landslide would further marginalise their influence. Nevertheless, they agreed to mute their hostility towards Tony Blair during the campaign. 'The discipline of the left in the run-up to the election was absolute,' Ken Livingstone would assert. That was not quite accurate. He could not resist urging a 'greedy bastard tax rate' of 99 per cent on those earning over £2 million; and Corbyn agreed that taxes should be increased, because 'the rich should pay for the social consequences of the Thatcher and Major years'. But there was a surprise in store. At the last moment, he found himself fighting to avoid deselection. Islington's corruption had at last caught up with him.

The previous year, a New Labour group within the constituency led by Stephen Twigg, an ambitious Balliol-educated councillor, had successfully appointed Leisha Fullick as the council's new chief executive in an attempt to rectify the borough's dilapidation and its crippling financial situation. Intelligent, honest and efficient, Fullick was greeted by Alan Clinton, a veteran Trotskyist and the council's Labour leader, with a damning 'She'll change nothing, even over my dead body.' Twigg, supported by about forty Blairites allegedly financed by Lord Sainsbury of the supermarket family, attempted to overthrow Clinton, but the hard left was still in control of the council, and he failed by one vote. Undeterred, he next sought to deselect Corbyn. The moderates complained about their MP's Marxist opposition to New Labour and his blatant disregard for Islington's problems. Corbyn dubbed them 'bedsit reactionaries'.

Fullick's responsibilities covered both Islington constituencies. During her first year, she discovered in her regular meetings with the two local MPs that Corbyn, unlike Chris Smith, never mentioned Islington's failures in housing, education and corruption. 'Jeremy,' she told a Blairite subsequently, 'is not interested in improving local services or performance. He's not even interested in the latest district auditor's report about the lack of street cleaning. He never asks for the plans to sort out the mess. He's only interested in South American liberation groups.' There was one exception to this lack of interest. Whenever a council employee was threatened with dismissal for incompetence or dishonesty, Corbyn intervened to protect them.

New Labour's accusations against Corbyn were of disloyalty to the party and negligence over conditions in his constituency. Twigg's move was once again unsuccessful, and he abandoned his campaign, although Corbyn was shocked by the attempted coup. Changing Labour from representing the working class, he said, to a party of middle-class Blairite clones was 'a pretty appalling vista for a party rooted in local democracy'. Local members rather than Labour officials at headquarters should decide the suitability of a candidate.

The failed coup was forgotten after Labour's landslide victory on 1 May. Unexpectedly, Stephen Twigg was returned as MP for Enfield Southgate, evoking that night's most memorable image – Twigg's incredulous smile and the forlorn face of Michael Portillo, the defeated former defence secretary. Blair's triumph excited Britain. Even Corbyn could not resist celebrating Labour's return to power after eighteen years, but he did not rush to join New Labour's election-night party on London's South Bank: he would have been among enemies. His personal majority increased to 19,955. The other good news for Corbyn was the election of John McDonnell, one of 145 new Labour MPs.

McDonnell's route to the Commons had been fraught. Since the abolition of the GLC he had worked for Camden council and the Association of London Authorities. Before the 1987 election he had been repeatedly rejected by constituencies, and had also been trounced when he stood for a place on the NEC. In 1992 he had stood for Hayes and Harlington, a seemingly safe Labour seat, but lost by fifty-three votes to the Conservative Terry Dicks. Afterwards he was sued by Dicks for having claimed in a leaflet that Dicks was sympathetic to Saddam Hussein. At the last moment McDonnell agreed to pay £40,000 damages and Dicks' legal costs of £30,000. The source of the money was never revealed, arousing suspicions about McDonnell's contacts. Over the next five years his agitation for direct action by the masses became noticeably more aggressive. 'Don't expect the change [to society] coming from Parliament,' he told one Trotskyite meeting. 'We have an elected dictatorship, so I think we have a democratic right to use whatever means to bring this government down. The real fight is in our communities, it's on the picket lines, it's in the streets.' McDonnell never renounced this passion for violence, nor his contempt for Parliament; but to secure his nomination as a candidate he continued to mask his convictions with postures of innocence. Successfully elected as the Member for Hayes and Harlington in 1997, in his maiden speech he condemned Terry Dicks as racist, corrupt and malignant, only this time from the safety of the Commons, meaning that he was immune to legal action. He provided no evidence for that defamation. His one indication of conformity was his marriage in 1995 to Cynthia Pinto, a Goan from Kenya. McDonnell's arrival in the Commons strengthened Corbyn, the Liverpudlian's education and understanding of Marxism compensating for Corbyn's intellectual deficits. Neither intended to express any loyalty to Tony Blair.

Their first opportunity to rebel arose earlier than expected. Chancellor Gordon Brown had embraced the Tories' agenda to deter the feckless and fraudulent from living on benefits. Corbyn was appalled. 'We must not press ahead down the road of compelling people to work,' he said. In his opinion, welfare benefits were an entitlement. No one, he argued, should be penalised for refusing to look for work. Those accused of 'fiddling' their benefits, he said, were victims of 'sharks' who condoned tax avoidance and evasion, or protected the rich from higher taxes. The government's suggestion that MI5 would be used to expose benefit fraud was, he said, 'desperation in the post-Cold War era to find something for MI5 to do'. Its officers would be better off pursuing large-scale tax evasion by the wealthy in offshore tax havens. The cure was for the government to impose higher taxes, provide 'quality jobs' and restore benefits to asylum seekers. He was among forty-seven Labour MPs to vote against the government. About twenty-five others abstained.

With a majority of 179, Blair had nothing to fear, but, intolerant of Corbyn and 'the usual suspects', he enquired about the possibility of deselecting Corbyn before the next election. But was told that the truculent communist would stand as an independent, and win. Later, Blair would also ask about deselecting McDonnell, only to be halted by stories published in the *Guardian* that his popularity would guarantee victory over any official Labour candidate. The opinion polls cited by the paper to prove McDonnell's strength were bogus, concocted by his supporters to stymie Blair, who now conceded that it would be best simply to ignore the rebel MPs.

The prime minister's own ignorance of history played its part. Devoid of historical context, Blair was unaware of the battles fought by Clement Attlee and Hugh Gaitskell against communist infiltrators, or about Harold Wilson's warnings to Jim Callaghan that union leader Jack Jones was Moscow's agent. Instead of following the example of his predecessors by expelling the far left and deselecting disloyal MPs, he asked the party chairman to allow only candidates committed to New Labour to appear on the approved list of prospective parliamentary candidates. That, he believed, would remove any long-term danger. But the immediate irritation remained.

In June 1998, Corbyn joined thirty other Labour MPs to vote against Blair's proposal to introduce student tuition fees.

(Ironically, nineteen years later those fees would galvanise the young to vote for Corbyn.) Blair's patience snapped. He wanted obedience rather than debates that would stir trouble in the constituencies. Two left-wing MPs in Scotland were deselected, and other like-minded candidates dropped from the approved list. Persistent rebels, Corbyn was told, would be monitored by a committee chaired by Margaret McDonagh, a loyal Blairite. Corbyn again protested about draconian discipline and the NEC's 'big purge' of persistent critics. Blair's threats, he complained, would stop 'radical voices' emerging. He also opposed a suggestion that NEC votes should no longer be secret. Ballots, he protested, must be private to defend members from the leadership. 'Any change,' he warned, 'will be strongly resisted.' Eighteen years later, when he sought to assert his own control over the NEC, Corbyn proposed that the secret ballot should be abandoned, reducing two women at the meeting to tears. So often, his 'good bloke' image was tarnished by the truth.

For his news, Corbyn relied on the *Morning Star* and occasionally the *Guardian*. He never read *The Times* or the *New York Times*. 'Many of the supposedly well-informed major commentators in our media', he said, were 'shallow, facile and ill-informed'. His dislike of the media had been shaped by their ridicule of Tony Benn as leader of the 'loony left' during the 1970s. His ideological consistency extended to disdain for the aspirational white working class who had fled Islington, and for people who lived in country towns. Young people, he began to argue in 1997, should not assume that education was necessary for self-advancement. Those passing through university were artificially regarded as superior, to make people like him feel inferior. He also disliked the consumerism and competition encouraged by schools. Students should be taught that 'getting rich at the expense of others was wrong'. Instead, he wanted education to increase social interaction and improve communities. His goal was equality of poverty, not equality of opportunity to earn wealth. To create the Marxist ideal, he believed in universal confiscation of the middle class's wealth to benefit the poorest. Undiluted socialist equality, he believed, would cure his constituents' problems.

By 1998, new arrivals from Somalia, Pakistan and Bangladesh had packed into Islington North. Queues of migrants and asylum seekers at the Red Rose sought Corbyn's help to obtain homes, welfare benefits, character references for bail, help to reduce their sentences after criminal convictions, and intercession to avoid deportation. He was focused on them. There was one revolution that he despised: the one that had spawned Amazon, Google, Apple and Microsoft. To him, the IT techies' wealth insulted the seventy nationalities struggling to survive within his constituency. He distrusted the internet's empowerment of individuals, raged against the American titans he could neither understand nor control, and disputed any benefit of globalised markets, preferring to rely on organising labour in factories and offices. To him, the operation of capital markets dictated in nanoseconds by computer algorithms was a threat. None of those developments had been analysed by Karl Marx in 1867, but Corbyn assumed they offended socialism. In his debate-free zone, his convictions suffocated any evidence that every Marxist government of the previous hundred years had produced miserable poverty. He ignored the educated Chinese and Indians, driven by the profit motive, who had raised their country's living standards by embracing the market economy, and disregarded the massive reduction of global famine, although the numbers employed in the agriculture industry had plummeted. Only communist Cuba and North Korea suffered constant food shortages, but in his world it was the bankers who were to blame. That was the message he repeated in the Commons.

Dressed in a series of new sports jackets – one was burgundy – bought, some assumed, under the influence of a girlfriend after his separation from Claudia, he endured mockery from Andrew Roth, the author of *Parliamentary Profiles*, as 'a pastiche of the bearded Spartist fantasist still fighting fights in his own head at least'. He was regularly reminded that his cause had become out of date, and his own party had ditched Clause 4. 'He speaks with great conviction,' said one Tory, 'and over the years has undoubtedly convinced himself. However, it is a comfort to know that people like him survive in Parliament as a reminder that some will not compromise their principles.' Corbyn's strength was his stubborn conviction that socialism would eventually prevail. The doomed Marxist cause in Chile could always be resurrected to prove that he was right.

Fifteen years after the murder of Salvador Allende there was a chance for justice. In 1998, Augusto Pinochet, the eighty-two-year-old former dictator who had led the coup against Allende, quietly arrived in London for medical treatment. Unexpectedly, on 16 October a Spanish arrest warrant was delivered to a British court requesting his extradition to stand trial for the murder and torture of thousands of Chileans during his seventeen-year presidency. Pinochet could not plead innocence. In an interview with the *New Yorker*, he had admitted that crimes had been committed both under Allende's rule and during his own dictatorship. However, he said, he could not be held responsible for all of them. Pending the British court's decision, he was placed under house arrest. 'It will be the first time this ghastly dictator has faced questions,' said Corbyn. 'He is one of the great murderers of this century.' British judges denied Pinochet's argument that as a former head of state he had diplomatic immunity from prosecution. 'He wanted human rights for himself,' said Corbyn, 'but not for his victims. None of his victims ever had the chance to go to court. They were merely shot and murdered during his disgraceful regime.' His plea that Britain should not be a safe haven for dictators sat uneasily with his own support for similar tyrants in Russia and Cuba. Nor did it explain why the 3,197 innocents brutally murdered by Pinochet's regime caused him more concern than the thousand killed by the IRA in Britain.

Tony Blair was faced with a similar contradiction. In the halcyon early days of his prime ministership, his government had adopted what he called an 'ethical foreign policy'. At the same time, he was drinking tea with the IRA killer Martin McGuiness. To make any progress, he had learned that a government needed to compromise, fudge and accept that half a loaf can sate one's hunger. In the case of Pinochet, there was no advantage for Britain in preventing his return to Chile. After the former dictator had been in detention for fourteen months, four doctors declared that he was unfit to stand trial. Pinochet returned to Chile to live in peace until his death in 2006, aged ninety-one. Corbyn's outrage was even dismissed by the *Guardian*. 'It can be ignored like any Socialist Worker placard in a demonstration,' wrote Simon Hoggart.

At that moment, Corbyn's passion for human rights – he had urged that Pinochet should be prosecuted at the International Court of Justice in The Hague – did not extend to the prosecution of the Serbian dictator Slobodan Milošević for atrocities against Albanians in Kosovo. To stop Milošević's ethnic cleansing, Blair supported the American bombing of Belgrade between 24 March and 10 June 1999. In the Commons, Corbyn would call the allegations of genocide 'fraudulent justification' for the so-called 'humanitarian' invasion – and voted against the military action notionally under NATO's command. He blamed American bombing for causing a refugee crisis, and accused Germany of starting the Balkan wars in a plot with Croatia against Serbia, its historic enemy. Even after the war, he disputed the veracity of the atrocities – 'They never really existed,' he said, although about 100,000 civilians were reliably reported killed. He did not comment when the Bosnian Serb commander Ratko Mladić was arrested in 2011 and later convicted of genocide at The Hague. Previously, the International Court of Justice had always attracted Corbyn's praise. In his hatred of America, he ignored the fact that the US and Britain had protected Muslims from a fascist dictator. Among Corbyn's critics was his usual ally Ken Livingstone, who in this case supported the bombing. Corbyn hated disloyalty. As a result, for the next three years the two barely spoke.

The same dilemma – whether a murderer could be an ally because he opposed Anglo-American imperialism – faced the left over the fate of Saddam Hussein's factories that were reported to have been producing weapons of mass destruction

(WMDs). The dictator's continued defiance of a 1991 United Nations resolution that the alleged factories should be demolished prompted American and British aircraft to bomb them in 1998. Corbyn opposed the destruction. Using the same arguments he had deployed against the Falklands War, the invasion to liberate Kuwait and the protection of Muslims in the Balkans, he denounced Blair for causing 'innocent deaths'. Britain should settle the disagreement, he said, through the UN. He and twenty-one other Labour MPs ignored Saddam's disregard of several UN resolutions. To every challenge about the selectivity of his moral crusades, Corbyn replied that he was a pacifist, and did not elucidate further.

In particular, he did not reveal the extent to which British Muslims were beginning to influence his calculations. The procession of petitioners through the Red Rose reinforced his conviction that Britain should allow unrestricted immigration. Empathising with his ethnic constituents, he thought that Britain's electorate should welcome the ending of immigration controls, offer the destitute of the world the economic benefits available in Britain, and condemn any critic of unlimited entry as racist. On that issue, he and Tony Blair for once agreed. In 1997 Blair had abolished the primary purpose immigration rule, which had restricted Muslim and Hindu families seeking to join their relations living in Britain. Within two years, an additional 150,000 migrants from the Indian subcontinent would be arriving in Britain every year. Neither Blair nor Corbyn seems to have considered how mass migration would depress wages, place pressure on public services, increase rents, aggravate the housing shortage, swell the cost of welfare benefits and alienate the white working class.

Both men supported multiculturalism, and refused to attempt to persuade Muslims to integrate into British society. Neither seemed concerned that the doctrine placed liberals and socialists in an ideological straitjacket. Their blind spot was self-inflicted. Both denigrated their country's history and ridiculed the notion of British traditions unified by a common language and culture. Despite the evidence that poor Muslim ghettos spawned Islamic terrorism, Corbyn tolerated segregated Muslim audiences at his meetings, and voted against the anti-terror laws aimed at Islamic extremists. He rejected the argument that such laws saved lives because potential terrorists could be identified before their atrocities were committed. In his opinion, so-called terrorist organisations were legitimate resistance movements to destroy imperialism. Similarly, he opposed a law criminalising the incitement of religious hatred. He made no public protest when crowds of his constituents flocked to the Finsbury Park mosque to hear Abu Hamza's racist sermons, and claimed that there was 'zero support' for the preacher in the area. In his regular visits to Friday prayers at local mosques, said the atheist Corbyn, he had never met anyone who did not condemn terrorism.

Corbyn had reached a watershed. Over the previous twenty-five years he had endorsed communist groups fighting against America and Britain, and had championed the IRA to unite Ireland. Without exception, all his causes had been either contained or defeated. In Islington, Haringey and the Labour Party he had championed Trotskyist agitation, but despite some successes, Margaret Thatcher and then Tony Blair had eventually marginalised him and his fellow hardliners. Patiently he plodded on, a pulp politician with a guaranteed income and status at Westminster, dreaming of an opportunity to seize power. In 2001 he did not imagine that a Muslim fundamentalist inhabiting a cave in Afghanistan would set in train events that would eventually dethrone the Blairites, or that his lifelong denigration of Israel would lay the foundations for an alliance with enemies of the Labour Party.

7

Circle of Fear

In March 2001, Western intelligence was monitoring al-Qaeda, the Islamic terrorist group led by Osama bin Laden, a rich Saudi national. Bin Laden was held responsible for the 1998 bomb attacks on two American embassies in East Africa that killed 224 people, and also for an attack on an American warship in Aden in 2000, killing seventeen. In alliance with America, the Labour government banned members of twenty-one Islamic terrorist groups from entering Britain. Corbyn, in unison with McDonnell and Abbott, voted against that order.

Six months later, on 11 September 2001, bin Laden's followers flew three passenger jets into New York's World Trade Center and the Pentagon, killing over three thousand people. At first, Corbyn doubted that Muslims were involved. Once the evidence proved irrefutable, not least because bin Laden publicly boasted about his success, Corbyn condemned the mass murder, but went on to praise the pilots who flew into the Twin Towers for showing 'an enormous amount of skill'. The attack appealed to Marxists. In Corbyn's opinion, America and Britain were to blame for bin Laden's widespread popularity among Muslims because of the West's responsibility for 'Israel's occupation of Palestine' and 'the unbelievable poverty and misery in Afghanistan'.

In the midst of the global shock, Corbyn felt that nothing should be done by American or British military forces to bring bin Laden to justice or prevent further attacks. 'I do not believe that the Pentagon or NATO are bodies that can administer world justice,' he explained. Only the UN and the International

Criminal Court could be trusted. He refused to explain how either of those bodies could arrest bin Laden, and since he had long argued that the British Army should be disbanded, he offered no solution to end bin Laden's murderous campaign. On the contrary, in the name of 'progressive socialism', Corbyn demanded that the US should not bomb bin Laden's bases in Afghanistan.

The certainty that America would retaliate sparked a uniquely diverse coalition among the left. Lindsey German, a Trotskyist, Kate Hudson, the general secretary of CND, Andrew Murray, a member of the Communist Party and a journalist at the *Morning Star*, and Mike Marqusee joined with Corbyn to create the Stop the War Coalition. At the outset, the group seemed destined to exist only briefly before disappearing like so many of its predecessors. The difference was Muslim interest in joining.

By coincidence, during the first week of September 2001 a UN World Conference Against Racism had met in Durban, South Africa. At the initiative of Muslim delegates, Zionism was identified as the world's most evil form of racism for forcibly separating Jews and Arabs. Israel was classified as an agent of Western imperialism, deliberately positioned in the region to stifle 'progressive' Arabs. A country the size of Wales, with a population of just seven million, threatened the lives of one billion Muslims. The conference classified the most totalitarian Muslim states as the 'good oppressed' – the victims of Anglo-American imperialism. Labelling Israel uniquely as a 'racist state' was the climax of twenty-five years of lobbying started by Labour MP Peter Hain, the former student anti-apartheid campaigner, who accused Israel of oppressing the Palestinians even more than South Africa had oppressed blacks under apartheid. Over that period, and especially during the year before they met in Durban, the anti-Zionists' language had become increasingly anti-Semitic.

At the beginning of 2001, the groups that were to meet in Durban had celebrated the final collapse of the peace process between Israel and the Palestinians. To their satisfaction, the Palestinians launched a second intifada, seeking to kill as many

Israelis as possible. Eight months later, at the climax of the Durban conference, thousands of activists and delegates marched through the city waving placards reading 'Kill All Jews' and 'The Good Things Hitler Did'. Against that backdrop, many British Muslim sympathisers of bin Laden ended up in an unnatural alliance with Corbyn and the Stop the War Coalition. 'I am not prepared,' said Lindsey German, 'to … regard the state of Israel as somehow a viable presence.' Born in 1951 and active for nearly thirty years in the Trotskyist Socialist Workers Party, German agreed with Corbyn to forge an alliance with fundamentalist Muslims to fight Zionism, despite their holding illiberal opinions fundamentally contrary to Corbyn's own, such as asserting the supremacy of a Muslim god over non-believers and rejecting gay rights.

In approving Corbyn as the group's vice chairman, the Coalition's Muslim members assumed that his anti-Zionism chimed in with their anti-Semitism. 'The Israeli tail wags the American dog,' Corbyn had written. In his view, Israel was the keystone of global imperialism, controlling America and the rest of the world. He shared the Muslim belief that Israel's creation was a crime, and should be reversed. Zionist Jews had rarely featured in his personal life since his employment by the tailors' union in 1973. With only 260,000 Jews living in Britain, just 0.4 per cent of the population, he had become more familiar with what he called 'the wonderful faith of Islam'. An atheist, he never spoke about 'the wonderful faith of Christianity', nor Judaism or Hinduism.

Corbyn did not seek to understand the history of the persecution of Jews after their forcible expulsion from Palestine two thousand years earlier. According to those who had talked about the subject to him, he was clearly unaware how anxious Europe's Jews had been to escape oppression. Their survival, the Zionists believed, could be guaranteed only by a return to their ancestral home.

In the wake of the Holocaust, the left, including Stalin, had supported the UN decree of 1948 to replace Britain's Mandate over Palestine by two states – Israel and Palestine. The Jews agreed, but the surrounding Arab states rejected the proposal. In radio broadcasts from Cairo, Palestinians were urged to leave their homes while Arab armies invaded the fledgling Israeli state to kill off the occupiers. During that war, America and Britain refused to supply any weapons to the Jews. Their salvation was Stalin's approval of sales of weapons by communist Czechoslovakia. After the Arabs' defeat, the US declared that Israel had a right to survive. By default, the nascent Palestinian state had been destroyed by the neighbouring Arab states. In 1967, Egypt's President Nasser massed his army on Israel's border and closed the Straits of Tiran to Israeli ships. To end the threats and the continuous Arab attacks, Israel launched a surprise invasion of its three neighbours. Six days later, each of the Arab governments surrendered. Thereafter, the Soviet Union and other communist governments sided with the Arabs – except that even Russia recognised Israel's right to exist. By contrast, on his return to Britain from Jamaica, the young Corbyn had aligned himself with the anti-Zionists' denial of Israel's existence. He preferred to ignore the fact that Israel was created by the United Nations and fulfilled all the legal requirements for international recognition. In the early 1970s he had defined Zionism as racism. He accused Jews of acting as supremacists, oppressing Arabs in what he called 'Israel's apartheid occupation' of Palestine. Pertinently, he never complained about the creation of Pakistan in 1948, when the partition of the Indian subcontinent had caused millions of deaths and the persecution of Hindus in the new Muslim state. In Corbyn's eyes, only the Jewish state had no right to exist.

Singlemindedly, he condemned the British government's refusal to support 'the inalienable rights of the Palestinian refugees to return', an opinion shared by the London Labour Briefing group. In 1982 the *Labour Herald*, which Ken Livingstone co-edited, had printed a deliberately provocative cartoon captioned 'The Final Solution', showing Menachem Begin, the Israeli prime minister, dressed as an aggressive Nazi officer, squashing a pile of Arab corpses under his jackboot. An article in the magazine also suggested that Zionist Jews had collaborated with the Nazis during the Second World War. 'Basically, your Zionist argues with the Nazis that Jews cannot be assimilated into Gentile society,' it claimed. In other words, the Holocaust was the Jews' fault. And, he continued, by exploiting 'the sympathy stirred up … after the Holocaust for their own devious ends', the 'Jews needed a land of their own, not just any land, either, but only the land of Palestine'.

Corbyn's anti-Semitism was never that overt, but like Livingstone's, it was deeply ingrained among the far left. One source of anti-Semitism in left-wing literature was 'On the Jewish Question', an essay written by Karl Marx in 1843. Despite Marx being himself Jewish, he denounced Jews as 'hucksters' whose 'worldly God' was money. It was 'the jealous God of Israel … The bill of exchange (or loans) is the real god of the Jew.' To liberate humanity, Marx concluded, the Jews should abandon their existence as a separate culture: 'In the final analysis, the emancipation of the Jews is the emancipation of mankind from Judaism.' He confirmed that opinion in an article for the New York *Daily Tribune* in 1854. Describing Jerusalem, Marx estimated that the town's population was four thousand Muslims and eight thousand Jews. 'Nothing equals the misery and suffering of the Jews at Jerusalem,' he wrote, 'inhabiting the most filthy quarter of the town … and [being] the constant objects of Muslim oppression and intolerance.' Although Jews were the city's majority population, Marx believed they should integrate with the Muslims.

His antagonism towards the assertion by Jews of their own identity cast him as a self-hating Jew. (Less well-known, Leon Trotsky, also a Jew, late in his life supported the idea of an independent Jewish state.) Marxist-Trotskyists like Corbyn imbibed Marx's sentiment without explicitly acknowledging its anti-Semitism, but the virus influenced Corbyn's language so that he automatically challenged the right of Israel to exist. 'The power of the Israel lobby is truly phenomenal,' he would say, referring to his conviction that there existed a global conspiracy of rich Jewish bankers, especially in New York, to orchestrate Zionist influence. He was not interested in comparing Israel, a democracy built in the desert, with the neighbouring undemocratic Arab dictators. He also ignored the fact that many Arabic Jews had fled persecution by Muslim governments in Egypt, Syria, Iran and Iraq to find sanctuary in Israel, and that Palestine had never been a state. Finally, he was indifferent to the legality of Israel's existence. Most countries were created by international treaties or conquest, including Russia, India, China, the USA, Canada, Australia, and all the Arab states. But Corbyn singled out Israel as uniquely illegal.

During the early 1990s, parallel with his support for the IRA, he had embraced the PLO, the Palestinian organisation responsible for scores of terrorist attacks across the world. While presenting himself as a man of peace, he accepted the PLO's use of bombs and murder to further its agenda. Accordingly, in 1995 he supported Samar Alami and Jawad Botmeh, two Palestinians living in London who had detonated car bombs in the capital the previous year, one near the Israeli embassy in Kensington Gardens, and another outside Balfour House, a Jewish community centre in Finchley. Explaining in court the discovery of an arsenal of bomb-making equipment and pistols in their home, Alami and Botmeh said that they were researching explosives to help the Palestinian cause in the occupied territories. In their appeals after their conviction by a jury, both asserted that they had been the victims of a political trial. Their appeals were rejected. Corbyn led a campaign to secure their release, arguing that their convictions had been a miscarriage of justice. He did not make any comment about the damage caused by their bombs.

There was a motive for Corbyn's sympathy. One day in 2000, Paul Eisen, a Jewish anti-Zionist (in public meetings he had denied that the Nazis had murdered six million Jews), called unannounced at Corbyn's home. Might he support Deir Yassin Remembered (DYR), an organisation that commemorated the victims of a notorious massacre in April 1948 by Jewish paramilitarists of about a hundred defenceless Palestinian civilians living near Jerusalem. 'I wanted him to join,' recalled Eisen. 'I'd hardly begun my feverishly rehearsed pitch before his chequebook was on the table.' Corbyn attended several DYR meetings until April 2013.

With that mindset, in 2001 Corbyn did not consider that the Stop the War Coalition's discussions about an alliance with Muslims posed a dilemma. At pro-Palestinian rallies he openly associated with Muslim activists who rejected equal rights for women and homosexuals, and opposed socialism and secularism. He adopted Lenin's maxim that to achieve the revolution socialists were justified in allying themselves to any group dedicated to the same goal. Like Corbyn, the Islamic extremists denigrated Britain's institutions and were dedicated to destroying Western liberal society.

With Corbyn's support, the Coalition opposed the American invasion of Afghanistan to topple the Taliban regime. Military action, they all argued, would not produce peace or justice. Food and kindness, rather than bombing, would win over the Afghans. Tony Blair rejected those arguments, and denied Corbyn's claim that civilian targets had been bombed. In a Commons vote, Corbyn's side was defeated by 373 to thirteen. One week later, about 20,000 supporters of the Stop the War Coalition marched through London. Attracting that number to Trafalgar Square to condemn America as a terrorist state for bombing Afghanistan was reckoned a huge success. In Corbyn's eyes, the fall of Kabul and the liberation of Afghanistan from Taliban rule – just two months after the 9/11 attacks – confirmed the evil power of American imperialism. Next, he predicted, President George W. Bush would link the terrorist attacks and the 'axis of evil' – Iraq, North Korea and Iran – to justify an invasion of Iraq. His prediction was ridiculed by the media and the majority of MPs.

Over the following year, Trotskyites and communists met frequently at a succession of parties in north London. These were often hosted by the Communist Party journalist Andrew Murray at his large house in Kentish Town. Regular guests included Seumas Milne, the *Guardian*'s opinion editor who championed Muslim fundamentalists, George Galloway, Corbyn, Tariq Ali, Ken Livingstone and Simon Fletcher – all

Corbyn's fifteen months in Jamaica in 1967–68 as an eighteen-year-old voluntary teacher forged his extreme left-wing ideas, but in the aftermath also raised questions about his credibility. On a minor matter, he wrongly claimed to have grown a beard while teaching on the island; and more important, his repeated claim to have stayed two years is untrue. He has never explained why he suddenly left Jamaica and what happened during the missing seven months.

His romance and marriage to postgraduate student and councillor Jane Chapman in 1974 ended in divorce. She blamed his misogyny, anti-feminism and unreasonable behaviour for the breakdown of their relationship.

Keith and Val Veness (far left and far right with Corbyn in Deal) formed a close political relationship with Corbyn after his return from Jamaica and have remained trusted friends. Nevertheless, Keith Veness is critical of Corbyn's disorganisation and lack of financial competence.

Corbyn was first employed in London in 1973 by the National Union of Tailors and Garment Workers, reporting to Alec Smith (below left). Smith denies Corbyn's boast that he challenged employers who were 'scumbags' and 'crooks' to recover members' unpaid wages.

Corbyn's successful organisation of Hornsey Labour Party during the 1970s included acting as agent for Trotskyist Ted Knight (front row centre), the Labour candidate in the 1979 general election. Their extremist manifesto was the foundation of a lifelong alliance to turn Britain into a communist country.

As Hornsey Labour Party's senior officer, contrary to the party's rules, Corbyn welcomed Marxists as members. Among them was Tariq Ali, a charismatic intellectual. Three times Labour HQ rejected Ali's application; and Knight was rejected by Hornsey's electorate, and sent back to Lambeth, a corrupt borough.

Corbyn slammed over Ali vote meeting

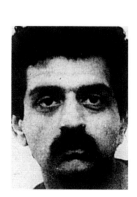

Under the mentoring guidance of Tony Benn, a Labour government minister during the 1960s and 1970s, Corbyn feigned loyalty to the Labour Party although, as a communist, he opposed nearly all its policies, and repeatedly voted against the party as an MP.

Through London Labour Briefing, a Trotskyist group, Corbyn supported Ken Livingstone's (left) coup in 1981 to seize control of the Greater London Council. Both actively supported Gerry Adams (centre), the Sinn Féin leader, and sympathised with the IRA's violent campaign – a strange posture for Corbyn, a self-professed pacifist.

Ever since he arrived in London in 1972, Corbyn regularly joined demonstrations and trade union picket lines, and gave hundreds of speeches across the country to any group protesting against what he deemed to be injustice and inequality. Occasionally he was arrested – as in 1984 during a Trotsykist-organised picket against apartheid.

Elected to the Commons in 1983, Corbyn forged a close relationship with Tony Banks (bottom), the left-wing MP for Newham, and was later joined by Diane Abbott, a former girlfriend, and Bernie Grant (centre), an aggressive ex-Haringey councillor who had persuaded Corbyn that Britain should not impose limits on immigration.

In 1997 they were joined in the House of Commons by John McDonnell, an established Trotskyist who had struggled to get elected as an MP.

Corbyn's second marriage in 1987 to Claudia Bracchitta, the daughter of Chilean exiles, started amid great romance and delivered three sons. But by 1996 Bracchitta was exasperated by Corbyn's behaviour and asked their mutual friend Reg Race (left), a former MP, to advise about her husband's financial incompetence. Their chaotic, debt-ridden lifestyle ended their marriage rather than, as Corbyn and Bracchitta told the media, a dispute about their son's education.

Corbyn overwhelmingly defeated his three Blairite opponents in the election for the Labour leadership, which was confirmed on 12 September 2015 in the Queen Elizabeth Hall, Westminster. His victory was aided by Jon Lansman (left), the founder of Momentum.

Corbyn's relationship with his third wife, Laura Alvarez, who he married in 2013, appears to be more stable than his previous two marriages.

untroubled that Murray's lavish hospitality was financed by his wealthy family and that, as an employee of Novosti, the Soviet-owned news agency, he was known to favour North Korea, and limited his criticism of Stalin for having been a little 'harsh'. But Murray's good food and wine strengthened the bonds between all these comrades-in-arms – even if their new Muslim allies were not invited.

By September 2002, the mood had changed. The government's publication of an intelligence dossier describing Iraq's ability to fire WMDs within forty-five minutes of the order at a British military base in Cyprus convinced the majority of Britons about the danger Saddam Hussein posed. To win parliamentary approval for the invasion of Iraq, Blair repeated that 'fact' three times in the Commons. A sizeable minority of MPs, including Corbyn, was suspicious of anything written by Labour's director of communications Alastair Campbell and signed by Blair. The WMDs, they were convinced, had been invented to justify Blair's agreement with Bush to topple Saddam.

In planning London's next Stop the War demonstration, Corbyn welcomed the support of the Muslim Association of Great Britain. The group was attached to the Muslim Brotherhood, a terrorist organisation sponsoring suicide bombers to impose Sharia or Islamic law across the globe. Some on the left questioned the coalition of Marxists with political Islamists, but after a debate the union was approved as a tactical advantage by Andrew Murray, Lindsey German and Corbyn, the latter explaining that the alliance was forged by a mutual opposition to Zionism. On the proposed march, protest banners against the war would be given equal billing with Muslim Association placards urging the destruction of Israel. The two, said the Muslim organisers, were linked: Zionists were planning the imminent invasion of Iraq. Corbyn agreed, and on 15 February 2003 at least 750,000 people – some said over a million – marched through London.

In the days before the Commons vote to approve the invasion, the country was electrified.

'Tony, just one question,' said Corbyn during a rare meeting with the prime minister. 'Why are we doing it?'

'Because it's the right thing to do,' Blair replied testily.

'That's not an answer,' said Corbyn, who would thereafter accuse Blair of committing Britain to an illegal war.

'It's the only one you're going to get,' said Blair.

With Tory support, he comfortably won the Commons vote; but the Labour Party, like Britain, was divided. On the eve of the invasion, MI6 chief Richard Dearlove came to Downing Street.

'Are you sure Saddam has WMDs?' asked Blair.

'Yes, absolutely,' replied Dearlove. 'Categorically.'

Over the previous six years, Blair had corrupted Whitehall's capacity to offer accurate advice on all policies, including those relating to the NHS, education and immigration. Distrustful of the civil service from the outset of his government, Blair had excluded independent senior officials from his inner sanctum. The constitutional checks and balances to preserve honest management had been deliberately dismantled. Consequently, the distortions that led to the Iraq war were not an aberration, but were characteristic of the unscrupulousness pervading his entire administration. The Ministry of Defence was helplessly excluded as Blair's secrecy denied the military the chance to plan the post-war occupation of Iraq, obtain sufficient money to buy adequate equipment, or train personnel to understand their mission.

There was little cheer in Downing Street in the days after Saddam's statue in central Baghdad was toppled on 9 April. Despite the military victory, Blair was fretting. 'Any news about WMDs?' he asked. 'No, prime minister,' replied Admiral Boyce, the chief of the defence staff. Saddam's defeat prompted Corbyn to announce a new demonstration. Under the banner 'Stop the killing. No occupation of Iraq,' he demanded that American and British troops should leave the country, transferring authority to the UN. Soon after, the UN mission in Baghdad was blown up by an extremist's bomb. Twenty-two people died, over a hundred were injured, and all UN personnel were evacuated. At the end of the month, Blair faced the awful truth that no WMDs existed. 'We were taken to war on the basis there was a real threat,' said Corbyn. 'He's ridiculous.' Previously, Blair had dismissed Corbyn's extreme convictions as politically irrelevant, but after his monumental mistake in Iraq, the discredited leader found himself vulnerable to Corbyn's attacks.

Twenty years after entering Parliament, the Honourable Member for Islington North was finally winning recognition, if not admiration. Opponents of the war were not even surprised by his praise for those killing British and American soldiers as waging 'an increasingly successful and popular guerrilla war'. His campaign was enhanced by the revelations of the torture of Iraqis by American army personnel in Abu Ghraib prison, near Baghdad, and the fact that British officials had suppressed the truth for about two months. Accused by Corbyn of duplicity, Blair faced a party revolt which was magnified in July by the suicide of David Kelly, a government weapons inspector. Kelly had effectively accused Alastair Campbell of 'sexing up' the government's intelligence dossier in 2002 to prove the existence of Iraqi WMDs. The official inquest into Kelly's death, Corbyn hoped, would expose the conspiracy between Blair and Campbell to shame the hapless civil servant in order to distract the public's attention from Campbell's guilt. 'I suspect that Downing Street has been involved from the very beginning,' he concluded about Kelly's death. A genuinely independent inquiry into Blair's conduct would, Corbyn knew, be enough to depose the prime minister, but at Blair's behest Whitehall circled the wagons. Those selected to serve on four successive investigating committees were trusted to fillet the truth, and Britons were denied the satisfaction of a final, accurate explanation. Many loyal Labour Party members were not deceived. Disenchanted, they drifted away, discounting the government's achievements. Widespread anger about Blair's deception could have been the turning point for Corbyn and the left, but traditional Labour voters were not attracted to his new group, Labour Against the War, once they saw it was linked to Britain's enemies.

Corbyn's new ally, the Muslim Association of Britain, appreciated his belief in unrestricted Muslim immigration, segregated faith schools and Muslim women wearing the full-face veil. As an expression of his sympathy, Corbyn opposed the government's invitation to Ayad Allawi, Iraq's new prime minister, to address Labour's annual conference in 2004. 'Allawi,' he explained, 'has introduced the death penalty and banned a television station in Iraq.' That argument generated yet further distrust of Corbyn among mainstream Labour voters. Those same criteria had not deterred his trust in the Iranian ayatollahs, the principal supporters of the Muslim Association, who imprisoned political opponents, brutalised women and executed adolescents for drug offences.

The glue cementing Corbyn to Iran's leader Ayatollah Ali Khamenei was Israel. 'The Zionist regime,' said the ayatollah in 2003, 'is a true cancer tumour on this region that should be cut off.' Khamenei's ultimate weapon to annihilate the Jewish state, Corbyn knew, was a nuclear bomb. Although a self-proclaimed pacifist opposed to all nuclear weapons, Corbyn did not comment on the International Atomic Agency's confirmation of Iran's secret nuclear programme, or criticise Iran's development of the bomb. Yet in May 1986 he had told the Commons: 'There is an inextricable link between the production of civil nuclear power and the warheads which result from it.' But he did criticise Israel for threatening to destroy Iran's underground factories to forestall the existential threat. As ever, his moral indignation was selective. Aligning himself with Muslims, he urged the British government to 'end its shameful complicity with Israeli and US policies and reverse Britain's historic betrayal of the Palestinian people from Balfour to Blair ... All who abhor Israel's outrages should support such key policies as economic sanctions, boycotts and an end to arms trading.' Iraq and Israel had widened the gulf between Blair and Corbyn.

In January 2004, Blair's government was in danger of defeat despite its 159-seat majority. In response to Blair's promise to 'quicken the march of progress' on foundation hospitals and the privatisation of public services and education, Corbyn reinforced the revolt to stop the government's rush to entrench Thatcherism. Although his Campaign Group had fewer than a dozen hardcore MPs, he drew on the dissatisfaction of many Labour Members who were opposed to Blair in principle rather than on ideology. A vote to introduce student fees was on a knife-edge, and potential rebels were invited to meet the prime minister, although Corbyn was pointedly excluded. Despite seventy-two Labour MPs rebelling, Blair scraped home by five votes. 'This isn't over yet,' warned Corbyn. Reflecting Blair's loosening grip before another vote, a Labour MP stood by the entrance to the opposition lobby in the Commons shouting, 'Line up, line up! This way for the rebellion!'

Unlike other Labour MPs, Corbyn felt no compunction about voting against his own party. He had done so eighty-seven times since the 2001 election, 148 times since 1997. For most of his colleagues, his dissent was a 'self-inflicted wound', the product of 'a psychological flaw on the left'. For a brief moment the rebels exercised some power, but would then be forgotten.

In the run-up to the 2005 election, the left hoped that Labour's majority would be slashed to just fifty, giving Blair 'a bloody nose' before he was replaced by at least a token socialist. To embarrass him, Corbyn made a rare appearance at a PLP meeting. People on the doorstep, he told the prime minister, were concerned about Iraq. Labour MPs heckled him, but failed to dent Corbyn's self-confidence. 'He's got to show a degree of contrition about the language he used in the run-up to the war,' he went on. Blair accused Corbyn, who had just voted once again against the Prevention of Terror Act, of protecting Britain's enemies: 'These people would kill thousands of our people. It is terrorism without limit.' The prime minister's supporters spoke about 'show trials' to deselect rebel MPs, but Blair lacked the strength to demand obedience. Historians compared his plight to Robert Peel's after the Tory revolt against the Corn Laws in 1846, which had led to the Tory Party being in disarray for twenty years. Labour's own days of reckoning would come before long.

The general election on 5 May 2005 brought few surprises. A disorganised Tory campaign led by Michael Howard assured

Labour of a third successive victory. Although Blair won a majority of sixty-six, he was a lame duck. In any controversy, Corbyn and fifty Labour rebels were certain to oppose the government. Corbyn even opposed chancellor Gordon Brown's demand for higher productivity from the public sector. Critics noted the irony that, while he rebelled against every change proposed at Westminster, especially those related to the NHS and education, he had remained absolutely silent when the management of Islington's failing schools was handed over by the council to Cambridge Education Associates, a private consortium.

Corbyn's constant rebellion made him vulnerable to one irrefutable criticism: that his political heroes were tyrants who rewarded their followers with poverty. In 2005, that prejudice was reconfirmed when Corbyn found a new hero – Hugo Chávez, alias *Il Commandante*, elected Venezuela's president in 1999. The former soldier turned populist politician was waging war against the oil-rich nation's middle class with 'socialism of the twenty-first century', a mixture of nationalist fervour and Marxism.

Corbyn had been unaware of Chávez until Alan Freeman, a British Marxist and the editor of *Socialist Action*, persuaded Ken Livingstone, who was by then London's first elected mayor, that Chávez was 'very important'. Three years earlier, Freeman had established the Venezuela Information Centre in Bloomsbury to explain Chávez's revolution to a largely indifferent British population. Chávez had won popularity by promising to provide new homes, improved medical care, cheaper food and more jobs by redistributing the nation's wealth from the upper and middle classes to the poor. He removed 19,000 managers of the country's oil industry, responsible for developing the world's largest reserves, and replaced them with three times that number of his own loyalists. Few of those high-paid cronies understood the complexity of oil exploration. Simultaneously, Chávez expelled foreign oil corporations and confiscated their assets. Rapidly, Venezuela's oil production fell by 50 per cent. By 2005 the country's plight was following a familiar pattern. To satisfy his followers, Chávez confiscated private property and imposed high taxes. Then he began imprisoning critics, and would later ignore a nationwide referendum that rejected giving him dictatorial powers. Despite the oppression, Tariq Ali proclaimed that Venezuela was the most democratic country in Latin America. Its inhabitants disagreed, and staged an unsuccessful coup. In the aftermath, Freeman persuaded Livingstone and then Corbyn to protect socialism in Venezuela. (After their falling out, the two had re-bonded over their opposition to the Iraq war.)

Later that year, Corbyn urged the annual Labour Party conference to support a motion: 'Hands off Venezuela.' He accused America of threatening a democratically elected leader, but his campaigning sat oddly with his poor grasp of the country's history. George Galloway recalled being with Corbyn as they left Bolívar House in London's Fitzrovia, a Venezuelan cultural centre since 1986, and pointing at the impressive statue of General Francisco de Miranda outside the building. 'Who's that?' asked Corbyn; he had no idea that Miranda was the Venezuelan revolutionary leader during South America's wars of independence in the nineteenth century. Bolívar House had been Miranda's private home, and was where he had designed Venezuela's flag. Corbyn had walked past the statue dozens of times without showing the slightest interest in Venezuela. Now he embraced Hugo Chávez as his inspiration for the overthrow of capitalism in Britain, and would extol him for 'seriously conquering poverty by emphatically rejecting neoliberal policies of the world's financial institutions'.

Corbyn's admiration grew during a private visit Chávez made to London in May 2006, organised by Alan Freeman. In a three-hour speech in Bolívar House Chávez explained how, in the name of socialism, his government had nationalised foreign oil corporations, increased taxes, attacked 'profiteers' and imposed price controls. He described his tactic of securing popularity by rewarding supporters with thousands of jobs, high wages and increased benefits. His destruction of market capitalism to reverse the conspiracy against the poor was judged by Corbyn to be the heroic path for Britain. Friendly cooperation in the community would replace competition. Corbyn's adulation was echoed by John McDonnell, who in his book *Another World is Possible* praised Chávez for creating 'alternatives to the market economy'. Both he and Corbyn applauded the politics of buying voters.

Not surprisingly, Chávez had not mentioned in his speech the consequences of expelling foreign oil corporations. As oil production crashed, Venezuela's budget deficit had grown, inflation was rising and corruption had become blatant. High taxes and the confiscation of farms for the benefit of Chávez's cronies had persuaded the middle class to flee the country. Inevitably, industry, business and agriculture suffered, as happens in all Marxist states. Venezuela was experiencing the first food shortages in its history, and a sharp increase in murders. Chávez was convinced that his country's ballooning debts would be covered by a rise in the price of oil from $100 to $250 a barrel. So was McDonnell. Neither understood the old adage: what goes up eventually comes down. In 2009, the price of oil fell to about $40 a barrel. Chávez's socialism had set Venezuela on the path to becoming the world's most indebted nation. Unsurprisingly, those developments did not undermine Corbyn's adulation.

8

Lame Ducks

The four bombs that ripped across central London on 7 July 2005 shocked Britain. Fifty-two people were killed and over seven hundred injured as four British Muslim suicide bombers blew themselves up. In the wake of the tragedy, Blair introduced a Bill with unprecedented powers, including the right to detain suspected terrorists and their sympathisers for ninety days without charge. Having issued no public statement regretting the carnage, Corbyn opposed the move. The threat of rebellion and defeat for the government, he said, had caused 'an enormous panic' at No. 10. In the subsequent vote, forty-nine Labour rebels contributed to the government's defeat by thirty-one. Blair shook his head in disbelief. 'You do have a group of people who are utterly determined to punch Tony Blair on the nose,' observed Charles Clarke, the home secretary, about Corbyn and his allies. 'They're serial rebels hell-bent to defeat the government.'

With a renewed sense of self-importance, Corbyn called for the prime minister's resignation. Failing that, he asked, would Blair stay and bring the temple down? 'I would much rather we had proper debate and an election within the party,' he said. 'After all, these are very important and very serious times.' His definition of 'serious' differed from most. Despite the responsibility of Islamic extremists for the London bombs, he denounced any criticism of Muslims opposed to the government's 'war on terror' as 'demonisation'. His embrace of political Islam was exceptional, even among the parliamentary hard left. In an attempt to prohibit incitement to religious discrimination, the government introduced the Racial and Religious Hatred Bill to protect Muslims. Corbyn and McDonnell voted against it, and were joined by MPs opposed for other reasons. The government was defeated by one vote.

Sleaze sapped what remained of Tony Blair's credibility. A police investigation into the alleged sale of peerages to party donors justified McDonnell's accusation that Blair had lost his moral authority. 'This is a defining moment in the history of the Labour Party,' he thundered. Newspapers published a long list of Blair's dodgy financial deals, starting with his acceptance in 1997 of £1 million from Bernie Ecclestone to exempt Formula One from a ban on tobacco advertising in sport. The final blow was the vote in March 2007 by ninety-three Labour MPs against the renewal of Trident, which led to the final collapse of Blair's authority.

Labour MPs accepted that Blair's resignation would be followed by Gordon Brown's coronation, in spite of his constant plotting against Blair over the previous decade. Those who lamented Blair's failure to bequeath a popular successor to continue the 'Third Way' were helpless. David Miliband, their only candidate, was too cowardly to challenge Brown, and was derided by Corbyn as 'shallow' because his proposed manifesto failed to mention housing or pensions. Corbyn also mocked Brown, observing that the chancellor's support for renewing Trident was 'sad and absurd … Brown has got a reputation for being an Iron Chancellor but now he says that he is prepared to write a cheque for £25 billion for American weapons. His obsession with being more New Labour than Tony Blair is getting the better of him.' Such criticisms did not resonate with the public – thirty years earlier, 400,000 anti-nuclear protesters had marched through London. Now, only a handful cared. Similarly, despite his worship of bankers, Brown's management of the economy was judged a success, and only the left openly expressed disgust at his esteem for City fat cats, highlighting the perk of one HSBC executive who received more from the bank for his annual dental care than a cleaner at its London headquarters was paid in a year.

Corbyn and his supporters decided to make a stand. To oppose Brown for the leadership, the left's candidate needed nominations from at least forty-four MPs. Although in the aftermath of the Iraq war Corbyn had become the left's de facto leader, he gave way to John McDonnell. However, the Trotskyite's extremism had alienated most MPs. He had pledged his support for IRA violence to defeat Britain, and would tell a rally of trade unionists in 2009, 'I'm trained in all the dark arts on how to kill a movement, how to destroy a public meeting, how to ensure a march never takes off the ground, all that sort of stuff.' He was also disliked by journalists for seeking to manipulate the media by giving out statements that he knew to be untrue. 'I wouldn't trust him as far as I could throw him,' said Anthony Longden, the editor of the *Uxbridge Gazette*, his local newspaper. Longden had been violently berated by McDonnell – 'the hairdryer treatment', as he characterised it – for refusing to publish distorted stories. McDonnell never pretended to be other than he was, the journalist recalled: he emanated 'pure intimidation'. With just twenty-two nominations from MPs, McDonnell failed to make the ballot. Corbyn's plan to stand as deputy leader had to be abandoned.

Brown not only won the leadership, he survived his first year despite 103 Commons rebellions. In the name of the Socialist Campaign Group (SCG), Corbyn led the dissidents to oppose any restriction on trade unions' power to call strikes, and they also contested the commitment to fight in Afghanistan. The left was failing, but at least he was the leader in their failings.

In 2008, Brown's second year as prime minister, Corbyn again saw hope. During the summer, banks across the world crashed. Capitalism's long predicted crisis, he assumed, would persuade the working class to switch allegiance to the left. The poor would expect the government to let banks go bust rather than pay for the City's blunders. Instead, Brown diverted £850 billion to the banks, and was hailed as a saviour of international finance. The public was less impressed. One year later, Brown arrived at the Labour Party conference in a bad temper: opinion polls were giving the Tories, under David Cameron, a steady 15 per cent lead. Corbyn voiced no sympathy. Earlier that year, he had been one of Brown's most vocal critics during an attempted coup by cabinet ministers. 'There has to be a change in policies as much as individuals,' he said. 'Clearly if the party leadership and Gordon in particular are not prepared to move at all on policy, then other options become more [sic] inevitable.' When the general election was called for 6 May 2010, Corbyn hoped that the Tories would win, as that would trigger changes within Labour.

During his own election campaign, Corbyn praised the Tolpuddle Martyrs, the Chartists and other socialist heroes. He criticised Brown's lack of socialist commitment, but said nothing about the soaring debt that Brown had accumulated before the 2008 crash to pay for public services. He also ignored the protests in Labour's heartlands against Blair and Brown's unannounced admission of over four million migrants to Britain, particularly non-EU citizens from the Indian subcontinent. Like the prime minister, Corbyn had not foreseen the collapse of Labour's traditional vote in the north of England, Wales and Scotland. Brown's unguarded description of a Labour voter in Rochdale as a 'bigoted woman' because she criticised uncontrolled immigration earned Corbyn's approval. But he was soon back on the attack, describing the plight of poor children in Islington who had never travelled by Tube and seldom left their decrepit housing estates. 'They feel insecure,' he said, 'because they do not have enough money, or because they feel opportunities are not for them.' Like Hugo Chávez, he recognised low-income families, especially the migrant community, as his core vote. 'We can't win without them,' he said, contemptuous of middle-class citizens demanding value for their taxes. As in his personal life, he never considered financial realities.

On election day, Labour won just 29 per cent of the vote, its lowest share since 1983. Nationally, although the Conservatives failed to secure an overall majority and had to form a coalition with the Liberal Democrats, the swing to the Tories was 5.1 per cent, but in Islington North Corbyn won a 3.3 per cent swing his way, with a majority of 12,401 over the Lib Dems. As usual, he sang 'The Red Flag' after his victory, and thanked his party workers. While Ukip had collected nearly a million votes nationally, in Islington North its candidate received just 716 votes. Corbyn's popularity did not extend beyond his constituency, however. In the metropolitan south, traditional Labour supporters who identified themselves as 'English' demanded a limit to immigration, and voted Tory or Ukip. Corbyn blamed the racist media and the Tories for misleading the working class by blaming migrants for their problems. But at least the political divisions were clearer with David Cameron as prime minister. In health, education, housing, immigration and defence, the nation's new leader adopted Blair's legacy and perpetuated his errors, failing to appreciate the disarray he had inherited.

Brown duly resigned as Labour leader. In the election to replace him, John McDonnell was deemed a non-starter. Not only had he failed twice to be nominated, but he had made important enemies: Paul Kenny, general secretary of the GMB, regarded him as 'a duplicitous bastard', and he was not alone. Kenny alleged that McDonnell was 'manipulative, a mixer and masquerader who tried to entrap me. He was not straight.' McDonnell wanted 'to be the emperor, and he would sacrifice any principles for power'. Beyond those characteristics, his pronouncements had become more extreme. Asked what he would do if he could go back in time, he replied that he would like to return to the 1980s 'and assassinate Thatcher'. At a seventieth-anniversary commemoration of Trotsky's death organised by a group banned from the Labour Party, he had spoken about 'the importance of Trotskyism for the struggle against the bosses and the Tories'. Shortly after, he told a 'Unite Resistance' conference that Tory MPs were 'social criminals': 'I want to be in a situation where no Tory MP, no coalition minister, can travel anywhere in the country or show their face anywhere in public without being challenged by direct action.' Those exhortations gave credibility to the pastime he had listed in *Who's Who* – 'generally fermenting the overthrow of capitalism'. His enthusiasm for direct action, even violence, remained undiminished.

Ever since McDonnell became an MP, his bond to Corbyn had been growing closer. Corbyn lived up to his self-description as an 'anorak' – dull and dedicated – whereas McDonnell, more intelligent and better educated, was the firebrand who proclaimed Corbyn's unspoken sentiment, 'You can't change the world through the parliamentary system.' While Corbyn was uncertain how Marxist ideology fitted in with lip service to capitalist democracy, McDonnell admitted that he was a member of Labour only as 'a tactic', because it was a 'useful vehicle. I'm not in the Labour Party because I'm a believer of the Labour Party as some supreme body or something God-given, or anything like that. It's a tactic. It's as simple as that. If it's no longer a useful vehicle, move on.' Discounting the ballot box as a means to change the world, McDonnell explained, 'There's another way too which in the old days we called insurrection. Now we call it direct action. It's when the government don't do as you want, you get in the streets or you occupy and you take direct action against them.'

He was at least being honest. 'Change,' he said, 'doesn't come from people having tea at the Ritz. It comes from people storming the Ritz.' In 2014 he wrote, 'The elite will only become fearful when our talk moves on to action.' His support for violence included approval of Ed Woollard, a student jailed in 2011 for throwing a fire extinguisher at police from the roof of the Conservative Party's HQ on Millbank in the midst of a riot. In McDonnell's opinion Woollard was 'not a criminal', but had been 'victimised ... The real criminals are the ones actually cutting the education services and increasing fees. We've got to encourage direct action in any form it can possibly take.' He praised the protesters who had 'kicked the shit' out of the Conservative Party's building: 'We'll come into your offices, we'll come to wherever you are to confront you.' His reliance on others to undertake mob behaviour raised the unanswered question of whether he himself had ever been personally violent. Those searching into his past found a gap in his biography during the years before he came to London in 1976. All evidence about his time in Great Yarmouth and Burnley had disappeared.

Forty years later, Natascha Engel and other moderate Labour MPs believed that McDonnell would have 'no problem signing death warrants for people he disliked'. Corbyn would no doubt have agreed with him. He had lived his career supporting violence for the right causes.

The left's baton for the leadership election was passed to Corbyn's old flame Diane Abbott, a politician unusually insensitive to the antagonism she awakened. Like McDonnell, she had no chance of attracting sufficient nominations to reach the ballot. Astutely, the left played the diversity card. The party, said Corbyn, should allow a wide debate. To deny Abbott the chance to participate would discriminate against her race and sex. Despite Abbott's unpopularity, this appeal to fairness persuaded David Miliband, the outright favourite, to direct the necessary number of his supporters to nominate her, and she duly won a place on the ballot. However, the contest was focused on Miliband and his brother Ed, so exposing a division within the party magnified by the fallout from Tony Blair's controversial profiteering after leaving Downing Street.

Against David Miliband's pledge of undiluted Blairism, Ed Miliband minimised New Labour's supposed achievements and renounced its architects. In terms approved by Corbyn and supported by Len McCluskey, the Liverpool-born leader of the Unite trade union, representing 1.2 million employees in the engineering and transport industries, Ed Miliband blamed Blair for destroying Labour's values by appealing to the electorate's conservative instincts. Even New Labour's introduction of a minimum wage and statutory human rights, and its huge expenditure on public services, were disavowed by Ed Miliband. He characterised Blair as having capitulated to greed, and promised a left-wing programme to rebuild the party from the grassroots. That resonated with McCluskey and other trade unionists, and although David Miliband won the most votes from Labour MPs and MEPs, and from the party membership, the union vote meant that Ed was elected by a 1 per cent margin. After Abbott won a derisory 7.4 per cent vote, the leadership of the left was transferred by default to Corbyn.

There was no mystery about Corbyn's dislike of the new leader's tepid socialism. Ever since the Young Socialists' Skegness conference in 1972, he had been committed to the Trotskyite's disdain for the notion that change could be achieved through Westminster. Although he remained an ostensibly loyal member of the Labour Party, he (like McDonnell) was committed to destroying Britain's liberal democracy.

For twenty-eight years he had espoused causes rather than involving himself in the finer workings of a parliamentary system. And those causes – multiculturalism, immigration, pacifism, anti-globalisation and communism – were fashioned through his prism of resistance, all done in the name of the poor. He was a protester and a defender rather than a builder. While he had frequently asked questions about Ireland, the Western Sahara, South America and the fate of islanders expelled from Diego Garcia (a British territory in the Indian Ocean that is the site of an Anglo-American military base), he had rarely scrutinised legislation in a parliamentary committee, and had never seriously proposed any new law. His isolation was shared with Abbott and McDonnell. The three stood not just on the fringe of Labour, but of mainstream British society. Supported by a hinterland of far-left groups, the trio had remained unwaveringly loyal to their dream of radically changing Britain. As the least articulate of the three, Corbyn aroused the least antagonism.

To maintain the façade of loyalty to Labour, he spoke about the resurrection of the values championed by Clement Attlee and Harold Wilson. He eulogised about a return to that glorious era of class solidarity, trade union power, nationalised industries and civil servants in Whitehall dispensing care to Britons from cradle to grave. He blamed the 1979 nadir of Jim Callaghan's government, with its devaluation, hyperinflation, strikes and de-industrialisation, on Callaghan's betrayal of socialism. Since then, he portrayed Britain as one of the most unequal countries in the developed world, while membership of the EU was no more than a capitalist plot to hand power to 'an unelected set of bankers' intent on increasing unemployment. He was particularly outraged by the EU's restrictions on government investment, its promotion of the privatisation of public services, and its support for competitive postal services. 'The idea of competition in postal delivery is ludicrous,' he said. That 'crucial public service' should be a government monopoly. Federal Express, UPS and the thousands of independent delivery companies servicing Amazon and all of Britain's online retailers should be wound up. In thirty years, nothing had changed about Corbyn's ideal route to a socialist society: leave the EU, erect trade barriers to cheap imports, nationalise the banks and industry, and tax wealth. He promised security of employment, but other than government borrowing and high taxes, did not explain how he would generate the money to pay for all the additional benefits. Although there was no evidence that the poor get richer by the rich being made poorer, he never spoke about increasing individual wealth. Rather, like Hugo Chávez, he favoured imposing fairness by levelling down. He championed the 'equality' of poverty. Communities, he believed, would be much happier with less material wealth. He wanted to return to past certainties by attaching new labels to old enemies.

In a reversal of roles, the old, anti-red witch-hunt was replaced by the 'progressive' left's vilification of 'neoliberals'. Characterised as decadent, self-enraptured, warmongering, anti-government globalists, this political group was synonymous with red-toothed capitalism. As a term of abuse, neoliberals were deemed to have abandoned the working class. Corbyn's greatest hatred was of 'markets'. Asked whether he understood the challenges faced by entrepreneurs, he would reply, 'I'm friendly with the guy who runs my local caff.' He could not name a single businessman or industrialist he admired. The American titans who built empires by developing railways, motor vehicles, oilfields, medical drugs, aerospace and computer technology offended him. He was baffled by how companies like McDonald's, Starbucks, Google, eBay and Amazon became successful. The division between the creators of Airbnb and the uneducated employed in traditional workplaces defied the certainties of Bennism. Since he could not identify a class that was exploited by the creators of Google and Apple, his political certainties were confused by Silicon Valley's emancipation of people from spending their whole lives working in a factory or coalmine. The unacceptable cost of the Techies' triumph, he concluded, was the break-up of communities of workers. The anonymous masses were ignored while, to his disgust, the media placed the rich on a pedestal and praised the success of celebrities.

He disliked the cultural gap between himself and entrepreneurs like Elon Musk, who had created first PayPal then Space X, which successfully developed a better reuseable rocket than NASA. Yet he demanded that Musk and his ilk should be controlled. Those wealthy entrepreneurs, in his view, were obsessed by profits, and should be subject to workers' committees. The people should be empowered to direct James Dyson and other innovators on how to run their business. 'Those who contribute but have no wealth,' said Corbyn during a TV interview in 2015, 'should not be denigrated by the vested interests of the rich.' Successful industrialists, he insisted, would not leave Britain to avoid workers' control or higher taxes. Even if they did, an exodus of potential risk-takers did not trouble him. Equality was preferable to the disparity generated by high achievers. In his world, the ideal export was the sale of British skills to build railways in South America. 'British engineers,' he explained during the interview, 'built most of the railways in Latin America.' He ignored the facts that 150 years after those engineers sailed to South America, Britain's own rail manufacturers had ceased to exist, and South America's rail network was either decrepit or self-sustaining.

Economic matters also continued to be foreign to him. His reprimand to the PLP that 'people are being forced to borrow money from hedge funds' displayed his naïvety. He was more concerned that Ed Miliband had allowed the Conservatives to depict themselves as having inherited Labour's reckless deficit, for which the only cure was huge spending cuts. Cameron's call for austerity was a Tory trick, based on a myth created to harm the poor. Corbyn was appalled by the government's plan to cut welfare benefits, which were at the heart of any civilised society.

In his revolutionary vein, he advocated near-unlimited spending and direct action to solve the shortage of housing. Squatters, he said, should be allowed to occupy any of the UK's 'one million empty properties'. 'The government is trying to criminalise resistance,' he protested about a law to protect private property from illegal seizure. 'Campus and workplace occupations have played a pivotal role in trade union and student movements.' The squatters' violence was acceptable to further the cause.

Yet he continued to parade himself as a pacifist. He could not imagine, he said, 'any circumstances' in which he would deploy the army. 'I don't wish to go to war.' He ruled out Britain defending another European country if it were attacked by Russia. Among his many protests was an appearance outside RAF Waddington in Lincolnshire, a control centre for Reaper drones. Drones, declared Corbyn, were an 'obscenity' and should be abolished. In his world, there was no such thing as a just war. The First World War, in his opinion, was 'driven by big-power competition for influence around the globe', and the government's plan to spend £55 million on a 'truly national commemoration' of the centenary of the war's outbreak in 2014 was wasteful and wrong. Never having read any analyses of the causes of the Great War, he dismissed evidence that the Kaiser had wanted to dominate Europe, or that Britain had fought to protect the Continent's democracy. Even committing an army to combat Nazi Germany posed a problem for him. Blanket outrage sufficed.

The same simplified thinking shaped Corbyn's support of the Palestinians – the symbol of his ambition to shift Britain away from the United States and NATO, and align it with leftist and Muslim governments. He had never read any study that dispassionately discussed the Jews' acceptance in 1948 of a separate Palestinian state, or the Arab rejection of the UN settlement. Restricting himself to speaking to people who shared his views, he barely considered how sixty years later a Palestinian state might be established without either Israel's agreement or destruction. Nor did he take into account the fact that many Diaspora Jews across the globe relied on Israel's existence as protection from institutionalised anti-Semitism – and even another Holocaust. To further his cause, he encouraged some Islington schoolchildren to visit a festival organised by the Palestine Solidarity Campaign so they could 'understand the wealth and joy of Palestinian literature and a little of the history of the region'. He added, 'It is not in any way biased' – although the festival explicitly denied Israel's right to exist. To his disappointment, the Education Act requires children to hear balanced presentations, and the visit was cancelled.

Corbyn consistently invited anti-Zionists to the Commons, without ever offering Jews a similar privilege. Among his guests was Raed Salah, the leader of the Islamic Movement in Israel, which had described Jews as 'monkeys' and 'bacteria'. Salah had been convicted in Israel for saying that Semites had drunk the blood of non-Jewish babies, and used children's blood to bake bread, and had pronounced that the 9/11 attacks were a Jewish plot – proven by an order from Israel to all Jews working in the Twin Towers not to go in to work that day (an order that was certainly never made). Corbyn also described the Reverend Stephen Sizer, an Anglican vicar who later approved on Facebook an article entitled '9/11, Israel Did It', and was banned from social media by the Church, as a hero for daring to 'stand up and speak out against Zionism'. In 2009 he had told a rally in support of Gaza about his 'tears' on reading a message from 'my good friend Ewa Jasiewicz' about conditions in Gaza. Jasiewicz, known for having daubed 'Free Gaza and Palestine' on the walls of the Warsaw Ghetto, where 400,000 Jews had been interned before being shipped to Auschwitz, had also advocated that Palestinians should 'bump off' Israeli politicians.

On Holocaust Memorial Day in 2010, Corbyn had hosted a protest in the Commons to compare Auschwitz to Gaza, featuring a speech by Hajo Meyer, an anti-Zionist Auschwitz survivor, titled 'The Misuse of the Holocaust for Political Purposes'. He also invited Dyab Abou Jahjah, a Muslim extremist, to Britain to address a Stop the War Coalition rally denouncing Israel, America and Britain. Jahjah was arrested at Heathrow, but Corbyn successfully lobbied Jacqui Smith, the home secretary, to admit him to the country to deliver his speech. Any doubts about Corbyn's beliefs were dispelled by his own words.

On 3 March 2009 he said in a speech, 'It will be my pleasure and my honour to host an event in Parliament where our friends from Hezbollah will be speaking. I have also invited our friends from Hamas to come and speak.' In the lexicon of terrorists, few groups were more medieval than Hamas and Hezbollah. Both were committed to the violent destruction of Israel. According to Hamas's openly anti-Semitic charter, five million Jews would be pushed into the sea or allowed to flee. Corbyn never criticised Hamas's policy. Britain, he said, had made a 'big, big historical mistake' in labelling Hamas a terror group. Like Hezbollah, he said, Hamas was an 'honest' resistance organisation combating Zionist imperialism on behalf of the oppressed. The British government should negotiate directly with Hamas and Hezbollah to 'bring about long-term peace and social justice'.

Iran was the paymaster of Hamas and Hezbollah: both were armed by its regular dispatch of weapons to their 60,000 militia members in Gaza and Lebanon. Iran's plan, as Corbyn knew, was to use both organisations to replace Israel with a Shia Muslim Palestine and simultaneously to destabilise the Sunnis, especially Saudi Arabia, by establishing a military presence from the Mediterranean through Iraq to Yemen. In every way, Iran's aggression ran counter to Corbyn's pacifism. Nevertheless, in 2008 he would agree to appear regularly on Press TV, the Iranian state broadcaster, even though at the time the Iranian government was repressing the Green Movement's campaign for democracy in the country. He was paid £20,000. 'Not an enormous amount,' he said. Considering that his MP's salary was £60,277 and his expenses were low, the fee made up a considerable part of his income.

Corbyn's values further emerged in 2011 after Shia 'days of rage' protests erupted on the eve of a Formula One race in Bahrain. Knowing that the demonstration had been organised by Iran, he led the protests in Britain against the Bahrainis' 'suppression of dissent', and urged a boycott against the 'totalitarian regime'. He also criticised the British government for accepting £3 million from Bahrain to refurbish a hall at Sandhurst, the British military academy, which would then be named after King Hamad of Bahrain. 'I'm appalled,' he said. 'It's simply wrong to take money from the dictator who shoots demonstrators.' That year, Amnesty International reported that at least six hundred people, including juveniles, had been executed in Iran, mostly for drug-smuggling. At least three thousand more were held in appalling conditions on death row in Iranian prisons.

By chance, Corbyn soon had an opportunity to display his even-handed pacifism. In January 2014 he made a short visit to Iran with three other MPs. There was an early hiccup: he refused to fly business class. 'If you don't agree,' he was threatened by the former Tory chancellor Norman Lamont, who was one of his companions on the trip, 'then we're not going.' Corbyn gave way. Despite his insistence before leaving that his prime interest was to 'address issues of human rights', he remained strangely silent during the MPs' meetings with government officials about the regime's execution of gay men, juvenile drug-takers and political opponents. Back in London, he never mentioned human rights in Iran during his appearances on Iran's Press TV. Acting as the host on an Iranian television discussion programme, he made his consistent theme Zionist conspiracies. To one contributor who called the BBC 'Zionist liars', Corbyn asked if he had 'used his right as a licence-payer to complain about their coverage'. When Osama bin Laden was killed by American special forces in May 2011, he appeared again on Iranian TV to proclaim that the assassination was 'a tragedy that would make the world a more dangerous place'. Rather than being shot, he said, bin Laden should have been put on trial.

Corbyn's attitude towards murderous Muslims was, as ever, confused. Also in 2011, David Cameron agreed with the American and French governments to destroy an armoured column advancing on Muammar Gaddafi's orders to Benghazi to quash a rebellion in Libya's second city. Had Gaddafi's soldiers not been killed by allied aircraft, the uprising would have ended in a massacre. Corbyn not only opposed that operation, he did not comment about the refusal of neighbouring Arab governments, especially Egypt, to come to the aid of Gaddafi's opponents in Benghazi. Instead, he attacked Cameron for criticising multiculturalism as a source of terrorism, and for branding British Muslims murdering Britons as the new 'enemy within'.

And then Cameron made a mistake.

Rather than ending British intervention after saving Benghazi, he agreed to continue air strikes to topple Gaddafi. Singling out the Libyan tyrant while tolerating other dictators drew criticism. 'Just because you can't do the right thing everywhere,' replied Cameron, 'doesn't mean you shouldn't do the right thing somewhere.' Lacking accurate intelligence about Libya's tribal society after forty-two years of dictatorship, he made no attempt to develop a plan for governing the country after Gaddafi's fall. Arabists, including George Galloway, predicted chaos, but were ignored. Corbyn, leading a protest outside Downing Street against Tory 'imperialism', focused on money. 'The stench of hypocrisy is overwhelming,' he said. Always convinced that American and British foreign policy were shaped to win commercial advantage, he insisted: 'The war is about oil – the theft of that country's oil and resources.' The evidence was the opposite: BP had just concluded an oil deal with Gaddafi that would now be lost. Corbyn brushed aside that inconvenient truth and disregarded the enthusiasm of exiled Libyans about the removal of a mass-murdering tyrant. As usual, he also ignored the UN resolution authorising the allies' intervention to save lives – but not Gaddafi's eviction. In the Commons vote, Cameron's intervention was supported by 557 for, with thirteen against, the nays including Corbyn and McDonnell. Cameron, warned Corbyn, was ignoring the lessons of the Iraq war.

After Gaddafi's death in October 2011, Cameron walked away, and Libya fell into a bloodbath. Corbyn was not credited for his accurate prediction. His motives were suspect after he explained the main reason for his opposition: the British people, he said, were worried that each rocket had cost £500,000, at a time when public services were being slashed. It appeared that he was preoccupied by money, and not by the liberation of Libyans from oppression.

His contradictions multiplied over the following year. Daily, Islamic fighters attached to ISIS were raping both men and women, burning civilians, forcing young Christian girls into sexual slavery, orchestrating public beheadings and drowning opponents in cages. Corbyn blamed the existence of ISIS on the Anglo-American invasion of Iraq and support for Saudi Arabia. He condemned British volunteers fighting for ISIS only insofar as he condemned all violence. 'It's wrong to make value judgements,' he said. After Reyaad Khan, an ISIS terrorist from Cardiff, was killed by a drone, Corbyn commented, 'I'm unclear as to the point of killing the individual by this drone attack.' He opposed any retribution. 'Yes, they are brutal,' he told the Russian television channel RT. 'Yes, what they have done is quite appalling; likewise what the Americans did in Fallujah and other places is appalling.' In Corbyn's eyes, there was a moral equivalence between the American army using excessive force against organised Sunni and Shia terrorist armies in Iraq that were responsible for planting huge bombs in Baghdad and other cities, and ISIS pushing gays off tower blocks.

In the summer of 2013 he was offered an opportunity to reconcile his opinions. On 21 August, President Bashar al-Assad of Syria dropped sarin gas on two suburbs of Damascus occupied by opposition groups. At least 281 people died in hideous pain. As punishment for breaking international law, David Cameron proposed joining America in a retaliatory bombing raid on the facilities manufacturing the gas. He required Labour's support in a Commons vote, and after Ed Miliband was briefed on the evidence and the proposed action, he agreed that his party would vote with the government. Over the following days, he reneged on that promise. Bowing to Corbyn's warning, he agreed that, as an ally of Russia, Assad deserved Labour's support. 'I don't think a bombing campaign in Syria is going to bring about their defeat,' Corbyn explained. 'It would make them stronger.'

To embarrass Cameron, he also mentioned Britain's 'double standards'. Saudi Arabia, he said, 'routinely beheads people in public every Friday ... We have very little to say about human rights abuses in Saudi Arabia because of the economic link-up with them.' On 31 August, without Labour's votes, Cameron was defeated in the Commons. Not only Assad but also ISIS was spared. Miliband also accepted Corbyn's argument against bombing ISIS strongholds because innocents would die, and 'the process spreads bitterness and violence'.

Outside Parliament, Corbyn was supported by the playwright David Hare. As the 'flipside of Cameron,' Hare wrote, Corbyn's objection to attacking ISIS showed that he 'at least recognised a moral problem'. Such a conclusion about Corbyn's moral probity was controversial. Was Hare suggesting that Assad's production of sarin should continue unimpeded, that he should be allowed to gas Syrians with impunity, and that Cameron's refusal to tolerate his breach of international law was immoral? Neither he nor Corbyn ever properly explained.

Some suspected that one reason for the sympathy Corbyn garnered was his anti-Zionism. On social media sites he had been a member of groups in which other contributors identified Mossad as responsible for terrorist attacks in New York and Paris so as to justify Western intervention in the Middle East, and described the theft of children by Jews to sell on the black market. Among many groups he had joined on the internet was Palestine Live, a secret Facebook group featuring Holocaust denial, conspiracy theories about Jewish power, and descriptions of Jews as 'Zios', 'ZionNazis' and 'JewNazis'. Other members included the former BBC economics editor Paul Mason, the Marxist MP Chris Williamson, and Jackie Walker, an anti-Semitic member of the Labour Party. He posted 'favoured' on several virulent anti-Semitic comments, but would resign from the group in 2015 – after his election as party leader. His sympathy with Muslim issues also led to an attack on Hindu nationalist politics. In 2013 he tabled a Commons motion calling for Narendra Modi, then the chief minister of Gujarat in India, to be barred from visiting Britain for failing to stop riots in 2002 that had caused the deaths of hundreds of Muslims. Two years later, Modi visited London as India's prime minister. Corbyn would refuse to meet him.

Amid his political joustings, Corbyn also reconfigured his private life. Following his divorce from Claudia in 1999, he had enjoyed relationships with a succession of younger women. Among the most prominent was Loraine Monk, a member of the London party executive who lived in Kingston-upon-Thames. Noted for dressing in Oxfam clothes, Monk asked Corbyn to take her to receptions, and to his friends' bemusement he agreed, although he had always refused Claudia's similar requests. Other women followed, including Ann Cesek, a lively blonde Marxist who had campaigned for his adoption as MP in Islington North, and another, a friend of Val Veness whom he later spurned. Years later, the tabloids reported some of Corbyn's other relationships under the headline 'Hot Trot'. Many were bewildered by how an unkempt, anti-social man, now in his sixties and dedicated to his allotment and jam-making, could attract any woman. The answer was partly that active left-wing women seek different qualities than domestic goddesses, and partly what Val Veness told Corbyn to his face: 'You couldn't pull all these women if you weren't an MP. They wouldn't be interested in an old man with a beard.' Those relationships had not strengthened his bonds with his three sons. To his surprise, they had grown up as inner-city kids interested in music and football. One, wearing a baseball cap backwards, lounged on the streets growling about 'an operation down West' – meaning London's West End – and dived into telephone kiosks to check if there were any forgotten coins. 'I didn't bring them up like that,' Corbyn complained, although there were times of happiness, such as when all four Corbyns watched Arsenal play in an FA Cup final.

Corbyn's lifestyle changed after he forged a new, long-term relationship. In 1999 he had helped Marcela Alvarez, a Mexican living in Britain, to find her son, who had been taken away by his father. In the midst of the custody battle, Marcela's sister Laura had arrived from Mexico to give moral support. Over the years Corbyn and Laura developed a transatlantic friendship, albeit Laura was twenty years younger than him. Unlike Claudia Bracchitta, she was not a middle-class intellectual but a small-town activist. Their relationship developed slowly, not helped by Corbyn's evident boredom during his visits to Mexico – he tended to go off on his own to send long text messages to people in England – but eventually they agreed to share his cramped house in Berriman Road, a quiet street in Highbury.

Like her predecessors, Alvarez soon discovered that Corbyn was 'not helpful with the housework', and was rarely at home, for all his objections about a 'very unequal society'. Nevertheless, they married in 2013. As before, none of his political friends knew in advance or were invited. He feared, he confessed, journalists investigating 'every last aspect' of his home life, and travelling to Mexico to interview his new wife's relatives. That would make his life 'very hard', he said.

The marriage ended any thoughts he may have been having about a complete change of life. Over some months he had spoken of abandoning politics and retiring to Wiltshire to keep bees, a new hobby. He seemed attracted by a return to his childhood interests of cultivating vegetables, rather than just his weekly visits to his allotment in East Finchley, and turning wood like his father. Laura, small and dark haired, seemed amenable to fitting in with his wishes. Unlike his previous two wives, she appeared undemanding, and relieved to have swapped her life in Mexico for London. There was no plan for the future other than to follow her husband's familiar routine of Westminster, events in Islington and speeches to far-left groups across the country, while she developed an interest in selling organic coffee. That could easily be done from Wiltshire. At the Islington North Labour branch's annual summer party in 2012, Keith Veness had encouraged that move. 'You're an old git,' he said. 'You'll drop dead in harness if you don't.' Not long after, Corbyn called him to discuss whether he should leave Parliament. In the end, he decided that he could not afford to resign. No alternative career seemed likely.

9

Party Games

Since his election as party leader, Ed Miliband had successfully maintained the appearance that all was well within Labour. The Blairites had not rebelled, while Corbyn, McDonnell and about fifteen other MPs on the left had limited their opposition. Despite his flaws, Miliband had crafted an alliance that produced a 2015 election manifesto for a united party. Convinced that Britain wanted to move left, he buried New Labour's confidence in markets, blamed Blair for Iraq, and pledged to spend much more on public services. In concert with his supporter Len McCluskey, he appealed to those angered by the 'Tory scum' and 'Tory toffs' who had enriched themselves during Cameron's so-called years of austerity. To reduce inequality, he pledged, Labour would end neoliberal economics and the profit motive. Corbyn watched and waited. Although he felt the manifesto was 'not fundamentally redistributive', the offer of at least some socialism attracted him. For the first time since 1981, he believed the party was moving his way.

In his unvarnished style, McDonnell was more forthright. The moderates, including Miliband's front bench, had not opposed *every* benefit cut: 'We've got to eyeball these bastards because they're supposed to represent us, not crap on us in the way that they are at the moment.' His villain-in-chief remained Tony Blair, the sorcerer who had welcomed globalisation and dismissed personal insecurity and excused inequality as part of the human condition. McDonnell's taste for revenge was unquenchable. 'We've got to destroy the government,' he insisted. 'We cannot cope with the re-election of a Tory government in whatever coalition form it is, because our *society* cannot cope with it.' Those who failed to mobilise were guilty of 'a dereliction of duty and cowardice'. Such zealotry attracted Andrew Fisher, a thirty-six-year-old communist who would become McDonnell's researcher. Fisher was built in his new boss's mould – he had called anarchist riots in Croydon in 2011 'aggravated shopping'. In the forthcoming general election, to be held on 7 May 2015, he planned to campaign in Croydon for the anarchist Class War candidate against Emily Benn, the Labour candidate and Tony Benn's granddaughter, part of Old Labour's aristocracy. Corbyn and McDonnell endorsed Fisher's sentiments.

Corbyn, ever the political optimist, started the campaign expecting a Labour victory. The success of Syriza, a Marxist party in Greece, and the growing support for Podemos, a populist leftist party in Spain, inspired hope for the British left. But they misunderstood the plight of their counterparts in Germany and France. Across northern Europe, voters were abandoning many basic socialist ideals in their anger at increased immigration. The drift to the right was hastened by the decline of trade union membership and the disappearance of traditional class consciousness. Corbyn also misjudged the British public's reaction to the Tories. Austerity may have been their proclaimed way forward, but the reality was different. Contrary to the government's pronouncements, public spending in 2015 was 10 per cent higher in real terms than in 2007. Government spending had outstripped growth by 4 per cent every year since 2000, even after allowing for inflation. As a result, contrary to ministerial claims, the nation's debt was not diminishing: it was doubling, as government expenditure increased. The beneficiaries of the extra money were the poor. Government statistics showed that the gap in earnings between the richest and the poorest had been closing since 1990, especially on taxed income. After excluding a handful of hugely-paid chief executives, Britain's highest earners were receiving only about four times more after tax than the lowest-paid. Corbyn's slogans did not match most people's experience; nor did voters agree about Labour's legacy.

He might blame Margaret Thatcher and Ronald Reagan for the financial crisis, but the majority of voters understood that in 2007, after fifteen years of unprecedented growth, Gordon Brown had borrowed excessive amounts so he could distribute welfare benefits, some to questionable claimants. It may have been charitable and socialist, but it was irresponsible.

Ed Miliband went into the final day of the campaign convinced that the following day he would be driving from his constituency in Doncaster to Downing Street. Either Labour would win an outright majority, or it would be the largest party in a coalition government. The TV exit polls at 10 p.m. shattered that illusion, prompting disbelief among the politicians of all parties. After midnight, the pattern of Labour's failure was irrefutable. The party had alienated the north, was weak in the Midlands, was ignored in the south, and had been wiped out in Scotland, where the SNP won fifty-six of the fifty-nine seats. Voters did not trust Miliband on immigration, welfare or the economy, and rejected him as ineffectual. Instead of hitting his target of 35 per cent of the vote, Labour won 30.4, two million votes behind the Tories. Miliband had raised his party's share by 1.4 per cent, but had lost twenty-six seats. His self-confidence wrecked, he instantly resigned. Stunned Labour MPs were plunged into another leadership election without time to digest what had gone awry.

Moderate MPs told a post-election party inquiry headed by Margaret Beckett that voters had rejected Labour's 'wrong message' about its economic competence. They blamed Miliband's insensitivity to working-class fears about immigration, Labour's disdain for middle-class owner-occupiers, its denigration of aspiration, and Miliband's contempt for those who took pride in England. Miliband disagreed, blaming the electorate's poor judgement in not embracing a 'progressive' manifesto. His other culprits were the right-wing media's 'determination to destroy' him, Tory lies about Labour's economic record, and the fallout from the Scottish independence referendum in September 2014, when Labour had lost support after allowing its spokesmen to share a platform with Tories.

None of those details mattered to Corbyn. Miliband's defeat, he said, was a failure of Blairism – a 'virus', according to Dave Ward of the Communication Workers' Union, a word Corbyn would not have rejected. He was convinced that Labour would have won had Miliband offered uncompromising socialism, and blamed the loss of Labour supporters on Ukip and the Tories and their racist, anti-immigrant propaganda. The solution was not to hanker after repeating Blair's three election victories, but to offer pure socialism.

At the Campaign Group's first post-election meeting, on 3 June, its nine members were in despondent mood. Unlike in 2010, there seemed no prospect that in the next twelve days they could persuade the required thirty-five MPs to nominate a left-wing candidate for the leadership ballot. There was also the question of who such a candidate could be. Diane Abbott had been humiliated after attracting minuscule support in 2010, and after two failures John McDonnell had ruled himself out, not least because nothing would persuade him to modify the hell-fire sermons he had been preaching over the previous forty years. Most recently, he had described himself as 'the last communist in Parliament', had pledged to disband the armed police and MI5, to abolish the monarchy and 'expropriate the banks', and exhorted the 'People's Parliament', a group organised by Seb Corbyn, Jeremy's somewhat sensible second son, to make the rich 'fearful' by 'direct action'. His diet was too rich for Labour MPs.

The one apparently pristine candidate was Jeremy Corbyn. Two years earlier he had told his local newspaper, 'I want to be able to criticise my party and I couldn't do that in a leadership race. I want to be able to look at myself in the mirror.' Even before he arrived at the post-election meeting he had jettisoned such contrived caution. 'What about if I do stand?' he asked. Then he announced unambiguously, 'I've decided to stand.'

'I thought we decided not to put up anyone from the left,' said a surprised McDonnell.

'Well, I have been lobbied by my constituents and trade unions, and we've decided that we need a debate,' replied

Corbyn. With his lifelong history of service, he implied, he was the ideal candidate. The only obstacle was obtaining the required number of nominations.

'It was my turn,' Corbyn told the *Guardian* shortly afterwards, suggesting that he was a reluctant runner who did not expect to secure the nomination of enough Labour MPs to stand. 'A few weeds are going to be springing up in my allotment, but I'll be able to get back to it shortly.' To fit the image of loyal but unenthusiastic compliance, he said that he had agreed to McDonnell's request. 'All right, all right, I'll do it,' he had supposedly told his colleague.

Four factors were in his favour. First, Abbott's earlier candidacy had established that the left should be allowed to run a candidate, in order to encourage a debate; second, while widely abhorred for his disloyalty to his front bench, Corbyn evoked little personal animosity, for all his dirty tricks in Hornsey and Haringey; third, after so many years in the trenches, both he and McDonnell were energetic organisers; fourth, his victory was unimaginable.

Corbyn's first move was to issue a press release demanding a full debate. If MPs, who made up just 0.1 per cent of party members, did not allow him to stand, that would be undemocratic. Thereafter, he called every Labour MP, asking for their support. 'He's a good bloke,' many agreed, mentioning that, unlike McDonnell, Corbyn was always polite, and never openly threatening. John Prescott weighed in: Labour MPs, he said, should lend Corbyn their votes to get him on the ballot. Only Corbyn, he suggested, could persuade the electorate that the party was not in the pockets of the trade unions, and destroy the Tory myth that Labour, rather than greedy bankers, had caused the financial crash. Gradually, Corbyn and McDonnell won over a few moderates who agreed to support his nomination, although none actually voted for him. David Lammy and Sadiq Khan, both of whom were vying to be the Labour candidate for London mayor, joined the nominees, as did Jo Cox, a feisty Yorkshire MP. Corbyn was on fertile ground with a handful of the most recent intake – prototype Corbynistas sponsored by

Unite, led by Clive Lewis, an engaging regional BBC journalist, and Cat Stevens, a thirty-year-old bisexual republican. Stevens who had studied gender studies at Lancaster University, represented the new politics – not of class but of identity: race, gender and sexuality. Every issue was interpreted through her rigid prejudices, oddly dubbed 'virtue-signalling'. Both Lewis and Stevens supported renationalisation, high taxation and the redistribution of wealth, including some confiscation of property.

Just twenty-four hours before the deadline, Corbyn still needed at least ten more MPs if he were to be allowed to stand. McDonnell would claim that it was he who cajoled the necessary support, but for a man so abhorred by his fellow Labour Members, that assertion rings hollow. During those last hours, Frank Field succumbed to his own logical thinking. Although he was a fierce critic of Corbyn, he believed that Labour's poor electoral performance was the equivalent of 'a political carpet-bomb operation'. Corbyn had sincere views which 'should be tested' to avoid another defeat. Bombarded by social media messages, former foreign secretary Margaret Beckett also signed Corbyn's nomination papers, although she had always been opposed to him. Thus, slowly, the numbers mounted, and by midday Corbyn was on the ballot. He had received thirty-six nominations. The majority of those would not vote for him, and all of them were certain that he would not be elected, including Beckett. In a career strewn with errors, especially as minister of agriculture under Blair, she would later say of her nomination, 'I probably regard it as one of the biggest political mistakes I have ever made.'

Showing no surprise, Corbyn, now a grizzled sixty-six, stood among a small group of allies in Parliament Square. 'I'm slightly surprised we made it, but there we are. At my age I'm not likely to be a long-term contender, am I?' He would rely on McDonnell for creating an organisation, and initially on his own credit card to finance his campaign. 'I'm not making any predictions,' the 200–1 outsider said. Owen Jones, a *Guardian* columnist and a like-minded socialist, thought Corbyn would do well to win 25 per cent of the vote. The feeling was widespread. 'Labour cannot afford another loser,' wrote Kevin Maguire, the *Mirror*'s left-wing columnist, anticipating that Corbyn was 'highly unlikely to wear the crown'. Even the prospect of Corbyn as a candidate horrified those moderate Labour MPs who despaired at the thought of a return to the 'bad old days of the 1980s' of Tony Benn and Michael Foot. Corbyn's platform as the anti-austerity candidate, said John Mann, a fifty-five-year-old former trade union official and examiner of the probity of bankers and civil servants, 'demonstrates our desire never to win again'. Mann received comfort from the *Sun*. 'Corbyn,' it forecast, 'has zero chance of becoming leader or – thank God – prime minister.' Everyone seemed in agreement.

Days later, Corbyn set off for his first campaign meeting, in Birmingham. His small team included Simon Fletcher, an effective operator who had worked with Ken Livingstone at County Hall; Kat Fletcher, an Islington councillor; Corbyn's election agent Carmel Nolan, a friend of George Galloway who would be his press spokesperson; and Harry Fletcher, a well-liked expert on probation recruited by McDonnell. (The three Fletchers were unrelated.) Corbyn showed no anxiety. After so many years campaigning, he looked forward to criss-crossing the country by train, and the pleasures of being recognised.

As he entered the hall, shabbily dressed as usual, he noticed a difference. Not only was the 1,500 crowd bigger than expected, its mood was excited. In front of him sat a broad coalition of public sector employees, minority groups, and then the victims – those dependent on welfare payments, protesters, Marxists in search of authentic socialism, and losers. Most were Labour's old grassroots, abandoned by the parliamentary party after 1983. For years they had sought a champion to dismantle Thatcher's legacy and destroy the muscle of the City of London. Like Corbyn, they regarded New Labour's legacy as a country riddled with hatred, fear and insecurity – a playground for the super-rich who ignored society's rules. Blair's grab for power had been followed, they believed, by Cameron slashing away at living standards, the destruction of public services, and greater inequality. Scattered among the Labour veterans were young people enraged by arrogant global corporations which they believed had denied them certainty and an identity in the world, and also the opportunity to acquire a decent home. They fumed that the workers were paying for the City's greed, that speculators and property spivs were getting rich on scams, and that no banker had gone to jail over the 2008 crash. In their eyes, the worst culprits were corporate directors earning vast salaries despite their poor performance. Above all, they complained of being saddled with the prospect of a £50,000 debt for university tuition fees.

Standing in front of this audience was an unscripted veteran – 'unscripted' because he had repeated the same slogans for forty years, and did not plan to say anything different now. During those decades, Corbyn had participated in so many demonstrations on wet, windswept streets that many would come to Birmingham – and to all his meetings over the following weeks – to repay his loyalty. He stood before them as the true believer who uncompromisingly upheld the gospel with a vision of 'straight-talking, honest politics'. To his audience, his inexhaustible rhetoric about the immorality of capitalism and his comradeship with the downtrodden won admiration. To the lost souls, he promised to 'aggressively redistribute' the ill-gotten gains of the rich. They identified with this self-effacing bearded man who in his thirty-two years at Westminster had submitted among the lowest expenses claims of all MPs, and who spoke enthusiastically about growing potatoes, broad beans, sweet corn and leeks on allotment number 33 in East Finchley. As he spoke, spurred on by the audience's enthusiasm, his team noticed that the familiar ramble was delivered with new confidence.

'The neoliberal era is in its death throes!' shouted Corbyn with the same certainty as that with which Karl Marx had predicted the imminent collapse of capitalism 170 years earlier. Responsibility for the world's ills was pinned on money-hungry entrepreneurs: 'The market will never provide a secure, dignified life for the vast majority,' ran his sermon. He promised the

'end of the era' of greed, shelter from moguls, control of globalisation, and curtailing mobile capital. In short, his audience
found a champion pledged to build a country in their
interests.

On the return journey to London, Corbyn joyously anticipated more admiration on the long campaign. 'Anything else
arranged?' he asked. 'You're speaking later today at a gay pride
march in Trafalgar Square,' replied Harry Fletcher. To join the
marchers, they got out of the Tube at Oxford Circus. As he
walked down Regent Street – beneath a banner proclaiming
'Jeremy for Leader' – Corbyn was grabbed time and again to
pose for selfies: the activists who mobbed him also worshipped
the very digital revolution he threatened to suffocate.
'Something's happening,' said Fletcher, struck by the adulation.
Not surprisingly, none of the national newspapers or TV
stations highlighted the day's events.

Political leadership contests are civil wars, but this one was
markedly different. Corbyn's three rivals – Andy Burnham,
Yvette Cooper and Liz Kendall – were lacklustre performers,
unable to escape their pedestrian pasts. All three had served as
senior ministers in Blair's government, and all three refused to
admit that its guiding ideology was discredited. Lacking imagination, they misjudged the membership's mood, and resisted
taking the risk of redefining themselves. In the wake of the 2008
crash, all three had failed to fashion an alternative vision for
living standards, homes and public services. All three did,
however, understand one legacy bequeathed by Ed Miliband. In
his bid to retain Len McCluskey's support, he had altered the
party's rules. Anyone paying £3 could vote for the leader, even
non-party members. The impetus behind the change was placed
on McCluskey, a former Militant sympathiser who was intent
on shifting power away from MPs to his Unite trade union.

The MPs' loss of control had started two years earlier, when
Unite officials rigged the ballot for the new Scottish parliamentary candidate for Falkirk in favour of a former nurse, Karie
Murphy, who just happened to be McCluskey's current partner,
and the mother of his son. Without their knowledge, Unite

members had been registered to join the Falkirk party, and had 'voted' for Murphy. Curiously, at that very moment, McCluskey was the target of allegations of corruption and vote-rigging by Gerard Coyne, a union executive who would soon challenge McCluskey for his post. In the uproar of allegations about Falkirk, Karie Murphy's candidature had been abandoned, and in exchange Ed Miliband had allowed himself to be persuaded by McCluskey to change the party's constitution. Instead of Labour MPs alone deciding, the party leader would be elected by the entire membership – one member, one vote. Since Miliband owed his own election victory to Unite, and since Unite contributed a fifth of Labour's income (over 80 per cent of Labour's funds came from trade unions), he ignored repeated warnings that the proposed new rule would allow the unions to overwhelm the party. Any undesirable consequences, he promised, would be solved later. Few anticipated the surge McCluskey had planned. At the beginning of June 2015, Unite and the other unions began to enrol 140,000 new members, then over the following weeks another 100,000.

In the leadership election, McCluskey initially supported Andy Burnham, the favourite, despite his monosyllabic style and colourless timidity. Corbyn was endorsed only by the two major rail unions, the RMT (Rail, Maritime and Transport Workers) and Aslef (the Associated Society of Locomotive Engineers and Firemen), and Unison, which had incorporated NUPE. Burnham's prospects slipped after the first televised debate between the four candidates. Unwilling to condemn Blair, he came over as a contaminated relic. By contrast, Corbyn fed his congregation's hopes. 'We have been cowed by powerful commercial interests,' he told them, promising to reverse Blair's 'promotion of the market economy rather than a planned economy'. Damning everything Blair had done, Corbyn asked: 'Why is it in Britain that the hundred richest people equal the total wealth of 30 per cent of the population?' His praise of immigration and of a planned economy provoked wild cheers from an audience packed with hard-left supporters. Compared to Corbyn's image as a free-spirited, romantic anti-politician, his

three opponents seemed leaden and lock-jawed. The next opinion poll slashed his odds from 200–1 to 12–1. 'Would it scare
you if you won?' he was asked. He closed his eyes. 'Scare me? It
would be a challenge.' He would still cycle or take the bus to the
Commons, he said, and he certainly wouldn't use the official
car. Nor, he added, keeping up the image of shy reluctance,
would he abandon his old clothes and dress up in a new blue
suit. Although he still did not sense that he might be victorious,
he played the modest leader-in-waiting for whom life would
not change.

His first obstacle was Labour's MPs. Here he was fortunate to
be presented with an open goal by Harriet Harman, the prim
acting party leader. Her misjudgement began when George
Osborne, the chancellor, blamed Gordon Brown's tax credits for
creating a dependency culture. High welfare benefits, he said,
deterred people from accepting offers of work. As part of his
£12 billion cuts to the annual welfare bill, Osborne targeted the
work-shy to save £4 billion. Government statistics suggested
that a quarter of the 2.1 million people who had received £135
billion in incapacity benefits over the previous ten years were
bogus claimants. Corbyn ridiculed that suggestion. Similarly, he
was outraged by the Tory plan to target those receiving more in
benefits than people in work earning the average wage. To highlight that anomaly, several newspapers featured photographs of
an unemployed single mother living with her six children by
several fathers in a multi-million-pound house in Kensington,
and relying on taxpayers to fund her weekly £2,000 rent and
overheads. Under the government's plan she would receive no
more than £500 per week – equivalent to an annual income of
£35,000 after tax. If taxpayers were expected to live within their
means, argued Osborne, there was no reason why the unemployed should enjoy standards of living higher than those at
work. The woman and her family would be relocated from
Kensington to a poorer area. That policy, countered Corbyn,
was 'inner-city social cleansing'. He refused to explain why the
feckless should enjoy an advantage over working people who
limited their expenditure to what they could afford.

Harriet Harman was in a dilemma. A clear majority of Labour voters supported Osborne's plan to limit child tax credits to two children. Ed Miliband's refusal to cut benefits was partly why Labour lost the 2015 election. Accordingly, she ordered Labour MPs to vote for Osborne's plans. Corbyn claimed that cuts would 'push more children into poverty'. The work-shy, he said, were not 'scroungers', and deserved to receive benefits. He would in good conscience therefore vote against Harman and the party.

As traditional loyalists, Burnham, Cooper and Kendall were also torn. Although all three recognised Osborne's trap, none was brave enough to say outright that a future Labour government should not make life better for skivers than for honest citizens. Burnham temporised, and was jeered. Finally, he 'flip-flopped', backing the spending cuts and pointedly refusing to accept money from trade unions. McCluskey switched his support to Corbyn, the favourite among Unite members. At hustings in Birmingham, Liz Kendall was booed for justifying austerity, and was written off. Yvette Cooper stood paralysed, as ever incapable of making a decision. Not one of them could describe an alternative to Marxism, or dared accuse Corbyn of tolerating moral corruption. Untainted by any ideological confusion, he was emerging as the champion of his tribe.

On 20 June, thousands of people gathered outside the Bank of England, for them the symbol of the guilty money merchants and shady property-owners. Under placards proclaiming 'Defy Tory Rule' provided by the Socialist Workers Party they marched to Parliament Square, where Corbyn would address them. The disgruntled and dispossessed had unexpectedly found a passionate luminary with a chance of becoming the Labour Party's leader. Alongside him on the platform was Martin McGuinness. 'Austerity,' shouted the IRA killer, 'is devastating communities.' He urged the crowd to support Corbyn to 'save ourselves from decades of yuppie rule'. While anarchists set off smoke bombs and daubed graffiti on the square's walls, the Welsh singer and TV presenter Charlotte Church warned that the Conservative government planned to sell off Britain's schools and hospitals. Corbyn, she sang, was their saviour, the anti-politician fighting the establishment.

Corbyn's success depended on tapping into images of misery, yet the usual grievances – high unemployment, inflation and industrial strife – were not mentioned, and for good reason. Unemployment was falling towards 1.65 million, the lowest for many years, and work opportunities were attracting thousands of migrants to Britain every week. Nevertheless, Corbyn claimed that his reforms would create a million new jobs. To a sophisticated audience, the image of a government generating wealth-creating employment was illusory. At Rolls-Royce's factory in Tyne and Wear, machines were running between twelve and forty-five hours at a stretch without any human intervention. Robots were producing parts in a quarter of the time of workers. Corbyn's supporters did not question his silence about the digital revolution. Rather, they responded to his favourite statistic, which he had borrowed from Oxfam: one person in five in Britain lived below the poverty level. The government's figures told a different story – the actual number was one in fourteen, meaning that about 4.6 million people were in long-term poverty. The Rowntree Foundation and the Institute for Fiscal Studies confirmed that the higher minimum wage and improved in-work benefits had reduced income inequality. Verified statistics showed that Britons had never been healthier, richer or more equal. The real truth that life had never been better for the majority passed over Corbyn's audience. Distrusting the torrent of unexpected data produced by the government and think tanks, they moaned that the world had become too complex, volatile and unpredictable. Global disaster was imminent, and here was a man of principle to confirm their gloom.

A poll of 12,000 people on the day of the general election, commissioned by the Tory peer Lord Ashcroft, showed that while 86 per cent of Tories optimistically believed that 'If you work hard, it is possible to be very successful in Britain, no matter what your background,' 62 per cent of Labour supporters took the opposite view. Corbyn supporters equated free markets with poverty, and doubted that creative innovation depended on a free market. In general, the left was pessimistic and disliked consumerism, home ownership, foreign holidays and Britain itself. They assumed that greater wealth for some meant inequality and increased poverty for the majority. While 71 per cent of Conservatives thought life in Britain had improved since 1979, 51 per cent of Labour voters thought life was better three decades ago. That was Corbyn's appeal: he offered to turn the clock back.

Against him, Andy Burnham offered no ideological certainty. In the welfare vote, he abstained, as did Yvette Cooper, a buck-passer in government. Instead of agreeing to unite against Corbyn, she and Burnham pursued a parallel course. Neither directly addressed the coalition of communists, Trotskyites and Greens joining Labour as members to vote for Corbyn. Both were silent about the entry into the party of Mark Serwotka, the Trotskyite general secretary of the Public and Commercial Services Union, previously barred from membership. 'Naughty people shouldn't join Labour,' Corbyn said on the BBC's *Woman's Hour*, but he welcomed the entryists. 'We will see what happens,' was his oft-used escape phrase. He showed the same nonchalance over his supporters' undisguised threats of violence against Cooper and Kendall. Two days later, a poll put him firmly as the future victor, nearly 20 per cent ahead of Burnham, his nearest challenger. After years in the wilderness, the lonely prophet gleefully approved his reincarnation as the left's catalyst to lead his flock to the Promised Land.

Fearing a repeat of Tony Benn's near-destruction of the Labour Party after 1979, Tony Blair, Peter Mandelson and Alan Johnson each appealed to the party's social democrats to reject an unelectable Marxist. 'Even if you hate me,' wrote Blair, 'don't take Labour over the cliff edge.' Abandoning the centre, he lamented, when Labour needed to win an additional ninety-four seats or achieve a 12.5 per cent swing to get a Commons majority, would be fatal. But he misjudged Labour's mood. Corbyn was appearing among crowds of fans wearing T-shirts with the slogan 'Jez We Can'. The resurgence of the left generated more media coverage, more converts, more celebrity endorsements and intense messaging on Twitter, Facebook, Google and Instagram – all this exposure provided by tax-avoiding American giants – with the headline: 'Warning: contains a new kind of politics'.

Older Labour members did not recognise anything new. Working from his Commons office filled with memorabilia from previous campaigns on issues including Palestine, CND, Stop the War and Ireland, Corbyn spoke about peace, the anti-apartheid movement and a return to Clement Attlee's state controls. His bookshelf was overflowing with works by or about Hugo Chávez – unread, but Corbyn's symbol of resistance to America. 'The thing about Corbyn,' observed the *Guardian* inaccurately, 'is that he is nearly always proved right – after the event.' In reality, he joined many campaigns long after they had started, and his 'new' approach was a repackaging of old policies. Around him were veterans who epitomised the truism that the hard left never disappears but, in their lifelong mission, regroup after every defeat to look for the next silver lining.

Added to the parliamentary inner core – Corbyn, McDonnell and Abbott – was Seumas Milne, Corbyn's fifty-seven-year-old intellectual *consigliere*, an alumnus of Winchester and Oxford, and the son of Alasdair Milne, probably the BBC's best post-war director general. At the next level was a handful of like-minded MPs and old comrades bound by relationships that stretched back over thirty years. Some, including Neale Coleman and Simon Fletcher, had worked with Ken Livingstone at the GLC or City Hall, while others such as John Ross, Jude Woodward and Kat Fletcher had been members of Trotskyist factions. In the background was Jon Lansman, a Cambridge-educated ally of Tony Benn. Steeped in Leninism, he presented himself as an agent provocateur in the vanguard of the class struggle to transform Labour into a revolutionary party. To strengthen Corbyn's bid for the leadership, he marshalled youthful idealists into Momentum, a new group whose mission was to infiltrate Labour. At Momentum's heart was Kate Hudson, CND's general secretary. Bound to Corbyn by a shared admiration for Russia, she had described the collapse of the Soviet Union in 1989 as 'a catastrophe for humanity'.

From his comfortable life in capitalist Britain, Corbyn still discounted the crimes and misery inflicted by Moscow. He had not protested when in February 2014 Vladimir Putin occupied Crimea, and he approved the incorporation of independent Ukraine within the Soviet sphere of influence. He showed no understanding of the legacy of Stalin's forced collectivisation programme, which had starved about four million Ukrainians to death between 1932 and 1933. Similarly apathetic about Poland's historic hostility towards Russia, he was against Poland's membership of NATO, believing that Russia had every right to determine its neighbour's fate. Like Livingstone, he opposed the threat of sanctions against Russia for providing the surface-to-air missile that pro-Moscow forces used to shoot down Malaysian Airlines Flight MH17 from Amsterdam to Kuala Lumpur in July 2014, killing all 298 people on board, as 'an awful lot of pandering to the hysteria that has been whipped up'. Often stuck for the appropriate words, he relied on others to articulate his disapproval of the West.

None of these allies was more important than Seumas Milne. Known as a 'Tankie' when he arrived at the *Guardian* because he supported the Soviet suppression of the uprisings in Hungary in 1956 and Czechoslovakia in 1968, Milne praised Stalin for offering 'socialist political alternatives'. The fact that he had murdered many millions was seen by Milne as necessary fallout from resistance to Western imperialism. There were lessons to be learned, he wrote, from the Soviet success: 'For all its brutalities and failures ... communism in the USSR, Eastern Europe and elsewhere delivered rapid industrialisation, mass education and job security and huge advances in social and gender equality. It encompassed genuine idealism and commitment'. Those who equated Stalin with Hitler, he believed, were peddling 'moral and historical nonsense'. Among them were the historian Robert Conquest. 'Stalinisation', observed Conquest, 'may be one way of attaining industrialisation, just as cannibalism is one way of attaining a high-protein diet'. In the same vein, Milne appeared indifferent to Vladimir Putin's murder of his opponents, suppression of critical media groups and wholesale transfer of billions of dollars of state money into tax-evading offshore accounts. American imperialism was at fault for demonising Putin, whom Milne admired as 'a powerful counterweight to Western global domination'. For all those reasons, Milne's political convictions and intellectual eloquence were indispensable to Corbyn.

The two were particularly bound by their unremitting hostility to Israel. After spending a gap-year 'holiday' in Lebanon in the early 1980s, witnessing ferocious battles between Israelis and Palestinians, Milne regarded Zionism as evil, without qualification. He shared Corbyn's belief that the Islamic attacks of 9/11 were explicable as acts of resistance. As part of the same mindset, he described the murder of Lee Rigby, a British soldier hacked to death on a London street by two Muslims in May 2013, as 'not terrorism in the normal sense of an indiscriminate attack on civilians', because Rigby had served in Afghanistan. Similarly, he agreed with Corbyn's denial that Bashar al-Assad had launched a chemical attack against civilians because the Syrian president had 'no rational motivation' for the killings. The video images of dead children with foam around their mouths, he said, could have been fabricated by the West. He was waiting to see the evidence.

Convinced that Western liberalism distorted the truth in order to conceal exploitation, Milne praised Nicolás Maduro, Chávez's successor as president of Venezuela, as 'a lesson to anyone interested in social justice and new forms of socialist policies'. This was in lockstep with Corbyn, who had tabled a motion in the Commons in 2013 congratulating Maduro on his election and his promise to 'continue Hugo Chávez's socialist revolution'. Corbyn spoke as an eyewitness, although on a recent visit to Venezuela with Diane Abbott he seems to have ignored the fact that the country was suffering 500 per cent inflation, and that Chávez's socialism was leading its people towards destitution. Maduro's dictatorial tendencies were likewise irrelevant to Corbyn. Anything was preferable to capitalism. In his opinion, Taliban rule in Afghanistan was perfectly acceptable, military intervention to protect Christian Yazidis in Iraq was unnecessary, and he would not protest against the oppression of those demanding democracy in Iran.

All these opinions, shared by Milne, attracted more admirers to Corbyn. Labour moderates, even as they understood the forces being unleashed, panicked. The party, warned the Blairite MP Tristram Hunt, would be 'hammered' at the next election. 'If Corbyn wins,' said John Mann, 'it would be catastrophic for the Labour Party. I don't think he will win. I don't think he wants to win. He wouldn't have a clue what to do. He has never run anything.' The mood, admitted one insider, was misery and depression. The opinion polls prompted Liz Kendall to warn, 'It would be disastrous for the party, disastrous for the country – we would be out of power for a generation.' Margaret Beckett admitted that she had been a 'moron' for having nominated Corbyn. Emily Thornberry, another nominee, said she would vote for Yvette Cooper. David Lammy, Sadiq Khan and Tulip Siddiq, the MP for Hampstead, also withdrew their support despite having nominated Corbyn. But Tony Blair's renewed criticism only enhanced Corbyn's status. 'His rivals,' complained Abbott, 'are trying to paint him as the political equivalent of the bubonic plague.' Her defence was unnecessary. Teflon appeared to protect Corbyn from his critics, and to the metropolitan middle class his image remained that of a polite, scruffy gardener who posed them no threat.

Corbyn's own behaviour was hardly dignified. When asked on Channel 4 why he called Hamas his 'friends', he sneered: 'Thanks for the tabloid journalism.' Despite his supposed hatred of promotional spin, he allowed his spokesman to peddle exaggerations: he loved cricket, enjoyed reading Oscar Wilde and Yeats, and was a devoted Arsenal fan. Despite that one Cup final visit with his sons, his attachment to Arsenal was questionable: in 2006 he had urged fans to boycott the club because of its commercial relationship with Israeli tourism.

The division between party members and Labour voters had widened. An opinion poll reported that 86 per cent of Corbyn's supporters described themselves as left-wing, compared to 33 per cent of the country; 60 per cent were against the monarchy, while nationally only 22 per cent were republican; 85 per cent of Corbynistas wanted the redistribution of wealth, compared to 29 per cent of the electorate as a whole; and 86 per cent endorsed his demand for the renationalisation of the utilities, compared to 31 per cent of the public. Since the working class had no votes in the leadership election, their mistrust was irrelevant, and as Lenin had chillingly directed, their suspicions would anyway be cured by re-education.

To establish his credibility for a wider audience, Corbyn sought to rebut the impression that he was ignorant of economics. Inevitably, he concealed the consequences of mismanaging his own money – no one outside his innermost circle knew about his financial crisis in 1996. Towards the end of July he told a BBC interviewer: 'We can learn a lot from Marx. Marx analysed what was happening in a brilliant way.' Next, in a speech at the Royal College of Medicine, he presented himself as a financial expert, albeit reliant on Richard Murphy, an accountant specialising in combating tax avoidance who would become an architect of 'Corbynomics', and on the economic plan John McDonnell had composed in 2012. A Labour government, McDonnell had said, should impose a 20 per cent wealth tax on all Britons, plus additional income taxes on the top 10 per cent. 'We're saying,' he explained, 'just collect the money and make those who created the crisis pay for the crisis, and that way you overcome it.'

Corbyn and McDonnell favoured the tax policies of the Callaghan era, when the country's richest paid 98 per cent in tax. Although the top 1 per cent of British taxpayers already contributed 27 per cent of the nation's total tax, and the top 10 per cent paid 59 per cent, making British rates higher than Germany's – and higher than under Gordon Brown's government – Corbyn rejected a calculation by the independent Office of Budget Responsibility that increasing taxes would reduce revenue, or that the Tory cut from 50 to 45 per cent of the top rate of tax had generated additional revenues. Both Corbyn and

McDonnell scorned the experience of France and Venezuela, where high tax rates had persuaded the rich to flee. Rather, Corbyn proposed 'People's Quantitative Easing' as the 'sound economics of public investment'. Under this system, the Bank of England would simply print sufficient money to finance the government's requirements. He denied the obvious consequence: hyperinflation. Just as in Weimar Germany in the 1920s, Zimbabwe after 2010, and Venezuela at that very moment, Britain's currency would be destroyed, and wages would be worthless. He also was deaf to the derision that the Tories heaped on Richard Murphy, who had predicted that a crackdown on fraud and tax evasion would raise an extra £119 billion a year. After scrutinising his calculations, the Inland Revenue (HMRC) found that Murphy had double-counted VAT and used the wrong tax rates, leading to his claimed revenue increase being exaggerated by £75 billion. Moreover, HMRC's aggressive tax collection had already increased revenues to a record amount.

At the heart of Corbyn's message was the proposal that Britain should replicate the 1970s arrangement whereby a new national investment bank pumped hundreds of millions of pounds into Britain's motor industry. He did not mention that all that money had been wasted, because the car factories were either closed down or sold off for a pittance. 'The route to prosperity,' he said, 'is a collective purpose between workers, public investment and services, and yes, often innovative and creative individuals.' He derided as a myth the suggestion that wealth creation was 'due to the dynamic risk-taking by private equity funds, entrepreneurs or billionaires bringing their wealth to the UK'. He also dismissed the evidence that new jobs and wealth had followed the privatisation of BT, British Airways, BP and the road haulage industry, and that many iconic British companies had been sold to foreign corporations because British tax laws prevented individual Britons from accumulating sufficient wealth to buy them. None of the voters attracted to Corbyn were concerned by those lessons from history. They focused on his pledge to renationalise the railways, an increasingly popular option as fares increased and trains' reliability was degraded by strikes and mismanagement. (In 2016, although only 10 per cent of all travel in Britain was by train, there were 1.718 billion journeys on National Rail, making the British network the fifth most used in the world.)

To Corbyn, every industrial disagreement was a justified expression of working-class rebellion against capitalism. Aslef and the RMT, the two major rail unions, had instantly donated money to Corbyn's election fund, knowing that he would support a twenty-four-hour London Tube strike opposing the introduction of all-night services. On the strike day, 8 July, Corbyn described the government's treatment of Tube workers as 'disgraceful', and said that it should not dictate to the unions. 'It's for them to determine their rules,' he said. The unions should manage the Tube. He dismissed as insufficient the Tube drivers' annual pay of £49,673 for a thirty-six-hour week, plus forty-three days' holiday. In his opinion, although Britain's six million public sector workers earned on average 13 per cent more than the twenty-four million in the private sector, their pay was inadequate. Unsurprisingly, the national media was unimpressed by Corbynomics.

To bolster the credibility of Corbyn's plans, John Ross, a Trotskyite, drafted a letter of support from eminent academics. Among them were Thomas Piketty, a best-selling French economist; Yanis Varoufakis, the charismatic Marxist who as Greece's finance minister for five months had contributed to the collapse of his country's banks; Joseph Stiglitz, the winner of the Nobel Prize for Economics in 2001, who in 2007 praised Hugo Chávez's management of Venezuela's economy, in 2010 advised Varoufakis as Greece plunged into crisis, and in 2014 encouraged the Scottish government to believe that an independent Scotland could flourish rather than collapse into bankruptcy, regardless of falling oil prices; and finally David Blanchflower, a former member of the Bank of England's monetary committee who in 2009 predicted that George Osborne's policies would push unemployment to five million (instead, nearly 800,000 new jobs were created in 2014 and unemployment fell to a

record low). In 2011 Blanchflower wrote: 'Britain now looks as
if it is headed back into recession … too bad the government is
in such deep denial.' The following year, Britain's growth was the
highest of the G7 nations.

Six weeks before the new Labour leader would be
proclaimed, Corbyn had become the outright favourite. 'It is
still probable that Mr Corbyn won't win,' wrote Philip Collins,
The Times's Blairite columnist. And anyway, 'if he wins, he will
soon be gone'. Collins, a member of Corbyn's Islington North
branch, could still not believe the mounting evidence that his
local MP had become the party's hero. 'It is hard to imagine,'
he wrote, 'a serious party doing anything more stunningly self-
harming than picking a reluctant leader running on a
programme that was out of date thirty years ago.' The truth
was hard to digest. Addressing packed meetings across the
country, Corbyn enjoyed a massive lead in the polls – over 20
per cent in some reports. 'It is pleasantly surprising, the way
in which the campaign has grown so fast,' he admitted. Yet one
poll reported that only 10 per cent of his supporters believed
that 'he understands what it takes to win an election'. In
interviews with the *Spectator*, critics spoke about 'the suicidal
charge of the red brigade'. 'Off a cliff and into oblivion',
predicted Jack Straw. 'Suicidal and madness', said Alan
Johnson. 'A potential catastrophe for Britain' and a 'car crash',
foresaw Alastair Campbell. Peter Mandelson called the
prospect 'Zimbabwe-style ruin', and 'the sad and possibly final
chapter' of Labour.

No Blairite wanted to acknowledge that Corbyn's popularity
was caused by revenge directed against them personally. New
Labour had created the crime of the Iraq war, while Corbyn had
championed the truth. 'The tribal Labour culture retains a
residual attraction,' wrote Collins in desperation. 'Labour won't
split or die. We are witnessing the prelude to paralysis.' To stave
off that fate, the *Guardian* urged its readers to vote for Yvette
Cooper, even though at that point only 7 per cent of its readers
supported her. Similarly, the *Mirror* ignored the evidence and
endorsed Andy Burnham. The editors of both newspapers knew

the truth, but could not bring themselves to acknowledge the horror. The MP for North Antarctica was heading for the winner's enclosure.

10

The Takeover

The climax of the four-month campaign was staged on Saturday, 12 September in the Queen Elizabeth Hall, Westminster. The few Labour MPs who attended looked morose. Dressed in black, the staff of Labour headquarters appeared similarly depressed. Only Jeremy Corbyn had the air of a satisfied man. Dressed in a dark suit and open-necked blue shirt, he spoke with conviction about the 'huge democratic exercise', then repeated himself over five minutes about the 'change' prompted by his victory. Just forty-eight hours before the official result was declared, his rivals had conceded to the landslide. Out of the 422,664 votes cast, Corbyn won 59.5 per cent, Burnham 19, Cooper 17 and Kendall 4.5. Just 0.5 per cent of Britain's population had resoundingly rejected Blairism. The Blairite MPs in the hall were jeered amid chants of 'Old Labour not New Labour.' 'The party is on a road to nowhere,' retorted David Blunkett, one of those present. 'It's a party deserting the voters.'

Fearing permanent destruction, the Old Guard shuddered at the inevitable move by Abbott, McDonnell and other Marxists from the back seats onto the front bench. Welcoming that prospect, Ed Miliband hailed 'a great opportunity for our party'. Writing in London's *Evening Standard*, David Hare judged Corbyn's supporters as 'united by a visceral loathing of David Cameron [who] belongs in a separate class of nastiness'. They voted for Corbyn, wrote the playwright, who occupied a large house in Hampstead, 'because he belongs so unequivocally to those who hate Toryism from the gut'. 'All piled in against Corbyn,' gloated Ronan Bennett, the pro-IRA Irish writer once employed by Corbyn, 'with frantic antics by Blair and Mandelson on the sidelines looking ever more ridiculous and irrelevant. And the joke ended up being on them.' Before leaving the building, Corbyn took a call from Cameron. He politely accepted the prime minister's congratulations and pledged to work with the government as leader of a loyal opposition.

At the nearby Sanctuary House hotel, supporters roared as their new leader arrived with Len McCluskey. In his speech to teachers, doctors and young professionals, the pale-faced victor held up a tea towel adorned with Tony Benn's face. As usual, he spoke about the Tolpuddle Martyrs, the Durham Miners' Gala, media intrusion, and giving power back to the trade unions. He embraced McCluskey, who had contributed money, accommodation and staff to his campaign, then sang his signature tune, 'The Red Flag'. He made no mention of reuniting the party. After bidding farewell, he joined a refugee solidarity march through Westminster. His next stop was Labour headquarters in Victoria Street. Eating a baguette and looking dazed, he walked through a silent crowd fearful for their jobs. Oblivious, he spoke to Iain McNicol, the party's general secretary. The two antagonists had little to say. McNicol acknowledged that the left was now within the citadel, but pointedly told the new leader that he was subject to the party's constitution. Corbyn nodded. He lacked the votes on the NEC to replace McNicol, but the party took second place to his 250,000 supporters. McNicol could wait.

Next he headed to Troia, a Kurdish restaurant on the South Bank, to join his family and about fifty allies. There he asked Tariq Ali, 'Did you ever think I'd be the leader of the Labour Party?'

'No,' replied Ali.

'Nor did I.'

In a speech to the gathering, Seumas Milne called Corbyn's victory 'a chance to change the balance of power and break open the political system'. Seizing control of Britain was the priority, he added: 'The challenge is to translate the insurgency into political power.' He was convinced that, because Labour had changed, Britain too had been changed, and 'for good'. All that stood in the way of total victory was the majority of anti-Corbyn MPs in the Parliamentary Labour Party. That hurdle would be cleared. Like Corbyn, Milne was dismissive of a snap YouGov poll reporting that a mere 17 per cent of the electorate believed Labour could win the next election, only 25 per cent trusted Corbyn to manage the economy and defence, and 50 per cent of those polled did not trust him at all.

'You're too nice to be leader,' Ken Livingstone told Corbyn. 'No one's scared of you.'

'John McDonnell will do all the scary stuff,' Corbyn replied.

By the time later that day that he was greeted in Islington by a huge crowd shouting 'Jez we can!' eight shadow cabinet ministers had resigned. He promised his supporters that his 'wonderful' party would deliver 'a more equal, a more decent Britain'. 'We want to install in Number 10 one of the best socialists,' said McDonnell. The meeting ended, yet again, with Corbyn's lusty, sincere rendition of 'The Red Flag'– an ensign shortly to fly over Britain.

Beyond Westminster, the Trotskyite Mark Serwotka shared the excitement: 'Corbyn needs six and a half million union members to ensure we have a vibrant campaign through strikes, demonstrations, occupations and everything else on the streets to topple this government.' Others spoke of adopting Marx's '51 per cent strategy': start on the extreme and recruit from the daft left, then the soft left, until finally you secure a majority.

The following morning, Corbyn rejected the BBC's request for interviews. Instead, he made his annual visit to the headquarters of the Camden and Islington Trust for mental patients behind St Pancras station. As usual on the trust's open day, he spoke solicitously to each patient, ignoring the media in the street outside. 'They're out to get you,' said a member of staff, referring to the Blairites. 'I know,' replied Corbyn. 'That's why I'm staying close to my friends.'

The following day, he made his way down the official opposition corridor at Westminster. To prove his purity, he chose to occupy a small office by a staircase rather than the large room usually allocated to the leader of the opposition. All the telephones, he ordered, were to be switched to answerphone. His staff were told to have no contact with the Tory whips, Downing Street or the speaker, all of whom, he explained, were bad people. The normal business of government and Parliament was junked. Next, he returned to Labour headquarters, where his team were provided with cakes and warm wine in the hope of silencing talk of a Corbyn 'coup' or a Blairite 'mutiny'.

The new leader's attempts at reconciliation soon evaporated. Back at Westminster, everyone was awaiting the announcement of his shadow cabinet. Discussions had started two weeks before the result, so Corbyn could promise the list within forty-eight hours of his election. Lenin would have expected him to act ruthlessly, but Milne told Russia Today, a favoured TV venue for his opinions, that although Labour MPs and frontbenchers were too right-wing, and 'there needs to be some recalibration' of the parliamentary party, it would not be 'in a bloodbath way'. Corbyn reluctantly agreed. Closeted with his new chief of staff Simon Fletcher, and Rosie Winterton, the chief whip, he had been persuaded to be placatory. 'For avoidance of doubt,' Milne said, in order to display the new leader's fluency in the art of wooing, his 'leadership will be about unity, drawing on all the talents – with women representing half of the shadow cabinet'. He added, 'We have won on the basis of policies, not personalities, without rancour.'

While Corbyn wrestled with the appointments, his office became chaotic. Telephones rang unanswered, messages remained unacknowledged and letters unopened, and arrangements for meetings disappeared because there was no diary. The few scheduled meetings that did take place were abandoned after Corbyn failed to appear, often because he was averse to making decisions. 'The atmosphere was fraught, tense and unhappy,' observed Harry Fletcher, 'because the staff were terrified of having power.'

Corbyn's first meeting with the PLP started in silence. 'Look, I know that I am not what all of you wish,' he told the sullen audience after a few words of thanks and a lame joke, 'but something amazing happened last week. I want to hear everyone's views.' Asked whether he would wear a pacifist white poppy to the Remembrance Sunday commemoration, he replied, 'I don't know what's going to happen this year.' That provoked heckles. His retort was familiar: 'I have never made personal insults or been rude about anyone, and if anyone is rude to me, I ignore them.' He sat down to some applause. Even his critics hoped that his promise of listening and promoting compromise would materialise.

The serial rebel who now demanded loyalty faced a Herculean task. Arch-Blairites including Tristram Hunt and Chuka Umunna morphed their Common Good group into 'The Resistance', and openly discussed how and when to trigger another leadership contest. Getting the necessary signatures – 20 per cent of the MPs – would not be a problem. 'The sooner the fightback begins the better,' wrote Roy Hattersley, a veteran of the successful battle to defeat Tony Benn in the 1980s. He knew better than most about Labour's litany of failed coups, yet even he was blind to the absence of an alternative moderate leader.

Several MPs resigned from the shadow cabinet, while others rejected the offer to serve. Some suspicious Members were lured by Corbyn's promise of a broad church. 'I don't know exactly where [he] will lead us,' wrote Tom Watson, elected deputy leader, 'but I'm looking forward to finding out.'

'Equivocate,' was Seumas Milne's advice. 'The Great Milne', as Corbyn described his adviser, suggested he should avoid sensitive issues.

'Can we speak about Trident?' one MP asked Corbyn.

'It's been nice meeting you,' the new leader replied, as ordered, and hastened away. His ambition to scrap Trident, Len McCluskey had warned, would be opposed by the trade unions. Unite's members built the submarines, and 40,000 members of the GMB union depended on the defence industry for their jobs. Compromise had featured little in Corbyn's life, but he now discovered that unless he made concessions to allow shadow cabinet ministers to oppose him on the EU, NATO and

Palestinian terrorists, the front bench would be half empty.

There were two other stumbling blocks. Many objected to McDonnell's appointment as shadow chancellor. 'If you appoint John,' a newly appointed adviser told Corbyn, 'you're going into the bunker and not reaching out. You're getting into factionalism.' The shadow cabinet, he insisted, needed balance. But Corbyn did not intend to reach out. McCluskey also urged that McDonnell should not be appointed, but Corbyn resisted. McDonnell was his counsellor and friend.

The second snag was Tony Benn's son, Hilary. 'He disagrees with you about everything,' another adviser told Corbyn. 'The EU, Trident, the Middle East and Russia. They're flash points. It's wrong to appoint him.' Once again, Corbyn resisted.

Assurances were offered, and from a mixture of motives Hilary Benn was appointed shadow foreign secretary, Andy Burnham shadow home secretary, and Lord Falconer, a Blairite, shadow justice secretary. Falconer accepted the role with misgivings, agreeing with Peter Mandelson that Blairites should wait before joining a coup. No woman was given a senior post, a failure criticised by Jess Phillips, the robust MP for Yardley. After describing the hours she had spent during the previous Parliament arguing with the government in the committee stage of the Welfare Bill to improve benefits and housing provisions, she loudly denounced Corbyn: 'I have never seen him rolling up his sleeves or doing anything to help. I have never seen Jeremy do anything but talk … He just made himself look good [by turning up to vote].'

Phillips understood Corbyn's antipathy to parliamentary committees. He had always disputed that change could be achieved through Parliament. 'All the shadow jobs are equally important,' he told Phillips about the absence of a woman in a senior post.

'Then why don't you just swap them all around?' she snapped back.

Diane Abbott rushed to Corbyn's defence. 'Don't be sanctimonious,' she publicly rebuked Phillips. 'You're not the only feminist in the room.'

'Fuck off!' Phillips replied. Sexism, racism and victimhood permeated the new leader's office.

Corbyn's debut at prime minister's questions came on Wednesday the following week. Dressed in a grubby jacket, creased trousers, a badly ironed shirt and a colourless tie, he entered the Commons chamber to sit between McDonnell and Abbott. Labour MPs were noticeably silent: not one cheered or offered encouragement. 'It was the first time I'd been on the front bench ever, in any circumstances,' Corbyn later reflected, 'and I looked around and the place was ram-packed. I'd never seen it so full, and I thought, "The majority of people here do not wish me well."' At the end of the thirty minutes he departed without glory but without serious damage.

Back in his office, he again struggled to complete his shadow cabinet. 'We're taking a fair amount of shit out there about women,' Simon Fletcher told him. 'We need to do a Mandelson. Let's make Angela shadow first minister of state.'

'Yes,' said another of those present. 'Do the Angela bit now.'

Embarrassingly, that conversation was overheard by journalists. Suddenly desperate to appoint one woman to a senior position, Corbyn made Angela Eagle his deputy, despite having neither respect for nor a relationship with her. That night he was filmed scowling at his humiliation, but he proved his authority by appointing McDonnell shadow chancellor. 'He's a very close friend of mine,' he said. 'He is a brilliant guy on economics and the ideas that go with it. I think it's very important that the leader and shadow chancellor are thinking in the same direction and we're certainly doing that.'

Others had different readings. David Blunkett believed that McDonnell's presence would mark a return to the 1980s. Back then, he recalled, there was 'thuggery, the attempt to intimidate, to bully, to manipulate the internal processes of the Labour Party in the interests of the few while proclaiming that this was for the benefit of the many'. There was a lesson, he warned: 'What we need to be aware of is the danger of the iron fist in the velvet glove.'

Len McCluskey denied that scenario: 'I am convinced that there will be no purges or witch-hunts, contrary to alarmist media speculation. Not only would that be against Corbyn's nature, it runs counter to [Corbyn's] intention to democratise Labour policymaking.' Everything in Corbyn's and McDonnell's past, McCluskey must have known, contradicted that assurance. And it was the past that caught up with both of them.

Corbyn first. Before his victory was confirmed, the *Jewish Chronicle*, on its front page of 12 August 2015, identified all the anti-Semites, Holocaust deniers and Palestinian terrorist representatives with whom he had associated. Stephen Pollard, the paper's editor, had previously called Carmel Nolan, Corbyn's media spokesperson, to ask the new leader to write an article about his commitment to anti-Semitism and his support for Britain's Jews. Corbyn rejected the offer. Pollard pressed Nolan. Why, he asked her, had Corbyn called Hamas 'our friends'? And why had Seumas Milne told a meeting in 2009 that Labour had a duty to support Hamas 'in a practical way' because Britain had committed a 'crime' in promising a homeland to the Jews? Did Corbyn endorse that opinion? Reluctantly, Nolan engaged. The result was the newspaper's publication on its front page of seven questions, together with Corbyn's replies. His answers were either outright denials or cop-outs. 'He's attended countless meetings,' was Nolan's explanation, 'and he cannot check the background of everyone he has met.'

Subsequently, the paper highlighted Corbyn's participation in October 2014 in a wreath-laying ceremony at a Palestinian cemetery in Tunis. Photographs showed him holding a wreath to be laid near the grave of three members of Black September, the terrorist group that had hijacked planes, murdered dozens of hostages and planted bombs across the West. Two of the group were particularly notorious: Salah Khalaf and Atef Bseiso had been the masterminds of the murder of eleven Israeli athletes and coaches at the Munich Olympics in 1972 – the carnage included the castration of an Israeli weightlifter. Other photos showed Corbyn holding out his hands in Muslim prayer, and later standing beside Maher al-Taher, a terrorist leader responsible for a series of murders including an axe attack in a Jerusalem synagogue one month later in which four rabbis had been killed. Some of the photographs had illustrated an article Corbyn had written for the *Morning Star* about the same trip. In his version, he had honoured the seventy-four victims of an Israeli raid on the PLO headquarters in Tunis in 1985. In both accounts, he represented himself as a peacemaker among Palestinians committed to killing Jews – although he refused to visit Yad Vashem, the Holocaust memorial in Jerusalem.

Pollard was not satisfied. In one of his replies Corbyn had said, 'I think to bring about the peace process you have to talk to people with whom you may fundamentally disagree.' Except that he did not disagree with the Palestinians. He had supported two of them who had detonated car bombs in London in July 1994. He had never wholeheartedly protested about Palestinian suicide bombers murdering Israelis. In further answer to Pollard, he replied that he could not be an anti-Semite because he was against racism and supported 'a more tolerant and kinder society'.

For years, most people assumed that Corbyn was honest, but that image had been contradicted by his welcome in 2011 to the fundamentalist Muslim Raed Salah, who opposed every universal human right, as 'a very honoured citizen' at a meeting of the Palestine Solidarity Campaign. Salah had been convicted in 2008 for racist incitement in Israel. Asked if he had made a misjudgement in meeting Salah, Corbyn replied, 'You're putting a lot of words into my mouth about misjudgements.' Describing the meeting, he explained: 'We had quite a long conversation about multi-faith objectives.' That was as questionable as his denial on BBC Radio 4 of having met Dyab Abou Jahjah at a Stop the War Coalition event in 2009. 'I do not know who this person is,' he said. The production of a photograph of the two in the House of Commons undermined that claim. Depicted as a friend of extremists, the man who prided himself on never losing his temper became noticeably irate for the first time in public. A new truth about Corbyn emerged. His nature was to reject any blame for an error. When exposed, he lost his temper.

'Until my dying day,' he said in an attempt to repair his image, 'I will be opposed to racism in any form.' But lying in the shadows were relationships with other anti-Semites. Corbyn did not anticipate the repercussions when they were exposed.

John McDonnell faced a similar reckoning over his enthusiasm for violence. He was asked about his praise of Ed Woollard, the student jailed for throwing a fire extinguisher at police in 2011, and the demonstrators who had 'kicked the shit' out of the Conservative Party's headquarters. 'John's tongue-in-cheek remarks,' one of his spokesmen explained, 'have been taken out of context.' Corbyn also defended McDonnell's remarks, although he did say, 'They are not the words I would use. I would prefer to use words that are parliamentary.'

Other illustrative past actions included a party in 2014 with the theme of 'killing' the royal family, which McDonnell had enlivened. As part of his guest speech, he told his fellow partygoers about a visit he had made to the Liverpool constituency of Esther McVey, a cabinet minister whose sin was to be a Tory. 'Why aren't we lynching the bastard?' he quoted a supporter as asking, and basked in the laughter. Asked about McDonnell's endorsement of a threat of violence to a woman, Corbyn just spoke about the party itself: 'It was a great event. I really enjoyed it.' McDonnell refused to apologise to McVey. He had no regrets, he snapped, for his 'honest anger'. As the reproaches accumulated, Corbyn tried to distance himself. 'I don't do personal attacks,' he said. 'I tend to see the best in people all the time. Is that a weakness? I don't know.' He also denied in a Sky TV interview that he had served on the Trotskyite *London Labour Briefing*'s editorial board in '1984 or later', contradicting the accounts of both Keith Veness and Reg Race, and the fact that his name featured in the paper as a member of the board.

Such reinventions caused complications. As the leader of the opposition, Corbyn received a pay increase of £58,000. His obligations included attending religious ceremonies, which he had always avoided. On the day after MPs heard that he might wear a white poppy on Remembrance Day, he was required to stand in the front row in St Paul's Cathedral at a service to commemorate the Battle of Britain. To be surrounded by servicemen, clergy and Britain's establishment in a public commemoration of the country's national identity was anathema to Corbyn. Moreover, a recently discovered video from 2012 revealed that he had told a small group that it would be 'wonderful' if the British Army were abolished. As a man with a sense of his own destiny, he was impatient with military heroes being hailed for symbolising the best of British values. At best, he thought, patriots should be consigned to the margins. 'I won't go,' he told his aides. After an intense argument with his closest advisers, he was finally persuaded that not appearing would be disastrous. None of them anticipated what would follow. Corbyn stood in the cathedral in stubborn silence, refusing to sing the National Anthem. He preferred to sing 'The Red Flag'.

Shortly after he left St Paul's, the media reported anger across the nation at his behaviour. His office immediately declared his pride in the Battle of Britain pilots, accompanied by a reference to his mother's endurance during the war. Few were fooled, not least because his parents spent the Blitz in the safety of Wiltshire. 'Has he killed us on Day One?' yelled McDonnell. 'John's in crisis mode,' admitted an aide. By then, several servicemen had mentioned how Corbyn, as he left the cathedral, had snatched sandwiches set out for the veterans, which he would eat on his journey to the TUC conference in Brighton.

Corbyn was flummoxed when he arrived at the conference. Unaccustomed to such high-level duties, he got lost behind the stage, walked late into the spotlight, then delivered a confused speech about the Tories as 'poverty-deniers', and an attack on Western capitalists' culpability for workers' injuries in Chinese factories. By the time he returned to London, his conduct in St Paul's was dominating the news. Unsympathetic newspapers had discovered a *Morning Star* column he had written in 2002 describing white Britons as reactionaries steeped in smug xenophobia. 'Football supporters singing "Rule Britannia",' he wrote, 'would not realise that they are parroting nineteenth-century imperial propaganda and racial superiority.' None drew the contrast with his enthusiastic rendition of 'The Red Flag', a murderers' anthem. But some did recall that his last speech in Brighton, near the site of the IRA's attempted murder of Margaret Thatcher, was to praise a Sinn Féin politician who had shot a British soldier during the Easter Rising in 1916.

To limit the damage, McDonnell took control. Trimming and repudiating his and Corbyn's past, essential to their survival, had become his speciality. Corbyn's silence in St Paul's, he explained, was the effect of being overcome by such a moving event. An interview was hurriedly arranged for Corbyn to say that he would sing the National Anthem on the next occasion. 'Of course I am a patriot,' he insisted. The firefighting coincided with his admission that he 'welcomed' members of revolutionary organisations, including Trotskyites and other banned extremists, into the Labour Party. 'I'm not concerned in the slightest,' he told a TV interviewer. The uproar intensified. 'Sorry, I didn't do well today,' he told his staff.

That evening, the past again caught up with McDonnell. A member of BBC TV's *Question Time* audience accused him of being an 'IRA terrorist sympathiser' for saying twelve years earlier that the IRA should be 'honoured' despite killing and injuring nearly eight thousand people. 'If I gave offence,' said McDonnell, 'and clearly I have, from the bottom of my heart I apologise, I apologise.' His intention, he claimed, had been to sustain the peace process, albeit by praising violence. 'I'm a plain speaker,' he said. To modify his image, he toned down his message. Until then, he had proposed to borrow an extra £500 million for industry and infrastructure. Now, to show that Labour would 'live within our means', he supported the government's 'charter for fiscal responsibility' and planned to eradicate the deficit. Labour's highest tax rate, he announced, would be 50 per cent rather than 60. That night, there was tumult in Corbyn's office. McDonnell's familiar machinations to conceal his true intentions had gone too far. He was ordered to recant. The following day, the façade was abandoned. 'You can't understand the capitalist system,' said McDonnell, 'without reading *Das Kapital*. Full stop.'

On day seven of his leadership, Corbyn wandered around Westminster exhausted and bewildered. Managing hostility was testing for a man unaccustomed to scrutiny, and whose skirmishes in Haringey bore no comparison to Westminster's all-out warfare. 'The Labour Party,' wrote the Lib Dems' Vince Cable, 'has chosen [a priest] with absolutely no idea how to realise what his congregation wants.' The *Guardian* columnist Owen Jones, an important ally of Corbyn's, had noticed in the run-up to victory that 'many felt anxious' about whether the new leader had the 'ability to take on such a demanding position'. Helpful advice, Jones would later lament, was being ignored. 'Terrible missteps played directly into the Tory narrative.' Corbyn's 'missteps' increased his vulnerability. Just fifty-one MPs were needed to start another leadership election, and he would certainly not find thirty-five to nominate him again. In the standoff, the moderates constantly discussed overthrowing Corbyn, but, still without an alternative leader, had failed to act.

For a man who required adulation, the anxiety produced by constant criticism became intolerable. In a new opinion poll, only 15 per cent of potential Labour voters described themselves as supporters of their leader. Corbyn looked to Milne and McDonnell for advice. His survival dominated their conversations. Milne was well aware that he was serving an indecisive man prone to change his opinion depending on whoever he had last spoken to. Corbyn's malleability played to his own strengths, but also required careful handling. Too many outside the room judged Corbyn 'thick'. At meetings, Milne sat expressionless when Corbyn asked the room nervously, 'What's wrong?' In response, there was silence. As Milne and McDonnell, both students of Lenin, understood, it was vital to be patient. Theirs was the art of proffering compromises to moderate MPs, while the National Executive resolved that every concession would be revoked once the danger of revolt receded.

To protect himself from a coup, Corbyn agreed to compromise over NATO, nuclear power, Trident, and welfare benefits. Contrary to his ideological antagonism towards the EU, he agreed to campaign to remain in the EU referendum that had been called for 23 June 2016, 'regardless of the outcome of David Cameron's renegotiation'. In the *Guardian*, Polly Toynbee, a high priestess of Blairism, hailed 'this unexpected Indian summer of warmth and comradeship under an auspicious red moon'. Although Toynbee and her newspaper opposed Corbyn's leadership, his swift makeover aroused no alarm. 'Details,' she wrote, 'are thin exactly on how he would balance the books … and why not? It's a long way to the next manifesto.' The *Guardian* praised his pledge to increase taxes to 'invest' in housing and welfare, although the paper's own £80 million investment in technology was contributing to its annual £60 million deficit. Reluctant to antagonise Seumas Milne, a friend of the editor, the paper supported his attack on the right-wing media's 'resistance to the democratic mandate' of Corbyn. Their character assassination, wrote Milne, amounted to treason. The nation, including the 11.3 million who had voted Tory in May, should applaud the wishes of 265,000 Labour supporters.

Few in the Labour Party, including some writers on his own newspaper, properly understood Milne's close collaboration with his leader. In the weeks after Corbyn's election, most outsiders were still unaware that Trotskyite groups were disbanding so their members could qualify to join Labour in targeted constituencies. Among those expelees returning to the party was Dave Nellist, a former Labour MP. Many came from Momentum. Their attempt to rejoin was supported by Len McCluskey, who saw the move as helping to purge the party of moderates – still unfinished business. Leaving his office (decorated with a large portrait of Lenin), the union leader set off to tell a meeting, 'We may lose some people along the way. All I can say to that is "Good riddance." I've got a little list here in my inside pocket with names of people I'd like to see go.' He was voicing the private thoughts of Corbyn, McDonnell and Milne. In public, all four spoke about a broad church and repeated the Brighton sermon about kindness. In private, they had begun to orchestrate a campaign of hatred on the internet. The conspirators were helped by the list of party members' names, email addresses and telephone numbers that had been handed to Jon

Lansman during the leadership election. It was now used by Momentum, Trotskyites, communists and McDonnell's Labour Representation Committee to flush out their foes. The first traces emerged in mid-October: Hilary Benn was voted off the NEC and replaced by Rebecca Long Bailey, a loyalist. Next, Corbyn supporters challenged moderate Labour councillors in Portsmouth, Lambeth and Brighton. Corbyn denied any responsibility. 'I want to make it crystal clear,' he told questioners, 'I do not support changes to make it easier to deselect MPs.'

His perfected trick was to appear above the fray, in no way involved in the dirty work undertaken by others. He relied on Momentum to politicise local problems, create dissent and, as Jon Lansman explained, develop the 'new politics made by Jeremy'. But, as Lansman adroitly added, while Momentum was 'incredibly supportive' of Labour, the group was 'not under its control'. Whatever the truth of that nice distinction, in a pincer movement between the party and Momentum, the coup to take over the party was under way. The showcase to rally the believers would be the annual conference in Brighton.

In its 115-year history, Labour had never faced a similar problem. On the eve of the hundredth anniversary of the Bolshevik Revolution, Marxism was derided in Russia for having caused misery to millions, yet Corbyn was heading for the party conference to preach the virtues of a discredited ideology. Undisguised Marxists had already arrived in Brighton to distribute leaflets demanding the 'intimidation' of Blairites, the 'reselection' of MPs, and, targeting one individual, the expulsion of Peter Mandelson as a 'traitor'. That label again.

Corbyn's conference speech would need to address a coalition of feminists, environmentalists, Europhiles, teachers and trade unionists – all repulsed by New Labour. United by defining themselves against others, they were attracted to their maverick new leader who spoke about democratic community participation, demolishing the leadership of personalities and empowering the grassroots against the political class. In what would be called 'a progressive alliance', they were the dispossessed angered by the cult of individuals, consumerism, markets and profits.

Their common purpose was to transform Britain irreversibly. The market economy would be destroyed forever. Corbyn's record was their lodestar. They were not concerned by his words at a rally at the start of the conference, when he had criticised the producers of the hit BBC TV show *The Great British Bake Off*, who had just sold the programme at a higher price than that offered by the BBC to Channel 4. As prime minister, Corbyn warned, he would ban both the sale of TV programmes to the top bidder, and the BBC from buying programmes from independent producers. This promise to return to the 1970s excited some of his new followers. Others demanded that he go further to 'democratise' the BBC, imposing the power of citizens and staff to dictate its policies and administration. Two years later, in a speech in Edinburgh, he duly argued exactly that.

In preparing for his conference speech, Corbyn planned to renege on the compromises he had made to his shadow cabinet. To crown his victory, he hoped to bind the party against Trident, since 'a nuclear-free world is a good thing'. He intended to proclaim that his election represented a mandate to remove the scourge of capitalism and to introduce 'a politics that is kinder, more inclusive'. He would promise 'a real debate, not necessarily message *discipline* all the time. But above all, straight-talking. Honest.' And, still thinking of the St Paul's debacle, he inserted into his speech a short paean of patriotism: 'I love this country and its people.' Reflecting his passion for Palestinian rights, he included a furious attack on human rights abuses in Saudi Arabia, but remained silent about the same horrors in Iran. He pledged that all schools would be brought back under the control of local education authorities. The party was certain to cheer his pledge to abolish parental choice. Since both he and McDonnell were educated at grammar schools, and Seumas Milne, a Wykehamist, sent both his children to selective schools rather than a nearby comprehensive, he preferred to skate over how children's education would be improved by returning to the failed model. The politics were more important than performance. For the rest, he adopted a speech written by Richard Heller, a freelance speechwriter, in the early 1980s that had been repeatedly offered to every Labour leader since Michael Foot, and always rejected as too extreme.

The mood in Corbyn's office in the days before his appearance was apprehensive. The media were certain to scrutinise his plan for the economy. Peter Kyle, the new Labour MP for Hove who had supported Liz Kendall in the leadership contest, had asked Corbyn, 'How does your economic policy differ from Ed Miliband's?'

'It's quite simple,' Corbyn had replied. 'I'm against austerity.'

Many laughed, until they realised that was the sum of his understanding. For the rest, he relied on McDonnell. Their friendship was being tested amid suspicion that the shadow chancellor was already plotting to inherit the leadership. A tell-tale sign was his creation of a separate office down the corridor at Westminster. Corbyn ignored the rumours of a prospective coup, not least because Seb, his twenty-five-year-old second son, was working for McDonnell, as was Andrew Murray's daughter.

Among those who doubted McDonnell's loyalty was Paul Kenny, the general secretary of the GMB union. 'Untrustworthy' was his judgement after experiencing McDonnell's aggressive manoeuvres to insert Trotskyists into the GMB's executive. That was exactly the failing that McDonnell intended to conceal. To distance himself from his *Who's Who* declaration of interests – 'fermenting the downfall of capitalism' – he intended to dress in a bank manager's blue suit and deliver judicious words in comforting tones, thus presenting himself as a trustworthy technocrat offering prudence rather than revolution. That image became more important after the emergence of a recording of a speech he had made to trade unionists in 2011, in which he could be heard encouraging his audience to spit in their employers' tea. Getting past such blips required reticence, but excited Marxists besieged him with advice. On the extreme end was Paul Mason, the former BBC TV economics editor, who was confident that Marx's prediction that capitalism was 'finished' was already proving true. In his opinion, Apple, Google and all the other privately owned technology corporations were destroying the world's economy. He urged McDonnell to advocate their dismemberment, accompanied by stimulated hyperinflation to destroy world debt. Also convinced that capitalism was on the brink of a worldwide crisis, Seumas Milne suggested that McDonnell make an outright pledge to cripple the City. To replace casino capitalism by state control, he believed, all banks should be nationalised so as to stop 'the transfer of wealth from the poor to the rich'. From the chaos, a new order would emerge.

McDonnell wholeheartedly agreed with both visions. By taxation and regulation, he wanted to destroy the City of London. To create pure Marxism, he would forsake the City's annual £70 billion profits and dismiss the 'class-ridden klepto-crats' who were managing Britain's financial services. Symbolically, he would move the Bank of England to Birmingham. Next, he would 'end' – or confiscate – the private ownership of production and property. Instead there would be 'public, co-operative and stakeholder ownership'. In *Another World is Possible: A Manifesto for 21st Century Socialism*, a sixty-four-page paperback, McDonnell described his plan to crush private share ownership and eliminate the 'unregulated, law-of-the-jungle, inherently class-ridden (capitalists) exploiting work-ers with low wages' while they pocketed £93 billion in unholy subsidies. He was unconcerned if the fat cats abandoned Britain and moved to New York or Singapore. To hasten their depar-ture, he intended to levy a so-called 'Robin Hood tax' on all the City's financial transactions. Those who remained would pay up to 70 per cent in income tax, plus a wealth tax and increased inheritance taxes. His targets, however, remained anonymous. He hated the lot of them. McDonnell could not name a single business mogul or Tory MP he respected. Above all, he told his staff, 'We're going to stuff Osborne.'

Umentioned was the French experience, which would accu-rately predict what such policies led to. After presidents François Mitterrand and François Hollande had imposed similar taxes, financial professionals had fled to London, causing a slump in France.

Before heading for Brighton, McDonnell had decided against spelling out his true agenda. Instead, he would promote a moderate rise in taxes to 'invest in infrastructure' and finance an 'Innovation Policy Council'. Whitehall officials would be trusted to outsmart Silicon Valley's free marketers to 'boost research and development spending' in technology. But his disguise went only so far. To please his followers, he could not resist inviting the world to recognise the genius of Karl Marx. McDonnell believed that the British would be inspired by the philosopher's prediction of the 2008 banking crash. In purposefully anodyne language, he lamented Marx's misfortune to be 'unfairly linked to brutal totalitarian regimes', and would urge his audience to sympathise with Marx's 'branding problem'. In another phrase he particularly liked, he would appeal for a mass movement of the far left, attracted to 'socialism with an iPad', and believing in his promises of increased welfare benefits, higher wages, a shorter working week and rent controls.

McDonnell gave his speech; it crashed. The audience disliked his monotone delivery, devoid of any bloodcurdling threats to capitalists. The angriest critics were Neale Coleman and Andrew Fisher, who let fly in Corbyn's Brighton hotel room. McDonnell, they complained, had failed to offer a Marxist analysis of the class conflict. After reading printouts from the internet, Corbyn had to agree. Surrounded by his Praetorian guard, he was genuinely angry.

'You've gone too far,' he told his friend. 'You sounded like George Osborne. Just read the *Guardian*'s report.'

'We need to be credible,' McDonnell replied, defending himself. Corbyn's purism, he said, was harming the party's chances of winning an election, and he urged him to fashion a deal with the Blairites. Diane Abbott, present as always to protect Corbyn, interrupted. Any change, she said, was unacceptable. McDonnell switched to immigration. To win more votes, he said, Corbyn should be less strident. Abbott interrupted again. On principle, she always disagreed with McDonnell – violent Trotskyists did not appeal to her – and on immigration she agreed with the new party line: no compromise. Corbyn was implacable. Their argument would continue until McDonnell surrendered. 'From now on, clear your speeches with Corbyn's office,' he was told.

To compensate for his shadow chancellor's equivocation, Corbyn stiffened his own speech, a team effort drafted by Milne, Coleman, Simon Fletcher and others, with an appeal to fight 'the forces of repression'. Despite the party's splits and the unconvincing brave faces of defeated Blairites on the platform, the mood of his audience was buoyant, and surprisingly receptive to the message that Britain was on the brink of disaster. The Tories were blamed for stagnating wages, dismal productivity, falling living standards and a growing deficit – up from £820 billion in 2010 to £1,500 billion in 2014: 'Some people have property and power, class and capital and even sanctity,' he told his followers, 'which are denied to the multitude.' The audience's standing ovation confirmed him in his righteousness, even if some murmured that the Conservatives had little to fear.

Steeped in the ways of Islington politics, Corbyn had for years represented people without savings and with low life expectancy. Less than 30 per cent of his constituents owned their homes, compared to over 65 per cent across the rest of the country. 'The British people don't have to take what they're given,' he repeated – six times – in his speech. He was thinking of the refugees in his borough, threatened by cuts to their benefits. Six weeks earlier, three thousand migrants, mostly from Libya, had attacked fences guarding the entrance to the Eurotunnel near Calais, causing thousands of lorries to be stranded in Kent and France. David Cameron had described the migrants as a 'swarm' across the Mediterranean; and Philip Hammond, the chancellor, cautioned that Europe could not protect itself from millions of 'marauding' African migrants who posed a threat to the Continent's standard of living and social structure. Outraged by such 'inflammatory' and 'scaremongering' language, Corbyn told his cheering audience to open their hearts to unrestricted immigration as 'nothing but a plus'.

Instinctively, he could not resist praising Venezuela as 'a cause for celebration'. Hugo Chávez's devastated country remained his model of a socialist idyll, glorified since the dictator's death in 2013. By following Chávez's path, he told the conference, Britain would be transformed. Not surprisingly, he omitted the latest effects of Chávez's populism: unemployment in Venezuela was rising, and as the government printed money to finance 'investment in infrastructure', inflation was heading towards 1,000 per cent. Immersed in a cycle of power cuts and rationing, Venezuela's hospitals had run out of medicines, infant mortality was rising, queues formed at 3 a.m. for basic food, and there was not even lavatory paper. Despite possessing the world's largest oil reserves, the country was being plunged into penury. As Margaret Thatcher said, 'Eventually, socialists run out of other people's money.' Corbyn ignored the evidence of Venezuela's spiral into darkness. Socialists, he repeated, must never flinch from the struggle. He had apparently forgotten his own homily, preached about fifteen years earlier: 'We should never forget our history, and learn from it.'

Sticking to the faith, he spoke about restoring Clause 4 of the Labour Party's constitution, to achieve 'the common ownership of the means of production, distribution and exchange', and an end to the private ownership of shops. Supermarket chains should be replaced by people's collectives. No one dared question his future agenda. They were focused on his more immediate plans, some of which they did not approve. The unions vetoed his promise of a debate about Trident, and others forced him to abandon an Iraq 'apology' by pointing to the hostility to such a move in opinion polls.

Then there was the continuing problem that Corbyn was an exceptionally poor speaker. During the unusually hectic preparations for his speech, he had been assured by Milne that the headlines would focus on his offer of socialism through 'a kinder, gentler politics'. His address, however, received very different coverage. 'As a piece of oratory,' commented the *Guardian*, 'it lay somewhere between mediocre and abysmal.' The Tory media dismissed Corbyn's familiar ramble; but unexpectedly, after the *Mirror*'s editor met him for thirty minutes, the newspaper tempered its criticism and predicted that the new Labour leader could one day be prime minister. The next opinion poll showed the opposite: Cameron was 24 per cent ahead. Tellingly, in 1980, one year after her first general election success, Margaret Thatcher's party had been 24 per cent behind Labour in the polls. Those who assumed Corbyn must feel vulnerable were mistaken. Journalists who were allowed to meet him during those days mentioned his 'arrogance'. He made no attempt to seduce or charm people he regarded with contempt. That particularly included journalists. All British newspapers, he judged, if not Donald Trump's 'enemies of the people', still peddled lies. He left Brighton combative, besieged, truculent.

The Tories, arriving in Manchester for their conference eager to celebrate the election of the first Conservative majority government since 1992, were relishing Labour's self-inflicted wounds. Diehard Tories could not understand the attraction of returning to the gruelling 1970s. Defeating Corbyn at the next election, wrote Tim Montgomerie in *The Times*, 'should be a cakewalk for the Tories because the middle class has too much to lose'. Few at the Manchester gathering understood the Labour leader's appeal to the millions of disillusioned people struggling against 'in-work' poverty, or that younger voters were untroubled by Corbyn's refusal to push the nuclear button.

Any Tory joy was anyway short-lived. The delegates became disheartened by George Osborne's promotion of the government as 'the builders', with a social programme to reduce inequality. Pushing Labour to the left was clever politics in a city without a single Tory MP or councillor, but it confirmed that Tory beliefs were unclear. 'I'm not a deeply ideological person,' Cameron had said in 2005, casting doubt on his principles. That doubt remained.

In his keynote speech, the prime minister played the patriotic card. After excoriating Corbyn's description of bin Laden's death as a 'tragedy' equal to the tragedy of over three thousand people in New York being murdered by terrorists, Cameron warned: 'We cannot let that man inflict his security-threatening, terrorist-sympathising, Britain-hating ideology on the country we love.' He was politely cheered. His oratory did not embarrass Corbyn, who was simultaneously addressing a demonstration in the same city. On the contrary, Corbyn's youthful audience bonded with him over their shared hatred of the establishment. Earlier that day, some of his audience had screamed 'Jewish Tory scum!' at delegates entering the rival conference. Others had sent online abuse to Blairite MPs, especially women. 'Kill yourself, you bigoted scum,' Jess Phillips was told. Corbyn stayed silent. Letting others attack his enemies was a win-win tactic. But to keep their support, he decided, required him not to betray his supporters by compromising his faith. On that score, appearances were critical.

As leader of the opposition, he was to be sworn in as a privy councillor. That required him to kneel in front of the monarch and swear 'by Almighty God to be a true and faithful servant unto the Queen's majesty'. As a republican, he believed that the monarchy should be abolished when the Queen died. His office told the palace that he refused to take the oath, an unprecedented snub. Instead of arriving at the palace on the appointed day, he authorised a spokesman to disclose that he had a 'prior engagement' – at his wife's insistence, he was on a walking holiday in Scotland.

However, unless he took the vow, he was ineligible to receive top-secret security briefings. One week later, he agreed to a compromise: he would swear the oath without kneeling, and would kiss the Queen's hand. Contrary to his pledge before his election, he also accepted a government car and a £58,000 pay rise.

He still had his principles, however, and drew the line at wearing the white tie and tails required for a state dinner at Buckingham Palace for President Xi Jinping of China. McDonnell and Seb Corbyn were summoned. 'You're the leader,' said McDonnell. 'We can't have arguments about things that don't matter.' Seb joined in: 'We've got a case to be made to the British public. We can't be diverted by these trivia.' At first the great leader was implacable. 'No,' he said. 'People would say that I've sold out to the establishment.' But gradually his resistance was worn down. A tape measure was produced and an aide, Gavin Sibthorpe, was dispatched to hire the necessary outfit.

'I'll wear it if I can cycle to Buckingham Palace,' said Corbyn defiantly.

'You can't,' said an aide, 'because there won't be enough time. You're meeting Xi first, and the dinner follows after that. You can't get back and change.'

At the last moment, Corbyn fell into line. Six months later, he showed he had learned his lesson, and effusively congratulated the Queen in the Commons on her ninetieth birthday.

In anticipation of the Labour leader's meeting with Xi, the Chinese ambassador had visited Corbyn's office at Westminster to be briefed. Corbyn, he was told, wanted to raise human rights and steel-dumping. On the day, both issues were duly raised, but Xi's inscrutable face gave Corbyn no clue as to whether he was being taken seriously. Xi must have been perplexed by his explanation of Labour's 'future direction'. Thanks to its embrace of capitalism, China was now remarkably prosperous, yet Corbyn intended to abandon capitalism, the foundation of Britain's wealth.

Laura Corbyn had played no part in the 'white tie' saga, but now she stepped in on the matter of her husband's wardrobe. On her orders he appeared at prime minister's questions in a dark suit, a clean light-blue shirt bought at House of Fraser, and a red tie. His beard was trimmed. That November, dressed to look like the other attendees, he wore a red poppy to lay a wreath at the Cenotaph, and sang the National Anthem. The result was mixed. In the next opinion poll the Tories were at 37 per cent, with Labour just five points behind; but Cameron's approval was at 41 per cent and Corbyn's at 22. The poll results coincided with the formal appointment of Seumas Milne as Labour's director of communications and strategy. His arrival had been complicated by lengthy negotiations over his pay-off from the *Guardian*, and the question of his new title. Charming and pleasant as a colleague, he was proudly inflexible as a Labour theoretician.

Milne introduced ideological discipline to Corbyn's office. Suspicious of Neale Coleman and Simon Fletcher, he objected to their nomination of Sarah Owen as Corbyn's political secretary. Her two supporters had chosen the soft-left former adviser to Alan Sugar to build bridges between Corbyn and three crucial groups – MPs, moderate trade unions and the NEC. Milne persuaded Corbyn and McDonnell to appoint Katy Clark, a hard-left bruiser, instead. Clark was expected to reach out to the party's leftist hard core and to distrust the rest. To assist her, Corbyn appointed the Trotskyist Andrew Fisher, who was advised to delete blogs describing his enthusiasm for violence.

Clark's arrival aggravated the office chaos. Meetings arranged to start at 9 a.m. were delayed because no one arrived until eleven, and some staff, without explanation, did not come to work at all. 'They were lazy and pissed on £100,000 a year,' said a member of Corbyn's team. If, by chance, sufficient numbers had arrived by midday, the next hurdle was to find Corbyn. People were dispatched around Westminster, calls made and scripts prepared. The leader, his aides discovered, lacked the mental agility to chair a meeting without a clear brief of what he was to say. In an attempt to end the shambles, Simon Fletcher listed a series of topics to be discussed before the end of October. Every one of them would still be outstanding the following February. The problem was not helped by the stubborn refusal of Nicolette Petersen, Corbyn's personal secretary, to move into his new office. She liked her old one, and Corbyn refused to order her to move: demanding obedience was still foreign to him. To some, sanity prevailed only when Laura Corbyn arrived with food and dispensed sympathy to those with complaints. Although not knowledgeable about politics, she understood her husband's way of life and his inability to care for his staff.

The prospective rebellion against Corbyn simmered until, just two weeks after the Brighton conference, moderate Labour MPs exploded. The cause was McDonnell's announcement – on Corbyn's orders – to reverse his support for the government's budget. Without explanation, McDonnell committed Labour to borrow-to-spend, the old Gordon Brown strategy. He also denounced Labour MPs who voted to deny welfare benefits to illegal immigrants. Over twenty of them refused to go along with McDonnell's somersault. 'Embarrassing, embarrassing,' he had to admit in the House. 'A shambles,' said a moderate MP at the next PLP meeting, conjuring the image of McDonnell drunkenly lurching from pillar to post. 'You're like a student union president,' Ian Austin rebuked Corbyn. 'Being a leader means you have to *lead*.'

11

The Purge

Labour's moderates were reluctant to propose an alternative leader until they were confronted by the ultimate moral quandary – a question of life and death. In the aftermath of more atrocities in Syria, a number of Labour MPs intended to support the government's proposal to bomb the perpetrators. To prevent more suffering, argued Jo Cox, the British Army should intervene, as it had in Bosnia, Kosovo and Sierra Leone. As an opponent of the army, Corbyn replied that he would never support military action. The establishment struck back. General Nicholas Houghton, the chief of the defence staff, declared on TV that if the Labour leader became prime minister he would worry about the credibility of Britain's deterrence. Corbyn protested at Houghton's prejudice. 'It is essential in a democracy,' he said, 'that the military remains politically neutral at all times.' Constitutionally, he was right – except that since he was an extra-parliamentary agitator himself, his stance was hardly convincing.

Four days later, his position became more difficult. At 9.51 p.m. on 13 November, a Reaper drone guided from Nevada fired a Hellfire missile over Raqqa in northern Syria, seven thousand miles away. The target was Mohammed Emwazi, alias 'Jihadi John', a British Muslim member of ISIS who had boasted on video about beheading two British hostages. Emwazi was vaporised. Cameron described the death of the 'barbaric monster' as 'self-defence'. The spotlight switched to Corbyn. He had never publicly expressed any outrage about Emwazi's crimes, and two years earlier had called drone strikes against ISIS fighters 'an obscenity'. Executing those murderers, he believed, was wrong. Now he repeated that killing Emwazi was obscene, and 'the ultimate in sanitised warfare'. (It was unclear what was wrong in making warfare sanitised.) Bringing him back to Britain for trial, he said, would have been 'far better'.

'Look,' tweeted the Labour MP Ian Austin, with deep sarcasm, 'why couldn't the police go and arrest Emwazi? It's not as if it's a really dangerous war zone and I'm sure he'd have come quietly.'

The ridicule bounced off Corbyn. If only the imperialist West had not interfered in Muslim countries, he said, there would be no bloodshed. 'A succession of disastrous wars,' he planned to say at a conference, 'has increased, not diminished, the threats to our own national security.'

On the eve of making that speech, late on Friday, 13 November, he was told that a Muslim group had carried out a series of attacks in Paris, killing 130 people and wounding hundreds more. Ninety had died while attending a rock concert at the Jewish-owned Bataclan theatre. Among the dead were the disabled, shot while immobilised in their wheelchairs. Corbyn's first response was to complain that the massacre was getting more media coverage than the effects of a simultaneous bomb blast in Beirut. Some were surprised by his reaction. After twelve journalists were slaughtered in the office of the satirical magazine *Charlie Hebdo* in Paris in January 2015 for publishing a derogatory cartoon of Mohammed, Corbyn had tabled a motion in the Commons expressing his sympathy for the journalists. Ten months later, he had evidently had second thoughts. After hearing details of how the French police had shot dead the seven Muslims responsible for the Paris murders, he sat through a series of meetings over the weekend to consider his response. 'We needed time to think hard about how to look sensible,' recalled an adviser. Charlie Faulkner, Angela Eagle, Hilary Benn and other shadow cabinet ministers were summoned. By Sunday night Corbyn finally announced, 'We must condemn the attack and go to the French embassy to show solidarity.'

The following day, Seumas Milne arrived at the office. Corbyn, he declared, must do the circuit of TV studios in Millbank. Corbyn obeyed, but, unwilling to disappoint his supporters, in his fifth successive interview, he vented his true feelings on the BBC: 'I'm not happy with the shoot-to-kill policy. Surely you have to work to try and prevent these things happening.' Shooting gunmen, he said, even as they killed innocent people, was 'quite dangerous', 'counter-productive', and would lead to 'war on the streets'. The real blame, he continued, lay with the West's interventionist wars. Western imperialism had produced 'the people's poverty' in Muslim countries, and, he implied, it was the West that was to blame for the mayhem in Paris. At Scotland Yard, police chiefs questioned whether Labour was on their side. 'Has it not come to something,' Cameron asked the House of Commons, 'when the leader of Her Majesty's Opposition is not sure what the police's reaction should be when they are confronted by a Kalashnikov-waving terrorist?' There was no obvious solution to Corbyn's predicament. Although the invasion of Iraq, and other Western wars in the Middle East, had undoubtedly caused damaging repercussions, his extreme inflexibility lost him credibility. Accordingly, his demand for an apology from Cameron was ignored.

Isolated in his office, Corbyn feared that he was 'being pushed off his pedestal'. That night, Monday, 16 November, there was silence as he entered the PLP meeting. Blaming the West for Muslim poverty when Arab dictators had squandered trillions of dollars of oil revenues over the previous sixty years was too rich for most Labour MPs. Asked three times whether he would in any circumstances approve drone strikes in national self-defence, Corbyn refused to answer. Finally he replied that he would need to read the legal advice. However, if a massacre like that in Paris occurred in Britain, he would refuse to authorise the police to shoot to kill. Nor would he support bombing ISIS in Syria. The MPs erupted. Desks were banged, and Corbyn was shouted down. 'You're a fucking disgrace!' one Member yelled. 'It's perfectly reasonable,' Hilary Benn told his father's one-time protégé, 'to shoot to kill where there is an immediate threat to life.'

Corbyn's sole defender was shadow employment minister Emily Thornberry, who epitomised those who snobbishly mocked the white working class. She didn't help. 'It's like a virus taking the party over,' said one mutinous MP after leaving the committee room.

Corbyn was supported by the Stop the War Coalition. On its website, the group described the Paris attack as 'reaping the whirlwind of Western support for extremist violence in the Middle East'. When asked about that statement on BBC TV, Corbyn replied: 'I wouldn't use that language' – but he did endorse the sentiment. To John Woodcock, the Labour MP for Barrow and Furness, Corbyn's stance was the same as 'blaming the Jews for their deaths under the Nazis'. Corbyn, his face impassive, was unwilling to make any concession. Moral predicaments were alien to a Trotskyist. Events would not reduce his sympathy for any Muslim seeking to defeat the West. In his mind, force should never be used to stop the objectives of IRA, Palestinian or ISIS terrorists. Yet, at Milne's request, Stop the War's description was removed from the website – not because it was wrong, said Andrew Murray, but because of 'how it could impact on Jeremy'.

Murray, Len McCluskey's chief of staff, had been a committed communist from a young age, and his admiration of Russia remained undimmed. He had invited Boris Kagarlitsky, a Putin spokesman, to address a rally on 27 August 2014, at which he denied any Russian involvement in the shooting down of Malaysian Airlines Flight MH17 over Ukraine the previous month. Kagarlitsky also denied the presence of any Russian troops in Ukraine, or indeed any Russian interference in the country. Since Milne sympathised with that opinion, he found no difficulty in arranging for Murray's employment as an assistant in Corbyn's office along with Andrew Fisher. Ostensibly, the two appointments were intended to improve efficiency, but in reality the party had reached a new crossroads. At Corbyn's request, only trusted communists and Trotskyists would be employed in his office to manage the PLP. All that stood in the way of a complete takeover was the party's National Executive Committee. In a desperate last gasp, Blairite MPs demanded that the NEC investigate Fisher. Ken Livingstone was outraged:

To consolidate his authority across the Labour Party, Corbyn has appointed among his closest advisers in the leader's politburo Seumas Milne (above), a committed Marxist, and Andrew Fisher (right), a lifelong communist.

As a pacifist, Corbyn claimed that he was seeking peace in the Middle East during his regular meetings with a succession of radical leaders and preachers. In 2013 he met Ibrahim Hewitt, a Hamas supporter, in Gaza. Hewitt approved stoning adulterers to death and lashing gay men.

In 2014 Corbyn laid a wreath at the 'Cemetery of the Martyrs of Palestine' in Tunis. Laid on the tombs of PLO terrorists, not their victims, the wreath's 'martyrs' included the nearby grave of the mastermind of the murderous attack on Israeli athletes at the 1972 Munich Olympics. 'I was present when [the wreath] was laid,' Corbyn later said. 'I don't think I was involved.' He added, 'I don't share platforms with terrorists,' belying the countless photographs of him alongside Irish, Palestinian and other supporters of violence.

After the Muslim attacks on the United States in September 2001, Corbyn forged an alliance with the Muslim Association of Britain, an anti-Semitic group linked to Hamas. Corbyn made the Rabaa sign at an annual feast jointly hosted by the MAB.

In 2009 Corbyn invited Muslim extremist Dyab Abou Jahjah (above centre) to Britain to publicly denounce Israel, America and Britain. Soon after their meeting in the Commons, Corbyn spoke about 'our friends from Hezbollah and our friends from Hamas', both terrorist groups promoting violence in the Middle East.

In 2000 Corbyn contributed money to Deir Yassin Remembered, a group organised by Paul Eisen (right), a Holocaust denier and anti-Zionist. Although Corbyn attended several DYR meetings with Eisen until 2013, after his election as Labour leader he would deny knowing Eisen.

Few wield more influence over Corbyn than Len McCluskey (above right), the Unite trade union leader, waving the Palestinian flag at Labour's 2018 conference. McCluskey inserted into Corbyn's office Unite's chief of staff and lifelong communist Andrew Murray (above left, also waving the flag) as an adviser; Karie Murphy (below left), his partner and mother of his son, as office manager; and his former partner Jennie Formby (below right) as Labour's general secretary.

Corbyn had a contradictory attitude towards Saddam Hussein – defending the dictator's invasion of Kuwait in 1990 and opposing the destruction of his factories producing lethal weapons. However, his opposition to Tony Blair's 2003 invasion of Iraq established his credibility beyond the far left.

At the invitation of Ihsan Qaesr (below left), an exiled Kurdish activist living in Islington, Corbyn travelled in July 1991 to Iraqi Kurdistan soon after Saddam Hussein had killed many Kurds in a series of gas attacks. Despite showing Corbyn 'unforgettable' scenes of desperation, Qaesr recalled, 'I was frustrated by Jeremy's refusal to support military retaliation and the military defence of safe havens for the Kurds.'

Corbyn questioned in 2012 the removal by Tower Hamlets council of 'Freedom for Humanity', a mural by Kalen Ockerman, an American artist. A snapshot glance revealed to Corbyn the familiar caricature of Jewish financiers, here playing Monopoly on a board supported by naked blacks – a Marxist depiction of the worldwide Jewish conspiracy against the world's oppressed.

In 2018 anti-Semitism within Labour provoked an unprecedented protest in Parliament Square, with placards reading 'Enough is Enough'.

After Luciana Berger, a Jewish Labour MP, exposed Corbyn's sympathetic protest to preserve Ockerman's mural, she required police protection at the 2018 Labour conference from violent abuse by Corbyn's supporters. Louise Ellman MP's lonely campaign after 2001 against the far left's anti-Semitism resulted in gross intimidation by Corbynistas. Ian Austin emerged in Westminster as a vociferous critic of Corbyn's ostensible anti-Semitism.

'Beware the fury of a patient man,' warned John Dryden, the seventeenth-century poet. Corbyn's strategy in 2019 is patiently to await the Tory party's self-destruction over Europe and enter Downing Street as Britain's saviour.

'The people driving this are trying to undermine the leader who has just been elected, and that's completely unacceptable.'

At that moment, in advance of Iranian-armed Hezbollah troops invading Aleppo in north-western Syria, Russian planes were bombing militias opposed to President Assad – or, as the *Morning Star* reported, the city was being 'liberated'. Rebel positions, including hospitals, were hit by napalm, chlorine and barrel bombs (a crude device consisting of an oil drum filled with explosives, typically dropped from a plane or a helicopter). Defending Russia, Milne accused critics of diverting attention from American 'atrocities' against ISIS. His 'moral equivalence' was shared by Corbyn, who opposed any reference to 'Russian aggression' in the party's briefing notes. Peace, he said, depended on Russia's victory and 'opposing the West'. If Assad were defeated, Corbyn and Milne feared, a pro-American, pro-Israeli government would take over in Damascus. Both discounted the anger of exiled Syrians living in Britain towards the supporters of Assad's war, and both depicted the fundamentalist jihadists as resistance fighters. Neither would consider any compromise with Labour MPs, who Corbyn ruled would be denied a free vote, while the party would also oppose Britain bombing ISIS. His edict raised the temperature. Two years earlier, before the first vote about bombing Syria, Corbyn had preached that 'A free vote is the right thing to do.' Now, his fellow MPs fumed, the rebel was demanding their loyalty. Corbyn's habitual mutinies had been tolerated because he was of no consequence. Now the leader was rebelling against his own party – a battle to be won.

On 17 November, MPs gathered in the Commons to hear David Cameron speak about the Paris murders. To indicate that he would not be cowed by the surrounding hostility, Corbyn sat slumped on the front bench, looking at his mobile phone and yawning ostentatiously. 'You do not protect people by sitting around and wishing for another world,' said Cameron. Behind the scenes, in a display of his influence, Milne explained that Corbyn would support shoot-to-kill if it were 'proportionate and strictly necessary'. Of course, that was not necessarily true

– but the impression of his advisers struggling to accommodate their leader's noble principles did not harm Corbyn, although every step was fractious, especially on that day.

A ceremony had been arranged at that night's football match between England and France at Wembley to honour the victims of the Paris massacre. Corbyn turned down his invitation from the Football Association. 'I've promised to attend a residents' AGM in Islington,' he said, 'and I won't let them down.' Whether he was genuinely concerned for his constituents or unsympathetic to the French victims is uncertain. 'They'd want you to go [to the match],' said Seb of his Islington constituents, despairing that his father did not understand a leader of the opposition's duties. Twenty minutes before the deadline, Corbyn finally agreed to attend.

Within hours, that concession was eclipsed on the news by his appointment of Ken Livingstone to review the party's policy on Trident submarines. By then Livingstone had retired from front-line politics to care for his young children while his wife studied to become a teacher. A few warned Corbyn about the danger of entrusting the ex-London mayor with any authority. His reputation as a politician was mixed. Some applauded him as a charismatic populist adept at exploiting situations by telling people what they wanted to hear: 'Consistency is grossly overrated,' Livingstone had once said. Others on the left disliked his propensity for evasion. Tony Banks and John McDonnell, Livingstone's former allies at the GLC, had long ago labelled him a 'dodgy politician' and a 'cynical manipulator'. 'He's clever enough to deceive people without them knowing it,' Banks had observed. Corbyn did not agree. 'Ken,' he said, 'is disliked because he's famous outside Parliament. There's a personal loathing of Ken that isn't rational.' With that, he set aside Livingstone's reputation as a loner and opportunist who joined his own gang, not other people's. He felt sure that he could trust his old colleague, and did not disown Livingstone's controversial public statements: that Western propagandists had lied about Stalin's murders of millions of innocent people; or that Tony Blair, rather than the four Muslim bombers, was responsible for the deaths of fifty-two people in London in July 2005. At the end of a brief conversation the two men agreed that Livingstone's defence review would recommend the cancellation of Trident and Britain's withdrawal from NATO.

Corbyn's loyalty, however, was soon tested. Kevan Jones, the shadow minister for the armed forces, criticised the appointment. Livingstone instantly retaliated: 'I think he might need some psychiatric help. He's obviously very depressed and disturbed. He should pop off and see his GP.' Jones had spoken publicly about suffering depression. 'It doesn't matter what disorders he's got,' scoffed Livingstone when asked to apologise for his 'gravely offensive' slur. Eventually, he did show limited contrition, only to explain a few hours later on a TV appearance with Jones that he had apologised only because Corbyn opposed 'all the offensive backstabbing and rows'. John Mann weighed in, telling Livingstone 'You're an appalling bigot' on his live LBC radio show. Corbyn was unmoved, not least because he shared Livingstone's disdain for Mann and Jones, both of them 'red Tories' destined for removal by Momentum. And contrition had no place in an outright battle for power.

Moderate MPs hated McDonnell even more than they did Corbyn. The latest investigations had produced evidence of the shadow chancellor's endorsement in April 2015 of the disbandment of MI5, special police officers and the armed police. At first McDonnell robustly denied making that pledge, but his lie was exposed by a photo showing him smiling to the camera and standing by a placard published by the Socialist Campaign for a Labour Victory which was committed to abolishing MI5 and the military. The revelation put more pressure on Corbyn.

Under the headlines 'Corbyn's Leadership Explodes' and 'Corbyn's Nuclear Nightmare', the media predicted that he wouldn't survive. According to Philip Collins in *The Times*, 'The end of his leadership is now only a question of when, not whether.' 'So this is what it looks like when a political party dies,' wrote Dan Hodges in the *Daily Telegraph*. 'It's no longer a question of "if" but "how", not "whether" but "when",' agreed Rachel Sylvester in *The Times*, describing the terminal breakdown of trust between Corbyn and his MPs. 'This is definitely the end,' wrote Janet Daley in the *Sunday Telegraph*. Even Len McCluskey criticised Corbyn for failing to give proper leadership and instead perennially saying the first thing that came into his head.

To add to Corbyn's plight, George Osborne laid an ambush. In his autumn statement, the chancellor unexpectedly hit Tory voters by increasing taxes on businesses and councils, increasing government spending and cancelling cuts to tax credits. The lurch to the left took McDonnell by surprise, but rather than changing his script, he mocked Osborne in the Commons for wooing China in the hope that it would invest in Britain's new nuclear power stations. In a theatrical gesture, holding aloft Mao's *Little Red Book*, he advised the chancellor to read it before selling state assets to Chinese corporations. He then tossed the book over the dispatch box. Osborne laughed, but McDonnell was serious. Labour MPs were stunned by the unvarnished exhibition of his communist ideals. At Corbyn's request, Diane Abbott waded in. Mao, she said, deserved praise for 'doing more good than harm'. Endorsing a dictator responsible for the deaths of an estimated seventy million Chinese deepened the divisions among Labour MPs and the gap between Corbynistas and the electorate. The Tory lead over Labour increased to 15 per cent.

The crisis of Corbyn's credibility was discussed at a meeting of the NEC. Patrick Heneghan, the party's election guru, explained that Labour's white working-class voters were unhappy about their leader's refusal to sing the National Anthem, meet the Queen, and even to protect them from terrorism. The result would be a loss of seats in the May council elections, particularly in Scotland. That judgement was disputed by Kezia Dugdale, the youthful new leader of Scottish Labour. Although overwhelmed by popular support for the Nationalists, she saw hope for a limited recovery. SNP politicians were proving to be dishonest, and were failing to manage schools, the police and the construction of housing. But instead of supporting Dugdale, Corbyn gave the impression of not caring. He had refused to visit Scotland during the independence referendum in 2014, made careless mistakes about the ownership of Scottish railways and the defence industries, and encouraged Momentum to batter the moderate Dugdale for her failure to embrace the far left's agenda. There could be no compromise with the right wing. To Labour MPs he seemed on a death mission – but they were in for a surprise.

Towards the end of November, Heneghan's message and the humiliations at Westminster were neutralised by a YouGov poll which found that Corbyn's popularity among Labour members had increased to 66 per cent, while less than 20 per cent said he should resign. The chance of a putsch was reduced. Dutifully, the NEC asked MPs to show their loyalty. The effect of that request was to be judged on 26 November. The litmus test was Corbyn's attitude towards ISIS.

In the Commons, Cameron set out the case for bombing Syria: 'We do face a fundamental threat to our security. We have to hit these terrorists in their heartlands right now.' But he had his own rebels: twenty Tories threatened to vote against the government. The prime minister needed Labour support.

'My socialist heart opposes war,' Corbyn replied. The public, he knew, preferred non-involvement, and some agreed that Tony Blair should be prosecuted at The Hague for his role in the invasion of Iraq.

'I'm accused of being a war criminal for removing Saddam Hussein,' replied Blair, 'who by the way was a war criminal – and yet Jeremy is seen as a progressive icon as we stand by and watch the people of Syria barrel-bombed, beaten and starved and do nothing.'

Labour MPs were split. 'Inaction has a cost in lives,' Hilary Benn told Corbyn.

The stakes were raised by Diane Abbott's intervention. In his absence she entered Corbyn's office and sat behind his desk. Once he returned, she demanded that he impose a three-line whip against the bombing. He agreed. To make sure that he did not waver, she announced on the spot that she would appear on TV to announce Labour's opposition. 'She squished Labour into a corner on it,' recalled an eyewitness.

Hilary Benn was appalled. Rather than be forced to bow to

Abbott's demand, he told Corbyn, he would resign as shadow foreign secretary, a threat he followed up with other sharp messages. 'What will my friends think?' Corbyn asked repeatedly, uncertain whether he should impose a three-line whip or allow a free vote. Unwilling to debate further with his MPs, he continuously asked Milne how he should reply to Benn's numerous notes to him. Any answer was complicated by Milne's habit of rewriting Benn's memos before Corbyn saw them. Infuriated by such interference, Benn arrived in Corbyn's office for face-to-face shouting sessions with Milne. With their disagreement unresolved, the battle escalated to a personal confrontation between Benn and Corbyn. Corbyn became noticeably tense, grinding his teeth as sweat formed on his brow. The appointment of Benn, he realised, had been a terrible mistake. Not only was he a destabilising influence, but his aide Imran Ahmed, Corbyn fantasised, was organising a plot to remove him. Ignoring Benn's denials and protests, Corbyn declared that the death of innocents was preferable to compounding the West's invasion of Iraq and the original sins of colonialism. ISIS, he repeated, should be asked to negotiate 'a ceasefire'. Refusing to destroy the murderers put his fate once again on a knife-edge. In turn, Benn was warned by McCluskey not to 'play with fire' and attempt to stage a coup. But at least Benn did not resign.

Much should have depended on Tom Watson, the deputy leader. In 2006 he had become famous as a ruthless fixer for successfully plotting on Gordon Brown's behalf to accelerate Tony Blair's resignation. That reputation had recently unravelled after glaring errors of judgement. He had generated national newspaper headlines by asserting that 'clear intelligence' existed of a 'powerful paedophile network' in Westminster, involving child abuse, torture and murder by politicians and other establishment figures. Among the many named as paedophiles by Watson's now discredited source were former Tory home secretary Leon Brittan, Field Marshal Lord Bramall and Edward Heath. All his allegations would prove to be entirely false, the product of malicious fantasists. Those gross defamations marginalised Watson's threat to Corbyn that a whipped vote on Syria would provoke a revolt by dozens of MPs. 'It is the leader who decides,' Corbyn told BBC TV, satisfied that his critics were fragmented. And as for his decision? 'I will make up my mind in due course.'

Contrary to his promise in September, Labour's policy would not be decided by discussion. Abbott again insisted that Corbyn impose a three-line whip: a free vote would signal weakness. To mobilise support, the Stop the War Coalition pronounced that ISIS embraced the spirit of 'internationalism'. The ISIS militia who threw gays off roofs in Raqqa, said Corbyn's allies, were no different to the socialist volunteers who had fought in Spain against Franco. Extreme events required extreme remedies. Corbyn was not troubled by equating socialists with Muslim fanatics, nor was he concerned by Momentum's new round of threats. Those MPs disloyal to him, Momentum made clear, would find 'no hiding place', and would face compulsory re-selection. To tone down these comments, Corbyn told Channel 4 News: 'Any selection, reselection or deselection is at least three years away.' Few were persuaded by that reassurance in the countdown to the Syria vote, set for Wednesday, 2 December.

'Very draining,' admitted a member of Corbyn's inner circle over that weekend. On Saturday, Corbyn was unwilling to telephone any of the rebels. Personal persuasion had never been his style: everyone, he assumed, was as stubborn as himself. Milne insisted that Benn should face an ultimatum: surrender or resign. But before Corbyn left his home for Westminster on Monday morning, Milne admitted that their position was weak, and that instead of threatening Benn they might need to fashion a compromise. Outside Corbyn's house was a group of journalists. 'You're very rude, the way you behave,' he barked at the mute photographers. Stepping into his official car, he was clearly nervous.

He entered the shadow cabinet meeting at 2 p.m. 'I'm not going anywhere,' he told his enemies around the table. Every MP would have to decide whether to obey the whip or risk deselection. 'Disgraceful!' shouted one voice. 'You can't throw us to the wolves!' exclaimed Andy Burnham. A number demanded that

Corbyn not impose the whip. Abbott urged him to fight on. Rather than face more abuse, he abruptly got to his feet and left the room. Back in his office, he emailed MPs and party members that he opposed 'bombing Syria'. His choice of words was deliberately distorting. Cameron was proposing only to bomb ISIS positions, not the Syrian population in general. But Corbyn's enemies kept pressing. Once again McDonnell persuaded him that nothing would be gained by staging an open fight at that moment. The reality of a large-scale rebellion was confirmed by Rosie Winterton, the chief whip, and by the end of the afternoon Corbyn capitulated. His surrender unleashed the cyber bullies to spew a barrage of hate on the internet against the rebel MPs. The compromise worked out with Benn was straightforward: Corbyn would open the debate, explaining his opposition, while Benn would speak at the end to support the government.

In the debate, Cameron described Corbyn, Milne and their associates as 'a bunch of terrorist sympathisers', but his argument that the bombing would support an army of 70,000 moderate Syrians lacked credibility. Corbyn's reply was predictable. The unexpected highlight was Benn's oratory. In an impassioned speech urging that 'fascists need to be defeated', he established the moral high ground. The Commons erupted in cheering. Skewered, Corbyn sat stony-faced amid the acclaim for Benn. Then, in a display of petulance, he refused to move so his adversary could sit down. As usual, he could not tolerate a challenge, especially from his mentor's son. 'Parliament,' Corbyn snapped, 'is supposed to be serious. It's not a place for jingoistic cheering.' Despite Momentum's intimidation, sixty-six Labour MPs voted to bomb ISIS. Although the majority of Labour MPs supported Corbyn, he was bruised by a government majority of 174. Within minutes of the vote, Andrew Murray and Lindsey German encouraged their supporters to trash the disloyal MPs as 'warmongers' and (again the overstatement) 'traitors' ripe for deselection. Corbyn's threats, retorted the rebels, had made them 'a target for home-grown jihadists'. Even 'Bomber Benn' was not safe from Corbyn's militants. Tosh McDonald, president of Aslef, compared him to Hitler. To calm the argument, John McDonnell issued a warning: 'There is no place in political life for threats or abuse and we will not tolerate them.' No one took his words seriously; they reeked of hypocrisy.

For a brief moment, Corbyn's fate again hung in the balance, but days later he was saved. A by-election was held in Oldham, the first of the Parliament, caused by the death of the long-standing Labour left-winger Michael Meacher. Those predicting doom and dismay were trounced by Momentum activists and Corbyn's Muslim supporters. On a 40.3 per cent turnout, Labour won with a handsome majority of 10,835 votes, with Ukip beating the Tories into second place. Corbyn's alliance with the Muslim Brotherhood had paid a rich dividend, yet no one mentioned Labour's tolerance of misogyny during the campaign. At election meetings in Muslim areas men and women had been strictly segregated; Muslim women complained that Labour would not let them stand in council elections; and Corbyn remained silent when his supporters made sexist attacks on female MPs.

Five days later he travelled by Eurostar to Paris, where he had been invited to address four hundred environmentalists and trade unionists about climate change.

'What's your big argument?' he had been asked two weeks previously by his speechwriter Josh Simons. 'What do you want to say?'

Corbyn looked forlorn. 'What do you think, Seumas?' he asked.

'This is a key moment,' replied Milne. 'It involves the big corporations and their influence on the world.'

'Great,' replied Corbyn, relieved that something suitable could be prepared. However, as he read the draft of the speech, he became dissatisfied. 'There's a lot about markets,' he said, clearly confused about the political choice between relying on the state to improve the climate and relying on the marketplace. Disgruntled, he looked at Milne. 'Now's not the right time to engage in that,' soothed his adviser, to calm him. 'We need to be crowd-pleasing.' He allowed the word 'market' to remain in the

speech, not anticipating that it would continue to unsettle
Corbyn, always resentful of ideas he disliked. While addressing
the audience in Paris, he found difficulty in saying 'market' out
loud. Stumbling over the word, he lost track of his speech, abandoned the script and went off on a ramble about the threat of
extinction to certain species of fish at the bottom of the sea.
Sensing the audience's restlessness, he then reverted to slogans
about equality, justice and socialism. To his surprise, the crowd
cheered. Even better, the celebrated American activist and
writer Naomi Klein appeared from the audience and enthusiastically embraced first Milne, then Corbyn. That evening, Klein's
reassurances over dinner in a brasserie gave Corbyn reason to
feel that he had escaped without any damage. His safety net was
always the company of sympathetic admirers.

Accordingly, on 11 December Corbyn went to Stop the War's
Christmas party in a Turkish restaurant in Southwark. He
arrived with John Rees, a Trotskyite who had publicly
pronounced that the ISIS executioner Mohammed Emwazi had
been an 'extremely kind' and 'beautiful young man' until MI5
turned him into a murderer. Corbyn was welcomed by a standing ovation led by Lindsey German and Andrew Murray.
Surrounded by his own kind, he praised Stop the War as 'a vital
force at the heart of our democracy'. To further cheers, he criticised 'unjust wars'. (He meant Britain taking on ISIS in Raqqa,
not Assad bombing his opponents in Aleppo.) Before leaving,
he offered his Breton hat to be auctioned – it sold for £270. That
party was very different to Labour's own Christmas celebration
a few days later – a sulky standoff between warring factions
exchanging bad jokes.

The split over Syria did not damage Labour. Most Britons had
decided that the bombing would make their own country less
safe. A ComRes poll placed support for the Tories at 37 per cent,
down 3 per cent, and Labour up 4 per cent at 33. Corbyn's problems were that on the economy the Tories were 41 per cent
against Labour's 18, and his personal approval rating was only
29 per cent. 'I'm not going anywhere,' he said before flying off
for a holiday in Malta with his wife. She insisted he needed a

rest, while Corbyn could never resist an opportunity to board a plane to escape office routine and strife.

Two weeks later, a poll showed that while 60 per cent of the electorate as a whole were critical of Corbyn, 60 per cent of Labour voters approved of his performance. The Blairites despaired. Peter Hyman, a speechwriter for the former prime minister, wrote at the end of 2015, 'This is the biggest existential moment in Labour's history.' The party's existence as an alternative government, he lamented, was in doubt. While Labour was credible as the Ukip of the left, Corbyn would never win more than 28 per cent of the vote in an election, the same as Michael Foot. Not enough electors believed in pacifism, republicanism and anti-capitalism. 'Millions of Britons have been left stranded without a political home,' Hyman concluded.

Corbyn saw it differently: Labour's natural voters had recovered their party from the Blairites. Fired up, he returned from holiday determined to eradicate the last of that breed. Working from 'Taking Control of the Party', a document produced by Katy Clark and Jon Lansman, he summoned those he judged guilty of 'incompetence and disloyalty' to his office. Top of his list for dismissal were shadow defence minister and supporter of Trident Maria Eagle, chief whip Rosie Winterton, and Hilary Benn. During endless meetings, Milne particularly demanded Benn's dismissal. 'He wants revenge,' observed one member of the inner circle. To reduce the fallout, a newspaper was briefed that Benn was to be fired.

At this point Tom Watson re-entered the battle. In Corbyn's office, he directed his attack at the leader. To protect Corbyn, Milne interrupted him. 'Shut up,' snarled Watson. 'It's not up to you. You weren't elected.'

Eventually, several MPs were fired or resigned, but not Winterton or Benn, the latter agreeing not to oppose Corbyn openly. 'I haven't been muzzled,' he insisted. 'Sacked by Jeremy Corbyn for too much straight-talking, honest politics,' tweeted Michael Dugher, the shadow culture minister and a working-class MP. Pat McFadden, the Labour spokesman on Europe, was also fired, the fall guy for Benn. Unusually, McDonnell came clean about the dismissals. They were clearing out 'a narrow right-wing clique' that was pursuing a 'right-wing Conservative agenda'.

'You're comparing us to the British National Party,' John Woodcock told McDonnell in the voting lobby. 'You're a disgrace.' The shadow chancellor refused to apologise. Once again, some MPs discussed a coup against those in the bunker, while others predicted that Labour would be out of office until 2030.

In the fallout, Maria Eagle was replaced by Emily Thornberry. The CND-supporting Thornberry was accused by Labour MPs of knowing nothing about defence. She replied that since her brother-in-law Major General Richard Nugee was a 'top soldier', she could master her brief. Next she said that Trident was as outdated as the Spitfire, because drones could spot the submerged submarines. She was wrong, but within Labour that was irrelevant. Ninety per cent of the party's new members supported Corbyn's attendance at a CND rally against Trident. Only trade unionists were unimpressed. Paul Kenny, the general secretary of the GMB, reminded Corbyn that unilateralism had divided Labour in the 1950s and had kept the party out of power for thirteen years; 46 per cent of the country was in favour of Trident and only 28 per cent against. The party conference, said Kenny, and not Corbyn, would decide whether to keep the weapon. Even McCluskey told Corbyn to his face that Livingstone should be removed from the defence review and Trident should not be scrapped. Corbyn made an even more arbitrary compromise than usual: the submarines could go out on patrol, but without their nuclear missiles. At the end of the week he blamed the atmosphere of indecision on his 'great failing in life' – letting everyone talk. Some thought he could have mentioned other failings, but no one doubted his real ambition – to secure unchallenged power.

Mid-January 2016 was the moment those around Corbyn decided to ratchet up their takeover plans. Neale Coleman, an efficient organiser as Corbyn's head of policy, was judged by Milne to be too keen to collaborate with MPs. For his part, Coleman found the infighting and communism within the leader's circle intolerable. After a series of arguments provoked by Milne, he resigned. Intentionally, Milne also clashed with Simon Fletcher, Corbyn's chief of staff since the leadership election. Without discussion, Milne had approved a fly-on-the-wall documentary by Vice Films featuring himself and Corbyn. On discovering that the production was under way, Fletcher predicted that the result would be 'a huge embarrassment'. Milne replied that Corbyn needed to 'cut through the mainstream media'. The result proved Fletcher right: Corbyn and Milne were exposed as manipulative and impetuous. By then, the factional skirmishes started in 2015 could only be resolved brutally.

McCluskey inserted his live-in partner Karie Murphy into Corbyn's office. Murphy, a niggling bully but with a flash of humour, had been the gatecrasher in the failed vote-rigging scandal orchestrated by Unite in Falkirk. Unashamed by that debacle, McCluskey offered Corbyn a deal: if Murphy were employed as his office manager, Unite would pay her salary. In obedience to his paymaster, Corbyn acquiesced. Among Murphy's first victims was Jon Trickett, Labour's election supremo. Next was Simon Fletcher. To undermine him, Murphy habitually altered the items he had listed on Corbyn's monthly strategy meetings. In a matter of weeks, to McCluskey's satisfaction, Fletcher resigned. His replacement, Corbyn announced, would be 'a fantastic person', namely the soft-spoken Trotskyist Andrew Fisher.

The continuing campaign to remove enemies was directed from Corbyn's office. Milne, Karie Murphy and James Schneider – a new assistant co-opted from Momentum and educated, like Milne, at Winchester and Oxford – 'anonymously' briefed 'outriders' on the internet – social media websites including The Canary, Aaron Bastani, Novari Media and Squawk Box – to disparage those like Emilie Oldknow, who resigned in disgust from Corbyn's office after arguing with Milne, going on to work for the right-wing trade union Unison. Young Corbynistas, the 'outriders' knew, relied entirely on social media for their information, and would approve their mockery of Oldknow with the question 'When did you ever stand on a picket line?'

The vitriol was energised by Momentum, by then employing permanent staff and, strengthened by McCluskey's money, lobbying for places on the NEC. Among those selected to influence the new Labour Party was Michael Chessum, an organiser of the 2010 riots at Millbank. Chessum condemned Remembrance Sunday as 'murderers holding special funerals for their victims'. He demanded the 'exorcism' of the Labour Party and the deselection of what he called 'aristocratic' MPs. His ally was Cecile Wright, who described the 2011 riots in Nottingham as 'an uprising targeted at the police'.

Momentum's steering committee included a group of women suspended from the party, among them Jill Mountford, a member of the Trotskyist Alliance for Workers' Liberty. In 2010 Mountford had stood against Harriet Harman, who she described as a 'chemically pure Blairite apparatchik personally responsible for many of the government's attacks on the working class'. Five years on, she urged the expropriation of banks and the abolition of immigration controls, the monarchy and MI5 – very much the Milne list. Another unsmiling leftist was Christine Shawcroft. With Corbyn, she still supported Lutfur Rahman, the mayor of the London Borough of Tower Hamlets, even after his conviction for corruption and electoral fraud. Alongside Shawcroft was Marsha-Jane Thompson, convicted for forging electoral forms and sentenced to a hundred hours' community service; and Jackie Walker, an overt anti-Semite. 'To protect Jeremy's leadership', McDonnell helpfully told these women, Labour's 'compliance unit', which had excluded Trotskyites for 'spurious reasons', would be closed down. Endorsed by Corbyn and McDonnell, all three re-entered the Labour Party. Among other returnees were the Trotskyist trade union leader Mark Serwotka and Christine Blower, the general secretary of the National Union of Teachers who had stood as a Trotskyist against Labour in GLC elections.

All understood Corbyn's priorities. These were, first, to transform Britain into a genuinely multicultural country. 'I don't think too many migrants have come to Britain,' Corbyn said during a visit to 'the Jungle', a makeshift camp outside Calais for migrants attempting to enter Britain illegally. Unlimited numbers of migrants, he urged, should be encouraged to cross the Channel. MPs sponsored by Unite echoed his rejection of any restriction until 'saturation level' was reached. 'What does it matter if we have to wait another week for a hospital visit?' asked Rachael Maskell about admitting unlimited numbers of refugees. 'Or if our class sizes are slightly bigger? Or if our city is slightly fuller? Surely it is worth it to see those lives being restored again?'

Second, Corbyn found a new voice with which to attack the police. Just thirty-one years after the Broadwater Farm riots, he appointed Kate Osamor as Labour's new equalities spokeswoman. Osamor, the daughter of Martha Osamor, a close ally of Corbyn's among Islington's immigrant community during the 1970s, had asserted that Mark Duggan, a professional criminal linked by the police to ten shootings and two murders, had been 'targeted [with all Tottenham's residents] for a concerted attack by the repressive forces of the state'. Duggan had been shot dead by the police in Tottenham in August 2011 while under surveillance for being in possession of a gun. Osamor's scathing distrust of the police appealed to Corbyn until, two years later, she was accused of nepotism. Without revealing that her son had been convicted of serious drug offences, and subsequently lying about the extent of her knowledge, she sponsored his nomination and election as a Haringey councillor, and also employed him as an assistant at the Commons. Corbyn would initially refuse to take any action, but then accepted her resignation so she could spend more time with her family.

Third, Corbyn supported a political strike by junior doctors despite the possible harm to patients. Ostensibly the dispute was about reforming the NHS model created in 1948. The Tories had pledged to impose a new contract on doctors to provide improved seven-day care. The purpose, said health secretary Jeremy Hunt, was to end the waste of unused equipment over weekends and reduce the risk to emergency patients. Most employment contracts in Britain stipulated that Saturday was a normal working day, so there was no reason for doctors to receive special treatment. In Hunt's proposed contract, the junior doctors would lose overtime payments on Saturdays, but in compensation their employment would be cut from nine-ty-one to seventy-two hours a week, and basic pay would increase by 13.5 per cent. The British Medical Association, the doctors' trade union, opposed all those changes. The govern-ment, the BMA protested, was endangering the NHS, would undermine patient safety, increase stress, especially for women doctors if they were pregnant, pave the way for privatisation, and cut doctors' pay by 30 per cent. Under the control of Momentum, the BMA organised a series of strikes and threat-ened to withdraw emergency care. In a video for Socialist Appeal, Yannis Gourtsoyannis, a BMA negotiator, said: 'The Conservative government must fall. Lives depend on it.' Thereafter, Gourtsoyannis met the union representatives of teachers and rail guards at the National Shop Stewards Network (NSSN) to discuss joint action against the government. Linda Taaffe, NSSN's secretary, was a member of the Trotskyist Socialist Party and an executive of the National Union of Teachers, which was run by Christine Blower, a Trotskyist agita-tor. 'Now is the time to ramp things up,' said Gourtsoyannis. 'We need to defend Corbyn and show the government the door.' At a rally in Brighton, Sean Hoyle, a rail union leader, said that NSSN's task was to defeat 'this bloody working-class-hating Tory government'. To weaponise doctors against the govern-ment, McDonnell appeared on the picket line at St Thomas's hospital, the first time Labour had officially supported a strike. Consistent with his support for all strikes, Corbyn also endorsed the doctors' strike, despite the speciousness of the BMA's complaints.

An aggressive intolerance had been introduced into British politics. Most assumed the prejudice was confined to the class war – socialists versus capitalists. But they were mistaken.

12

The Jew-Haters

Few Labour MPs were more troubled by Jeremy Corbyn than Louise Ellman, elected in 1997 for Liverpool Riverside. A soft-spoken mother of two, she was born in Manchester and had joined the party at eighteen. It was seldom mentioned that Ellman was Jewish: at Westminster and in her constituency, her religion was irrelevant. That changed after Corbyn's election. The membership of her constituency soared from five hundred to 2,700, and at meetings the Corbynistas harangued her about Israel and Zionism. Older party members were disgusted by the anti-Semitic abuse. 'It's pretty nasty,' Ellman reported to party headquarters in London. She blamed the revived Militant faction, reincarnated as Momentum, for plotting to deselect her. No one at headquarters acknowledged her concern, which did not surprise her.

Ellman's predicament had arisen soon after the creation of the Stop the War Coalition in 2001. She was among the first to protest against its anti-Semitism. The criticism of Israel and Zionism was couched in language markedly similar to the myths parroted over the previous two thousand years about Jewish wealth dominating the world. Jeremy Corbyn had been seen at its annual Al-Quds (the Arab name for Jerusalem) event opposing Israel's existence, mingling among Palestinians distributing magazines featuring cartoons portraying Jews with large noses pulling the strings of puppet politicians, media moguls and bankers. 'Rothschild' was written on one 'banker' to illustrate the worldwide conspiracy of Jewish finance. The Nazi swastika adorned other placards to signal anti-racism.

Newspapers, Ellman discovered, both national and local, were reluctant to report her complaints after a leader of the Muslim Association of Britain, a branch of the Muslim Brotherhood, threatened a libel action following her denunciation on Radio 4 of the group's anti-Semitic activities. Just before Christmas 2003, she addressed an empty House of Commons about the 'rising tide of anti-Semitism'. Jews were being targeted as the tiny elite who had stolen the wealth of the masses. With their removal the world would be a better place. To the sympathetic understanding of former foreign secretary Robin Cook, she blamed Islamist groups for 'inciting racial hatred' against Jews under the guise of anti-Zionism. She named the leaders of the Muslim Association of Britain, all of whom were connected to Hamas or other terrorist organisations, for promoting the image of a Jewish global conspiracy. They had been invited to speak in Parliament and at British universities to threaten Israel with extinction, she said.

The reaction to her speech shocked her: 'I was regarded as a freak.' Letters published in the *Guardian* denounced her for identifying Muslims as anti-Semitic. The paper endorsed the complaint that all dispossessed Muslims were the victims of Zionism. At Westminster, several MPs shunned her. At the door of the Commons chamber the veteran Labour MP and out-spoken anti-Zionist Gerald Kaufman, himself a Jew from Manchester, snapped, 'Shut up. You sound like "Here we are, the Jews again."' In anger, Ellman shouted back at him. 'You need a long cup of tea,' Kaufman snarled. Anti-Semitism, he implied, was the Jews' own fault. Ellman assumed he wanted to please Muslim electors in his Manchester constituency. The hatred against her intensified. Israel was 'wagging the American dog', Corbyn wrote in the *Morning Star*. He was heard by a member of his staff mocking Ellman as 'the Honourable Member for Tel Aviv' – an allegation he later denied. Jewish students in a number of universities were suffering the same persecution.

Aggressive Muslim students, especially at the School of African and Oriental Studies (SOAS) in London, ignored Britain's established tolerance of free speech by threatening

Jewish speakers. The students called Jews 'Zios' and, comparing Israel with Nazi Germany, denounced its citizens as white supremacists living in an apartheid state 'intent to wipe out the Palestinian race'. Any defender of Israel was dismissed as racist, and the more extreme supporters of Hamas demanded that the country should actually be destroyed. Encouraged by leaders of the Stop the War Coalition, 'anti-Zionism' became interchangeable with anti-Semitism. By contrast, for instance, no one blamed 'Russianism' for the illegal occupation of large parts of Eastern Europe after 1945. 'Zionism' was used as a euphemism for 'Jews'. That conflation accelerated after 2010, under the leadership of Ed Miliband, who was himself Jewish. Ellman, for one, was unconvinced by Miliband's denial that there was a problem, and noted that his mother was an anti-Zionist. Equally disturbing to her was the refusal of other Jewish MPs, including David Winnick and Margaret Hodge, to attempt to counter the new persecution. 'I always felt alone,' she lamented. 'I had to rely on Tory MPs.'

By 2012 she had become aware that Jeremy Corbyn, sitting on the highest bench at the back of the Commons chamber, often spoke in favour of the Palestinians and against Israel. That year, at a time of intense fighting between Hamas and Israel around Gaza, he repeatedly protested about Israeli brutality, without mentioning provocations by Hamas or atrocities committed by Muslims against fellow Muslims. However, Ellman had no personal knowledge of his attitude towards Jews outside the Israeli conflict. She had not heard about 'Freedom for Humanity', a large mural that had just appeared in east London. The vivid image, painted by Kalen Ockerman, an American artist known as 'Mear One', portrayed Jewish financiers playing Monopoly on a board supported by the naked backs of the world's oppressed – mostly blacks. Even after a brief glance, no one could fail to grasp the familiar caricature of grotesque-looking Jewish bankers engaged in a worldwide conspiracy to manipulate subjugated slaves. The mural perfectly illustrated Malcolm X's damnation of 'Zionist dollars' bankrolling colonial oppression, an important influence in Jamaica at the time of Corbyn's stay there in the 1960s. After protests, Tower Hamlets council ordered the mural to be scrubbed out.

The matter came to Corbyn's attention. Looking at the mural on his computer, he saw rich white Jews, international power-brokers, exploiting oppressed blacks. Immediately he protested against the mural's removal 'on the grounds of free speech'. He also wrote to Ockerman, 'You're in good company,' referring to the removal of a mural by Diego Rivera in New York back in 1934: 'Rockerfeller [sic] destroyed Diego Viera's [sic] mural because it includes a picture of Lenin.' He apparently did not think twice about making what seemed to him an unexceptional remark about a class enemy. Except, to avoid accusations of anti-Semitism, he referred to Jews as 'Zionists' – although he had never publicly drawn a distinction between the two terms when voicing in public meetings his outrage at the treatment of Palestinians in Gaza. On those occasions he effortlessly lapsed into anti-Semitic language, convinced that a backbencher's prejudice would not attract attention beyond his loyal audience.

In that vein, soon after he had approved Ockerman's mural, he spoke without inhibition at a meeting of the Palestinian Return Centre (PLC), a group known to blame the Jews for the Holocaust. Among his audience was Manuel Hassassian, the Palestinian Authority's representative in Britain. In an unusually light-hearted manner, Corbyn addressed the difficulty British 'Zionists' experienced in coping with an alien culture. 'So clearly two problems,' he summarised. 'One is that they don't want to study history and secondly, having lived in this country for a very long time, probably all their lives, they don't understand English irony either … so I think they need two lessons which we can help them with.' Jews had lived in Britain since at least 1656, yet in making such statements Corbyn was employing classic anti-Semitic tropes describing otherness. The Wandering Jew, a cosmopolitan unaligned to any nation, was the age-old stereotype. Corbyn would never criticise any other religion in the same language.

With that mindset, he was unsurprised two years later, in February 2015, to hear that 'Zios' had been banned from Oxford's gay and lesbian clubs. The paradox was that Israel protected homosexuals, while in some Muslim countries they were murdered. Oxford's anti-Semitism came to a head after Corbyn's election as Labour leader. 'Some members,' Alex Chalmers, the co-chair of the university's Labour Club, wrote, 'have some kind of problem with Jews.' This anti-Semitism, Chalmers noticed, was driven by Marxists, in particular two Momentum activist members of the club: Max Shanley, a friend of Jon Lansman, and James Elliott, a contributor to Corbyn's youth manifesto.

After unsuccessfully seeking help from senior Labour officials, Chalmers resigned from the party. Iain McNicol, Labour's general secretary, asked Jan Royall, an academic and former Labour leader in the House of Lords, to investigate. On the basis of eyewitness testimony, including that of Labour Youth's representative on the NEC Jasmin Beckett, about James Elliott's anti-Semitism, Royall highlighted individual prejudice worthy of further investigation. 'I was dismayed and ashamed,' she wrote, 'that the ancient virus of anti-Semitism had infected our party.' Nevertheless, she concluded that endemic loathing did not exist in the club. In the final version of the NEC's report, Corbyn's political secretary Katy Clark removed all Royall's references to proven animosity towards Jews. Even with those omissions, Corbyn ordered that the report should not be published. Concealment, he agreed with Milne, would close down the problem. Shanley and Elliott were acquitted by the NEC of racism, but Jasmin Beckett was not protected, and Corbyn loyalists demanded that she be expelled from the party. Bombarded with verbal violence for telling the truth about an anti-Semite at her first NEC meeting, she needed Tom Watson's protection to escape the Corbynistas' intimidation. In December 2015 Louise Ellman mentioned Oxford's hostility in the Commons. Corbyn dismissed her protest. He abhorred anti-Semitism, he said, without explaining why he was targeted by so many allegations.

Among the casualties were members of his own family. His brother Piers criticised the calls for a crackdown on anti-Semitism within Labour as absurd. 'My brother isn't wrong,' said

Jeremy Corbyn, 'and actually we fundamentally agree.' Then his youngest son Tommy was revealed as the events manager of York University's Palestinian Solidarity Society: his group was celebrating 'Israel Apartheid Week' with a play called *Seven Jewish Children*, described by the *Spectator* as a 'ten-minute blood libel'. Tommy also failed to delete a series of violently anti-Semitic statements posted by others on his Facebook page until he was prompted to do so by the media.

Unsure how far the virus had spread, Jewish groups began to fight back, probing John McDonnell's record to discover that he too was tolerant of anti-Semites. In 2012 he had appeared on a platform with Gerry Downing, a Trotskyist who demanded that 'the Jewish problem' of Zionist Jews ruling the world should be addressed. With McDonnell's help, Downing had become a Labour Party member, and had appeared on BBC TV as the party's representative to complain that a 'number of millionaires and billionaires of Zionist persuasion within the American ruling class and within the European ruling classes in general' were committing 'heinous crimes' against Palestinians. Years before, in 1985, when McDonnell had been co-editor of the *Labour Herald*, the paper had compared Israelis to the Nazis and supported Palestinian terrorist attacks against Israel as the consequence of 'the racism at the heart of the Israeli state'. Like Corbyn, McDonnell was not overly troubled by anti-Semites in the party, although he did suggest that Labour must 'sit up and listen' to the concerns of Jews. To reinforce that impression, in the post-2015 makeover McDonnell's office had removed the links on his web page to 'Innovative Minds', a site that praised the Islamist suicide bomber who in 2001 had killed twenty-one Israelis in a Tel Aviv nightclub, one among many Palestinian attacks on Israeli civilians.

In 2014 Vicky Kirby, a Labour parliamentary candidate, had been expelled from the party after she tweeted, 'What do you know about Jews? They've got big noses and support Spurs. LOL.' She also wrote that Jews 'slaughter the oppressed', and that Hitler was 'a Zionist god'. Corbyn agreed that Kirby should be readmitted to the party. Soon after, she became a vice chairman of the branch in Woking. Once her past was exposed, Corbyn reluctantly conceded that she should be suspended. Kirby looked forward to having that suspension raised after Benazir Lasharie, a Labour councillor in Kensington and Chelsea, was readmitted despite blaming Jews and Zionists for the 9/11 attacks on America. The party's new tolerance also benefited Khadim Hussain, a former Labour mayor of Bradford who had complained on the internet that Britain's schools 'only tell you about Anne Frank and the six million Zionists that were killed by Hitler'. Aysegul Gurbuz, a Labour councillor in Luton, tweeted in 2011 that Hitler was the 'greatest man in history', and hoped that Iran would use a nuclear weapon to 'wipe Israel off the map'. Two years later she tweeted, 'The Jews are so powerful in the US. It's disgusting.' She too was temporarily suspended. To Corbyn's frustration, Iain McNicol prevented him exercising any control over the party's disciplinary procedures.

For all his denials, Corbyn collaborated with anti-Semites. He had accepted £2,000 from Ibrahim Hamami, a London GP and a Hamas sympathiser, who applauded the stabbing of Jews and denied that Israel had the right to exist. Corbyn wrongly registered the donation in the Commons, and refused to explain what he did with the money. In 2013, Middle East Monitor (MEM) funded a trip for Corbyn and his wife to Gaza, and in 2015 he accepted an invitation from Ibrahim Hewitt, MEM's senior editor, to speak at the group's annual conference. Hewitt, another Hamas supporter, approved stoning adulterers to death and lashing gay men. At the conference, Dr Azzam Tamimi spoke about suicide bombers as noble martyrs. Hewitt said of Tamimi, 'I consider him to be a very good friend and I think he's done a fantastic job.' Corbyn's association with such people had gone largely unnoticed while he was on Labour's fringe. After his election as leader that changed, although he did not anticipate the investigation of his past alliances, or how they would be interpreted.

Asked about his association with the anti-Semitic Muslim extremist Dyab Abou Jahjah, he denied that he knew him. Shown a photograph of himself with Jahjah, he said that he had forgotten about a request he had made in 2009 for a visa for his 'friend'. His memory was also weak when in August 2015 the *Jewish Chronicle* asked him to explain his relationship with the Holocaust denier Paul Eisen. 'Paul Eisen,' replied Corbyn's spokesman, 'is not someone Jeremy Corbyn's office has any dealings with.' The production of another photo, this time of Corbyn at Deir Yassin Remembered (DYR), prompted his recollection. Some years previously, he admitted, he had been present at such an event, and had donated money: 'At that time I had absolutely no evidence that Paul Eisen was a Holocaust denier.' He also forgot accompanying Eisen to a DYR meeting in St John's Wood on 9 April 2013, at least five years after Eisen had made his views public. Then he was asked why he had called Hamas and Hezbollah 'our friends'. Again, he had difficulty recalling having done so, until a tape-recording was produced. He then explained that he used the term 'friends' towards both Hamas and Hezbollah 'in a collective way', and did not agree with 'what they do'. Asked why he spoke to either group, he replied that his ambition was to bring about peace. 'Does it mean that I agree with them?' he asked rhetorically. 'That's not the point.' He could not name a single Israeli politician with whom he had discussed peace, or explain why he suggested boycotts and reprisals only against Israel, and not against any other country. Nor could he explain why the Stop the War Coalition had allowed anti-Semitic banners at its annual Al-Quds event.

Linked together, Corbyn's encounters could not be dismissed as coincidental or arbitrary, but rather spoke to a pattern of association with Holocaust deniers, terrorists and outright anti-Semites. When Ivan Lewis, another Jewish Labour MP, accused him of 'anti-Semitic rhetoric' and association with racists, he replied that it was ludicrous to liken him to Holocaust deniers. The idea that he was anti-Semitic was 'appalling, disgusting, deeply offensive'. In his opinion, he, and not Jews, would decide whether his anti-Zionism was racist. During the Labour Party conference in Brighton in 2015 he made a reluctant appearance at a reception for Labour Friends of Israel.

Compelled to fulfil the leader's traditional visit, in his speech he condemned the 'siege of Gaza', without mentioning that Hamas was firing rockets into Israel, and noticeably refused even to use the word 'Israel'. His bias provoked Michael Foster, a generous Jewish donor to the party, to describe Corbyn's close aides as Nazi SS shock troops and Corbyn himself as an anti-Semite. With Corbyn's compliance, Foster was instantly suspended from the party.

That single act changed little. Luciana Berger, another Jewish Labour MP, revealed that she had received 2,500 abusive messages over three days, telling her to 'eat pork' or 'move to Israel', and had had a yellow star superimposed on an image of her face with the hashtags #filthyjewishbitch and #kike. Berger had been director of Labour Friends of Israel for three years before she became MP for Liverpool Wavertree in 2010. Manny Shinwell, her great-uncle, was famous in the post-war years as a pugnacious Red Clydesider Member of Parliament. In the weeks after Corbyn's election, the overt racism included online messages telling Berger that Hitler was right – six million times. Despite this vilification, she stood to be Labour's candidate for mayor of Liverpool. To her disappointment, Corbyn personally endorsed her opponent, and she was attacked by his supporters for being Jewish. 'It's completely unacceptable,' said Corbyn; but he ignored calls to do anything about it.

For the first time, the existence of anti-Semitism among Labour supporters attracted public notice, and anger against Corbyn grew. Lord Levy, the party's former fundraiser, was the type of prominent Blairite Corbyn instinctively disliked, so his expression of 'shock and horror' at the failure to condemn anti-Semitism was relatively easy to ignore. More awkward was the protest of Jonathan Arkush, the president of the Board of Deputies of British Jews. 'Most people in the Jewish community can't trust Labour,' he said. 'There's an ideological bigotry towards Israel prevalent on the far left that Israel can do no good.' Reluctantly, Corbyn agreed to meet Arkush and the Board of Deputies, complaining to his staff in the Commons that inviting the 'bourgeois' Arkush was 'unfair'.

Josh Simons, a policy adviser in Corbyn's office, noticed that as the staff prepared for the meeting, the mood was one of 'flippant disdain'. For Corbyn, Jews were automatically assumed to be rich capitalist financiers and bankers backed by Wall Street, and were all undoubted swindlers. They were not victims of racism, but the enemy of the working class.

The Board of Deputies' leaders arrived at Corbyn's office on April Fool's Day, 2016. Uncertain how to address them, he relied on a script given to him to read, and thereafter directed their questions to Seumas Milne. Ignoring that pass-off, Arkush asked Corbyn, 'What do you expect the Jewish community to feel when you meet people who are blatantly racist? Do you accept that it was inappropriate?' Corbyn hesitated, then finally replied that he would 'reflect'. But he refused to express any regret about associating with Hamas or Hezbollah. He would meet the Palestinians again, he said. Positioned to one side of the room, Milne was seething. In the presence of Jews, his body language had visibly changed. His language did not. Replying to the deputies' questions, he refused to say 'anti-Semitism', only 'anti-Zionism'. His blatant anti-Semitism, said one of the visitors, was 'frightening. Giving power to Seumas Milne is fearful.' The deputies knew that he had recently quibbled about printing Corbyn's Passover message to Labour supporters on cards that featured a Hebrew phrase. 'We must be careful,' Milne had said. 'There's a long history between the Hebrews and Zionism.' Corbyn could not be allowed to sign a card that gave any hint that he might be betraying the Muslims. Arkush left the meeting disturbed, and still uncertain about where Corbyn stood, despite his prejudices being increasingly on open display. Concealed beneath his benign exterior was anger: antagonism towards the Jews and fury about his opponents in Westminster. Speedily, those two groups merged. Jewish MPs were conspicuous among those in the PLP considering whether to launch a new leadership election. But their disunity remained his strength.

Without a leader or an ideology, many MPs were cowed by Labour's 'shock troops', led by Jon Lansman. Based in his office overlooking Euston station, Lansman claimed to control 90,000 supporters spread through a hundred groups – called by some 'Militant Reborn' – across the country. He spoke about 'permanent mobilisation' to defend Corbyn, not least action by Momentum's members to trigger 'mandatory deselection' of untrusted MPs. To root them out, in early 2016 Katy Clark drafted a 'loyalty list' to classify MPs into five categories, from 'core group' to 'hostile'. In between were 'core group plus', 'neutral but not hostile', and 'core group negative'. She listed only seventeen unquestioned loyalists, including McDonnell, Abbott, Clive Lewis, Dennis Skinner and Jon Trickett, a Yorkshire MP since 1996. Emily Thornberry was 'core group plus'; Rosie Winterton, the chief whip, was 'hostile'. Every Jewish MP was 'hostile' or 'negative', including Ed Miliband. Chuka Umunna, another 'hostile', was described by Marlene Ellis, a Momentum activist, as not 'politically black', by which she presumably meant he was a 'traitor' to his race. While authorising these classifications from his own office, Corbyn publicly ordered his MPs to cease their personal abuse, public sniping and anonymous briefings. His overwhelming mandate, he said, justified his demand for unity and loyalty. The overt hypocrisy encouraged the Tories' hopes for gains in the May council elections. The handicaps were their own splits over Europe, and what they recognised as a disastrous budget.

On 16 March 2016 George Osborne produced a statement before the House that was riddled with errors. His cuts to welfare provoked Iain Duncan Smith, who the week before had protested about Osborne's cuts to disability benefits, to resign as secretary of state for work and pensions. Pointedly, he accused David Cameron of lacking compassion. At prime minister's questions an open goal was awaiting Corbyn's shot. Instead, he spoke about refugees, Amnesty International and whether Turkey should join the EU. Baying Labour MPs heckled him for being a loser, unwilling to fight for Downing Street. 'We cannot go on like this,' John Woodcock wrote in the *Mirror*. 'How have we managed to turn one of the worst-ever weeks for David Cameron's Tory government into another humiliation for the Labour Party?' Criticising Corbyn for his 'lack of intellect' and inability to think on his feet, Woodcock called for a leader who could help the disabled: 'These people are being appallingly served by a leadership team who cannot even get its act together properly to stand up for disabled people when they are screwed over by the Tories.'

Corbyn's take was completely different. Back in his office, he, Milne and their team were joyous. 'They had deliberately ignored Duncan Smith's resignation,' noted an eyewitness, 'to subvert the system and the Commons. They refused to play the game.' Few beyond their group understood such an outlook. Conventional politicians, not for the first time, spoke about Corbyn's position as 'unsustainable'.

The best form of defence is attack. After pounding up and down the corridor, Milne came out fighting. In an unexpected appearance at a meeting of the Campaign for Labour Party Democracy, he urged the hard left to 'isolate those [moderate MPs] who want to create a feeling of confusion and failure'. He was supported by Lansman, who urged his supporters to accelerate the purge of moderate Labour councillors. 'This is our party now – we shouldn't allow others to take it away from us,' said Jackie Walker, Momentum's vice chairman, choosing to attack 'the enemies within the Labour Party' on RT, Russia's TV station.

At that moment, Katy Clark's secret loyalty list was leaked. Its categories, renamed 'Gallows', 'Gulag', 'Re-education', 'Jury's out' and 'Comrades', was a gift to Labour's critics. In the Commons, Cameron waved the list at the Labour benches. 'Hands up who's core support!' he shouted. His glee concealed his own weakness. Labour was now ahead of the Tories in the polls, and only 7 per cent of Labour supporters trusted 'Bullingdon' Cameron, the Old Etonian and Oxford toff, on Europe. By contrast, over 70 per cent of Labour supporters trusted Corbyn. Just as Bernie Sanders, the seventy-four-year-old Vermont socialist, was being taken up by 'betrayed' young Democrat voters in America, Corbyn was appealing to insecure young voters in a backlash against Britain's elite. Opinion polls in 2015 had shown Labour with a 16 per cent lead among eighteen- to twenty-four-year-olds. One year later, that had risen to 41 per cent. Cameron was blamed for rising house prices, increasing student loans, inadequate welfare payments, an underfunded NHS and a 10 per cent fall in average real wages between 2007 and 2015. Corbyn was applauded as he marched through Whitehall with Yannis Gourtsoyannis, the doctors' leader. Cheers also met his demand that Jeremy Hunt should negotiate during the junior doctors' all-out strike, the first in NHS history. The public ignored the seventy meetings between Hunt and the BMA over the previous three years. Facts never undermined Corbyn's support for a strike, especially after new statistics exposed an obscene inequality: the chief executives of Britain's top hundred corporations were earning on average 183 times more than the average employee. Those at the very top earned 810 times more, and no one could demonstrate that those stratospheric levels of income delivered better performance.

More ammunition was added to Corbyn's attack on the Tories by the media's publication of 'the Panama Papers', a vast trove of leaked confidential documents from an offshore law firm. Hundreds of the world's richest people were exposed as successful tax-avoiders. Among them was David Cameron's father Ian, a stockbroker who had died in 2010, long after he had deposited his family's funds in a firm based in the Bahamas. The prime minister himself had also owned shares in the tax haven worth £31,500, which were sold on his entering No. 10. Although his dealings were totally legal, his complicity in capitalism's amorality was stark. Asked for an explanation, his spokesman stonewalled: 'That's a private matter.' Following the 'omnishambles' budget, and with the cabinet deeply divided over Europe, Downing Street gave the impression of being mismanaged by a secretive, sleazy, multi-millionaire prime minister. 'There's one rule for the rich and another for everyone else,' Corbyn commented. 'The government needs to stop pussyfooting on tax-dodging.' Cameron, he sniped, was a wealthy Etonian leading the posh party to reward the rich at the expense of the honest poor. Cameron's personal ratings slumped below Corbyn's for the first time. The prime minister's credo of helping the poor to get rich and reducing taxes for those who worked was forgotten. To silence the uproar, Cameron belatedly published his tax returns, which showed that he had paid £400,000 in income tax over six years. His conduct had been irreproachable, but for Corbyn – pledged to levy punitive taxes to abolish the rich once and for all – his rival's conduct remained immoral.

In Corbyn's scenario, children should not inherit their parents' wealth. But to the Tories' glee, he appeared to have forgotten his own inheritance in 1987 of £37,478 – about £100,000 today – from his mother's estate, and he had also ignored how the Miliband brothers had avoided paying taxes on their parents' home by a deed of variation in their father's will. Moreover, the publication of Corbyn's tax return revealed both a £100 fine for late submission and his failure to include his state pension as income. That omission highlighted his prejudice against private income. Over the previous thirty years he had received an estimated £1.5 million from the state. His parliamentary pension, also funded by taxpayers, was worth £1.6 million, paying him about £50,000 a year on top of his state pension and his salary as leader of the opposition. But he was impervious to accusations of hypocrisy, and equally unembarrassed that Ian Lavery, his friend and shadow trade union minister, had not declared to HMRC his receipt of a £72,000 cheap mortgage from the National Miners' Union in 1994, and then refused to disclose whether the money had been repaid.

The public test of Corbyn's values would be the council elections on 5 May 2016. Since 1985, when Labour was in opposition it had never lost seats overall in any council election, but now the party faced a new situation. The white working class in the rundown northern cities blamed Labour and the EU for increased immigration. They complained that their incomes had fallen, public services were stretched, and their communities troubled by unwelcome changes. Nor did they like Corbyn's metropolitan contempt for English culture. Most had heard about Emily Thornberry's mocking tweet during a 2014 by-election: the caption 'Image from #Rochester' accompanied a photo of a house partly covered by the flag of St George with a white van on the forecourt – the symbol of a patriotic Englishman made good. The working class's concerns about an uncontrolled influx of foreigners produced the same answer as before – Labour wanted more immigration. Although 330,000 migrants had legally settled in the UK in 2015–16, and at least another 100,000 had arrived illegally, Corbyn was unfazed. The result, the BBC reported, was that only 16 per cent of voters over sixty years old would vote Labour. The party was predicted to be heading for 150 lost council seats, a considerable defeat.

Corbyn was unyielding, and agreed with Milne that the media, 'are obsessed with trying to damage the leadership of the Labour Party and unfortunately there are people in the Labour Party that play into that'. At a public meeting, Corbyn smiled as his supporters jeered the BBC's political editor Laura Kuenssberg for asking a critical question. For some time he watched her discomfort before asking for silence. He saw no reason to alter his image as the authentic anti-establishment icon. 'Don't do anything that could damage the party,' said Jon Trickett, reappointed by Corbyn to run the council elections campaign. But then, unexpectedly, anti-Semitism became an issue.

Sufyan Ismail, the chief executive of Muslim Engagement and Development (MEND), was known for using anti-Zionist language. Naturally, he sought a like-minded personality as the guest of honour at MEND's fundraising dinner on 22 April 2016, and invited Naseem 'Naz' Shah, Bradford's new Labour MP in succession to George Galloway. Two years previously the forty-two-year-old Shah had written on Facebook that Israel should 'relocate' to the United States, because 'America has plenty of land to accommodate Israel as its 51st state', and would 'welcome Israelis with open arms'. Once the 'transportation' was complete, she argued, evoking the image of cattle trucks arriving at Auschwitz, 'the Middle East would again be peaceful'. Her post, accompanied by a map, showed Israel plonked down in the southern states of America and concluded 'Problem Solved.' In another post, she added: 'Never forget that everything Hitler did was legal.' Employed on McDonnell's team, she had been encouraged by party leaders to seek membership of the Commons select committee inquiring into anti-Semitism. Clearly, she would have a particular contribution to make.

On Tuesday, 26 April, Corbyn's staff was asked by a journalist about Shah's Facebook post. Summoned to Corbyn's office, she waited for nearly an hour while a dispute raged inside. 'We forgot you're here,' she was finally told. Party general secretary Iain McNicol had demanded that Shah be suspended, but Corbyn had refused, hoping that an apology from her would be sufficient. Quickly composing a statement presented for approval to Seumas Milne, Shah claimed that the post had been written before she was elected to Parliament. Before the publication of this explanation on her Facebook page, Milne removed her reference to anti-Semitism. With that, he believed, the problem would go away; Corbyn did too. Neither considered how Shah would reply to racists if she were asked whether Britain's 'problems would be solved' by all the Shahs returning to their country of origin. Or, as Jonathan Arkush later noted, 'If a Labour MP was to propose the transportation of black people back to Africa, I just can't imagine the shock, the outrage if that person was allowed to remain in the party a split second.' Neither Milne nor Corbyn considered the question worthy of an answer. Both sympathised with Shah's anti-Zionism, and were unconcerned that she was also anti-Semitic.

By the end of the day, 26 April, their studied nonchalance fell away. Bowing to pressure from MPs, McNicol suspended Shah from the party 'pending an investigation'. Then, to Corbyn's irritation, the Jewish problem resurfaced. In another Facebook message, Malia Bouattia, the new president of the National Union of Students, described Birmingham University as a 'Zionist outpost' because it hosted 'the largest [number of Jews] in the country whose leadership is dominated by Zionist activists'. Bouattia, a Muslim whose parents were born in Algeria, would be criticised by an all-party committee of MPs for her 'smack of outright anti-Semitism', but as usual, Corbyn said nothing.

His silence was filled by Ken Livingstone. London's former mayor spoke as a member of the NEC and as a close ally of Corbyn, who, he knew, agreed with him about Israel and the Jews. The only difference was that Livingstone's anti-Semitism was undisguised. Before 1987 he had waged a bitter campaign against Reg Freeson, the Jewish Labour Member for Brent East. Livingstone wanted Freeson's seat, and did finally end the MP's twenty-three-year parliamentary career. In February 2005 his anti-Semitism had resurfaced when an *Evening Standard* journalist asked him an innocuous question after an evening event. 'Actually,' replied Livingstone, 'you're just like a concentration camp guard. You're just doing it because you're paid to, aren't you?' Oliver Feingold, the reporter, replied that he was Jewish. Two days later the *Standard*'s editor exposed Livingstone's racism. After he refused to apologise, he was suspended as mayor for one month.

Soon after, he cursed two Jewish property developers and suggested that they 'return to where they came from', which happened to be India; but that was not considered by an adjudicator to be anti-Semitic, just insulting. He survived to defend Naz Shah. 'I don't think her comments were anti-Semitic,' he said on radio on the day she apologised. 'This is an over-the-top comment about a horrendous conflict,' he added, referring to the Israeli-Palestinian war. Shah was the victim of a 'well-orchestrated campaign' by the 'Israel lobby to smear anybody who criticises Israeli policy as anti-Semitic'. He went on: 'Let's remember, when Hitler won his election in 1932 his policy then was that Jews should be moved to Israel. He was supporting Zionism before he went mad and ended up killing six million Jews.' Livingstone was suggesting that Hitler was in favour of a Jewish state in Israel, and that the Jews were contaminated by their preparedness to work with him, complicit in their own genocide. Not only was that wholly untrue – the fabrication of Lenni Brenner, an anti-Semitic American Trotskyist – but Livingstone ignored Hitler's explicit anti-Semitism in *Mein Kampf*, published in 1925, as well as all his speeches promoting hatred of Jews before 1932. He also distorted an act of desperation in 1933: to escape the doom they foresaw, representatives of Germany's 522,000 Jews did negotiate with the Nazi government for some of them to be allowed to emigrate with their possessions rather than depart penniless. That limited agreement was irrelevant to Zionism, but was twisted by anti-Semites to portray Jews as collaborators in their own destruction.

Livingstone not only also distorted this narrative, he went further, claiming that anti-Semitism did not exist in the Labour Party, and was instead a Jewish invention to mobilise support for Zionism. As 'progressive anti-racists', he argued, those on the far left could not be accused of anti-Semitism. He was following Corbyn's line that the champions of 'progressiveness' possessed the authority to declare that their anti-Zionism was not anti-Semitic.

On the day of Livingstone's broadcast, 28 April, Corbyn was on a train to Grimsby. As he posed with other passengers for selfies, his press secretary Kevin Slocombe whispered, 'Ken's said something on the radio.' It was soon clear what had been broadcast. After getting off the train, Corbyn called Milne. 'We need to talk to Ken,' he said before heading off to meet supporters. 'Ken must be suspended,' Slocombe told Milne. 'This is madness,' he added. Milne was immovable: Livingstone had to be protected.

At that moment, Livingstone was walking up the stairs in the Millbank studios in London, followed by live television cameras. He was confronted by John Mann. 'You're a disgrace!' shouted Mann, who by chance was in the building and had heard about Livingstone's comments. The ex-mayor, Mann continued, was 'a Nazi apologist' and 'a lying racist'. Watching the saga live on TV with others in his office, Milne laughed, as if to say: 'We're on the inside. We're resisting the powers-that-be.'

In LBC's studio, Livingstone had pronounced in his nasal monotone, 'It's over the top to think of anti-Semitism and racism as exactly the same thing.' He explained that 'Anti-Semites don't just hate Jews in Israel, they hate them in Golders Green as well,' by which he seemed to mean that since he hated only Israeli Jews, he was not an anti-Semite. He added that, 'as a statement of fact', Shah had been right to say that in ordering the Holocaust Hitler had acted legally. The Holocaust was not a crime. Livingstone believed that the Jews had cooperated, and ever since had exploited what had happened to them to justify the creation of Israel. To escape Mann, he locked himself inside a Millbank disabled lavatory. Milne would protect him.

Corbyn was preparing to lay a wreath on a workers' memorial in Grimsby. In more calls, he agreed with Milne that they had to defend Livingstone. As in all disputes about history, ideology and political strategy, Corbyn regarded Milne as the Keeper of the Line, the reliable intellectual who guarded their purity. 'Ken has a point,' Milne told Corbyn. To suggest that Hitler was a Zionist and the Holocaust was not a crime, said Milne, was not racist. Ken was not wrong to 'criticise Zionism, even if the Zionists happened to be Jews'. Their old comrade was the victim of Zionists, and was not anti-Semitic.

In Corbyn's office, Josh Simons, a policy adviser who was Jewish, watched as Milne seethed. Britain, exclaimed the Keeper of the Line, had committed a crime in 1917 by promising a homeland to the Jews. Another office member condemned the 'Jewish conspiracy to get Livingstone'. At this, Milne turned to Simons and in an interrogatory tone demanded to know his opinion as a Jew. His snap question followed a lengthy and detailed inquisition during a recent train journey about Simons's religion. Milne and the others, Simons concluded, neither understood two thousand years of anti-Semitism, nor wanted to.

By the time Livingstone emerged from Millbank onto the street, some Labour MPs were demanding his suspension. Their protests were parried by Milne, who wanted Mann, and not Livingstone, suspended. The protesters were also snubbed by Corbyn, who told them that the row had been created by his own opponents because they were 'nervous and jealous of his power'. Anyway, he agreed with Livingstone that it was 'over the top' to 'think of anti-Semitism and racism as exactly the same thing' – Labour 'does not have a problem with anti-Semitism'. He simply weighed his morality against others' immorality, and never found himself wanting. He had no desire to understand the complaints being voiced, or to enquire why Jews were so aggrieved. Like Milne and Livingstone, he refused to capitulate to Jewish complaints. Late that afternoon, Josh Simons walked out of the office and never returned.

Around the same time, Livingstone was approached by a journalist while out shopping in north London. People should calm down, he said. But they didn't; the pressure on Corbyn only increased. By the end of the afternoon he was forced to bow to Iain McNicol's insistence that Livingstone be suspended. In turn, he demanded that Mann should also be suspended for bringing the party into disrepute. After hearing that Mann had become the target of serious physical threats from Corbynistas, he was persuaded to tone down his punishment: Rosie Winterton was told to issue a reprimand. Along the leader's corridor, only McDonnell demanded Livingstone's expulsion from the party. Old hard-left vendettas never die.

In her Westminster office, Louise Ellman kept silent. 'I didn't want to dig because it was too scary to find the truth that people are truly hostile,' she recalled. 'I had a trauma about the whole thing. It was too horrendous to believe this existed in the Labour Party.' Corbyn never sought her out. Instead he spoke to the film director Ken Loach, who was responsible for making his election videos. Loach, a well-known anti-Zionist, had in 1987 directed *Perdition*, a play at the Royal Court depicting Zionists as collaborators with the Nazis in the extermination of Europe's Jews, although following protests the production was cancelled before its first preview performance. Years later he corrected himself, but in 2016 he emphatically denounced the persecution of Livingstone. Like Corbyn, Loach supported the Palestinians' return to their homeland, but to avoid overtly endorsing the destruction of the Jewish state, both men had supported a two-state solution until the creation of the Stop the War Coalition. Then, with their embrace of the Muslim Brotherhood, that solution – which implied the recognition of Zionist Israel – became unacceptable. By its silence, the coalition endorsed Hamas's demand for Israel's obliteration.

On his return to London, Corbyn was faced by irate Labour MPs. 'Vile, offensive and crass,' said Tom Watson about his leader's sympathetic reaction to Livingstone. In response, Corbyn denounced a 'witch-hunt' contrived to undermine his leadership. 'There is not a problem,' he told the *Guardian*, although he granted that 'It's not a happy day.' In a further public statement, he declared that he was 'absolutely against anti-Semitism', but during a telephone call he told Milne that an article by Jonathan Freedland in the *Guardian* urging him to confront Labour's problem was 'utterly disgusting subliminal nastiness'. His criticism was shared by Michael White, the *Guardian*'s former political editor, who on the paper's website condemned the 'idiots' who swallowed the Tory plot to construct phoney anti-Semitism in the Labour Party.

Beyond Westminster, the Corbynistas broke cover. 'Labour's Blairite right wing,' emailed Martin Mayer, a Unite representative on the NEC, 'have used the smear of anti-Semitism to undermine Jeremy Corbyn's leadership.' With fraternal loyalty, Piers Corbyn, an inveterate Trotskyist, could not resist joining the fray. Livingstone, he declared with assumed authority, was misunderstood, and his account of Zionists cooperating with Hitler was actually true. There was 'too much sensitivity around anti-Semitism'. The ex-mayor's critics, he continued, were 'pandering to Israel'. Jeremy Corbyn could also take comfort that his stance towards Jews was approved by the historian and Holocaust denier David Irving. 'Corbyn,' said Irving, 'seems like a very fine man.' He would also be praised by David Duke, the former grand wizard of the Ku Klux Klan, who stated: 'Corbyn has told the truth that it's not necessarily in the interests of the British people to support the Jewish state.' The enemy of my enemy is my friend, runs the fourth-century BC Sanskrit treatise on statecraft.

Approval from such right-wing supporters was not enough. Iain McNicol suggested that Corbyn ask Jan Royall, the Labour peer who had undertaken the investigation of anti-Semitism in Oxford, to report on whether the party had a wider problem. Trusted by the Jewish community, Royall would have been ideal. But Corbyn rejected her, and McNicol, a weak man, did not press him.

A more suitable candidate was soon found. 'Shami wants to come and help,' Corbyn announced to his office, referring to Shami Chakrabarti, the former head of Liberty, the civil rights group. In the days after the Livingstone debacle, Milne had phoned Chakrabarti. She took the call while standing on the tarmac at Heathrow, where she was about to board a flight for Dublin. Milne told her that the solution to the party's problems was an inquiry, and she instantly accepted his offer to undertake the face-saver. By the time she landed in Ireland she had agreed that she would not investigate individuals accused of anti-Semitism, but would instead conduct a 'thematic' review of the party's broader culture. To make it palatable to party members, she would also include complaints about Islamophobia, even though that was not an issue either in the media or at Westminster. In addition, to avoid any complaints that she was personally hostile to Labour, she would join the party. Her membership was completed on an app at Dublin airport. At Milne's suggestion, she agreed that she would not recommend any disciplinary action. Blandness was required, and Chakrabarti was content to oblige. The public assumption that the respected lawyer would remain staunchly independent was undermined by her own decision not to undertake an unbiased, judicial-style inquiry, but to be as partial as she deemed necessary.

Grateful for the lifebelt, Corbyn announced that Livingstone's comments were 'unacceptable', and that he had appointed Chakrabarti to investigate Labour's alleged anti-Semitism. 'She's trying to find a way into his office,' concluded one of Corbyn's staff about the lawyer keen to land a job. 'And he's trying to silence his critics.'

Over the following weeks, Chakrabarti listened to hours of harrowing testimony from Jews, not least from female Labour MPs describing the anti-Semitic abuse they had suffered from party members. As the evidence accumulated, she made no attempt to appear independent. 'Regularly,' said an eyewitness,

'Seumas Milne got calls from Shami. He gave her guidance about what he and Corbyn expected.'

Corbyn's priority, amid talk of a coup to save a broken party without any prospect of power, was to prevent a meltdown in the local elections that were to be held on 5 May. He could not imagine that anti-Semitism would influence the outcome. The raw statistic of 300,000 Jews and three million Muslims living in Britain spoke for itself.

Anticipating disappointment in the 124 council elections, four mayoral elections and two by-elections, the party searched for a scapegoat. The *Mirror* went back to heaping blame on Tony Blair. Len McCluskey also hit out at the Blairites, accusing Liz Kendall of being 'nothing short of treacherous' for criticising Labour for its attitude towards Jews, and berating Ian Austin for 'behaving despicably' to undermine Corbyn. Raking up anti-Semitism, said McCluskey, was a 'cynical attempt to challenge Jeremy Corbyn's leadership'. There was more than a whiff of old-style Soviet propeganda in this, blaming scheming Jews for the ills of society.

13

Stuck in the Bunker

On election night, Corbyn was happily ensconced in a pub festooned with Fidel Castro posters. He appeared relaxed. 'I am not a traditional party leader. I do things in a rather different way. Some people are slower at learning things than others.' His cryptic observation did not deflect from the results. Labour surrendered eighteen seats in England, lost its majority in Wales, and suffered humiliation in Scotland, where the Tories become the official opposition after the SNP lost its overall majority. Although Labour won more votes across Britain than the Tories (who lost forty-eight seats), the 2 per cent swing was well short of the 12 per cent needed in a general election to win a Commons majority. Since the party also lost support in marginal areas, there was no talk about a national revival. 'The clock is ticking,' said Jo Cox, echoing the foreboding felt by her colleagues that the party would be out of power 'until 2030' because of Corbyn's 'weak leadership, poor judgement and mistaken sense of priorities'. At daybreak, Corbyn clung to the one piece of outright good news, Sadiq Khan's election as London mayor with a 14 per cent majority. His victory, said Diane Abbott, 'was all about Jeremy', seemingly forgetting that Khan had deliberately distanced himself from her leader. Corbyn was wounded by the results, but no moderate MP volunteered to strike. 'I'm carrying on,' he said, repeating once again that two-thirds of Labour's members had voted for him.

On 10 May, Khan was invited to address Labour MPs in a Commons committee room. Few came, and with the leader's chair empty, it looked as if Corbyn had stayed away. In reality, he was sitting to the side of the dimly-lit chamber, arms folded, looking as if he were on the verge of a breakdown. As Khan entered, Corbyn was noticeably reluctant to clap. Many MPs judged the new mayor's speech to be lacklustre, but agreed with his warning that Labour could not win the next general election, scheduled for 2020, unless the party appealed to non-Corbynistas. At the end, their leader rose gracelessly for the standing ovation. Then he spoke – more hesitantly than usual – to berate any MP who disputed the party's 'victory' in the council elections. His distortion enveloped the room in an awkward silence. He also went on at length about Labour's success in Islington, and it was left to Peter Hain, now a member of the House of Lords, to break the spell. In Wales, he said in a voice that electrified the meeting, Labour had secured its smallest vote since 1908. 'Good spinning, Jeremy,' Hain ended up, 'but we won't win in 2020.'

Corbyn had welcomed David Cameron's announcement of a referendum on EU membership, to be held on 23 June 2016 – six weeks after the council elections. His hostility towards the EU was ideological. Europe, he had told President Nicolás Maduro of Venezuela in a broadcast conversation in 2014, had 'suffered appallingly' because the EU was a capitalists' club and a barrier to his life's commitment to 'build socialism and the fight against capitalism'. The EU, he believed, existed for greedy bankers and multinationals to exploit the working class. If Britain voted to leave, and freed itself from Brussels' control, a socialist government could prevent British investment abroad and control markets, tariffs and profits – all contrary to EU laws. Both Corbyn and McDonnell wanted to campaign for Britain to leave, but were challenged by Hilary Benn and others in the shadow cabinet. The majority of Labour MPs and the trade unions, said Benn, supported membership. Reluctantly, Corbyn agreed to campaign to remain.

His lifelong opposition to the EU was displayed during a conference of European socialist leaders in Brussels on 17 December. Organised by Jan Royall, the meeting was an ideal opportunity for him to forge relationships and influence the European debate. Instead, he showed his resentment at even being in the city. Detached from any interest in European socialism, he refused to engage in the discussions and fluffed his own presentation. Unable to master the technical details of EU membership without Milne's help, he retreated into a shell. 'Did you find it useful?' Royall asked. 'Yer,' he replied while texting his wife about a minor domestic crisis: while roasting a batch of coffee beans, Laura had set them on fire. Coping with that incident provoked the only moment of emotion in Corbyn's day. On his return to London, he was asked over dinner in King's Cross with his team, 'How did it go?' 'OK,' he replied. Milne came to his rescue with a positive summary, but even his brio failed to dispel the impression of an uncertain man.

The remainers' chances of success, Corbyn knew, depended on Labour voters. David Cameron's fate was equally bound up in the outcome. If Britain voted leave, Corbyn calculated, the prime minister would be humiliated and the Tories electorally weakened. Those were good reasons not to appear on any platform alongside him. Associating with Tories was repellent to Corbyn anyway, while political collaboration risked repeating Labour's error during the Scottish independence referendum. To Alan Johnson, appointed to lead Labour's remain campaign, Corbyn's reluctance to preach the advantages of EU membership was 'risible'.

Within weeks of Johnson starting his work, the complications intensified. According to him, three of Corbyn's closest associates in his office were undermining his efforts. Corbyn ignored him at meetings, and found regular excuses not to appear on the remainers' platform, while he continued to speak in favour of the IRA and Hamas, spent time protecting anti-Semites within the party, and justified the misery heaped on Venezuela: anything but Europe. He even denounced Sadiq Khan for 'discrediting' himself by sharing an event with Cameron. 'You're deliberately sending Jeremy to speak in areas where he's not needed,' a journalist told Milne. 'Don't be so stupid,' said Milne, laughing. He would not dream of 'scuppering the vote'.

Corbyn knew the contrary. For Labour supporters minded to vote leave, controlling immigration was critical, but to him those opposed to open borders were racist. True to the vision of Britain as the multicultural, non-white society spun by Bernie Grant forty years earlier, he wanted to ban only low-paid workers from central Europe, particularly in the construction industry – even if that meant fewer houses were built. His ambition, he said, was to protect British jobs and wages. To keep ideologically pure, he ordered party officials to remove every reference to immigration from Labour's campaign. As he knew perfectly well, his stance undermined the remainers' campaign.

Hilary Benn intervened. Entering Corbyn's office, he said, 'You need to think in the language of the national interest.'

Milne laughed. 'What's funny about the national interest?' asked Imran Ahmed, Benn's assistant. Milne's dismissive shrug sparked an outburst from Benn directed at Corbyn. Trashing Cameron, he said, was short-sighted. The referendum could be lost. Milne started to interrupt. 'Shut up!' Benn shouted, not for the first time. 'This is for elected people to discuss!'

Corbyn, unnerved, preferred Milne to recite his thoughts. 'We won't speak about immigration or the national interest,' Corbyn told Benn. Soon after, he removed from an important leaflet a personal endorsement written by a party official. The words he deleted ran: 'I am clear, just like my shadow cabinet, the trade union movement and our members, that it is in the interests of the people of this country to remain in the EU.' Corbyn's obduracy was buttressed by McDonnell, who refused to participate in any remain event and vigorously vetted Labour's literature. He too ordered a pro-European sentence to be struck out from a remain leaflet. Like Corbyn, he knew all too well the effect his personal refusal to participate would have on the remain campaign.

A detailed survey showed that only 20 per cent of voters shared Corbyn's opinion. During an uncomfortable session in his office, Alan Johnson urged him to avoid a destructive breach with traditional Labour voters. Stony-faced, Corbyn refused to budge. 'My socialist views are totally unchanged,' he said. He was even considering a visit to Syrian refugees in Turkey to promote open borders, an incendiary provocation for the remainers.

To Johnson's distress, he also insisted on speaking only in generalities, and, on Milne's advice, chose to star at the British Kebab Awards rather than attend a major remain rally. At the end of that evening he joked that he preferred the salad and not the meat. Pro-Europe Labour MPs were outraged by his sarcasm, and by his refusal to endorse a letter signed by over two hundred Labour MPs that stated, 'The Labour Party is united in arguing that we are better off remaining in the European Union.' Incandescent at that latest refusal of Corbyn to engage in the campaign, Johnson was even more indignant about his leader's appearance in a fur coat on *The Last Leg*, a Channel 4 comedy show. Not only did Corbyn deliberately look unserious, but, to harm the campaign still further, he told the audience that he was only '7 or 7.5 out of 10' in favour of Europe. 'I'm not a huge fan of the EU,' he said, smiling.

The referendum result on 23 June shocked everyone. Almost every British region except London and Scotland voted leave, including an estimated two-thirds of white working-class voters, especially in Labour's traditional northern heartlands. The puzzle on that momentous night was to locate Corbyn. He had disappeared – his staff assumed he had gone home to sleep, and had turned his telephone off.

Early the following morning, sterling fell to a thirty-one-year low, the FTSE share index tumbled 8.7 per cent, and David Cameron decided to resign. After getting up late, Corbyn was seen laughing over breakfast with his team. Although Milne and McDonnell admitted to voting leave, Corbyn would deny that he had done so. After a telephone conversation, Keith Veness believes that he did vote leave, not least because he sounded so delighted.

Before Corbyn arrived at his office that morning, he publicly demanded that the government should immediately apply for Article 50, the process that would terminate Britain's member-ship of the EU. He saw no reason to prepare for negotiations or for a transition period before Brexit. He wanted Britain out of the EU without establishing any relationship with the customs union or the single market, and emphatically ruled out a second referendum. To those who accused him of deliberately influencing the vote by encouraging immigration, he replied that Brexiteers suffered from 'a lesser understanding of diversity'. His flippancy sparked another outbreak of anger among Labour MPs, especially the remainers. Hilary Benn was seen holding his head in despair.

While Corbyn cheered the result, two Labour MPs, Margaret Hodge and Ann Coffey, had formally submitted a motion of no confidence in their leader. Both accused him of having failed to promote the EU's benefits for workers. 'His heart wasn't in it,' said Coffey politely, adding that he should resign, just as Cameron had done. The dam was broken, and other MPs quickly signed the motion. Among the first was Tristram Hunt, the historian MP for Stoke-on-Trent Central. Labour, he said, needed a credible leader for the snap election that was likely to be called within the year. Another pro-European mentioned 'the deepest peacetime crisis in our country for decades, and our party cannot afford to continue with self-indulgence'. By the time the shadow cabinet met later that day, about fifty-five MPs had signed the motion. 'It's not good enough,' said Ian Murray, the shadow minister for Scotland. Pointing his finger at Corbyn across the table, he snarled, 'You should resign.' While others joined the attack, McDonnell and Abbott remained silent. Only Emily Thornberry offered any defence.

Surprised by the hostility, Corbyn shrunk back. Insiders recognised the pattern of behaviour. In a crisis, his frame froze and his smile became glazed, as he was unable to conceal his dismay. His fate was listed for discussion three days later by the PLP. On Milne's orders, Corbyn later told Channel 4 News, 'I'm carrying on.' Under no circumstances would he resign. Although the Blairite challenge had split the parliamentary party, he said, the referendum had exposed the Blairites as wrong. The electorate had rejected Peter Mandelson and the London elite. With the party under his control, and most trade unions on his side, he was convinced he would survive. Even if the nation was wavering on the brink of a nervous breakdown, he was standing firm.

The following day, Saturday, Corbyn addressed a Gay Pride demonstration in London. Unlike the cheers he had garnered the previous year, this time he was booed. To shouts of 'Coward!' he reluctantly left the stage, saying quite inaccurately, 'I did all I could.' Soon after, he heard that Hilary Benn had asked other members of the shadow cabinet to join in a mass resignation if after a PLP vote of no confidence he still refused to resign. Among those who agreed with Benn was the Brexiteer Frank Field. But he did not personally confront Corbyn – with Milne and McDonnell as his protectors, few were given that chance.

On Saturday night, Corbyn's office heard that the *Observer* would report that Benn was canvassing shadow ministers. Katy Clark telephoned Benn. He did not take the call. At 1 o'clock on Sunday morning, Corbyn called him. 'Do you have confidence in me?' he asked. Speaking in a tone eerily similar to that of his father, Benn replied that his answer was 'No,' and that the leadership crisis had to end. Following the call, Corbyn announced that he had dismissed Benn. 'Hilary was really surprised,' recalled an eyewitness. 'He never thought he would be fired. He was fired for standing up for his beliefs by the man who prided himself on doing that all his life.' Benn's surprise summarised the moderates' naïvety, and their fate.

Early on Sunday morning, to stifle the revolt, McDonnell, Thornberry and Abbott bombarded the radio and TV studios to justify Corbyn's position. Their efforts were pointless. Soon after 8 a.m., the first of eleven shadow cabinet ministers announced their resignations, starting with Heidi Alexander, the shadow minister for health. 'I hated being a member of Jeremy's shadow cabinet,' she would say, 'because it was entirely dysfunctional. He would agree one thing at the shadow cabinet meeting and then his political assistant [Katy Clark] would telephone the next day to say "I know what he really thinks" and that he really meant the opposite.' She added, 'I wasn't part of a coup but just wanted to be part of a team.'

Just before 9 a.m., McDonnell found himself disinvited from BBC TV to make way for Benn. 'I wanted Jeremy to succeed,' Benn told the audience, 'but it is clear he's not succeeding and we have a wider duty to the party, and I think the country needs an effective Labour opposition.' Even as he was broadcasting, other resignations were announced, including Lord Falconer, Seema Malhotra (an aide to McDonnell), Vernon Coaker, Chris Bryant and Gloria De Piero – all Blairites. Their letters blamed Corbyn for Brexit and for endangering Labour's credibility. Lucy Powell, the latest to quit, wrote, 'Your position is untenable.' The only turncoat was Andy Burnham. In his desire to become Manchester's mayor, he pledged his support for his leader. Undaunted, McDonnell spoke defiantly on another TV programme: 'We are on a path of building a majority government for Labour – I think they should calm down and listen to their members.' His tactic to keep the flame alive was always to pronounce that Britain was on the verge of an election at which Labour was certain to be victorious.

Besieged by journalists outside his house, Corbyn remained resolutely inside. Stiffened by Abbott, he was ordered to conceal his anger from the public. Keeping power was vital. Resignations were bourgeois self-indulgence. By mid-morning another twenty MPs, including the Eagle sisters, had resigned from their party roles, bringing the total to fifty-six. Corbyn was told to dismiss the revolt as a blip. Despite his ratings falling below 20 per cent, and with no chance of winning a general election, he tried to ignore the *Mirror*'s damning headline – 'For the good of the party and the country, if you're not going to be prime minister, you're the wrong person for the job.' He took comfort from the image on Sunday-morning television of Tom Watson, his obese deputy leader, wading through mud at the Glastonbury Festival, seemingly unaware of any crisis. Once told about it, he was unable to get a telephone signal to call London, and remained isolated from the battle. Corbyn hung on to one truth: the attempted coup lacked a leader, a platform or any party support. At 2 p.m. that Sunday, he emerged from his house, but refused to speak to the press.

Others did that for him. 'Those Labour MPs plunging their party into an unwanted crisis,' warned McCluskey, 'are betraying not only the party itself but also our national interest at one of the most critical moments any of us can recall.' In any leadership election, he insisted, Corbyn must be a candidate, or the party would split. He went on to threaten the rebel MPs with mandatory reselection. Another ally, Jon Lansman, urged members of Momentum to join the Labour Party for an imminent leadership vote. 'We cannot let this undemocratic behaviour succeed,' he said, adding that Momentum had collected 200,00 signatures in support of Corbyn. Secretly, he sought more money from McCluskey to secure control of the party and protect Corbyn. By nightfall, Watson had returned to London – only to be barred from Corbyn's office while his leader was appointing unknown MPs to his shadow cabinet. 'I'm deeply disappointed,' Watson said of Benn's dismissal. He refused to endorse Corbyn.

At 9 a.m. on Monday, the three men finally met at Westminster. Watson insisted that Seumas Milne leave the room, then did not mince his words to Corbyn, who looked 'broken, puzzled and sorrowful'. Watson told him that having lost the PLP's support, and destined to lose an imminent general election, he should step down. Watson was devoted to the Labour Party, but to Corbyn it was irrelevant. This was a battle for power – Marxists versus Blairites. The counter-coup would be crushed. Watson's report to friends after the meeting confirmed his irresolution. He judged that Corbyn's intelligence was limited and his emotions permanently concealed, but he couldn't gauge whether his tenacity was feigned or genuine – and he was uncertain of the next step.

The four 'soft' left MPs who followed Watson into the office – Lisa Nandy, Owen Smith, John Healey and Kate Green – managed to get face to face with Corbyn, but it was still not he who did the talking. Just as they began to speak, John McDonnell entered the room and answered the questions they addressed to their leader. The previous September, McDonnell had said that Corbyn was reluctant to run for the leadership. Now, he said, he refused to resign. While Corbyn remained silent and immobile, McDonnell pleaded for loyalty, but failed to stop the four from leaving the shadow cabinet. After the meeting, Healey wrote to Corbyn that he was 'deeply disappointed with the discussion and by your failure to recognise that the turmoil after the referendum vote, a likely autumn election, the responsibility to hold the Labour Party together and the very wide – and ever widening – concerns about your leadership, require a fresh leadership election'. He received no reply.

Around that time, Jess Phillips (who had left the Labour Party during Tony Blair's reign, then returned in 2010 and five years later won a Birmingham seat for Labour) spotted Milne ordering coffee in the ground-floor atrium in Portcullis House, a modern office block for MPs opposite Big Ben. Ten days earlier, a week before referendum day, Jo Cox, the forty-one-year-old Labour MP for Batley and Spen, had been brutally murdered in the street by a right-wing fanatic. Labour MPs remained shocked. Phillips, a critic of Corbyn, approached Milne and told him about an online threat to point a blowtorch at her neck. 'Don't take it personally,' said Milne dismissively – he too, he said, had been the target of threats. 'This is fucking personal!' Phillips shouted in front of other MPs. Milne rushed upstairs. He would never admit that he bothered with the 'personal'.

The same applied to Corbyn. As he sat in the Commons chamber to hear Cameron's timetable for Brexit, he pretended to be unfazed by all the hostility. Taunted by calls to resign from the Labour benches behind him, and by jeers from Tories, he kept his cool. In the circumstances it was remarkable, but then he had overseen innumerable fractious meetings in Hornsey and Haringey, and had endured twenty-three years as a loner at Westminster, so his self-control was natural. 'The country,' he told the House, 'will thank neither the benches in front nor those behind for indulging in internal factional manoeuvring.'

Later that day, Labour MPs gathered for a PLP meeting, which quickly split into two contentious groups. Corbyn rose. Outnumbered by critics, he asserted that he would not resign – and sat down. 'For your sake,' said Robert Flello, the Member for Stoke-on-Trent South, 'but most importantly for the people who need a Labour government, do the decent thing.' Flello assumed that as a result of his speaking out, Momentum activists would seek to remove him. So did Ian Murray, who to protect him and others told Corbyn, 'Call off your dogs.' Hard-left activists, he complained, had threatened his staff.

Others were even more blunt. 'You can't offer leadership,' Helen Goodman told Corbyn, 'you're not a leader.' Jack Dromey, MP for Birmingham Erdington, spoke of the party being 'on the brink of a catastrophic defeat from which Labour may never recover'. To cheers, Alan Johnson attacked Corbyn's aides for refusing to support the remain campaign. 'At times it felt as if they were working against the rest of the party,' he said. 'Your office did not even turn up for weekly meetings.' A lone supporter, Barry Gardiner, a pedantic Cambridge graduate and MP for Brent North, started to defend his leader, but was interrupted by boos. Still Corbyn refused to bow, but he decided to escape. Rising quickly, he walked out of the room. MPs began to spill into the corridor. 'It was like a lynch mob without a rope,' said McDonnell. As Corbyn arrived back in his office, an eye-witness recorded, 'He looked the most unhappiest [sic] I've ever seen him. He internalised his grief.'

Outside the committee room, emotions were high. John Woodcock overheard Kevin Slocombe, Corbyn's official spokes-man, tell a journalist that the MPs' threats were 'a corridor coup' and 'irrelevant'. Outraged, Woodcock shouted back, 'It's extraor-dinary that you stand and slag us off to the media in a highly distorted account.' Close by, Chris Bryant, the shadow leader of the House, told another journalist about Corbyn, 'The writing on the wall is eight metres high, and if he can't see it he needs to go to Specsavers.' Letting off steam was no substitute for ousting the leader. Meanwhile, a thousand Corbyn supporters waving Socialist Worker placards and wearing T-shirts sporting slogans like 'Eradicate the Right-Wing Blairite Vermin' had gathered in Parliament Square. McDonnell, Abbott and Corbyn went out to meet them. 'Jeremy Corbyn is not resigning,' McDonnell announced.

Encouraged by the success of far-left parties in Spain, Italy and Greece, Corbyn's troops were posing as the vanguard of a new era, but their euphoria was fleeting. The following day, Tuesday, 28 June, an overwhelming 172 Labour MPs voted at yet another PLP meeting for Corbyn to go. By now, sixty-four frontbenchers had resigned. Just fifty MPs supported him. Corbyn visibly sank in his chair. In his office, McDonnell wailed, 'It's all over,' and suggested that Corbyn offer some sort of olive branch. Even Abbott feared he would be forced to resign. The villain, she suspected, was McDonnell, who she believed was organising a coup of his own. 'He's having talks with Jon Lansman,' she told Corbyn. 'He's not looking after your best interests.' Their safety net was that McDonnell would find it difficult to win a leadership election.

It was Milne and McCluskey who rescued Corbyn. Both appealed to the leader's faith. The left had waited a hundred years to control the Labour movement, and surrender was unimaginable. Nor was there scope for compromise or 'outreach' to the rebel leaders. They determined that the saboteurs who sought to de-legitimise him would be squashed. To manage the crisis, Karie Murphy barred some rebels from entering the leader's office. Even Andy Burnham was denied entry. At approved meetings, Abbott stood vigil to prevent her one-time lover tipping over the edge. Looking washed-out, Corbyn repeated, 'I'm not going to resign. I'm not going to damage the cause.' No one could decide whether he was a skilful strategist or an unimaginative simpleton. Finally emerging from his office into the corridor, he showed renewed defiance. 'Today's vote by MPs,' he said, 'has no constitutional legitimacy.' Unleashed, Momentum activists had begun to denigrate the 172 rebel MPs on Twitter, accusing them of betrayal and issuing stark threats of deselection, violence and even murder. Fearing for their safety, some MPs hesitated before leaving their offices.

During that prolonged hiatus, Tom Watson was certain that Corbyn could not be saved. 'He's going to resign,' he guaranteed newspaper editors. 'Go Now!' roared the *Mirror*'s front-page headline, unusually signed by the editor Lloyd Embley, a Labour loyalist who urged a 'persuasive contender' to come forward and save the party. 'Will he be prime minister?' asked Kevin Maguire, the newspaper's left-wing columnist. 'No.' The same forecast was offered by the *Guardian*: 'The Corbyn experiment is effectively over.' Few doubted that Labour's malaise was terminal. The choice, the *Guardian* reckoned, was between different captains of the *Titanic*. 'Labour,' it went on, 'is struggling to find an identity.' In reality, the party had an all too clear future identity: it would be Marxist, and its members would be re-educated to appreciate the new route to socialism. Both the *Guardian* and the *Mirror* misunderstood the party's new direction.

To show that Corbyn was in command, Milne invited Sky News's cameras to record the first meeting of the new shadow cabinet. Corbyn was flanked by the remain-supporting Cat Smith, an MP for just thirteen months, and by Tom Watson, even though he was still urging his leader to resign.

'This seems a bad idea, Seumas,' said Corbyn, spotting the flaw of being squashed between two critics.

'I'm not sure this is a great idea either,' agreed Milne.

'Can we do something later?' Corbyn asked the Sky journalist. 'OK?'

Fifteen minutes later, the Sky team returned to the room. The scene had changed. Corbyn was now flanked by Emily Thornberry and Steve Rotheram, his parliamentary assistant. Watson had disappeared completely – he was not even in the room. Airbrushing had been a familiar tactic in Stalin's era. Cynics would compliment Milne for mimicking the control freakery prevalent under Blair.

'Are you rolling?' Corbyn asked the journalist. 'We're going to do a short piece which I'll record,' he continued, 'then the microphone will be turned off and then there'll be some pictures of our beautiful faces.' Reports about the transition of a contrived but customary photo opportunity in the leader's office into chaos did not surprise Lewisham East MP Heidi Alexander. 'Whenever he appeared on TV to explain Labour's position,' she reflected some weeks later, 'the result was confusion or despair.' At shadow cabinet meetings, she observed, Corbyn would read out his position from a typed sheet of paper. 'I hated being part of something so inept, so unprofessional, so shoddy.' Good people recruited to his office soon left. 'It was a joke.' Corbyn rejected her criticism. His method, he explained, was to listen and summarise the conversation: 'It's a style she might be misreading.'

The following day he returned to the Commons for prime minister's questions. The fury in the Labour ranks behind him had intensified. Several Labour MPs muttered loudly that he had voted leave. After Corbyn mentioned the referendum result, the wounded Cameron told the House, 'I know the Honourable Gentleman says he put his back into it. All I can say is that I'd hate to see him when he's not trying.' Then, genuinely angry about Corbyn saying that the result would cause workers insecurity and poverty, he snapped, 'It might be in my party's interest for him to sit there – but it's not in the national interest. And I would say: "For heaven's sake, man, go!"'

Few politicians could have withstood such vitriol. Corbyn returned to his office and again contemplated resigning. Over the following hours, McDonnell kept him hostage. 'No matter how bad it gets,' he would later say, 'determination is what you need. We're doing something we've been working for thirty, forty years of our lives. And this opportunity has come. We didn't expect it. But now it's come we're making the most of it.' As he often did, he quoted the left-wing Italian philosopher Antonio Gramsci, this time his adage 'Pessimism of the intellect, optimism of the will.'

To destroy wealth and established power, Gramsci had written, socialists should ignore the state and Parliament, and attack the ruling elite. As students of revolutionary history, McDonnell and Milne resolutely discounted surrender as an option. They took comfort from knowing how the Bolsheviks had suppressed many rebellions before establishing their authority. By the evening, Corbyn, without apparent irony, issued a statement attacking the 172 MPs as disloyal. The snap response from the majority was unapologetic: he himself had voted against Labour 617 times since 1983, and had supported Tony Benn's attempt to overthrow Neil Kinnock in 1988. The loyalty of the 172 was to their constituents and the 9.4 million Labour voters, many of whom would refuse to back the current leader. In his riposte, Corbyn quoted the support of 248,000 party members. It was a stalemate, with still no Labour moderate daring to make an issue of either Corbyn's Marxism or his anti-Semitism. Instead, their fire was directed at John McDonnell.

Until Corbyn's election as leader, McDonnell had never concealed his appetite for revolution. He interpreted even moments of average turmoil as a prelude to Armageddon. 'This is a classic crisis of the economy,' he had told a group after a bank failure back in 2013, 'a classic capitalist crisis. I've been waiting for this for a generation. For Christ's sake, don't waste it. You know, let's use this to explain to people this system is based on greed and profit and does not work. We've got to demand systemic change. Look. I'm straight. I'm honest with people. I'm a Marxist.' His audience had cheered. Three years later, a recording of the speech emerged. To his face on BBC TV, Tory MP Anna Soubry accused McDonnell of being 'a very nasty piece of work'. Dressed in his adopted banker's uniform – blue suit, white shirt and tie – McDonnell soberly protested that his announcement of his communist leanings 'was a joke', and not for the first time denied that he was a Marxist. His audacity was noteworthy. Earlier that year he had told the *New Yorker* in a joint interview with Corbyn that although neither of them wanted to totally destroy capitalism, he did admit that one weapon they would use would be a wealth tax. 'People have had enough of neoliberal economics,' agreed Corbyn in the interview. 'They don't want to live in an unequal society any more.' Marxism, they volunteered, was the answer. But now, under siege, both men denied their core beliefs. Repudiating them had become critical to Corbyn's survival.

At that moment, few understood that Corbyn himself was the issue. Rather than draining the swamp, he had brought it with him. Among the many stains blighting his past was his subscription between 2013 and 2015 to 'Palestine Live', a Facebook page popular among Holocaust deniers. Noted for its vicious anti-

Semitic statements, it was just one of forty virulently anti-Zionist accounts Corbyn was following. His interest had been raised by his secretary Nicolette Petersen. In 2010 she had been instructed to submit to Palestine News a guide of how to deselect Labour candidates and MPs who were 'friends of Israel'.

Corbyn believed that Zionists were a malign influence across the world, but would not accept that his anti-Zionism had blended into anti-Semitism. Commissioning Shami Chakrabarti's investigation was intended to uphold that conviction and smother the backlash. The reason for her investigation had been complaints about at least ten explicit anti-Semitic attacks on Labour MPs and Labour supporters by party members. She decided not to investigate a single case. Rather, she described them as 'unhappy incidents'. To dilute any criticism even further, she refused to define anti-Semitism. Unusually for a lawyer, she avoided the distinction between justified criticism of the Israeli government's policies and the overtly anti-Semitic conflation of Jews, Zionists and Israel. She also deliberately discounted the adoption of the internationally approved definition of anti-Semitism formulated by the International Holocaust Remembrance Alliance (IHRA) in May 2016. 'I thought we should set the bar higher,' she said later. By those limitations, she effectively ignored the left's demonisation of Zionist Israel.

Towards the end of her inquiry, she interviewed Corbyn. 'I put to Jeremy the list of people he had met and shared platforms with in the past,' she would say, 'and he had good answers. He was searching for peace and trying to get reconciliation.' She concluded that his anti-Zionism was not anti-Semitic, but only passionately supportive of Palestinian rights. Faced with accusations by Luciana Berger and many other Jewish MPs and peers that her inquiry was biased, she would reply that while she would not judge Berger, she did not know if she was 'conflating'. It was an odd choice of word. Berger could have accused Corbyn of anti-Semitism, Chakrabarti was suggesting, just because she disliked Corbyn. In other words, she was 'weaponising' anti-Semitism. While criticising Berger, Chakrabarti asserted her own purity: 'I wouldn't work for Jeremy if I thought he was anti-Semitic.'

As she was writing her report, Chakrabarti discussed her conclusions with Milne – but she would deny that he vetted or influenced her. 'In Shami's opinion,' recalls an insider with the authority of a witness, 'she had delivered what Milne required to end the dispute. But she had failed to grasp the seriousness of the Jews' despair. She was out of her depth.' In the opinion of Jews who personally claim to have experienced Milne's ill-treatment of them, as well as of non-Jewish eyewitnesses, Chakrabarti ignored Milne's insensitivity – she would say that he did 'not have a visceral hatred of Israel and is not anti-Semitic'. Either way, her investigation was over, her job done. Milne assured Corbyn there was nothing to fear.

On 30 June, near the Aldwych in central London, Corbyn stood beside Shami Chakrabarti as she introduced her report to a hall packed with his supporters. Watching from the side were Milne and members of Momentum, and scattered among the audience were a small number of Labour MPs. In the spotlight stood Chakrabarti, smiling as she was congratulated by Corbyn. He had good reason to be relieved. She had reported that although there was 'occasionally a toxic atmosphere', Labour was not 'overrun by anti-Semitism'. To reach that conclusion she made no mention of Corbyn calling Hamas and Hezbollah his 'friends', ignored the Naz Shah and Ken Livingstone controversies, and disregarded Josh Simons's four-page account of repugnant comments by Corbyn's advisers. 'Thanks very much for this,' she had emailed Simons. 'I'll take this very seriously.' His evidence was ignored. To complete her work, she incorporated only an anodyne part of Jan Royall's report on Oxford's Labour Club, and did not cite Royall's conclusion of finding 'clear' evidence of 'the ancient virus of anti-Semitism' in the Labour Party. With those omissions, Chakrabarti absolved Corbyn of any responsibility, recommended that any future suspensions from the party be kept secret, ruled out lifetime membership bans, and declared that any Labour Party members who were guilty of anti-Semitism should not be disciplined.

At the end of her brief speech, Corbyn spoke. 'Our Jewish friends,' he said, aware of the implications of his comparison, 'are no more responsible for the actions of Israel or the Netanyahu government than our Muslim friends are for those self-styled Islamic state organisations.' In equating Israelis with ISIS, Corbyn was clearly stating that the barbaric atrocities committed by Islamic terrorists were no different from violence committed by Israelis against Palestinians, albeit that the brutalities were authorised by a democratic state in which Palestinians served as members of parliament and as judges in the supreme court, studied alongside Jews in universities, and were treated in the same hospital wards.

Before Corbyn had finished speaking, the former chief rabbi Lord Sacks accused him of spouting 'pure anti-Semitism'. Considering Labour's 'recent troubles', said Sacks, 'it shows how deep the sickness is in parts of the left of British politics today'. Any comparison of Jews and ISIS terrorists, he continued, was 'demonisation of the highest order, an outrage, unacceptable'.

Among those seated in the hall was Ruth Smeeth, the Jewish Labour MP for Stoke-on-Trent North, while standing in the aisle nearby was Marc Wadsworth, a Momentum member. Wadsworth was handing out a press release calling for the de-selection of MPs – 'traitors' – opposed to the leadership. He refused to give a copy to Smeeth, as in his opinion she ranked among the party's enemies. Her treachery was 'proven' when she asked a *Daily Telegraph* journalist seated next to her to read out the press release. To Smeeth's surprise, Wadsworth snapped at her that not only was she 'working hand-in-hand' with the right-wing media by speaking to the journalist, but she was also a Jew. Smeeth burst into tears. 'I was attacked,' she said later, 'by a Momentum activist and Corbyn supporter who used traditional anti-Semitic slurs to attack me for being part of the media conspiracy.' As the hapless MP visibly struggled with her emotions, the insult was compounded when, at the end of his presentation, Corbyn walked through the audience and greeted

Wadsworth. 'I outed Smeeth,' Wadsworth told him proudly. 'Bloody talking to the Torygraph.' Glancing at Smeeth, Corbyn saw that she was in tears, shared a laugh with Wadsworth, and walked out of the hall.

In the days after that incident, Smeeth received thousands of abusive messages, including death threats. 'It is beyond belief,' she later said, 'that someone [i.e. Wadsworth] should come to the launch of a report on anti-Semitism in the Labour Party and espouse such vile conspiracy theories about Jewish people while the leader stood by and did absolutely nothing.' In his own defence, Corbyn said that he had been misunderstood.

Shami Chakrabarti agreed. Presenting herself as a bridge between Corbyn, the party and his critics, she drew comfort from his supporters, especially a small, vocal group of anti-Zionist Jews. Allegations that Corbyn was anti-Semitic, they said, were 'smears against the leader'. Few Labour MPs offered support to Smeeth. Fearful of a backlash from Muslims in their constituencies, many did not want to risk deselection.

Beyond Parliament, within hours of the report's publication Chakrabarti's reputation was being shredded, partly on account of her failure to consider that Corbyn had not vocally opposed the forced segregation of Muslims at party meetings. She had also ignored male Muslim officials refusing to allow women to be selected as Labour candidates in at least two constituencies. In later interviews, including on the BBC's *Today* programme, she would expose her poor understanding of anti-Semitism by failing to robustly condemn those who disputed Israel's right to exist. Further allegations of her prejudices emerged, in particular over Moazzam Begg, a fundamentalist British Muslim who had been imprisoned at Guantánamo Bay. After his release she had called him a 'wonderful advocate ... for human rights and in particular for human liberty'. In Afghanistan, Begg had declared that 'Israel's crimes far outweigh the Taliban's who are in their own country. Zionist Israelis aren't.' On his return to Britain he associated with Cage, an organisation that defended British members of ISIS who had executed innocent civilians.

Chakrabarti was not embarrassed by her admiration for such a figure. By then she was also associated with Phil Shiner, a lawyer who had been found guilty of inventing hundreds of allegations of the abuse of Iraqis by British soldiers. Some would later say that she was as naïve about Begg and Shiner as she was about anti-Semitism.

The outburst of bitterness towards Chakrabarti and Corbyn took McDonnell by surprise. 'It's like warfare in *Lord of the Flies*,' he said. Amid new rumours that Corbyn might quit, Angela Eagle announced that she would stand for the leadership. Her declaration exposed the feebleness of those opposed to him. Not only did Eagle's unengaging personality and modest intellect make her unsuitable as a political leader, she also lacked the experience to challenge Corbyn's Marxism, and many of her supporters were Blairite peers without a vote. Even so, as a stalking horse for the anti-Corbynistas, she was a threat. Len McCluskey again stepped in. A new leadership election, he warned, would start 'a civil war that will be bitter and ugly and may never allow the party to reunite again'. Since there was an overwhelming majority of Labour MPs who opposed Corbyn, McCluskey's warning would normally have been ignored, but few moderates were prepared to risk deselection by supporting a lacklustre candidate, especially as the interventions of Momentum activists were intensifying.

At that moment, the moderate Labour MP Peter Kyle was battling against Mark Sandell, a Momentum agitator who was attempting to have him deselected from his Hove constituency. Sandell's next target was the Lewisham Deptford MP Vicky Foxcroft. The outcome was still uncertain. At the same time, Stella Creasy, an anti-Corbyn MP representing Walthamstow, discovered that Andrew Fisher had organised a Momentum rally in her constituency without telling her. Even Eagle's core supporters feared the end of their careers. Others muttered that she had voted for the Iraq war. With little immediate support, soon after she made her announcement she decided to withdraw. In just hours, the crisis had fizzled out. As before, Corbyn's strength was the absence of a convincing challenger.

Later that same day, to prove his patriotism, Corbyn went to Westminster Abbey for a service to commemorate the fallen in the Battle of the Somme. Across Parliament Square, his office was refusing requests from several MPs to meet him and press him to resign. 'We're not letting that happen,' said a Corbyn aide. 'He's a seventy [sic]-year-old man' who was owed 'a duty of care … There's a culture of bullying. Maybe it's a Blairite/Brownite thing.' The leader's office was once again being fenced off, although in briefings Kevin Slocombe insisted that Corbyn was enjoying the fight. His miscalculation was to assume that the Jewish question had gone away.

An all-party committee had been convened to consider the allegations against the Labour Party, and its swift report, unlike Shami Chakrabarti's, criticised Corbyn for allowing 'institutional anti-Semitism' to thrive in the Labour movement, permitting his party to become 'a safe space for those with vile attitudes towards Jewish people', and for his 'lack of consistent leadership' in challenging racism. The same MPs would condemn Chakrabarti's report as a whitewash. The reaction of those accused was predictable: Corbyn dismissed the MPs as biased and Livingstone scoffed that their report was 'rigged', while Chakrabarti sighed that Labour was not 'much worse than any other party', and that accusations of anti-Semitism had been used as part of Labour's civil war. Her report and its aftermath appeared to suggest her sense that the Jews' complaints were not credible.

The recriminations and plots within the parliamentary Labour Party were not festering in isolation. Westminster was the focus of a country plagued by recriminations about Brexit, anger about multiculturalism, and distrust of both politicians and businessmen. Britain's traditional tone of tolerant debate had seemingly evaporated. Both major political parties were mired by chaos and ill-feeling. Discounted as irresponsible and heavily criticised for his conduct as one of the leaders of the leave campaign, Boris Johnson, the favourite to win the Tory leadership once Cameron stood down, suddenly withdrew from the race after being dumped by his former supporter Michael Gove.

That was the story that dominated the headlines, but on the sideline, Corbyn's future still hung in the balance. In the hiatus, even the *Observer*, usually so loyal to Labour, concluded that he was 'finished as a credible national politician. [The cost of his] ideological self-indulgence is electoral irrelevance.' Amid fears that the party would split, Tom Watson met Corbyn on 4 July and once again asked for his resignation. Once again he was rebuffed. If there were another leadership election, said Corbyn, he would stand as the unity candidate. He doubted that the rebel MPs had either the courage or the leader to create a new party. Over the following day, Watson floundered. He was failing to broker a deal with his friend and former flatmate Len McCluskey, while McCluskey himself was secretly plotting with McDonnell to string out the crisis in the hope that it might be defused by splits among Corbyn's opponents. That secrecy was only disturbed by the warfare at the next meeting of the PLP at the beginning of July.

Pointedly, Corbyn boycotted the meeting, but his hard-left supporter Dennis Skinner, forever known as 'the Beast of Bolsover', provocatively mocked all his critics in the Commons. Party members, he scoffed, were more important than politicians. Incensed, former leader Neil Kinnock struck back: 'We are going to fight and we are going to win.' Thirty years earlier, he had defeated Tony Benn, Skinner and Militant Tendency. Now he was bruised that his victory seemed all for nothing. 'I'm bloody angry. It's bloody appalling,' he spluttered. And that seemed to be the climax of the meeting. McDonnell laughed in relief. At a rally of the left in north-west London he scoffed, 'The only good thing about it is, as plotters they were fucking useless.'

14

Squashing the Opposition

Spared the pressure of an immediate leadership election, Corbyn began another makeover. After finally agreeing with his staff to stick to the scripts he was given, master the autocue and be coached for prime minister's questions, he apologised for comparing ISIS to Israel during the presentation of the Chakrabarti report; and as for his calling Hamas and Hezbollah 'friends' in 2009, he said, 'I regret using those words.'

His actions belied his apologies. Buoyed by his critics' vacillations, he asked for Naz Shah's suspension to be removed, and simultaneously his office dismissed Josh Simons's complaint that Chakrabarti had dismissed his submission as 'false and part of the campaign against his leadership'. He also defended Jackie Walker, a black Jewish activist, writer and former vice chair of Momentum who had been suspended again from the party for saying that Jews were the 'chief financiers of the sugar and slave trade' in the West Indies. She had also spoken about Jews 'celebrating' the Holocaust, by which she meant that they were exploiting their own genocide for political advantage. It would be 'wonderful', she said, if Holocaust Day was not just about the Jews, an opinion endorsed by Momentum.

In Corbyn's opinion, none of those statements was anti-Semitic, and Walker's accusers were mendacious patrons of Israel, intimidating an honest critic. He did not consider that Rothschilds' bank, which he believed had been guiltily involved in the British Empire's commerce, was minuscule, and only became 'notorious' in Nazi propaganda. Without requesting an apology, he agreed that she should be reinstated as a member and consented to share a platform with her at a Momentum rally. Those who criticised him were silenced by an eruption of anger towards America and Tony Blair.

On 6 July, the fourth official report of the events leading up to the Iraq war was published. After a seven-year inquiry, a deeply unimpressive panel under Sir John Chilcot condemned Britain's military, intelligence services and Tony Blair for mistakes leading to the invasion and occupation. However, the report failed to address Blair's wholesale corruption of the machinery of government, so dozens of culpable civil servants escaped censure. Incapable of mastering the flaws of the report, Corbyn focused on the simple 'disastrous decision' to go to war, and blamed a 'small number of leading figures in the government' who were 'none too scrupulous about how they made their case', and apologised to the people of Iraq. His accurate predictions of disaster enhanced his status, but his credibility was challenged because he ignored the nature of Saddam Hussein. While the war itself was not justified, it had removed a brutal dictator who over thirteen years had disregarded seventeen UN resolutions while he gassed Kurds, murdered Iraqis and prevented inspectors from visiting his bomb factories. Corbyn's partisanship riled his critics, and put an end to the final attempt between Watson and McCluskey to resolve the deadlock over his future. Menacingly, McCluskey accused Watson of 'an act of sabotage fraught with peril for the future of the party'. In the Commons, Ian Austin heckled Corbyn as a 'disgrace' who should 'sit down and shut up'.

The revolt could no longer be contained. On 11 July, Angela Eagle decided after all to formally challenge for the leadership. Under the party's rules, Corbyn would need to secure the nomination of thirty-five MPs if he were to be on the ballot. Unlike in 2015, none of his opponents would oblige on this occasion. The left's tactic was intimidation. McCluskey warned the 'rebel' MPs not to use 'legal means' to exclude Corbyn from the ballot. If the anti-Corbynistas dared to insist on abiding by the rules, he threatened, the result would be 'a lasting division in the party', and worse. Countering his menace depended on

Eagle showing leadership. But instead of rousing the rebels, she was silent.

Corbyn's obstacle was the NEC. Only it could change the rules. To save the party from Marxist control, Iain McNicol appealed to the NEC's members to vote against Corbyn. His weakness, he knew, was the quality of Corbyn's challenger. Sharing that despair about Eagle's inadequacies, Owen Smith, an otherwise insignificant Welsh MP, offered himself as an alternative contender for the leadership.

Neither Eagle nor Smith had much idea about self-promotion. While both were inconspicuous over the weekend, Corbyn starred at the Durham Miners' Gala, 100,000 people cheering his defiance. And yet, beyond the faithful, his poll rating hit minus 41, a record. Labour's fate, rather than the national destiny, dominated the media – although on the same day, 11 July, Theresa May was by default confirmed as the Tory leader and the new prime minister.

Two days later, David Cameron made his farewell speech to the Commons. Corbyn showed no goodwill to the Bullingdon boy. As the ex-prime minister left the chamber in silence, he walked out too. Without a word to Cameron – magnanimity was not in his tool kit – he headed off to a meeting of the Cuba Solidarity Committee.

The outcome of the NEC's vote on whether Corbyn would be on the leadership ballot was uncertain. In the countdown, his bid to remove his enemies was ratcheted up. Shortly before the NEC met in Victoria, Jon Ashworth, the MP for Leicester South and a critic of Corbyn, received an email from Katy Clark telling him that he had been expelled from the NEC. This decision was overturned during a stormy meeting of the shadow cabinet. Miffed that at least one enemy was still there to confound him, Corbyn arrived at the NEC meeting along with Milne. The unusual sight of police officers at the building's entrance reflected the general atmosphere of hostility. Inside, Corbyn was asked to leave the committee room while his position on the ballot was discussed. He refused, and also insisted that the vote should not, as normal, be secret. Two women members protested, fearing violent threats if their decisions were publicised. Many female Labour MPs, they said, were terrified by Momentum's coercion. When Corbyn insisted on an open ballot, both women burst into tears. He was unmoved. Defeated in a vote, he finally agreed to leave the room.

The slight was meaningless. Outnumbered by the trade unions, the moderates on the NEC lost by four votes. 'I'm delighted,' said Corbyn as he posed for selfies on the street. 'That will strengthen our party in order to defeat this Tory government.' He repeated his pledge of 'kinder' politics, but no compromises would be offered to win over disaffected moderates. His next target, he agreed with McCluskey, would be Iain McNicol. His proposed replacement was Jennie Formby, a former Unite official, a member of Militant, and the mother of McCluskey's son. Formby's appointment would also suit Karie Murphy, who expected her orders to be obeyed. Without ceremony, McCluskey was enthroned as Corbyn's Godfather.

The first opinion poll put Corbyn 20 per cent ahead of Eagle. On 19 July she quit the race to allow Owen Smith a clear run. The former employee of the pharmaceutical corporation Pfizer offered neither originality nor authority. Worse, he lacked a national organisation to compete with Momentum. Even Smith himself recognised this insurmountable weakness.

Fearing impotence, he tried to reposition himself as further to the left than Corbyn. His ploy was threatened by over 100,000 new applications for membership, assumed to be from Corbyn supporters. To deter rogue voters, the NEC had increased the annual membership fee from £3 to £25, and claimed to have retrospectively barred 100,000 people who had joined in the previous six months. There was good reason to doubt such statistics. The party claimed to have removed Trotskyites and members identified by complainants for such actions as shouting 'Zio!' In reality, just 1,258 people had been barred, and Corbyn's popularity was increasing remorselessly. The media was unimpressed. 'The poison in Labour's veins is so deep, so toxic,' commented the *Mirror*, 'that nobody can see a way of ending this harmoniously.'

'I hold out the hand of friendship,' said Corbyn, then announced that all MPs would face reselection before the 2020

election. To minimise the threat to his candidacy, his spokesman denied his support for mandatory reselection, but the
purge had long begun. Hundreds of Momentum members, willing executioners, stormed into the annual meeting of Brighton
and Hove's Labour Party to deselect Peter Kyle. Momentum
directed similar tactics against Thangam Debbonaire, the MP
for Bristol West, while she was being treated for breast cancer.
Other women MPs accused John McDonnell of urging supporters at rallies to demonstrate outside their constituency offices.
As usual, McDonnell and Jon Lansman denied the eyewitness
evidence of their followers' threats of rape and even death. A
brick was thrown through a window of Angela Eagle's office.
She directly accused Corbyn of allowing a 'culture of bullying'
to develop. 'It's being done in your name,' one of the victims told
Corbyn. 'I don't allow bullying,' he replied. Owen Smith spoke
about a 'bear pit' of violence inspired by Corbyn and McDonnell.
By doing nothing to stop the aggression, snapped former home
secretary David Blunkett, Corbyn 'condoned the force'. His face
was visible at the foot of the scaffold.

As the threats against MPs accumulated, Len McCluskey
invoked a hoary canard: government agents, he claimed, were
operating in disguise and using 'dark practices' to bring Corbyn
and McDonnell into disrepute. 'There's a hysteria being whipped
up by MI5 in the social media,' he lashed out. He scornfully
brushed aside Eagle's fears: 'She was just a pawn.' On the same
day, Seema Malhotra, the MP for Feltham and Heston, who had
resigned from McDonnell's team, discovered that his aides and
Karie Murphy had twice broken into her Commons office.
Murphy, she reported, had been 'aggressive and intimidating' to
her staff. Corbyn, McDonnell and Murphy dismissed the unauthorised entries as 'a small matter of miscommunication'.
Margaret Hodge was struck by how much what was happening
recalled the 1980s: 'It is the politics of intolerance, bullying and
intimidation.' Corbyn resented the criticism, as he always did.
To counter accusations of misogyny, he posed for the media
with eight women: members of Momentum, Muslim activists,
hard-left teenagers and his wife Laura.

He ignored the wider electorate. 'He speaks only to his tribe,' complained a veteran Islington member. 'He's making no effort to speak to the wider public, to win them over.' Further evidence of this was a speech in the Commons in which, in defiance of the party's official policy, he once again opposed the renewal of Trident. Nuclear weapons, he said to heckles from Labour MPs, had failed to prevent genocide in Rwanda in 1994 and ISIS's atrocities in Iraq. He made no mention of the nuclear threat from Russia, North Korea and Iran. He also disputed that bombing would defeat ISIS in Iraq or Syria. He preferred negotiation. In a free vote, 140 Labour MPs supported Trident and only forty-seven voted with Corbyn.

Commentators criticised Corbyn's 'poverty of ambition' for failing to win the political centre, but they misunderstood. As unwilling as ever to compromise, he planned to defeat the PLP, transform Labour into a genuinely Marxist party, and win sufficient electoral votes to become prime minister. Just the one victory would be enough. Thereafter, McDonnell boasted, their changes would be 'irreversible'. The swift destruction of Britain's capitalist economy, mirroring Hugo Chávez's impact in Venezuela, cast doubt over the fate of Britain's democracy: Venezuela was just the latest example of the fact that no Marxist government had ever been democratically removed from office. Just as Corbyn and McDonnell intended to revise the Labour Party's rules to permanently protect their coup from any challenge by social democrats, they would change the British constitution to cement their victory. The result of the second general election would be a foregone conclusion.

Corbyn's second leadership campaign was far more relaxed than his frenetic first attempt. Dressed in slacks, a tieless crumpled shirt and Mexican sandals, he repeated the same speech at rally after rally. Consistently enthusiastic, his audiences were thrilled by his declaiming of socialist principles. Like religious converts, they embraced the endearing sixty-seven-year-old who claimed to be reading a book about Icelandic lore and admitted to his unfamiliarity with the TV presenters Ant and Dec. They rapturously applauded his pledge not to commit the British military to defend any NATO ally, but instead to disband the organisation as 'a danger to the world' that was deliberately 'escalating tension' with Russia. Others were enthralled by his long TV interview with the novelist and poet Ben Okri. Among the list of literary works he described as the source of his inspiration was Oscar Wilde's 'The Ballad of Reading Gaol', a confection created by his office to suit his audience. Few of them knew that the only books on his shelves at home dated from the post-war years and were about the Labour movement, and inherited from his parents. Similarly, after he admitted in another interview that 'I haven't been to the cinema in ages. I mean I don't mind the cinema,' his advisers told him to reply '*Casablanca*' when next asked to name his favourite film. His only honest reply to Okri was when he was asked to choose between power and revolution. His reply – 'Revolution' – drew admiring gasps. His fans still cheered even when he could not correctly answer how many MPs were needed for a party to have a majority at Westminster.

YouGov described the typical Corbyn supporter as a young, middle-class charity worker who spent fifty hours a week online, ate vegetarian curries and was interested in the NHS, homelessness and climate change. A Corbynista, according to YouGov's survey, would describe him or herself as ethical and personally prone to depression. That stereotype of an oddball who was also against Trident, angered by climate change and stridently anti-business matched the party which Corbyn was refashioning to represent idealists and losers. In despair, moderates believed that Corbyn's base was blind to their hero's frailties – an opinion shared by his first wife, Jane Chapman. Convinced by her personal experience that his limitations were being overlooked, she decided to vote against her former husband.

Ignoring the pinpricks, and proud to speak on behalf of YouGov's stereotype supporter, Corbyn posed as the heroic crusader for social justice besieged by right-wing barons to launch a classic demolition job of his opponent. His attack centred on Owen Smith's employment by Pfizer. Briefed by Corbyn's office, BBC TV asked Smith why he had supported the NHS's purchase of private services. The interviewer endorsed

Corbyn's argument that medical research should not be 'farmed out' to multinational pharmaceutical corporations, but undertaken by the NHS. Smith fell into the trap. Instead of defending his former career, he denied the facts that capitalist corporations rather than socialist governments had developed antibiotics, anti-cancer drugs and vaccines against shingles and malaria. The NHS had never produced a single drug. Having positioned himself on the extreme left, he refused to challenge Corbyn's plan to make Britain's drug companies state-owned. Nationalisation, Corbyn knew, appealed to his base, which favoured, as he put it, 'a new egalitarian economic model'. He was unconcerned that most pharmaceutical corporations and their researchers would move abroad to escape political control and reduced incomes. Playing to his supporters, he further pledged that every employer of more than twenty-one people should be subject to a 'compulsory pay audit' to prevent discrimination against women, transgender people and ethnic minorities.

The enthusiasm of Corbyn's supporters masked what the country as a whole was feeling. The latest opinion polls showed that 51 per cent of voters supported Theresa May as prime minister, and just 16 per cent Corbyn. That sparked Tory calls for a snap election, but May rejected the idea. Asked on BBC TV whether Corbyn would resign if he lost the next general election, John McDonnell replied, 'That would be inevitable. Of course he would. Any Labour leader who loses an election usually goes.' Corbyn contradicted his ally. 'Nothing is inevitable,' he said; the party would decide. Encouraged by the huge crowds, he was sure that any chance of his being defeated in the leadership election had evaporated. New anti-Corbyn groups, including Labour Tomorrow, which had a £250,000 war chest, were feeble. His criticisms of Britain – whether highlighting job insecurity at companies like Sports Direct or the greed of the arch-capitalist Philip Green – resonated even among those close to Theresa May. At least 255 constituencies endorsed Corbyn, while only forty-nine backed Smith.

In the instability caused by Brexit, British politics had become contrary. No senior Tory politician challenged Corbyn's manifesto, or asked him to identify a British corporation that required government investment. Ideology-lite Tories ridiculed Marxist promises of economic security, but lacked the intellect to argue for capitalism's advantages. Accelerating the drift, the *Spectator*'s editor Fraser Nelson openly disparaged David Cameron's record – the creation of 2.6 million new jobs, historically low unemployment (4.9 per cent), the fewest children living in workless households, the bottom 50 per cent paying just 10 per cent of all income tax while the richest 5 per cent paid nearly 57 per cent, and Britain enjoying one of the world's fastest rates of growth. In the ideological vacuum, May's team fashioned speeches in imitation of Labour's 'progressive' goals of reducing poverty and injustice. For stealing Labour's policies, they won Nelson's praise.

Just as some Tories were losing self-confidence, Corbyn's economic advisers Thomas Piketty and David Blanchflower complained that he should have quit after the 172 MPs voted against him and announced their own resignation. Corbyn, wrote Blanchflower, had 'no chance of winning a general election'. And if there were the 'slightest prospect' of him becoming prime minister, 'the bond and equity markets would eat him for lunch'. Although he never met Corbyn and encountered McDonnell only once, Blanchflower was appalled by their idea that the dividends of any company found guilty of failing to pay 'a living wage' would be subject to additional taxes. That, he said, would encourage corporations to move abroad. Nobody in their right mind, he wrote, would serve as governor of the Bank of England under a prime minister who failed to understand the realities of capitalism.*

The desertions of his two advisers had no impact on Corbyn's re-election rollercoaster. This time Tony Blair, Gordon Brown and Neil Kinnock did not speak out against him. With no enthusiasm for Owen Smith, they accepted Corbyn's victory. Instead of delivering a bloody nose, the challenger had given

---

* Blanchflower's own credibility was questionable after he asserted, quite wrongly, that 'the UK appears to be already in recession' following 'a major economic crisis caused by the shock Brexit vote'.

Corbyn a blood transfusion. Nevertheless, some critics refused to be cowed. The leaders of several London Labour councils voted for Smith, as did mayor Sadiq Khan, who called Corbyn a 'disastrous' leader who should take his share of blame for Brexit. 'I'm afraid that we simply cannot afford to go on like this,' he wrote. Corbyn's ratings were 'the worst of any opposition leader'. Khan's criticism was repeated by the Newcastle MP Chi Onwurah, one of two shadow cabinet ministers for culture. 'There's nothing socialist about incompetence,' she scoffed, adding how she had been singled out for discrimination. After her appointment, Corbyn had refused to speak to her, and had simultaneously given the same post to Thangam Debbonaire. 'No one knew what he wanted us to do,' complained Onwurah. In reply, Corbyn's spokesman denied that she had been 'singled out'. Certainly everyone was suffering from the same ineptitude, even if that was not what the spokesman had meant.

The day after Khan's denunciation, Corbyn spoke to a huge crowd in Kilburn, north London. His mention of Khan's name provoked loud boos, and the converted roared their adulation of their leader. He was noticeably thrilled. The party was being refashioned in his image, and his critics were being silenced.

With Shami Chakrabarti's report, critics of Jews and Israel were given renewed licence. After the report's publication, Grahame Morris, the Labour MP for Easington and chairman of Labour Friends of Palestine, posted images of Israel's flag with the caption 'Nazis in my village', and compared British Jews serving in Israel's army with British Muslims joining ISIS in Iraq. In the past he had hosted an event with Sameh Habeeb, who had edited a journal which contained Holocaust denial material (which Habeeb said he had not approved, and had removed when it was discovered). Morris was not reprimanded.

Chakrabarti's reward was a peerage, which critics described as 'a shameless kick in the teeth for all who put hope in her wholly compromised inquiry'. Baroness Chakrabarti explained that her elevation to the Lords had been discussed over the past decade, and that the party required a young, qualified lawyer prepared to spend time in the upper chamber. Few saw the appointment so benignly, not least because Corbyn had pledged not to nominate anyone to the upper house. 'The whitewash for peerages,' said a Jewish critic, 'is a scandal that raises serious questions about the integrity of Ms Chakrabarti, her inquiry and the Labour leadership.' The once respected Chakrabarti, said John Mann, had 'sold herself cheaply'. She continued to protest her innocence. 'Jeremy Corbyn,' she said, 'is not a corrupt man and I am not a corrupt woman. There was nothing remotely transactional about it.' Initially she refused to disclose when Corbyn had offered her the peerage, before finally claiming that it was on Cameron's last day in the Commons. Corbyn refused to confirm this. He was fed up with all the whiners.

Only the complaints kept mounting. Tom Watson had heard that officials at the party's headquarters had spotted suspected Trotskyists applying to join Labour – still officially forbidden. Sifting through '180,000 new applications' for membership, the staff noticed 'entryists' sponsored by left-wing constituencies. In a lengthy submission to Corbyn, Watson enclosed a newspaper published by the Trotskyist Alliance for Workers' Liberty with the headline 'Flood Into the Labour Party'. The Alliance had officially disbanded in November 2015 to allow its members to join Labour, radicalise young people and attack older, right-wing party members. Other Trotskyists were infiltrating Labour as members of the 'rabble' called Momentum. Did Corbyn approve of identified Trotskyists – who opposed parliamentary democracy – joining the party, contrary to its rules? 'Some old hands are twisting young arms,' wrote Watson. 'That's how Trotsky entryists operate. Sooner or later, that always ends up in disaster.'

Among those 'old hands' was Jill Mountford of the Trotskyist Alliance, suspended from Labour in February 2016. As an official of Momentum's steering committee, she was organising the telephone banks for Corbyn's re-election campaign and addressing rallies in his support. Corbyn dismissed Watson's complaint. Mountford, he said, was welcome in Labour's big tent. Even Corbyn's brother Piers, despite campaigning in May's council elections for Michelle Baharier, a Marxist standing against the official Labour candidate in Peckham, was allowed to join the party. Nothing had changed in Jeremy Corbyn's world since the early 1970s – his dislike of Jews and favouring Trotskyists to set up their own organisation within Labour. Similarly, he resurrected his old habit of knifing his enemies. Watson, his elected deputy, was criticised for being a 'Trot-hunting … straw man' peddling 'absolute fantasy'. Watson, he said, as a product of his 'vivid imagination', was promoting 'baseless conspiracy theories' that 300,000 new members were 'sectarian extremists … who have suddenly descended on the Labour Party'.

The vilification of Watson increased. Len McCluskey's Unite was financing Momentum. Together, the union leader and Jon Lansman controlled Labour, and by extension Jeremy Corbyn. When Watson made his discovery public, McCluskey accused him of inhabiting 'a world of skulduggery, smears and secret plots'. At the same time, McCluskey was accused by Gerard Coyne, his challenger as Unite's leader, of using exactly the same tactics. The battle to control Labour was brutal.

Corbyn was remarkably consistent in the way he fought his campaigns. As well as adopting the same tactics he had crafted during the 1970s, he championed the same policies, including renationalising the railways. But in promoting that radical change, he revealed two particular characteristics: he ignored the facts, and he was starkly dishonest. Investment in the rail network had gone up by 900 per cent since privatisation in 1997, and the daily experience for some travellers, on new trains and in refurbished stations, had improved. Corbyn ignored key statistics: the number of passengers had increased from 750 million to 1.6 billion a year; British trains were faster and safer than most of those in Continental Europe; fares had risen much less than under nationalisation, while the state subsidy was about the same;* most delays were caused by Network Rail, which was owned by the state; and ticket prices had to be approved by the government. He was convinced that if French and German

---

* In 2014 the railways received £3.8 billion in subsidies and £3.7 billion for track infrastructure. This was at the same level – 29 per cent – as in the final year of the nationalised British Rail.

nationalised rail operators could run British Rail, then British civil servants could perform the same task, and the privatised rail companies would not pocket profits of no less than £240 million in 2014. There was a madcap consistency in Corbyn's ignoring such figures. Put simply, privately financed modernisation offended him. Just as he had objected to the renovation of King's Cross and St Pancras stations, he opposed the construction of HS2, the high-speed train from Euston to the north, because 'it benefits the few and not the many'.

To prove his point, on 11 August he boarded Virgin's 11 a.m. train from London to Newcastle. He was accompanied by Yannis Mendez, a TV director, and Anthony Casey, a writer. Together, they would produce a campaign film to illustrate Corbyn's promise of a 'clear plan for a fully integrated railway in public ownership'. Although this plan was never made public, he guaranteed that, once renationalised, British Rail would never cancel a single train.

As the train left King's Cross, the three men walked through a fairly empty carriage, then a carriage of reserved seats that were also unoccupied, until they reached a third carriage. There, Corbyn sat on the floor outside the lavatory to recite a prepared piece for Mendez's camera about overcrowding on that particular train: 'This is a problem that many passengers face every day … Today, this train is completely ram-packed.' Mendez posted this fabrication on the *Guardian*'s website, with his report of Corbyn joining 'twenty other seatless commuters [on the floor] on a three-hour journey'. In truth, after Corbyn had been filmed for about fifteen minutes he had got up, returned to the carriage he had just walked through, and sat in one of the many unoccupied seats for the remainder of the trip.

Twelve days later, Virgin Trains exposed Corbyn's lie. The proof was in its CCTV footage. The company's chairman Richard Branson personally accused the Labour leader of hypocrisy and spin. Corbyn's staff struggled to establish a rival version, but he was not there to help them explain away his conduct – he was at home making jam. Eventually, Labour's spokesman said that Corbyn had been 'unable to find unreserved seats' and that he was later seated 'after a family were upgraded ... after the first stop'. That was untrue, because the first stop was an hour after Corbyn had sat down on the carriage floor. At a press conference at the end of that day, he still refused to admit what had taken place. 'Can we move on, please?' he said, plainly irritated.

Assuming that the electorate shared his own hatred of Branson, Sam Tarry, Corbyn's campaign director, threatened to renationalise the 'tax exile's' trains. To Tarry's misfortune, his attack provoked newspaper exposés of his own life. As a councillor in Barking, Tarry was required to live in the borough, but neighbours at his registered flat there said a female tenant was the actual resident, while he was regularly seen with his wife at their own house in Brighton. A councillor failing to live at his registered address in the borough – which Tarry denied doing – was acting illegally. To divert attention from this embarrassment, John McDonnell turned on Branson, who as a tax exile, he said, should be stripped of his knighthood for 'not acting in the spirit of our country'. Some Labour MPs wondered whether McDonnell's support for the IRA was in the 'spirit' of Britain. Corbyn's paid appearances on Iran's Press TV were equally open to criticism.

Corbyn finally spoke – not about his deceit on the train, but to explain that the reason for his appearances on Press TV was to 'address issues of human rights'. That was also untrue. On none of the available tapes had he criticised Iran's mistreatment of women and children or the regime's political opponents. Two months later, the *Guardian* apologised for publishing Corbyn's fabrication. After a year of crises – rebellions, resignations and mockery – he was exposed as an unrepentant liar.

On the eve of the leadership election, Corbyn's team met at Esher Place, a conference centre in Surrey owned by Unite. McCluskey, the host, was still under pressure from Gerard Coyne for his alleged unethical behaviour. Also present were Karie Murphy, Andrew Murray, Diane Abbott, John McDonnell, Seumas Milne, Jon Lansman and the former BBC TV journalist Paul Mason. Their agenda was to consolidate the hard left's control over the party. McCluskey suggested that disloyal MPs should be 'held to account' and deselected. That strategy was agreed, and a new list was drawn up: thirteen MPs who had 'abused' Corbyn would be pressured to resign.

Among them was Ben Bradshaw, the MP for Exeter. After the list was exposed, Bradshaw denounced Corbyn as a 'destructive combination of incompetence, deceit and menace'. John Woodcock, another on the list, reviled Corbyn and McDonnell for having 'set themselves up as the high priests of honest and straight-talking politics. Yet as soon as they are challenged, their operation squirms, spins and distorts like the very worst of anything that came before.' As usual, Corbyn would deny any involvement in the proposed purge. 'As you know,' he said, 'I never abuse anybody, tempting as it sometimes is.' Tongue in cheek, he continued, 'I'm very keen on providing olive branches,' and then revealed that he was growing an olive tree on the balcony of his office. 'It's doing very well. It's thriving.' But he refused to discipline those who abused the thirteen MPs. To save themselves from deselection, the listed MPs were instructed in Soviet style to pledge their loyalty to Corbyn – even if they disagreed with his policies.

In that vexed atmosphere, on 24 September a dribble of Labour MPs headed to the Labour Party conference in Liverpool to hear the election results. Outside the security gates, Trotskyists demanded the deselection of 'traitors of our Labour Party'. Inside the dimly-lit, half-empty hall sat the defeated old guard, watching with renewed despair as history repeated itself. Corbyn won 61.8 per cent of the votes, up from 59 per cent in the previous election. The cheers were muted, not least because most of his supporters, disdainful of old-style party conferences, had gone instead to a Momentum rally that same day featuring the Sex Worker Open University and Black Lives Matter. 'We are all part of the same Labour family,' said Corbyn to his cowed audience. He promised to wipe the slate clean if everyone united behind him. 'We certainly can't carry on as we did,' he said with a hint of menace. His old life had been in opposition. Now he was perfecting his skill as executioner.

Officially, the chaos was over. The threat by the 172 MPs had been overcome, the Blairites buried. Tom Watson's appeal to the conference that 'capitalism is not the enemy' and 'we need to win elections' was jeered, and his denunciation of the folly of trashing Blair's achievements drew heckles. Now Corbyn would dictate the agenda. For a start, he did not formally object when the NEC forbade the conference to discuss anti-Semitism, and did not impose a ban on the distribution of leaflets advocating the expulsion of the Jewish Labour Movement. He ignored appeals for help from abused women MPs. However, at the last moment he did allow Seumas Milne to alter the text of defence spokesman Clive Lewis's statement about Trident. Only as he stood in front of the autocue on the stage did Lewis spot how Milne had blurred the party's commitment to renew the missile. Lewis, a passionate Corbynista, was incandescent. But the lesson was explicit: ideological purity superseded electoral politics. The party would unite on Corbyn's terms.

In his own well-structured speech, delivered with confidence and some humour, Corbyn declared that the state knew best how to manage the economy. Labour would fight the next election, he said, to remove all controls on immigration: 'It is not our objective to reduce the numbers.' He blamed 'repeated Western military interventions' for immigration, although the migrants coming to Britain from Nigeria, Somalia, Albania and Pakistan were not escaping 'invasions'. There would be no compromise: 'We cannot abandon our socialist principles because we are told this is the only way to win power. That is nonsense.' He basked in the loud applause.

Next stop was a Socialist Workers event. Among Trotskyites, Corbyn condemned American intervention in Syria and repeated his opposition to 'Prevent', the government programme aimed at dissuading Muslims from joining terrorist groups. It wrongly obstructed their radicalisation, he said. Britons travelling to Syria to join ISIS should not be demonised as terrorists, because that was a value judgement. They were merely 'expressing a point of view', and were not a threat to Britain's security. 'Islamic terrorism', he went on, was an unconscionable label.

Those who wanted to return to Britain after fighting with ISIS should not be prosecuted as terrorists.

Among those Corbyn would have readmitted without redress was Imran Khawaja, a British jihadist who had travelled to Syria, where he posed with several severed heads before faking his own death. After his surreptitious return to Britain he had been convicted under the 2006 Terrorism Act, which Corbyn opposed. Similarly, on his website Corbyn praised Marwan Barghouti, convicted of attacking Israeli citizens and sentenced to five life terms, as 'an icon', and similar to Nelson Mandela. The Trotskyists applauded all those sentiments, as they did Corbyn's eulogy for Fidel Castro, by then close to death. Like Corbyn, they refused to recognise the failures of Cuban communism, and expected every opponent to be deposed. Accordingly, in a telephone call the day after the conference, Rosie Winterton, the chief whip, was fired. Insulted by Corbyn's apparent misogyny, she insisted that after six years' service she was at least entitled to a personal meeting. He agreed, but the dismissal remained in force. To underline Corbyn's appeal for unity, she was replaced by Nick Brown, Gordon Brown's former henchman. Although not of the hard left, Brown could be trusted to twist arms where necessary.

The new shadow cabinet included Diane Abbott as shadow home secretary, Shami Chakrabarti as shadow attorney general, and also some MPs who had earlier resigned in protest over a 'catastrophic' leader. That left Kezia Dugdale, the moderate Scottish leader, as an exceptionally free-spirited opponent. Ever since her promotion after the 2015 general election debacle, Dugdale's relationship with Corbyn had been tempered by Labour's humiliating wipe-out. Neil Findlay, a Marxist Member of the Scottish Parliament, had organised Corbyn's leadership campaign rally in Aberdeen. After hearing him speak about socialism, Dugdale realised that he regarded Scotland as a foreign country. He had refused to campaign there during the EU referendum, and neither understood nor cared that Scottish Labour rejected the far left and was preoccupied with maintaining the Union. To her dismay, on a visit to Glasgow he would say that a second independence referendum was 'absolutely fine'. Blasted by Dugdale for contradicting Scottish Labour's opposition to a new vote, he somersaulted three times over two days, finally opposing a second referendum unless the Scottish Parliament came out in favour. 'A gift for the Tories,' complained a Dugdale adviser. 'How dare you preach unity,' Dugdale asked Corbyn after he had tried to get her expelled from the NEC, 'and try to undermine me as Scottish leader?' For the moment, she survived. In due time, he calculated, she would be pushed aside. The fact that Labour could never secure a Commons majority without winning in Scotland was irrelevant to him. As in all matters, ideology, not political calculation, was decisive.

Leaderless, the moderates could only hope for a ruinous general election defeat. One after another, they recorded their fears. 'I'm in despair at this calamitous situation,' confessed David Blunkett. 'I can't honestly see how we're going to get out of it ... That's my worst possible nightmare – a Labour Party that doesn't connect to the lives of ordinary working people.' Fuming on the sidelines, Tony Blair warned that Britain would become a one-party state. Peter Mandelson said he was praying for an early election, in which Labour's inevitable heavy defeat would lead to Corbyn being deposed. Many Tories were also urging Theresa May to break her pledge and call a snap vote. In the most recent opinion poll, she had scored 44 per cent against Corbyn's 19. Labour needed to win an additional 140 seats in England and Wales, with 40 per cent of the vote, to form a majority government – and that was impossible without Corbyn and Momentum attracting Tory voters with compromises they refused to consider. Professor John Curtice, Britain's pre-eminent psephologist, predicted that in a general election the Tory majority would increase from twelve to forty-four. May was tempted, but a warning note was sounded by a handful of Tories. In 1992 John Major had won a record fourteen million votes, but the Tories' lead in the opinion polls was wiped out soon after by a financial crisis, and then its unity was splintered by Europe. Now, twenty-four years later, the same could happen in the wake of Brexit.

In the past, Corbyn had feigned to be unconcerned by the polls. Now, his transition from a protester to the leader of a political party committed to an election victory meant that he scrutinised the indicators of the public's voting intentions. Reality broke in on 8 December. Labour had recently been routed in two by-elections – in Richmond and Sleaford – and another was imminent, caused by the resignation of Jamie Reed, the Labour MP for Copeland. Over the previous thirty-five years no sitting government had won a by-election in a constituency that had been held by the opposition, but Labour was unusually vulnerable in Cumbria. The constituency's principal employer was the Sellafield nuclear power plant. As an implacable opponent of nuclear power, Corbyn had advocated its permanent closure, at the expense of thousands of local jobs. Contradicting his beliefs would break a lifetime's habit, explained his admirers. 'It is appalling,' he had said in 1998, 'that countries that desperately need money for education, health and development spend money on nuclear weapons.'

Despite the danger of electoral suicide, Corbyn's best offer to Copeland was 'an investment plan' for a nuclear-free zone. With a new poll giving him a 16 per cent chance of becoming prime minister, he agreed under pressure from his staff to give ground on at least one major policy. He chose immigration. 'Labour is not wedded to freedom of movement,' he announced. But then he added off-script, 'I don't want that to be misinterpreted. Nor do we rule it out.' Just before Christmas, Diane Abbott acknowledged that Corbyn had a year to turn the party round, no more. Her forecast was echoed by Len McCluskey, although he gave him two years. Corbyn's consolation was to win, for the seventh time, the Parliamentary Beard of the Year competition. 'I started wearing a beard when I was nineteen and living in Jamaica,' he told the audience. 'They called me "Mr Beardman".' That small untruth was evidently too good to be given up.

Life was so much easier among trade unionists. At the Aslef Christmas party in Conway Hall, Corbyn was surrounded by his closest comrades – among them Tosh McDonald, the union's president, famed for leading ruinous strikes, and its general secretary Mick Whelan, who had threatened the government with 'ten years of industrial action'. One area where the three were notably united was in their opposition to British Rail's modernisation plans. Corbyn supported the strikes against driver-only trains by a thousand RMT train drivers on Southern Rail, despite their disrupting the lives of 500,000 commuters. He knew that the unions' argument that driver-only trains were unsafe was bogus – a third of all British trains ran without a guard, and most commuter trains into London were driver-only. Some London lines operated without any driver, and not a single accident had been caused by the new technology. But modernisation offended Corbyn's gospel. Labour's next election manifesto, he pledged, would ban driver-only trains and order the reintroduction of guards. Protecting workers' monopolies and restrictive work practices was true socialism. In return, over the previous year the rail unions had donated £185,000 to Labour. With sincerity, Corbyn led the standing ovation for Aslef's president, and pledged to 'replace the capitalist system with a socialist order'.

There was less comradeship at the Christmas party for Labour's MPs, a karaoke evening held at the Westminster Kitchen Bar, a restaurant across the river from the Houses of Parliament. Many of the songs were deliberately chosen to insult the party's current leader – Ruth Smeeth sang Tony Blair's anthem, 'Things Can Only Get Better', and Mike Gapes intoned the Beatles' 'Back in the USSR'. Corbyn took it all in good part, and his benign expression reflected how secure he felt. He welcomed Trotskyists joining Momentum, which by then boasted 15,000 members, joining the 100,000 new Labour members. They were his trusted allies to change Britain. Like Donald Trump, newly elected as America's president, he represented both the new populist era and the revival of a bygone age. Like Trump, he lampooned his critics as manufacturers of fake news, and like Trump he championed the underdogs, the losers in society. Unlike Trump, however, he had failed to win new voters, rebuild his party or win credibility among the wider electorate. Labour under a Trotskyite leader appeared doomed.

15

The Coming of St Jeremy

At the beginning of 2017 the news was bad. Instead of reviving the working-class vote, Labour was certain to lose Copeland, a seat it had held for eighty years. The *Mirror* described the looming defeat as 'Labour's deep hole'. Salvation had depended on Corbyn abandoning his opposition to nuclear power, but he repeatedly refused to compromise. Finally, to save the seat, John McDonnell said that Labour had given the workers 'assurances'. As usual, that was not true. In July 2012 he had predicted that within the first hundred days of the next Labour government, 'You announce no more nuclear power … we have built up support for those policies.' Corbyn's future depended on holding Stoke-on-Trent Central in another by-election on the same day, caused by Tristram Hunt's resignation.

To relaunch Labour for the two battles, Corbyn pitched himself as the scourge of the super-well-off. 'The economy is rigged for the rich,' said Steve Howell, Seumas Milne's new deputy, a former member of the Communist Party and an admirer of Soviet Russia and East Germany. In an attack on 'fat-cat Britain', Corbyn promised to impose a maximum earnings limit. 'If we want to live in a more egalitarian society and fund our public services, we cannot go on funding worse levels of inequality,' he declared on BBC radio. In socialist Britain, the workers could determine their bosses' pay, and even Premier League footballers would have their earnings cut. His models for success were the government wage caps in Cuba, Venezuela and Egypt.

The reaction was not entirely favourable. Richard Murphy, Corbyn's tax adviser, called the idea absurd. David Blanchflower described it as 'totally idiotic'. Multinational corporations, he went on, would move their headquarters abroad, and footballers would refuse to come to English clubs. Corbyn did not understand how globalised markets would throttle draconian controls of the type last used by Harold Wilson. The digital world had marginalised the nation state. Venezuela's fate was ample proof, only Corbyn ignored it. By the end of the day, his spokesman said that he had 'misspoke'. The embarrassment was compounded by McDonnell's proposal that everyone earning over £1 million should publish their tax returns 'to rebuild trust in our society. People don't have trust in the establishment. I just want openness and transparency'. McDonnell's championship of 'transparency' went awry after the Tory Party examined Corbyn's own 2015–16 tax returns, and discovered that he had omitted the entire additional £58,000 he had been paid as leader of the opposition.

That blip, probably the result of incompetence rather than a wish to defraud, was less damaging than his indecision about the EU. With Labour split almost as badly as the Tories, Corbyn could not fix on an agreed policy. He confused the customs union with the single market, and was undecided about that: on a single day the previous December, he had changed his position four times. There was good reason for his cartwheeling. While he supported Brexit, two-thirds of Labour's electorate had voted remain; and whereas most Labour MPs were remainers, most of their constituencies voted for Brexit. Marxism provided no answer to a problem that could be resolved only by compromise, and ultimately a parliamentary vote.

For a few weeks, Corbyn could not decide whether Labour MPs should be ordered to vote with the government in support of applying to leave the EU. On referendum day he had declared that Britain should do so instantly. Now, seven months later, he prevaricated. Discussions in the shadow cabinet left everyone perplexed. One morning he had agreed to control immigration and not support the train drivers' latest strike, but that same afternoon he reneged. Immigration should be uncontrolled, his office announced, but then he went ahead and supported the strike. On the vote to invoke Article 50, the instrument for Britain's departure from the EU, he finally imposed a three-line whip to vote with the government. Fifty-two MPs defied his order, including seventeen frontbench remainers. Four shadow cabinet ministers resigned. Even pro-Corbyn MPs opposed a hard Brexit. His prevarications sapped his authority. The usually supportive *Guardian* journalist Owen Jones was among the disillusioned. Surveying the chaos, he blamed Corbyn for ignoring good advice. 'A coherent strategy, a coherent vision and a clear message never emerged,' he would write. 'It is soul-destroying to watch great ideals and policies being dragged down not by their own merits, but through a lack of strategy and basic competence.' This did not just apply to Brexit. Among Corbyn's misjudgements was his promise of universal free school meals, the beneficiaries of which would include the rich. The dilemma for Jones was fundamental: 'If Corbyn fails the cause will fail with him.' Without a rescue plan, he concluded, the leader would have to go.

On the eve of the Stoke and Copeland by-elections, Corbyn's Westminster office was even more chaotic than usual. To his good fortune, Ukip's challenge in Stoke was mired by sleaze, and Labour won. But in Copeland, Corbyn had so alienated Labour supporters that the Conservatives won with a majority of 2,147. If the 6.7 per cent swing were repeated nationally, the Tories would have a majority of over a hundred seats. 'Labour's collapse among working-class voters is catastrophic,' concluded YouGov in a new opinion poll.

Asked if he were to blame, Corbyn replied, 'No.'

'Why not?'

'Thank you for your question,' he replied and walked on.

Holly Lynch, the Labour MP for Halifax, told Corbyn to his face that her current slender majority of 428 would be wiped out because of him. 'I've just been re-elected,' he shrugged. As usual, he refused to take responsibility. McDonnell blamed disunity among Labour MPs for the defeat in Copeland. He also accused the Blairites of conspiring with the Murdoch empire, citing in evidence Peter Mandelson's admission, 'I work every single day to oust Corbyn.' In McDonnell's imagination, Mandelson was secretly orchestrating a coup, so he invited the supposed traitor for tea to forge unity. 'I know I have got a pugnacious approach,' McDonnell volunteered in a moment of rapprochement. Corbyn offered no similar concessions. 'Comrades,' he told a conference in Scotland, 'let us never forget it's not called the struggle for nothing.' Believers knew, he said, that the capitalists would eventually be defeated and replaced by workers' control. A YouGov poll found that just 13 per cent wanted Corbyn as prime minister, compared to 51 per cent for May. The Tories, at 43 per cent, were eighteen points ahead of Labour, which was predicted to lose the skilled working class, and, as in 1983, to win no more than 27 per cent of the vote. Some of its MPs again spoke about ousting Corbyn to save the party.

The temptation was too great for Theresa May. On 18 April she announced a snap election for 8 June, to 'remove the uncertainty' over getting Brexit legislation through Parliament. 'Crush the Saboteurs' was the *Daily Mail*'s headline. Under electoral law, a premature election required a two-thirds majority of the Commons, and Labour joined the Tories to vote in favour. In the *Guardian*, Polly Toynbee slammed Corbyn for approving an election that would surely see Labour crushed. 'Will this be the last disastrous service he does to his party?' she asked. The Tories, she feared, would successfully portray him as a metropolitan Marxist and terrorist ally. Jonathan Freedland in the same paper understood May's decision: 'It's about the surest bet any politician could ever place ... May will win and win big.' In *The Times*, Philip Collins was equally convinced: Corbyn had 'no charisma and little intellect ... it is a recipe for catastrophe and the only question is how bad it gets. Labour is putting a cast-iron solid dud in front of the British people.' Some Labour MPs despaired about the inevitable massacre – the polls showed that even those with majorities of eight thousand were at risk. Others were gleeful that the election would end Corbyn's reign. Few were more antagonistic than John Woodcock, who had won his Barrow and Furness constituency in 2015 with a majority of just 795. In a recorded video he pledged, 'I will not countenance ever voting to make Jeremy Corbyn Britain's prime minister.' In unison, everyone ignored John Curtice's revised prediction. May, the pollster reckoned, could find it hard to increase the number of Tory seats, let alone win a majority of a hundred, because only seventeen Labour seats were marginal, compared to forty-nine Tory ones.

That truth was made more evident within hours of May's announcement. Corbyn arrived in Croydon, a Tory marginal with a majority of 165. Looking dapper in a suit, and with his beard trimmed, he uttered a prepared line: 'I want an economy that works for all' – a perfect Tory slogan. By the end of the first day of campaigning, May's Brexit theme had been pushed aside: inequality had become the issue. 'This election,' said Corbyn, 'is the establishment versus the people. Instead of a country for the rich we want richer lives for everyone.' Fluently, he recited his familiar sermon against greed, the cosy cartels and the crooked bankers. The faithful applauded thunderously. After a life on the fringe, the thrill of fighting to be prime minister had injected a sizeable adrenaline dose into the sixty-seven-year-old Corbyn.

To control the campaign, he separated his election team from the staff at Labour headquarters. The Marxists around Corbyn distrusted those who had served Blair and Brown to preach the required degree of socialism. Three communists wrote the manifesto: Steve Howell, Andrew Fisher and Andrew Murray. Without a blush, Seumas Milne chose 'For the Many, Not the Few' as Labour's campaign slogan – Tony Blair's mantra. Unmentioned but noted were the Labour candidates who refused to feature Corbyn's photo on their election leaflets, and promised on the doorstep that Corbyn would not win. Never before had Labour entered an election so divided.

On May Day, John McDonnell stood in Trafalgar Square surrounded by communist banners, Stalin's photo and the flag of Assad's Syria. Few could understand his benign attitude towards Stalin's reign of terror, but like his predecessors during the 1930s – Ramsay MacDonald, George Bernard Shaw, and Sidney and Beatrice Webb – he believed that Stalin's atrocities had been exaggerated. 'Much better be ruled by Stalin,' G.D.H. Cole, a Labour economist of that interwar era, had written, 'than by the restrictive and monopolistic cliques which dominate Western capitalism.' Similarly, the Marxist historian Eric Hobsbawm had believed that the 'sacrifice of millions of lives' was justified to build a communist state. Some eighty years later, mimicking that host of legendary spirits, McDonnell repeated their philosophy. Defeating the capitalists required violence and also loyalty to comrades, especially those targeted by the hated media.

Some of the criticism was mere buffoonery. Kelvin MacKenzie, the former editor of the *Sun*, told the *New York Times*, 'I think the fake news headline which would give this country the most joy would be "Jeremy Corbyn Knifed to Death by an Asylum-Seeker".' In the same vein, Corbyn was denounced by Boris Johnson as a 'mutton-headed mugwump', a reference to US Republicans who had deserted their party in 1884 to support the Democratic candidate. More serious, in Corbyn's opinion, was the media targeting of his closest allies. Labour's Constitutional Committee had concluded that Ken Livingstone's anti-Semitism had brought the party into disrepute. After he refused to apologise he was barred from holding office for two years, but allowed to remain a party member.

Corbyn could be judged by his support for Livingstone. He welcomed his ally's anticipated return in April 2018, and declared that the media had maliciously weaponised anti-Semitism against him. Jewish MPs were appalled. Even the *Guardian* called Corbyn's promise of zero tolerance towards anti-Semitism 'a lie'. 'Shameful decision today,' tweeted Yvette Cooper. Under pressure during a TV interview, Corbyn bad-temperedly accused the media of being 'utterly obsessed' with the status of his leadership, and refused to criticise Livingstone.

He was similarly protective of Diane Abbott. In an election interview with LBC's Nick Ferrari, Abbott had said that Labour would recruit ten thousand more police, at a cost of £300,000. When challenged about the figure, she revised the number of recruits to 25,000, then corrected herself again to say it would be 250,000 policemen – adding as an afterthought that that figure included policewomen. When asked whether 250,000 extra police was realistic, she replied, 'I mean two thousand.' Finally, after searching through her brief, she said the cost would be £298 million, then belatedly added an additional £130 million for training and inflation. 'I'm not embarrassed in the slightest,' Corbyn told journalists later, reiterating his distrust of the capitalist media burrowing into his past. 'Let's just keep going.' Only McDonnell smiled. He loathed Abbott, and the feeling was mutual. Karie Murphy was dispatched to order Abbott to stop giving interviews.

The good news for Corbyn was Len McCluskey's re-election as leader of Unite. On a turnout of 12.2 per cent of the union's members, McCluskey received 59,067 votes against Gerard Coyne's 53,544. Coyne complained about irregularities in the polling, and was instantly suspended from the union by McCluskey, who, secure for another four years, pledged £4.5 million to Labour's election fund. In return, he successfully demanded that several Unite members be selected as Labour candidates. Among them was his 'bag-carrier' Dan Carden, chosen in Liverpool Walton. Reflecting his partisanship, McCluskey refused to back Siôn Simon as Labour's mayoral candidate in the West Midlands because he was close to Tom Watson. Simon would lose to a Tory by six thousand votes of over half a million cast, for which he blamed McCluskey. The reckoning was harsh.

Three days after Abbott's humiliation, Labour was routed in the local council elections, losing 382 seats. The Tories gained 563 seats, with 38 per cent of the vote, 11 per cent ahead of Labour. In Manchester, Andy Burnham was elected mayor, but abandoned his own celebration party after hearing that Corbyn was heading north to be photographed alongside him. Steve Rotheram won the mayoral battle for Labour in Liverpool, but told his supporters that Corbyn was 'Marmite' for voters – he was either liked or loathed, there was no in-between. 'It's difficult,' Corbyn agreed, but refused to apologise for the council results. With the Tories soaring in the polls to 47 per cent of the electorate, Labour MPs openly speculated about their futures outside Parliament. Corbyn's only potential lifebelt was John Curtice's caution about extrapolating from the council elections to predict a Conservative landslide in the general election, because the council elections had been held in the Tory shires, not in Labour's cities.

The pressure on Corbyn intensified, and the media demanded that he explain where he stood on defence. After denying in a speech that he was a pacifist, he refused six times in an interview to say whether or not he wanted Britain to leave NATO. Similarly, McDonnell denied on BBC TV that he was a Marxist, despite the evidence of a recording from 2013 in which he had admitted precisely that. Four years later, he would only admit, 'There's a lot to learn from Marx.' Labour's draft election manifesto reflected that philosophy: more and higher taxes, more welfare benefits, rent controls, widespread nationalisation, no university tuition fees, no immigration controls, the demilitarisation of Britain, support for the Palestinians against Israel, and the destruction of the City. In McDonnell and Corbyn's vision, Britain would erect barriers to imports to protect British industry.

On 11 May, all these details were leaked. Labour MPs in marginal seats led the resultant panic. Few could agree about the identity of the culprit. Was it Corbyn, with the intention of bouncing the party into a Marxist manifesto? Or was it the anti-Corbynistas, trying to pre-empt the meeting that would finalise the policy document? To avoid answering that question, Corbyn agreed that the final programme should hint at 'fair' controls over immigration, remove criticism of Israel, and be positive towards NATO. But the financial plan remained unaltered. 'Jeremy Corbyn's and John McDonnell's sums,' wrote Joe Haines, Harold Wilson's acerbic press spokesman, 'are clearly based on the same mathematics that Diane Abbott practises.'

The official launch of Labour's campaign was staged at Bradford University on 17 May. Surrounded by Abbott,

McDonnell, Chakrabarti and Milne, Corbyn entered the hall to wild cheers. His flock of five hundred loved his attack on grammar schools and fox hunting, and roared as he went all out for the biased media. Young Marxists were convinced that the public was shifting towards Labour. The independent Institute of Fiscal Studies estimated that, despite the higher taxes it would impose, Labour's financial plan would be £30 billion short in revenues every year, the highest gap since 1949. Corbynistas were unconcerned. The next morning, the party's ratings rose to 32 per cent.

On the same day, the Tories launched their manifesto. Risk-averse as ever, Theresa May never trusted those beyond her immediate circle, and the programme had been written in unusual secrecy. In turn, serving a woman without noticeable intellect, emotional intelligence or charisma, her advisers ignored the traditional Tory guarantees to cut regulations and taxes. Instead, the party pledged to increase both. Insensitive about the fact that home ownership had fallen from 73.3 per cent in 2008 to 63.5 per cent in 2016, May forgot those dreaming of their first home or longing for a move up the housing ladder, whose hopes had been extinguished by rising prices and stagnant incomes. Inexplicably, she also adopted Ed Miliband's price cap for energy, which the Tories had convincingly ridiculed four years previously, and said she would cut welfare benefits. Only during the lacklustre manifesto launch did these vote-losing policies become obvious. Then it got worse. Under the slogan 'Strong and Stable', May embarked on a campaign focused on herself, isolated from the public and highlighting her inability to engage in unscripted debates or small-talk. Fatally for a leader lacking stamina, those flaws were exposed in a negative campaign she herself had chosen to last seven weeks rather than three.

Lynton Crosby, the Tories' Australian election guru, expected voters to be appalled by the Labour leader's sympathy for terrorists. 'Corbyn has spent a lifetime siding with Britain's enemies,' said Ben Wallace, a Home Office minister. But Crosby did not reckon with Corbyn's stubborn nonchalance. Five times he was asked to denounce the IRA 'unequivocally', and each time he refused. Instead, he condemned 'all bombing'. He quibbled about his support for the IRA. 'I did nothing wrong,' he repeated. 'I campaigned for peace in Northern Ireland.' Too late, the Tories realised that most people just ignored the damnation of Corbyn as 'an odious individual' by Northern Irish politicians, or the songs of praise uttered by Gerry Adams. IRA terrorism had ended twenty years earlier. 'People don't care,' Corbyn was told by his pollster. 'Especially young voters. They want to know how you'll improve their own lives.'

In theory, Labour's tax-and-spend was the Tories' strongest card. But May refused to engage with Corbyn about his offer of a speedy path towards Venezuelan-style socialism. She also chose to remain silent about McDonnell's assertion that 'Everything is fully costed,' although he could not estimate the size of the increased deficit, or guarantee that the extra taxes would pay for his promises. The only certainty was that at least 400,000 City jobs would be lost as financial institutions abandoned London to avoid McDonnell's taxes.

On 22 May, the last day on which people could register to vote, Labour promised to scrap university tuition fees in the autumn, a year earlier than previously promised. The total cost of £11.2 billion, said Corbyn, would be covered by taxation. Asked about the accumulated student debt of £100 billion, he replied, 'I will deal with it.' That was interpreted as meaning that Labour would cancel the liability. Believing the promise, at least 714,000 first-time voters were among the estimated three million people who registered on the electoral roll after Theresa May had fired the starting gun. In an appeal to youth, Corbyn proclaimed, 'Fewer working-class young people are applying to university.' The truth was that working-class applicants had increased from 10 to 25 per cent of the total over the previous decade. After the election, McDonnell admitted that Corbyn's pledge about student fees and debt was phoney. 'I don't want to promise something we can't deliver,' he would say. 'We never promised to do so,' said the Labour MP Angela Rayner. During the campaign, the Tories failed to extract that confession.

Instead, on the same day that Corbyn uttered his tantalising guarantee, Theresa May crashed.

Her manifesto proposed to rewrite the financial contract between the generations. The pensioners' winter fuel allowance would be cut, some pensions would be reduced, and the old would be compelled to sell most of their assets to pay for their personal care. That commitment to what became known as the 'dementia tax' caused uproar. Four days later May abandoned the plan, but by then her campaign had unravelled. Rather than 'strong and stable', as she liked to characterise herself, 'the Maybot' was exposed as indecisive and brittle.

Adopting Hugo Chávez's tactics, Corbyn was meanwhile appealing to the disgruntled: trade unionists, public service workers, students, the conscience-stricken, and disappointed home-seekers – above all, to those aggrieved about their situation. In his exhaustive tour around Britain, he wooed crowds seeking salvation from deprivation – real or imagined – associated with health, housing, schools, race or gender. Mixing joyfully with the masses, 'Uncle' Jeremy played on people's fears and anger to offer idealism and hope. He was the authentic anti-establishment politician with a moral cause: 'You cannot trust the Tories. The worst pay squeeze in two hundred years', he declared. Few Britons understood his worship of Chávez (the first of what would eventually be two million Venezuelans were fleeing their country to find food and work, and to avoid murderous violence), but they did accept his narrative: that only the rich would benefit from May's re-election. The Tory lead in the polls fell again.

Late on that day, 22 May, with Corbyn's campaign rolling and May's stuttering, a Muslim suicide bomber attacked young girls and their parents at the end of a pop concert in Manchester, killing twenty-three people. Corbyn's instant reaction was to deny the truth, that Islamic terrorism was to blame. 'Terrible incident', he tweeted. His communist advisers recognised the error. Credibility was at stake for a man vying to be responsible for Britain's security despite voting thirteen times since 9/11 against anti-terror laws. The makeover was swift. The attack, he said just hours later, was 'an abominable and atrocious act'. To correct any damaging impressions, he also condemned the IRA's murders as 'completely wrong', and denied outright ever having met any member of the organisation. He then jumped on a train for Manchester.

With him was Karie Murphy. In her usual bullying manner, she told Andy Burnham and local Labour MPs during the journey that Corbyn would pose with them for the media, and participate in their vigil for the victims of the attack. The MPs refused to collaborate. To assert her authority, she yelled her orders, provoking some MPs to tears. When they reached Manchester, she bulldozed aside police objections to Corbyn visiting the arena, a crime scene, for media photos. Once again, Corbyn had eclipsed May on what should have been her own turf of law and order.

Days later, he took a step to assert his authenticity. Sensing that few cared about his relationship with the IRA, he reaffirmed his convictions in a public speech written by Milne and Andrew Murray, blaming first Britain and America and their intelligence failures for what had happened at the concert in Manchester; then the Tory government's relationship with Saudi Arabia and the Gulf states for funding extremists. British foreign policy, and not Muslims, he told his audience, was responsible for the atrocity. His solution was to remove barriers to Muslims entering Britain, and to welcome Islamic teaching. The Tories believed that this speech was an own goal, but their attacks on Corbyn's sympathy for terrorism caused a backlash among young voters. Those uninspired by May identified with Corbyn's empathy for the underdog. Capitalising on that emotion, Corbyn's team accused the 'nasty party' of launching a 'vicious campaign' to score 'cheap points' by 'brutal assaults'.

Then came Labour's major counter-attack, Corbyn switching the focus onto Theresa May's cut of 20,000 police officers when she was home secretary. He promised to increase police numbers by 10,000. None commented on the absurdity of Corbyn, a life-long enemy of the force, offering to increase its strength. Helped by an army of activists knocking on doors and bombarding social websites, a surge of support reduced his negative ratings. Compared to the cool gamesmanship of Corbyn's team, the Tories continued to flounder. Monosyllabically, May scrambled to rescue herself. Two weeks before the election, her advantage in the opinion polls slumped to 5 per cent.

The two leaders' ultimate test was forty minutes of live TV – half in front of a studio audience, and half in an interview with Jeremy Paxman. In her unconvincing appearance, May stumbled. Next, in Corbyn's segment, Paxman set out to tear his prey apart. Why, he asked, did the Labour manifesto not pledge to abolish the monarchy? 'There's nothing in there because we're not going to do it,' Corbyn said, smiling, then explained that he had no wish to impose his will on Labour. 'I'm no dictator,' he said disarmingly. Carefully rehearsed by Milne, he justified his association with the IRA as being in aid of 'the peace process', and described any future use of drones to kill Islamic terrorists as 'hypothetical'. Lifelong principles melted away. To be elected required the very compromises he had spent thirty years in Parliament eschewing. He also concealed his ambitions to scrap Trident, remove limits on immigration and nationalise the banks. Asked after the programme whether Milne had coached Corbyn, a Labour spokesman replied, 'Jeremy's uncoachable.' He also proved to be untouchable. Neither the studio audience nor the interviewer landed a serious blow. Paxman's agitated interruptions put many voters on Corbyn's side.

Next morning, the coaching unravelled. Corbyn had chosen free childcare as Labour's theme for the day. Asked on BBC *Woman's Hour* to say how much thirty hours of such childcare would cost, he came unstuck. 'I presume you have the figures?' he was pressed by Emma Barnett. 'Yes, I do,' he replied. There followed a long pause. Everything was costed, he repeated, unsuccessfully searching through his notes for a number. Minutes after the interview ended, Corbyn's supporters attacked Barnett on the internet as a 'Zionist shill' and a Jew.

This further example of anti-Semitism was buried by Corbyn's team having ratcheted up its media campaign. Over the previous weeks, Labour had presented slick online mini-dramas featuring attractive middle-class people troubled by student fees, their children's inability to buy a home, and a fear of NHS cuts. The videos were tapping into people's feelings with tempting idealism. Messages on Facebook, Twitter and Snapchat overwhelmed any critical questions posed by the traditional media about Corbyn's record. In a rigorous operation supplemented by troll factories based in Russia, the Facebook pages of Tory candidates were deluged with hate mail. Defamatory abuse generated by supporters was 'liked' and shared by thousands. Celebrities including Stephen Fry and singer Harry Styles posted messages urging their followers to vote Labour – except that the posts were fabricated by unnamed people. 'Fake news' targeted the prime minister's husband Philip May, claiming that he was a director of G4S, a private security company that paid no corporation tax despite making billions of pounds from government contracts, and falsely alleging that it had benefited from corrupt relationships. Saira Hussain, an architect who placed the post, also boasted about having met Baroness Uddin, who in 2010 had been suspended by the Labour Party for falsifying her expenses. Hussain's story about Philip May was a complete lie.

Across the country, Tory candidates were swamped by similar fabrications. 'A lie told often enough,' said Lenin, 'becomes the truth.' The reward was a poll prediction that Labour would gain seats, and May would fail to get an overall majority. Despite the threat of defeat, she refused to participate in a live TV debate with Corbyn. Fearful of speaking without a script, she assumed that he would not agree to appear without her, but at the last moment his advisers persuaded him to snatch the opportunity and take a free run. He appeared with Amber Rudd, the home secretary, pulled in as May's substitute. He did not shine, but Rudd failed to land a telling blow.

That good news for Corbyn was undercut by another terrorist outrage. On 3 June, two weeks after the Manchester massacre, three Muslim men rampaged through Borough Market in London, murdering eight young people and injuring forty-eight before police shot them dead. In the emotional aftermath,

Corbyn's Islamophilia once again threatened his standing. Memories were fresh about his refusal to outrightly condemn all the extremist madrasas (Islamic schools), preachers and groups like Hamas that motivated Muslim murderers, and his enthusiasm for 'the wonderful faith of Islam'. But rather than sensing any vulnerability in his own position, he called for May to resign because she had cut police numbers. He knew his criticism was nonsensical – the real shortcoming had been inadequate intelligence from MI5 and MI6, two agencies that he had pledged to shrink or abolish outright. To that purpose, he had recently refused to discuss with Keir Starmer, the former director of public prosecutions and a Labour MP since 2015, the provisions of the Investigatory Powers Bill to supervise the intelligence agencies. Abolition, not reform, had been his policy.

In the tumult, other voices were drowned out. Lord Carlile, for ten years the government's independent reviewer of terrorism, accused Corbyn of seeking to mislead the public. Cressida Dick, the commissioner of the Metropolitan Police, also contradicted his claims. A specialist police team, she pointed out, had arrived at Borough Market eight minutes after the first alarm, proving that London's police were well-prepared. Corbyn ignored her testimony, adroitly shrugged aside Theresa May's characterisation of him as unpatriotic and a friend of terrorists as 'utterly ridiculous' and 'offensive', and again blamed the government's police cuts. May's refusal to confront him head-to-head about his ideological convictions protected him from a potentially damaging contest.

For political reasons, Corbyn had always disputed that the vast majority of British terrorists were Muslims radicalised in city ghettos. To Muslim applause at many meetings across the country, he opposed the Prevent programme and condemned David Cameron's description of madrasas as places where children had 'their heads filled with poison'. In concert with his Muslim allies, he dismissed the government report by Louise Casey, director general of Troubled Families and previously deputy director of Shelter, that radicalisation could be partly cured by the supervision of Muslim faith schools and by encouraging integration. Since May had failed when home secretary to implement Casey's recommendations, she relied on former MI6 chief Richard Dearlove to criticise Corbyn in the *Daily Telegraph* as 'not fit for No. 10' because he had been 'hugging, supporting' terrorists. As none of Corbyn's supporters read the *Telegraph*, and Dearlove's attack was ignored by the rest of the media, Corbyn once again escaped untouched. 'I hear some people have said nasty things about me,' he told a rally. 'I forgive them all.'

In the last days before the vote, May staged televised meetings with loyalists in a bakery, on a farm and in a factory. At each event, barely a dozen people were corralled around her. At the same time, Corbyn was addressing huge crowds in Birmingham, Brighton, Glasgow and finally in Camden, north London. Similar numbers had greeted him at over ninety rallies with chants of 'Ooooh Jeremy Corbyn,' to the tune of the White Stripes' 'Seven Nation Army'. Hundreds were still queuing outside the Camden venue when he finished his speech and headed for a glass of red wine in a nearby pub. Nothing he said over the previous seven weeks was memorable, no phrase was savoured as evidence of genius, but his audiences had departed in their thousands filled with enthusiasm.

The campaign had also transformed Corbyn himself. The veteran protester understood that politics was no longer just a series of battles within the Labour Party, but actually about winning real power. His new ambition was to become prime minister. On polling day, 8 June, he returned home to watch the results coming in with Milne and Karie Murphy. He anticipated a Tory victory, but not a landslide. Murphy disagreed. She had already chosen the clothes she would wear on her trip with Corbyn to Buckingham Palace for his enthronement as prime minister. Immediately after the polls closed at 10 p.m., he heard the BBC's prediction: no overall majority for the Tories, and a hung Parliament. He was 'shocked'. He may not have won outright, but the 'Corbyn surge' had secured his leadership of the party. In their euphoria, he and his team convinced themselves that May would resign, and Labour would form a coalition government with the SNP.

The following day's arithmetic told a different story. The Tories had won 318 seats, a loss of thirteen. Labour had won 262 seats, including the gains of thirty-two 'safe' Conservative seats that took in Canterbury (Tory since 1918), Kensington (Tory forever), Croydon, Brighton, Reading and Portsmouth. Moreover, in the Labour seats specifically targeted by the Tories, Labour's vote had increased. Diane Abbott's majority had risen to 35,000, and Corbyn's was 33,000, up by 12.7 per cent. Momentum took the credit in Hampstead and Kilburn, claiming that its thousand volunteers there had transformed Labour's majority of forty-two in 2010 to 15,560 for Tulip Siddiq in 2017. Contrary to every prediction, Labour had won 3.6 million more votes than in 2015, giving them 40 per cent of the total. That was an increase of a record 9.6 per cent in just twenty-five months. Set against the prediction seven weeks earlier that Labour would win only a quarter of the votes, the difference reflected Corbyn's personal success. Much of the swing was attributed to a 'youthquake' triggered by his promise to scrap student fees, and to urban middle-class professionals irate about Brexit and the Tories' tolerance of the super-rich. (Later analysis would reduce the importance of the youth vote.)

Reports from Conservative headquarters of Theresa May collapsing in tears, her ministers in disarray and a raft of antic-ipated resignations fuelled Corbyn's certainty of a terminal Tory rout. McDonnell urged him to capitalise on the enemy's insta-bility by pronouncing victory. 'Demoralise and divide them,' he urged, 'and force them back to the electorate, and this time we'll have a majority.' His bellicosity was encouraged by Karie Murphy. 'Keep the excitement going!' she shouted. 'We're going to win!' Infected by their hyper-confidence, Corbyn gloated on leaving his house early that morning, 'Politics has changed. Politics isn't going back into the box where it was before.' Labour, he proclaimed, had 'won this election'. May should resign and make way for him. Stoking the fire, McDonnell told the public that morning, 'I don't think the prime minister is stable ... I can't see her surviving.' He added, 'The responsibility is on

Theresa May now to stand down and let a Labour government take its place.'

As usual with Corbyn and McDonnell, the truth was different. Labour was well short of the 320 MPs needed for a Commons majority. Worse, for the third consecutive general election it had lost to an increased Tory vote, 5.5 per cent more than in 2015. In 130 English seats, especially in traditionally safe Labour areas, there was a swing to the Tories because Labour voters mistrusted Corbyn. Most people over fifty-five, especially the working class, voted Tory. For those over seventy the figure was 69 per cent, despite Labour promising increased pensions and benefits. Tony Blair would have won over many of those disaffected older voters. The only conspicuous Tory victory was the defeat of the Scottish independence movement. Repelled by Corbyn, Scottish Labour supporters switched to the Tories. Just 401 additional votes in eight British constituencies won by Labour would have secured a Tory majority in the Commons. On the same basis, Labour would have needed 52,000 votes in the right places to win the extra sixty-four seats it needed for a majority. Corbyn's calculation was different. If Labour had won just seven more seats, he argued, he could have formed a minority government with the SNP. The blame was heaped on the Blairites for undermining his reputation. But in those hours after the results, no one spoke about Labour's defeat.

At 8.15 a.m. Corbyn was thanking party workers at Labour headquarters for producing 'an amazing achievement'. Once he had finished, Karie Murphy was blunt. True socialism had triumphed over Blairism, she asserted. If the moderates in the party had believed in Corbyn, Labour would have won an outright victory. The fate of those turncoats was now sealed. On the TV screens in the room, Emily Thornberry was accusing May of 'squatting in Downing Street' and calling on her to resign. But despite their despair, the Tories refused to surrender to Labour's propaganda. Faced with that obduracy, McDonnell told his claque that they were victims of a coup.

Among those disciples, Owen Jones echoed McDonnell's outrage. 'Progressive' forces, he urged, should 'take to the streets

... Organise.' Convinced that the Tories were in fatal disarray, he described Britain's mood as being in transition from Thatcherism to true socialism. That shift, he believed, would accelerate as voters were exposed to the overpowering arguments in favour of removing the ruling class. 'This is a dangerous time for the prime minister as she seeks to smother any challenge,' Jones wrote, without a scintilla of doubt. Theresa May was clinging on 'in the hope that her opponents lose or relinquish the initiative'. His justification for an uprising against the Tories was their 'arrogance and recklessness'. He jeered at Corbyn's critics at Westminster for suggesting that the middle class had increased Labour's vote. Labour, he wrote, got its 'largest support among working-class voters under thirty-five'. This finessed the truth that there had been a 12 per cent swing of all working-class voters to the Tories.

With his familiar extremism, the former BBC economics editor Paul Mason concocted a conspiracy of 'active sabotage' by the 'British elite' to abandon Brexit in order to stop Jeremy Corbyn. 'The global kleptocrats,' he proclaimed, wanted 'ten years of disruption, inflation and higher interest rates' so as to create the 'perfect petri dish for the fungus of financial speculation to grow'. With conviction he asserted: 'The Tories decided to use Brexit to smash up what's left of the welfare state and to recast Britain as the global Singapore. They lost.'

Amid the frenzied language from the left, Corbyn's sober critics were perplexed by his success. 'I was wrong,' admitted Peter Mandelson. 'An earthquake happened in British politics. I acknowledge he has been able to inspire a lot of voters.' Wistfully, he added, 'He's not going anywhere.' Stephen Pollard, the editor of the *Jewish Chronicle*, was dumbfounded: 'It's obvious now that I no longer understand [my country]. It never crossed my mind, despite the baggage of his deplorable alliances and views, that 12.8 million voters would decide they really rather liked the idea of him in No. 10 ... One has to wonder where the red line now lies that voters will not allow to be crossed.'

Even the veteran Marxist journalist Martin Jacques was confused. Convinced, as all 'progressives' had been over the previous century, that capitalism or neoliberalism was in its death throes, Jacques was perplexed that despite allegations of falling incomes and rising inequality, the working classes had voted for Brexit and Donald Trump. One reason, he understood, was their loss of trust in conventional politicians, which had been fomenting ever since Thatcher and Reagan created a global free market. But to his distress, instead of Corbyn being the working class's champion against bankers and Wall Street, they chose Brexiteers to lead their revolt. Jacques wondered: had the new populists damagingly highlighted the fact that Corbyn's 'feet of clay' were a throwback to the 1970s?

New cheerleaders offered a more positive interpretation. Polly Toynbee, previously a fierce critic, now hailed him as 'the new man beaming with confidence, benevolence and forgiveness to erstwhile doubters'. In his 'week zero', she wrote, 'his past is cauterised and there will be no point dragging it out again', because 'Labour can relish the political spectacle from now on while preparing for government'. Briefed that Corbyn was offering moderates an olive branch, she accepted without demur his assertion that they would return to the front bench. 'I'm sure we can reach an accommodation,' he said, expecting disgruntled MPs to hold their tongues.

At the first PLP meeting there was no hint of bloodletting. Welcomed by cheers, Corbyn spoke optimistically about unity. Later, in the Commons, Labour MPs again applauded his entrance. 'Democracy is a wondrous thing,' he baited the prime minister as she sat glum-faced and struggling to agree 'a coalition of chaos' with the Ulster Protestant DUP. Then the purification began.

'No jobs for traitors,' declared McDonnell, as intolerant as Corbyn towards those who refused to conform. Seeing Chuka Umunna interviewed on TV provoked all his fury. Umunna, McDonnell seethed, was not one of 'our people'. He demanded that the Nigerian-Irish MP and another fifty rebels planning to defy a three-line whip and vote to remain in the European single market should be crushed.

Momentum turned against those fifty MPs not only for their

EU stance, but for failing to praise Corbyn during their election campaigns. Unite officials too challenged them for failing to pledge allegiance to their leader. The pressure was intense and unpleasant. Although she was on maternity leave, Luciana Berger was told by a Unite official who had recently been elected onto her constituency's executive committee to 'get on board quite quickly now', and apologise to Corbyn. She duly succumbed.

The intimidation of Berger was not unique. Many female Labour MPs, particularly Jews, complained of renewed abuse by the left. As in Haringey thirty years earlier, Corbyn did nothing to protect them. He inspired the attacks, then stood back. Now was the moment, he agreed with Jon Lansman, to revive the deselections interrupted by the election. Momentum members in local branches were empowered to remove Blairite MPs. To smooth the process, the left needed to dominate the NEC. Here Corbyn's first step was to oust Tom Watson as Labour Party chair, an honorary title usually given to the deputy leader, and to have him replaced by Ian Lavery, a controversial former miner who supported deselection.

Next for removal was Kezia Dugdale in Scotland. Although she had won seven seats for Labour, her campaign had focused on the SNP rather than on Corbyn. Her unforgivable crime, his supporters believed, was her failure to embrace him and so win more seats. She replied that Labour's vote in Scotland had gone to the Tories for the first time because of Corbyn's Marxism. In his book, to hold that view was treachery. One more push, he ordered, would sweep her aside. Exhausted by the intrigue and secrecy, Dugdale hesitated, unable to decide whether Corbyn was a clever strategist or a coward. Was he in control, delegating others to do his dirty work, or a puppet with others pulling the strings? Either way, she could no longer protect her position. She too was ousted, to be replaced by Richard Leonard, a Marxist.

By then, Corbyn's confidence about his destiny had been boosted by an unexpected disaster that played to his advantage. Seven days after the election, on 15 June, he witnessed a scene of class warfare that for him symbolised the rottenness of Tory

Britain. Once again, he truly expected Theresa May to fall. Grenfell Tower, a twenty-four-storey block of flats owned by the Royal Borough of Kensington and Chelsea, had been destroyed by fire the previous day. The tower, officially home to about 250 people, had recently been refurbished by the council in response to a Labour government directive to improve the outward appearance of housing blocks. Starting in a faulty refrigerator on the fourth floor, the flames had taken hold because of a delay in calling the fire brigade. Then, uncontrolled by incompetently led firefighters, they had spread into the building's new cladding before erupting into an inferno. In horrendous circumstances, seventy-one people died – although the precise number was unknown when Corbyn arrived at the scene.

Mingling with grieving survivors, he identified with the message on Socialist Worker placards waved in front of the news cameras: 'Tories have blood on their hands.' Agitators pronounced that up to four hundred residents had been burned to death – slaughtered by austerity, Tory toffs, property hucksters, and racists. Councillors in Britain's richest borough were damned for neglecting poor people in social housing. Among the litany of deliberate distortions dominating the media, the councillors were accused of having rejected a tender of £11.3 million to use safer but more expensive cladding, in favour of a bid of £8.6 million. In fact, to meet the tenants' requirements, the council had increased the budget to refurbish the building from £6.9 million to £10.3 million. However, the protesters were right that cheaper cladding had been used. Relying on government-approved experts, the councillors had been told that the inferior cladding satisfied the existing fire regulations. They could not have known that, dating back to 1997, the statutory safety standards had been weakened by government orders, and that the manufacturers had possibly certified the cladding as safe on the basis of falsified regulatory tests. Grenfell was not unique. Dozens of local authorities, including nearby Camden, a Labour council, had used the same cladding on at least 306 tower blocks, and it had also been fixed onto at least 130 private developments.

Emotionally, Corbyn hugged Grenfell residents of all nationalities, and accused Kensington council of social cleansing. In
truth, over the previous twenty years the council had increased
the number of tenants who had been granted social housing,
while Islington had cut its numbers by 4,500. Corbyn had never
protested on his own constituents' behalf. Kensington's councillors, however, were vulnerable to historic complaints. They had
ignored warnings from Grenfell residents about shoddy work-
manship and fire risks, although none had specifically
mentioned the cladding or the corrupted building regulations.
Slow and inept in its own self-defence, the council's outstanding
response to the surviving residents was drowned out by the
agitators' screams of odium, widely reported in the media, especially by Jon Snow on Channel 4 News and Kirsty Wark on the
BBC's *Newsnight*. As one, the media conjured up an image of
rich politicians trampling on the traumatised poor.

In the stampede to judgement, Corbyn looked wonderfully
humane compared to Theresa May. When she visited the scene,
fearing that Grenfell would bring her down, she avoided meeting the residents at all. The image was of desperate survivors,
having lost their possessions, their homes and often family
members, being ignored by a heartless Westminster insider.
May had seemingly learned nothing from her electoral failure.
Panic-stricken, she committed £80 million to rehouse the
tenants within weeks, she said, setting an impossible
timetable.

Before Grenfell's embers had cooled, Corbyn's activists were
inciting revolution. One day after the fire, crowds chanting
'Murderers!' stormed the council's headquarters and pronounced
with certainty that over two hundred people had died. By then,
the police and fire services were convinced that the true figure
was no more than eighty. Their estimates were dismissed by the
left as a conspiracy, and rejected by Jon Snow on Channel 4. He
was supported by David Lammy, the Labour MP for Tottenham.
Stoking anger against the Tories, Lammy wildly condemned the
police estimate of deaths as 'far, far too low', and accused
Downing Street of orchestrating a political cover-up to mini-

mise 'anger and unrest'. Diane Abbott added yet more poison. 'Those hundreds of people who died,' she said, 'are a direct consequence of Tory attitudes in social housing.' Nothing less than 'murdered by political decisions' was John McDonnell's judgement. Just as Corbyn had cited police cuts as the reason for Muslim terrorism, McDonnell blamed the Grenfell deaths on 'austerity … as the price paid in public safety … in the disregard for working-class communities'. Supervising the scene of the fire, Dany Cotton, London's fire chief, denied that money or cuts to her service had in any way contributed to the deaths. In those early hours, no one dared mention the fire service's ineptitude. The stage was dominated by the agitators' yells for 'days of rage' against 'corporate genocide'. Moderate Labour MPs were shocked. 'That is the language of the hard left,' snapped Margaret Hodge, 'which is not done in my name.' Corbyn dismissed her comments with contempt, an opinion shared by the *Morning Star*, which called her a member of 'the devious, dinosaur faction'.

As passions rose, Corbyn became convinced that the anger over Grenfell would topple May. Thatcherism, he spouted, was disintegrating. 'Britain's old order is crumbling,' repeated Owen Jones, always quick to climb on board. Rather than allow 'a few politicians pulling levers at the top' to organise relief and discover the truth about the tragedy, he and Labour's leaders smelled the whiff of revolution. Grenfell's tenants, said Corbyn, represented the 'power of the dispossessed'. Here was an instant army of downtrodden victims eager to challenge the ruling class. To harness their power, he presented them with identifiable enemies and answers. 'The brutal and inescapable truth,' he said, 'is that the fire simply would not have happened if the occupants had been wealthy.' Those who had been made homeless should be immediately rehoused by requisitioning all Kensington's empty properties, especially those 'owned by the rich'. Four years earlier, Corbyn and McDonnell had supported legislation to empower squatters to occupy uninhabited buildings, and to be protected by lawyers financed by legal aid. The reality of Corbyn's 'kinder, gentler politics' was his admission that, had Labour won the election, the state would have weaponised grief and confiscated over a hundred local homes. Or, as McDonnell urged the 'politicised, mobilised population' – to take control.

Consistent with his opinion that democracy had broken down, McDonnell called on the trade unions to 'mobilise one million people to protest in London on 1 July' to force May to hold another election. The Trotskyite shadow chancellor never ceased to encourage instability. He also urged the rail unions to restart their strikes against driver-only trains. He might have felt a moment of trepidation when a 'May Out' march by 'Grenfell victims' from west London to Parliament Square on a 'Day of Rage', 21 June, attracted fewer than three hundred people, mostly Trotskyists imported from around the country; but any doubts were brushed aside by the opinion polls. Grenfell had pushed Labour 8 per cent ahead of the Tories.

Corbyn's lead was boosted by his appearance at the Glastonbury Festival three days later. While May was watching the annual Armed Forces Day parade, Corbyn stood on Glastonbury's stage to introduce Run the Jewels, an American hip hop duo notorious for loving 'drugs and bitches' and urging their followers to 'carry a blade and a firearm'. The Labour leader visibly glowed as he received a rock-star welcome from 150,000 fans joyfully chanting 'Ooooh Jeremy Corbyn.' Enjoying this demonstration of his immense popularity, he apparently forgot that those waving 'We love you Jeremy' banners had paid £238 each for their tickets to the festival. Above their cheers, he shouted that Theresa May would be forced into an early election. Her staying in office, he bellowed, was ludicrous. 'He told me he would be in Downing Street in six months,' Michael Eavis, the festival's eighty-one-year-old founder, confided to friends in his hospitality tent. 'He really is the hero of the hour.' On the platform, Corbyn smiled. He was a saint. His life story was of failure metamorphosing into success. Victory and Downing Street were just a matter of time.

Tory MPs were apoplectic about BBC commentators praising Corbyn's Glastonbury appearance as 'brilliant'. Reading the media reports about 'giddy optimism', 'the cult of Corbyn' and 'hysterical support', the man himself might have been forgiven for not being able to believe anything else. The adulation – the mugs, badges, T-shirts and scarves all bearing his name – as well as the perks of leadership, was intoxicating. Convinced that the government would soon collapse, Corbyn planned to spend the summer campaigning in seventy-five Tory marginals. Excitedly, the staff along his Westminster corridor indulged in confident chatter about the Tories' desperation. None paused to consider that May had set off for a three-week holiday in the Alps, while no one told Corbyn that Glastonbury had employed seven hundred litter pickers on zero-hours contracts, about half of whom were prematurely fired before the end of the festival.

On 1 July, McDonnell's 'one million march' through London attracted 20,000 people. His threat of a summer of strikes had not materialised. As usual, his predictions of imminent power were empty threats. But the momentum could not be slackened. To keep the comrades marching towards victory, Owen Jones exhorted: 'There can be no going back … A retreat to Labour's old formula would be a tragedy and a fatal mistake … Labour's role is to tear down a bankrupt social order, not defend it.' Three months later, the reality was still ignored at the party conference in Brighton. From the platform, McDonnell spoke as ever about 'mobilising the counter-power – creating extra-parliamentary resistance – to lead a popular movement to retaliate against hostile private business, the City and the media'. To keep the pot boiling, he cried: 'Comrades, we must win!' To his way of thinking, the final triumph was only moments away.

16

Game-Changer

The tense standoff between Corbyn and his critics reignited in March 2018. The reason, once again, was his past.

On 4 March, Sergei Skripal, a former Russian intelligence officer, and his daughter Yulia were found near to death in a park in Salisbury, Wiltshire. Britain's security services established that they had been poisoned by novichok, a chemical nerve agent. Scientists at Porton Down, Britain's centre for chemical warfare, established that the poison had been manufactured in a secret Russian government laboratory. Britain's intelligence services concluded that Skripal had been the target of an attempted murder directed by the Russian state.

On 12 March, Theresa May outlined those findings to the Commons. Two days later, she announced that the intelligence services' conclusion, endorsed by the governments of Britain's NATO allies, including President Trump, would result in sanctions being imposed on Moscow's diplomats in London. The spotlight switched to Corbyn. How would the former *Morning Star* columnist respond? Automatically, he consulted Seumas Milne, and together they composed an ideologically watertight response.

British intelligence, Corbyn told the Commons, was unreliable. Considering their errors before the Iraq war, there was no reason to trust the scientists in Porton Down. He urged May not to 'rush way ahead of the evidence', but to take a 'calm and measured' approach. She must avoid a 'McCarthyite intolerance of dissent' against Russia that risked a 'drift to conflict' and a 'new Cold War'. Resolutely, he refused to accept the Russian state's involvement. Having cast doubt on Moscow's culpability, he switched the blame onto the Conservatives for accepting £800,000 in donations from Russian oligarchs. Few were persuaded about the equivalence between Moscow's attempted murders in Salisbury and shady money, but Corbyn's prejudice would become even clearer a month later, after British intelligence reported that President Assad had launched a chemical attack on the Syrian city of Douma. Just as with the Skripals, he accepted Russia's denials of responsibility.

Corbyn's ridicule of Britain's security services came only weeks after the exposure by the *Sun* of his relationship in 1986 with the Czech intelligence officer Ján Sarkocy. Corbyn was portrayed as having been a Russian agent. Furious, he accused the press of publishing 'lies and smears', and threatened that once elected he would control the foreign ownership of Britain's media. 'We've got news for them,' he warned Rupert Murdoch and others. 'Change is coming.' Portrayed as anti-British and pro-Russian, he watched as his poll ratings fell – and he was then hit by another demon from the past: the taint of his anti-Semitism.

With Corbyn's blessing, Naz Shah's suspension from the party had been lifted, and Ken Livingstone's was about to expire without further investigation. Both were protected by Christine Shawcroft, who was responsible for the NEC's disputes panel. All the allegations of anti-Semitism, Shawcroft had said, were attempts to 'smear' Corbyn. The Jews, she implied, were to blame. Livingstone's fate was the litmus test of the NEC's willingness to eradicate anti-Semitism. Corbyn gave the answer: 'Ken has a right to be heard in his defence,' he said, anticipating his ally's return to the party.

By then, David Collier, an assiduous internet researcher, had discovered Corbyn's positive comments on websites which described Jews as stealing children to sell on the black market, and variously asserted that the terrorist attacks on 9/11 and in Paris were orchestrated by Mossad to justify Western intervention in the Middle East.

Amid growing impatience about Corbyn's protection of anti-Semites and the constant fear, particularly among female

Jewish Labour MPs, of abuse, on 23 March Luciana Berger resurrected her unanswered query about Corbyn's defence three years earlier of the anti-Semitic caricatures of bloodsucking Jews in 'Freedom for Humanity', the mural by Mear One in Tower Hamlets. Before he sent his commiserations to the artist, Corbyn must have asked himself why the mural was so offensive that the council had demanded its removal. A millisecond's glance at it would have revealed the caricature of bloodsucking Jews. Clearly, Corbyn had not found the anti-Semitism offensive, or he would not have sided with the artist. Now he did reply to Berger. He had protested against the mural's removal, he said, as it was an affront to the right of free speech. 'I didn't notice the anti-Semitism,' he added. The Jewish community erupted. Repeatedly, said the Board of Deputies of British Jews, Corbyn had 'sided with anti-Semites rather than Jews'. Corbyn 'cannot seriously contemplate anti-Semitism because he is so ideologically fixed with a far-left world view that is instinctively hostile to mainstream Jewish communities'. They continued, 'At worst, it suggests a conspiratorial world view in which mainstream Jewish communities are believed to be a hostile entity, a class enemy.'

For Jews, Corbyn's approval of the mural's right to remain was the turning point. One lesson of the Holocaust had been the folly of Europe's Jews in complying with the Nazis' orders. With little resistance, they had walked into the ghettos, then obediently boarded trucks and trains for transport to their destruction. Since then, Israel's survival in the face of Arab invasions had shown that Jews were not weaklings or cowards. Yet, because they had prospered, Israelis were blamed for all the Arabs' tribulations – incessant wars, oppression, poverty and inequality. By approving Mear One's mural, Corbyn had wrapped up the Arab world's misfortunes and Palestinian rights as exclusively the fault of the Jews and their paymasters. That was a step too far. Britain's usually reticent Jews decided a line had to be drawn.

An unprecedented demonstration was summoned outside Parliament on 26 March. By then, Corbyn had refashioned his excuse about the mural. 'I sincerely regret,' he said, 'that I did not look more closely at the image I was commenting on.' The thousand protesters heading for Parliament Square doubted him. They believed he had looked at the mural and seen no problem with its message – Jews were global financiers keen to exploit the world's oppressed.

'Enough is enough!' chanted the crowd. The thirty Labour MPs and peers who stood among the demonstrating Jews knew the risk they were taking. Momentum activists in their constituencies would demand their deselection, and they could expect no support from Corbyn or the majority of the NEC. Among the MPs present were David Lammy, John Woodcock, John Mann, Louise Ellman and Luciana Berger.

Familiar voices defended Corbyn. Diane Abbott accused Jews of a 'smear campaign', and Chris Mullin, the former Bennite Labour MP, tweeted, 'Sorry to see Jewish leaders ganging up on Corbyn.' A Zionist mob, Mullin suggested, was causing grief to an innocent man. Ken Loach demanded that the thirty MPs who joined the demonstration should be 'kicked out of the party', and accused the Jews and MPs of weaponising anti-Semitism. All three were confident that they were speaking on behalf of the majority of Labour members. Eighty per cent, according to one opinion poll, believed that anti-Semitism in the party had been exaggerated to damage Corbyn. Israel, most believed, was a worse influence than Iran. Shocked by that hatred, Margaret Hodge, previously reluctant to recognise what was happening, accused Corbyn of having 'allowed himself to become the poster boy of anti-Semites everywhere'. Anti-Semitism, she said, had only become legitimate in the party after he was elected leader.

To forestall further criticism, Corbyn wrote to Jonathan Arkush, the president of the Board of Deputies, and other Jewish leaders conceding the 'hurt and pain' caused by the anti-Semitism, and said he would 'redouble' his efforts to 'bring this anxiety to an end' so that Labour would 'do better' on the issue. He also invited Jewish leaders to meet him. 'Jeremy is utterly committed to driving anti-Semitism out of the Labour Party,' said his office while his staff sifted through his Twitter and Facebook links to remove any endorsements of anti-Semites. In advance of his meeting with the Board of Deputies, the *Evening Standard* published an article by Corbyn giving 'an apology' for 'pockets of anti-Semitism' in Labour. 'My party and I are sorry for the hurt and distress caused,' he wrote.

His ostensible regrets were undermined four days later. In a show of defiance, he celebrated Passover, the most important religious holiday in the Jewish calendar, at a dinner organised by Jewdas, a heretical group of vocal anti-Zionist Jews and deniers of the existence of anti-Semitism in the Labour Party. He embraced Jewdas, well aware of its description of Israel as 'a steaming pile of sewage which needs to be properly disposed of'. That was the prelude to an unusual Commons debate in the late afternoon of 17 April. To embarrass Corbyn, the government decided to devote three hours to anti-Semitism, the first time the subject had been debated in Parliament's history.

Quoting the Italian author and Auschwitz survivor Primo Levi, the communities secretary Sajid Javid set the scene by repeating his stark warning: 'It happened, therefore it can happen again.' Looking straight at Corbyn, Javid said, 'Enough is enough.' Thereafter, one MP after another stood to condemn Labour's anti-Semitism. Many were reduced to tears as Luciana Berger ended her speech with the words of Jonathan Sacks, the former chief rabbi: 'An assault on Jews is an assault on difference, and a world that has no room for difference has no room for humanity itself.' Soon after, Corbyn walked out of the chamber. He failed to hear Ruth Smeeth's description of the hatred heaped upon her by his supporters. 'The gallows would be a fine and fitting place for this dyke piece of Yid shit to swing from,' one Corbynista had written. 'Hang yourself you vile treacherous Zionist Tory filth, you're a cancer of humanity,' wrote another. Corbyn also missed Margaret Hodge declaring, 'I have never felt as nervous and frightened of being a Jew as I feel today.' Nor did he return to hear Diane Abbott's summing up. She attempted to minimise her fellow Labour MPs' suffering by equating it with the abuse directed at her, rebuked the Tories for making use of anti-Semitism in an attempt to gain 'party political advantage', and defended her friend: 'Nothing is gained by accusing the leader of Her Majesty's Opposition of being an anti-Semite.' She was ignored. Amber Rudd, the home secretary, ended the debate with a message directed at Corbyn: 'He has an obligation to take action. We expect nothing less.'

One week later, on 24 April, filled with considerable doubts, Jonathan Arkush and his delegation arrived in Corbyn's office. At the last moment, Seumas Milne had tried to change the terms of the meeting, suggesting a round-table discussion for the following day to include members of Jewish Voice for Labour, an anti-Zionist group that believed Corbyn was the victim of Jewish defamation. Setting up Jew to fight Jew suited Milne, but was vetoed by Arkush. The round-table discussion was abandoned.

Milne was in the room when the group arrived. On their previous visit, he had sat silently glowering at a separate table. This time he was positioned beside Corbyn, intending to participate. Jennie Formby, the party's new general secretary, sat on the leader's other side.

The pleasantries were brief. Then Arkush asked the blunt question: 'Why do you portray Israel as a uniformly bad place? Why can you not acknowledge a single positive attribute?' Corbyn looked at Arkush in silence, then in discomfort. He disliked being challenged. In a monotone, he replied from a prepared statement, suggesting, Arkush observed, that he was 'too unemotional or intellectually incapable to understand the complaint that he had failed to combat anti-Semitism. He did not engage, either to agree or disagree. He looked as if he was shrinking into a shell from which he did not want to come out.'

The conversation moved on to Israel's fate. Arkush said he had noticed that Corbyn 'approved the dictum "From the river to the sea" – the Palestinian state would extend from the River Jordan to the Mediterranean'. That meant the elimination of Israel. Corbyn did not comment. 'He refused to say what would happen to the six and a half million Israeli Jews,' recalled Arkush. 'That didn't seem to trouble him.' He also drew attention to an inconsistency: 'You've said that you believe in the two-state solution. That means you're a Zionist.' Corbyn looked shocked, but said nothing. 'Zionism,' Arkush continued, 'is nothing more than the UN's fundamental right of people to self-determination.' In the exchange that followed, he noticed how, sitting with his head cupped in his hands, Corbyn appeared 'bored, uninterested and condescending. He could not articulate any defence of ideological points of view, but he was going to hang on to them. He would not accept the legitimacy of the other side of the argument.'

Arkush's thoughts were interrupted by Milne, who declared: 'Israel is an example of ethnic cleansing. Israel was born in bloodshed in 1948.' Labour, he implied, would not accept Israel's right to exist. There would be no compromise. Corbyn nodded his agreement. Arkush was shocked. 'Any definition of anti-Semitism must cover the slur that the creation of Israel was a racist project,' he said. How, he wondered, would Jennie Formby respond to Milne's outburst.

Formby interrupted Arkush before he had an opportunity to ask that question. Two weeks earlier she had fired John Stolliday, the head of the NEC's compliance unit responsible for rooting out anti-Semitism. His replacement, Gordon Nardell, a lawyer who had publicly denied the existence of anti-Semitism in the party, was an ally of Ken Livingstone, Jackie Walker and Ken Loach. Formby now went on to describe in endless detail Labour's process to investigate the charges. The Board of Deputies' delegation silently recognised that this was a ruse to take up the meeting's allotted time.

When she finally finished, her comments were ignored. Arkush looked at Corbyn: 'You need to take a personal lead to remove anti-Semitism.'

Milne interrupted. 'That's just what Jeremy has always done.'

'We don't want words. We want action,' said Arkush. Labour, he insisted, needed to endorse the internationally accepted definition of anti-Semitism by the IHRA, which included eleven examples. In 2016 the NEC had adopted the definition, but had deleted four of the examples, which Corbyn had demanded should be rephrased to suit his opinion. According to him, it was not anti-Semitic to accuse British Jews of dual loyalty – being more loyal to Israel than to Britain (which embraced the old allegation of Jews being members of a worldwide, super-national conspiracy). He also wanted the freedom to say that Israel was a racist endeavour because in his opinion it had been founded on the basis of race. Labour members, he believed, should be allowed to call Jews 'Zio' or 'Zionist Nazis', as long as their intent was not anti-Semitic. And it was justifiable to compare contemporary Israel's policies to Nazi Germany's.

'Labour only accepted the IHRA's definitions with qualifications,' explained Milne. The best they would do was to rely on Gordon Nardell to monitor the complaints.

'You cannot cherry-pick the definition,' replied Arkush, 'and say that some forms of anti-Semitism are permissible.'

They had reached a dead end. Corbyn failed to agree to any of their suggestions. 'Corbyn,' Arkush told his colleagues afterwards, 'has anti-Semitic views, but that does not mean he is anti-Semitic. He just has a blind spot about anti-Semitism.' Later he would acknowledge his mistake. There was no blind spot.

In a public statement, Corbyn described the meeting as 'positive and constructive'. The Board's spokesman called it 'a disappointing missed opportunity'. Labour's leader, he said, had failed to grasp that he not only had to 'build trust' with Jews, but bring about 'strong actions in order to bring about a deep cultural change in his supporters' attitude to Jews'.

Corbyn was not worried. The opinion polls showed little damage from the latest arguments. Three days later, he voiced no protest when his supporters harangued Ruth Smeeth after she gave evidence in a disciplinary hearing against Marc Wadsworth for his anti-Semitic outburst in 2016. Nor did he comment about the fact that she had to be protected by Labour MPs and peers as she left the building. He was focused on the council elections on 3 May, in which Labour was predicted to make huge gains. 'Tories are Bracing Themselves for Disaster in London' was the *Spectator*'s headline. 'Red London', pronounced the magazine, 'terrified' the Tories. The flagship Tory councils of Westminster, Wandsworth, and Kensington and Chelsea were expected to fall to Labour because of Grenfell Tower, Theresa May, Brexit, and Momentum's mass mobilisation of activists.

The polls were wrong. Labour failed to gain a single London council, and across the country the Tories lost only twenty-eight seats (mostly to the Lib Dems), while Labour gained just fifty-seven. Labour won just 35 per cent of the vote. There was talk of 'peak Corbyn'. Defeated Labour candidates blamed their leader's sophistry about Russia and the Salisbury attack, but most importantly his anti-Semitism.

But surrender to the Jewish demands was inconceivable. Although Corbyn had encouraged Ken Livingstone to resign from the party before he was expelled, and Christine Shawcroft had been persuaded to step down from the NEC, Gordon Nardell was not encouraged to hasten his inquiries. The wider public, Corbyn calculated, was not interested in a debate about the IHRA's guidelines. At a series of events during the early summer, the faithful reassured him of their loyalty. In Islington, party members cheered his thirty-fifth anniversary as their MP, and at a fundraiser organised by his wife for 'Justice for Mexico', his South American friends were oblivious to any problems. To an extent, so was Corbyn.

At the start of his act at the Mexican event, the alternative comedian Jeremy Hardy quipped, 'I've been a member of the Labour Party since 1980 – with just a short break between 1985 and 2015' – the sort of comment that went down well with a London audience.

Corbyn turned to a friend and asked, 'Why 1985?'

'That was the year the miners' strike ended, we lost the rate-capping campaign, a lot of strikes were crushed, and Kinnock attacked Militant.'

Corbyn nodded. His understanding of history remained vague. The highlight of the event was the auction, which included two autographed jars of Corbyn's home-made blackberry jam. They were sold for £55 and £75. In all, £750 was raised for the cause, which a friend called 'staggering'.

Corbyn's immediate problem, however, was that the Jewish community refused to return to its usual placidity. His insistence that he be free to say 'Zio', call Israel a Nazi-style racist state, and accuse them of disloyalty, continued to outrage British Jews. By 16 July, tensions were at breaking point. Labour MPs – both Jewish and non-Jewish – were incandescent about the anti-Semitism in Corbyn's office.

Margaret Hodge finally realised that her leader could not solve the problem of Labour's anti-Semitism, because he himself was the problem. Denying that truth had become pointless. Corbyn regarded British Jews as different from everyone else. His leadership had cast them as pariahs, making them unsafe in their own country. He had betrayed the reason she had joined Labour, the natural home for Jews to fight racism and intolerance. His rejection of the IHRA's guidelines was the final straw. Spotting him that afternoon in a Westminster corridor, the diminutive Hodge stood in his way.

'You're an anti-Semite and a racist,' she said to his face.

'I'm sorry you feel like that,' he replied in a flat tone.

'It's not what you say,' she continued, 'but what you do, and by your actions you have shown you are an anti-Semitic racist.'

This time he made no reply.

Elsewhere at Westminster, Ian Austin spied Ian Lavery, the party's chairman and a Corbyn loyalist. Austin, an intemperate man, was fuming as he approached him. Labour's failure to tackle anti-Semitism, he snarled at Lavery, was 'a bloody disgrace … The party has become a sewer.' Lavery reported the attack to Formby and Milne.

Milne insisted that Hodge and Austin should be disciplined – he would not tolerate criticism from Zionists. The usual websites echoed his anger with outbursts of indignation. 'Zionist agent Hodge' was accused of acting 'under orders from her paymasters in Israel', and of using the Holocaust as a 'weapon' against Corbyn. Unlike the party's nonchalance towards anti-Semites, retribution against Hodge and Austin was quick. Both received letters from Formby informing them that they would be formally investigated for breaking Labour's code of conduct. Milne hoped that they would be silenced, and possibly deselected.

For the Jewish community, the Rubicon had been crossed. On 25 July the three Jewish weekly newspapers published identical front pages: 'United We Stand'. A Corbyn government, all three declared, would pose an 'existential threat to Jewish life'. Since Corbyn became leader, 'the stain and shame of anti-Semitism has coursed through Her Majesty's Opposition'. Either Labour would accept the IHRA's definition, or the party would 'be seen by all decent people as a racist, anti-Semitic party'.

The battle lines had been drawn. John McDonnell blamed Hodge for 'a complete misinterpretation' of the NEC's rejection of the IHRA guidelines. 'She'll admit it,' he wrongly announced. 'She was angry, she lost her cool.' 'He's distorting the truth,' replied Hodge, recognising McDonnell's need to bury the problem. The left-wing musician Billy Bragg joined in. British Jews, he warned, had 'work to do to build trust' with the Labour Party. At an NEC meeting, Peter Willsman, a Momentum activist, accused Jewish 'Trump fanatics' of 'making up duff information' and fabricating claims of anti-Semitism 'without any evidence at all'.

One week later, the row exploded yet again when newspapers republished photographs showing Corbyn in 2014 at the 'Cemetery of the Martyrs of Palestine' in Tunis, standing near the mastermind of the murderous attack on Israeli athletes and officials at the 1972 Munich Olympics. 'I was present when [the wreath] was laid,' he said. 'I don't think I was involved.' He was paying his respects, he claimed, to 'a fitting memorial to everyone who has died in every terrorist incident everywhere, because we have to end it'. He seemed to have forgotten that the wreath was laid on the tombs of the PLO terrorists, not their victims. 'I don't share platforms with terrorists,' he added, belying the countless photographs of him alongside Irish and Palestinian murderers.

At this point, Len McCluskey – who would wave the Palestinian flag at the party conference – came to the rescue.

The Jews, he said, were to blame for everything. 'The more Corbyn has sought to build bridges,' he complained, 'the worse the rhetoric has become.' The Jews were 'refusing to take "yes" for an answer from Corbyn's commitments'. They had 'wildly exaggerated' everything, showing 'intransigent hostility and utter refusal to engage in a dialogue about building on what has been done and resolving outstanding difficulties'. They should 'abandon their truculent hostility, engage in dialogue and dial down the rhetoric'. McCluskey did not criticise Corbyn for refusing to accept the IHRA definition of anti-Semitism, but instead blamed Blairite MPs for seeking to weaken the party leader. Andrew Murray, now his chief of staff, would go further. A 'deep state' in Britain, he would claim, was working to prevent Corbyn becoming prime minister. Mark Serwotka fuelled the debate. Israel, he said, could have 'created a story that does not exist' about anti-Semitism in the party. Labour's leaders had adopted the centuries-old allegations against the Jews: conspiracies, disloyalty, distortion and dangerous.

Corbyn could not have anticipated the next blow. Just one week later, newspapers were sent a video of him speaking in 2013 at a meeting of the Palestinian Return Centre. The group, which was allied with Hamas, blamed the Jews for the Holocaust. At the meeting he had addressed the problem of British 'Zionists' criticising Manuel Hassassian, the Palestinian Authority's representative in Britain, who was in the audience. 'So clearly two problems,' he said. 'One is that they don't want to study history, and secondly, having lived in this country for a very long time, probably all their lives, they don't understand English irony either … so I think they need two lessons which we can help them with.' From his own mouth came the declaration that 'Zionists', alias Jews, were not genuinely British.

Amid the cacophony of outrage, no one was more virulent than Jonathan Sacks. Corbyn, he said, was an 'anti-Semite', a supporter of 'racists, terrorists and dealers of hate who want to kill Jews and remove Israel from the map'. The Labour leader's remarks were the 'most offensive' since Enoch Powell's 'Rivers of Blood' speech in 1968.

Corbyn's office openly mocked Sacks's comparison. The former chief rabbi, it was suggested, was just another wailing Jew. Disgusted, two days later Frank Field resigned the Labour whip. In his letter to Corbyn he blamed 'Labour's leadership becoming a force for anti-Semitism in British politics'. Corbyn was delighted. Ridding the party of Field had always been one of his aims. The next to be toppled was Joan Ryan, the MP for Enfield North, after she criticised Corbyn's failure to tackle anti-Semitism. Her defeat in a vote at her constituency was filmed and broadcast by Press TV, Corbyn's Iranian outlet. For some Labour MPs this was too much. 'Call off the dogs,' Chuka Umunna told Corbyn, who he blamed for turning Labour into an institutionally racist organisation.

Corbyn was as unapologetic as ever, using the recent killings of over 160 Palestinian protesters, including children, by Israeli soldiers on the Gaza border to justify his anger. He arrived at the decisive NEC meeting on 4 September, which had been called to decide whether Labour would accept all the IHRA guidelines. Clutching a five-hundred-word statement approved by Milne, Corbyn argued for nearly three hours that he should be allowed to say that Israel was a racist state without being accused of being an anti-Semite. McDonnell and union leaders agreed with him, but refused to sacrifice a possible general election victory to a matter of principle. Speaking as if an election were imminent and victory inevitable, McDonnell resisted Corbyn's arguments. 'We've got to speak as if we're going into government,' he repeated. 'We've got to take ourselves seriously, and can't have this row going on any more.'

Worn down by the opposition, Corbyn eventually relented, and agreed that Labour would accept the full IHRA definition. The party dropped the disciplinary proceedings against Margaret Hodge, albeit the announcement inaccurately asserted that she had apologised. To draw a line under the dispute, Corbyn agreed to appeal to the Jewish community at the party's annual conference in Liverpool.

At that conference, the moderate MP Stella Creasy took a swipe at her leader. Addressing the Jewish Labour Movement, she said, 'I was going to start with a joke about what it must feel like to be a Jew in the Labour Party. But somebody told me you guys don't get irony.'

17

Resurrection

Liverpool, 25 September 2018: the four hundred Palestinian flags waving over the heads of the packed conference centre confirmed Corbyn's victory. After years of struggle and humiliation, the Labour Party was firmly under his control. Over three days, the 1,300 delegates in the hall endorsed their leader's left-wing policies. Even their profound division over Brexit had passed without the emotional explosions that had embittered the ideological battles of previous decades. The delegates understood that election victory required the image of unity, and also a collusion to obscure the proposed seizure of private wealth. The word 'socialism' was barely uttered in front of the television cameras by either Corbyn or McDonnell. In his speech to the delegates, the shadow chancellor introduced the dictatorship of the proletariat under the banner of 'industrial democracy'. He proposed to confiscate 10 per cent of all private businesses with over 250 employees from the owners or shareholders. This was presented as 'mainstream' and 'common sense'. Eventually, all those enterprises would be owned and managed by the workers. By then, McDonnell's ambition to replicate Hugo Chávez's Venezuelan achievement in Britain would be fulfilled. Time, however, was short. At sixty-seven, he was impatient for an election and his arrival at No. 11 Downing Street as chancellor. 'I'm having to do all the hard things,' he had recently complained to aides beyond Corbyn's hearing. The atmosphere in Liverpool justified his sacrifice. Filled with confidence, at the end of his rousing speech he was unable to resist raising a clenched-fist salute – to a standing ovation.

The Trotskyist shadow chancellor had obeyed the ideologue's manual. Every defeat over the previous thirty years had been a reason to move on to the next challenge, until the unimaginable happened and the party had been captured. Ever tightening control, the purge – so often denied by Corbyn, McDonnell and McCluskey – had reached a new intensity. In Hampstead, Enfield, Lewisham, Hastings, Mansfield, Stoke and Brighton, moderate Labour MPs were under siege. The first stage was motions of no confidence; deselections would follow. Jon Lansman personally demanded expulsions in Ealing and Sheffield, and encouraged his team to complete the eviction of Frank Field, who had represented Birkenhead since 1979. In Haringey, members of Momentum intimidated the moderate councillors to succumb to a 'democracy review'. Claire Kober, the borough's popular Labour leader, resigned after ten years because the activists' anti-Semitism and misogyny, she said, 'got too much'. Richard Horton, the chairman of Haringey's Stroud Green branch, complained of aggressive Marxists who, in the name of democracy, pursued 'a narrow sectarian view of what the Labour Party should be which was destroying my mental health and damaging my family life'. He too departed. Laura Parker, Momentum's national coordinator, made the movement's intentions clear to MPs who supported the government on Brexit. 'There is no room for Labour MPs,' she said, 'who sided with the reactionary Tory establishment.'

A slew of other Members – all critics of Corbyn – were suspended from the parliamentary party for alleged sexual misconduct. John Woodcock was accused of sending 'inappropriate texts' to a former employee, a charge he strenuously denied. After seeing that the disciplinary proceedings were rigged against him, he resigned from the party but remained an MP.

His fate was markedly different from that of Leicester East MP Keith Vaz, a friend of Corbyn's. As chairman of the Commons Home Affairs Committee, Vaz was renowned for his tough questions to public figures about their moral conduct – this, despite his own suspension from the Commons in 2000 for dishonesty. In 2016, a further cover-up was exposed by the *Mirror* – he had been secretly filmed discussing drugs to enhance sexual performance with Romanian male prostitutes. The video showed Vaz offering to pay for cocaine before having sex with the men. 'Well, he hasn't committed any crime that I know of,' Corbyn said, dismissing the incident as 'a private matter'. Vaz escaped formal investigation of his behaviour for 'health reasons'. Thus were Corbyn's old allies protected and moderates crushed. The Liverpool Trotskyist Derek Hatton was readmitted to the party, while Owen Smith was fired from the shadow cabinet after he called for a second referendum, a policy supported by Keir Starmer, Labour's Brexit spokesman.

Radical democracy, however, had limits. The battle for control within Labour was as old as the socialist movement, having started in the nineteenth century with Marx, Lenin and their opponents. The lesson taught by the Bolsheviks was to promise empowerment to the grassroots – but only after the revolution was completed. For Corbyn, the next step was to force Iain McNicol out of office. As the person controlling the party's membership, selection of MPs, and discipline and finance, McNicol was blocking the left's final triumph. The bastion fell after the NEC elections in January 2018. Three new hard-left candidates won places, giving Corbyn control of the majority of votes. Soon after, McNicol meekly tendered his resignation, with a promise of silence in exchange for a peerage.

The departure of the moderates' last defender prompted Jon Lansman to bid to become McNicol's successor. Ironically, even he did not understand the nature of what was being plotted, Labour's Godfather was not Momentum's creator, but Len McCluskey. The union leader demanded that Jennie Formby, now his former partner, replace McNicol. Meekly, Corbyn acquiesced and Lansman surrendered. Unite's control of Labour tightened. Admission to the party, the selection of MPs, and the composition of election manifestos all now fell under Formby and McCluskey.

The conspirators skilfully confused the opposition. Like McDonnell, Lansman presented himself at the party conference as a 'social capitalist', a sham phrase designed to give the impression that a Trotskyist could work with capitalists for society's benefit. In a speech to a fringe meeting of 'Labour Business', Lansman boasted to an audience of sixty businessmen about his childhood involvement in his grandparents' East End rag-trade business, his family's property investments, and, to gild the fantasy, his 'commercial genius' in creating Momentum as 'a start-up business'. Momentum, he said, 'wants to work with business'.

None of his audience, mostly low-level managers of small businesses and local entrepreneurs, appeared to realise that this apparently sympathetic organisation was a Trotskyist group. They applauded Lansman with the same conviction which minutes earlier they had shown when McDonnell had delivered the same message: businessmen and the City had nothing to fear from a Corbyn government. 'We want to work with you,' he said. Amid the beauty of Liverpool's regenerated docklands, the audience had seemingly forgotten that the Titan city of the nineteenth century had been destroyed by Marxist-led strikes after 1945, then wrecked again during the 1980s by the Labour council whose deputy leader was McDonnell's ally Derek Hatton. The city had been rebuilt by the arch-capitalist Michael Heseltine, but it remained a shadow of its past imperial self. They also appeared not to realise that thirty-two years previously Hatton had been expelled from the Labour Party for demanding the same Marxist agenda as McDonnell was presenting in 2018.

That evening, at the Pullman Hotel inside the conference centre, Milne and others were polishing Corbyn's speech for the following day. They decided that his approach had to be less doctrinaire than McDonnell's. To Labour's misfortune, the government's official statistics showed that both household incomes and employment had hit record highs, pensioner poverty was decreasing, and ever more young people were entering higher education. Attempting to outbid the government would barely generate favourable headlines, but that was less relevant than restoring Corbyn's reputation. An insurrection against his anti-Semitism by party members during the summer had dented his celebrated authenticity.

To end months of turmoil, he agreed to bite the bullet. Milne would insert into his speech a substantial passage appealing to Jews to treat Labour as 'your ally'. Corbyn would admit that anti-Semitism had caused 'immense hurt and anxiety in the Jewish community and great dismay in the Labour Party'. That would be the limit of his olive branch: just a few twigs. Unyielding as ever, he would not admit to one truth: that his fate depended on overcoming the serious doubts raised during the preceding months about his character and political values. There would be no specific apology, but an appeal to 'draw a line under the issue'.

That same evening, ninety people crammed into a small room in the conference centre for a meeting hosted by the Holocaust Educational Trust. Protected by two heavily armed policemen in the corridor outside, they would be unimpressed by Corbyn's appeal, especially Luciana Berger, who in her address described the vindictive abuse directed at her by party members. After recalling Labour's anti-Semitic hatred in 2018 she introduced the eighty-eight-year-old Susan Pollack. Seventy-four years previously, like 424,000 other Hungarian Jews, Pollack had been transported in a railway cattle truck to Auschwitz. Unlike her parents, the attractive teenager was spared an immediate death in the gas chambers. For months she watched the smoke pour from the chimneys of the four crematoria: evidence of the incineration of five thousand Jews every day – a fact disputed by Paul Eisen and the other Holocaust deniers with whom Corbyn willingly associated.

The mass deportation of Hungary's Jews in which Pollack had been ensnared in 1944 had been masterminded by Adolf Eichmann, one of the architects of the Holocaust. Over lunch in Budapest's Astoria Hotel, Eichmann had boasted to SS major Wilhelm Hoettl that rounding up and murdering Hungary's Jews in just eight weeks would rank among the Final Solution's most efficient operations, albeit by that stage of the war Germany's ultimate defeat had become inevitable.

'How many Jews have we killed in total?' Hoettl casually asked.

'Including this lot,' replied Eichmann after a moment's calculation, 'six million.' Staggered by that number, Hoettl would cite the conversation during his testimony at the Allies' trial of leading Nazis for war crimes in Nuremberg the following year. Incriminating his former superiors, the unrepentant Hoettl had correctly calculated, would save his life. By sheer chance, Susan Pollack had not been one of the six million.

Her ordeal had ended at Bergen-Belsen. As the end of the war approached, with the Red Army nearing Auschwitz, many of the surviving inmates had been force-marched to Germany. 'A British soldier saved me,' she told her audience. 'They had just liberated the camp. He lifted me up and fed me. One more night and I would have been dead.' One of her listeners asked her for her thoughts on Corbyn's attitude towards Jews. 'I say to Mr Corbyn,' she replied, '"Stop the anti-Semitism."' Her audience, bruised by the revelations of the previous months, could only murmur their agreement. Not one of Corbyn's circle heard Pollack deliver her account, which had been allocated a slot at 8.30 p.m., at the very end of the conference's fringe events.

Twenty minutes after that meeting, just outside the conference centre, Corbyn was walking down a curved staircase onto the packed dance floor of the Revolución de Cuba restaurant, the venue for the annual *Daily Mirror* conference party. Loudspeakers blared 'Ooooh Jeremy Corbyn'. On a TV screen, a loop replayed Theresa May's robotic 'dancing' on her recent trip to Africa. Less than two minutes later, Corbyn left the restaurant. His short address to the *Mirror* journalists and other guests was limited to a familiar pledge to make Britain 'fairer and more equal'. Nothing more. He did not mention the threats he would make to the media in his speech the following day. 'Here, a free press has far too often meant the freedom to spread lies and half-truths,' he would say, 'and to smear the powerless, not take on the powerful.' He would blame 'the billionaires who own the bulk of the British press [and who] don't like us one little bit. No, it could be because we're going to clamp down on tax dodging. Or it may be because we don't fawn over them at white-tie dinners and cocktail parties.' He suppressed his anger about the media's criticism of himself, and in particular that summer's condemnation of his anti-Semitism.

The following day, Corbyn's pledge to Britain's Jews was received by the delegates with a sprinkle of unenthusiastic clapping. His animated pledge to the conference a few minutes later justified their scepticism. On appointment as prime minister, he promised, he would instantly recognise the Palestinian state. Wild cheers greeted those words, despite the fact that there was no such entity.

In the hours after his speech, the opprobrium that had dogged Corbyn since early March 2018 subsided. Against the odds, the conference had been a success. As a man of principle, he hated compromise and surrender. He had lost the Jewish vote, but the sea of Palestinian flags waving in the conference hall represented a far bigger constituency. The incalculable question was whether he could fully recover from the summer's setbacks. The Tories, despite their civil war over Brexit, remained 4 per cent ahead in the polls, with Theresa May's personal ratings still substantially higher than his.

On his way back to London from Liverpool, Virgin's trains were running nearly ninety minutes late, the result of faulty signals. Those delays, tweeted Corbyn confidently, would not happen once the railways were nationalised. The question was whether he realised that Network Rail, responsible for signalling, was already a nationalised business.

Over the following weeks, Theresa May led Conservative Party members into open warfare among themselves. In her customary secretive manner, reflecting her insecurity, she had put together a withdrawal deal from the EU without sensitively negotiating the crucial terms with the Brexiteers or Remainers in her own party, or consulting the DUP about the 'backstop' – to prevent the imposition of a 'hard' border between Northern Ireland and the Irish Republic – even though her government depended on the Ulster Protestants for a majority in the

Commons. Neither strong nor stable, May led an irretrievably split cabinet as she approached the 'meaningful vote' in the House of Commons on 11 December to secure Parliament's approval for the agreement. She faced certain defeat, an abyss she refused to acknowledge. The alternative to her deal was either a hard Brexit or remaining in the EU. Every option offered either chaos or humiliation.

Daily, the spectacle of a prime minister tossed around by a rabble of Tories deadlocked about the nation's fate allowed Corbyn to ridicule 'a shambolic government'. Few disagreed with him. His tactics, agreed with McDonnell and Milne, were to sit tight, waiting for the Tories to make a fatal mistake, and meanwhile to urge the electorate to focus on the catastrophic mess created by extremist Tories blind to the country's social and economic problems. Once the government had self-destructed, Corbyn's team calculated, Labour would step forward as the nation's saviour. As the seventeenth-century English poet John Dryden warned in his great political poem 'Absalom and Achitophel', 'Beware the fury of a patient man.'

But patience, many Labour MP's believed, was a strategy mired by contradictions. Corbyn's preference for leaving the EU was opposed by the majority of his party – both MPs and the membership, which favoured a second referendum. To avoid losing support, he called for a general election, and only if that failed, a second referendum to oppose the solution to the impasse. Unable to agree a consistent policy, he also floundered when he spoke about his pledge to renegotiate May's deal, admitting that he had not actually read the 585-page draft agreement. Since all the EU leaders had pronounced that the deal had been finalised, and could not be renegotiated, his boast about his ability both to negotiate an exit from the EU and simultaneously to enable Britain to remain in the customs union and the single market lacked conviction. The recitation by the party's front-bench spokesmen of those unrealistic demands did not enhance Labour's credibility as an alternative government, and May retained a 10 per cent lead over Corbyn in the opinion polls. And yet, if the Brexit imbroglio was put aside, the undertaking by Corbyn and McDonnell to control capitalism's excesses and failures resonated among the young, and even among some middle-class Tories outraged by their party's fratricidal warfare and disgusted by its silence about the nation's poor and uneducated.

On Monday, 10 December, the Tories moved one step closer to self-destruction. Faced by certain defeat in the Commons over her deal with the EU the following day because of fears that the 'backstop' would sacrifice Britain's sovereignty in perpetuity, Theresa May postponed the 'meaningful vote' until January 2019. Two days later, over forty-eight Tory Brexiteers formally challenged her leadership, accusing her of having botched the withdrawal negotiations from the outset, and prompting a vote on her position. By 9 o'clock that evening, she would know whether her premiership was over.

Soon after making a defiant statement outside 10 Downing Street, May headed to the Commons for the weekly prime minister's questions. Corbyn was waiting. Facing each other across the dispatch box were two similar politicians – both stubborn, and deaf to all voices bar those of a coterie of trusted advisers. In such a political crisis, a divided British minority government might expect to be dealt a mortal blow by the leader of the opposition, followed by a successful vote of no confidence and a change of government. Corbyn's strength was the apparent unity of his backbenchers. Most of the 172 rebel Labour MPs had buried their animosity so as to avoid being held responsible for sabotaging the prospect of a Labour government. Even mainstream social democrats had given up the fight. The party's new rules, they knew, made the left impregnable. Corbyn's Labour was the only alternative to the Tories. However, a new weakness had emerged. A great deal depended on Corbyn's performance, yet in the days before the vote he addressed no public meetings and gave no TV interviews. Except for prime minister's questions, he had rarely spoken in public, prompting wild speculation among some Tories that he was seriously ill.

In the event, Corbyn's animated anger as he read out his

prepared questions to May dispelled the gossip, but singularly failed to deliver the mortal blow. The wounded premier's confident responses flummoxed him. His moment was lost. Eight hours later, having promised to resign before the next general election, May secured a victory of sorts. In the party's leadership election, two hundred Tory MPs voted in her favour, while 117 called for her resignation. It might have been expected that the opposition of about 40 per cent of her own MPs should have ousted May. Her fate depended on Corbyn tempting the DUP and Brexiteer Tories to support a motion of no confidence in the government, triggering a general election.

The scenario was not altogether fanciful.

For weeks, some extreme Tory Brexiteers, fearful of the referendum result being reversed, had become tempted to join Corbyn in voting against their own government. Not only had May signed the 'backstop' against official advice and without consulting the DUP, but she had botched the 2017 general election, failed to achieve any social reforms, and clearly lacked the imagination and character required of a successful leader. The DUP, with good reason to distrust her, were also pledged to vote against May.

Their combined inclination to turn on the prime minister was upended by Corbyn himself. First, he refused once again to negotiate with his opponents. Hatred suffocated his own self-interest. Second, in an attempt to seduce floating voters, John McDonnell had tried to mitigate his own promise of 'irresistible change' by mouthing soothing platitudes about cooperating with industry and supporting the government's tax cuts for the middle class. To McDonnell's frustration, Corbyn refused to kick the ball into an open goal. Rather than obfuscate for political advantage, and so grab power, he reasserted Labour's ideological purity. There could be no tax cuts, he insisted, until the welfare benefits freeze was removed. McDonnell was left fuming, wondering whether Corbyn wanted to be prime minister at all. But even he could not avoid revealing his own Trotskyist beliefs. In the midst of the Tories' crisis, he pledged to legalise sympathy strikes by British workers for any cause in the world, guaranteeing a return to the industrial anarchy of the 1979 'winter of discontent'. Wavering Tory Brexiteers were shocked by the Labour leaders' unvarnished commitment to communism. Any ideas of supporting Corbyn so as to save Brexit disappeared, at least for the moment.

On 19 December, Corbyn's dilemma was exposed. Urged by his party to initiate a vote of no confidence in the government, he resisted because he knew that after a government victory he would be under pressure to push for a second referendum, which he opposed – as did May, who was desperate to retain the loyalty of Brexit voters. Neither leader would openly declare on which side they would campaign in a second vote. Corbyn dithered for hours, until his advisers produced a solution. He should table a vote of no confidence in May personally for delaying the 'meaningful vote'. Only the far-left activists in Corbyn's office, dismissive of parliamentary procedure, could have failed to ascertain that the speaker would refuse to call a motion which lacked any constitutional importance. Mocked by his own MPs for his indecision, and by May for backing a 'stunt', he faced a boisterous prime minister in the Commons.

'I have to say,' declared May, looking at Corbyn with a glint in her eye, 'that it is a bit rich for the Right Honourable Gentleman to stand there and talk about [the government's] dithering. Let us see what the Labour Party did this week. They said they would call a vote of no confidence, and then they said they would not. Then they did it, but it was not effective. I know it is the Christmas season and the pantomime season, but what do we see from the Labour front bench and the leader of the opposition?' With that she launched into comic mockery before snapping at Corbyn, 'Look behind you. They are not impressed, and neither is the country.'

Furious as usual about any criticism from a Tory, Corbyn glared angrily at May and mouthed the words 'Stupid woman.' The government benches erupted. Four hours later, at the very same time as Fiona Onasanya, the Labour MP for Peterborough, was convicted for persistently lying to avoid a speeding ticket, he returned to the Commons to claim that he had said 'Stupid people,' and not 'Stupid woman.' The contrary judgement by professional lip-readers, he implied, was wrong. To divert attention from this latest fiasco, he announced the next day in an interview in the *Guardian* that he supported Brexit and opposed a second referendum. With that shot, the majority of Labour MPs became targets of Tory remainers urging them to unite with them to defeat both May and their own leader, and to prevent Brexit.

The nation entered the new year of 2019 amid unprecedented uncertainty. Both major parties, led by their extremist wings, were promising to make Britain poorer. Yet the divisive argument over Brexit, which was disrupting relationships in families and between friends, was being conducted in the best tradition of British democracy – without riots or bloodshed. History suggested that, eventually, a solution would be forged and the nation would be reconciled. But that seems far off at the time that this narrative reaches its end on 4 January.

At the beginning of 2019, nobody knew how long Theresa May would be able to survive as prime minister, what would follow the defeat of her deal in the 'meaningful vote' in mid-January, and whether the Commons would take control by voting for a second referendum and thereby delaying, or even overturning, Britain's exit from the EU. Alternatively, faced by May's resolution to crash out of the EU without a deal if her agreement was rejected, would the EU give way in the hope of avoiding chaos in Europe, and agree to a fixed time limit on the 'backstop'?

The only certainty was Jeremy Corbyn's patient expectation of the Tory Party's self-destruction. On the edge of a historical breakthrough, he believed that he would witness the end of liberalism and capitalism in Britain, and lead his followers to the red dawn of a new era. If he was successful, future generations of British schoolchildren would learn to hail Corbyn, The Leader and The Hero.

Two years earlier, Corbyn had named Oscar Wilde's 'The Ballad of Reading Gaol' as his favourite poem. His enthusiasm for it was dubious, not least because Wilde himself was no believer in socialism.

> He walked amongst the Trial Men
> In a suit of shabby grey;
> A cricket cap was on his head,
> And his step seemed light and gay;
> But I never saw a man who looked
> So wistfully at the day ...
>
> So with curious eyes and sick surmise
> We watched him day by day,
> And wondered if each one of us
> Would end the self-same way,
> For none can tell to what red Hell
> His sightless soul may stray.

Acknowledgements

This book was written more out of a mission than out of love. Faced by a warring Tory Party, Britain would normally switch to the opposition for a sane administration. Indeed, the country's democracy requires regular changes of governing parties. Unusually, at the present time that automatic move has been stalled by Labour's leader and his associates. Jeremy Corbyn's lifelong rebellion arouses disquiet. That concern is magnified by his concealment about his past and his directive to close associates to refuse to help journalists and authors to understand it. Similar orders have been issued by John McDonnell and others in their tight circle. Tolerating a smokescreen put up by those who seek to become Britain's rulers is unacceptable. I therefore set out to discover whether Corbyn's own version of his life is accurate, and, equally important, what principles he would apply to what he and McDonnell have pledged themselves to achieve in government – 'the irreversible change of Britain'.

Undoubtedly, many Britons share Corbyn's ideals. They long to live in a truly socialist or communist society. Others, namely the floating voters and the young, may well be attracted by those values if only to be rid of the fractious Tories. The question is, what will be the real outcome of Labour's government under Corbyn and McDonnell?

In setting out to discover the truth about Jeremy Corbyn, no author could succeed without the generous help of many people, especially those who have been close to him over the past fifty years. Fortunately, many of them gave me their insights and recalled their eyewitness experiences. As usual, so many wanted to remain off the record that I decided it was best not to reveal any sources. The text often makes the source clear, and on those occasions where it obfuscates the truth, that is intentional. I have also not acknowledged all those people individually here. For legal reasons, it was also deemed best not to reveal other sources, so unusually the book has no references.

Among those I can name, my principal debt is to Claudia Wordsworth for her remarkable research. Perceptive and brilliantly persistent, she delivered nuggets of gold. She is a true ally. I am also grateful for research to Janis Finch, Sarah Fletcher and Andy Kyle.

Among those who can be named for giving me help I am grateful to David Blackburn, Janet Daley, Liz Davies, Andrew Gilligan, Miriam Gross, Mark Hollingsworth, Andrew Hosken, Tim Rayment, David Rich, Daniela Richterova and Katerina Saturova.

My books always rely on the best lawyers, and for that I am indebted to Tom Jarvis and Simon Dowson-Collins at HarperCollins, and to David Hirst.

I owe a lot to Richard Cohen, a valuable partner, for his outstanding editing, and then to Robert Lacey, a legendary editor at HarperCollins, for his meticulous work. Also at HarperCollins I am grateful for the enthusiastic support of Arabella Pike, my editor, and Katherine Patrick, my publicist.

The steadfast rocks on whom I always depend are Jonathan Lloyd, my long-time agent at Curtis Brown, and the most important, Veronica. This book could not have been written without their support. I am really grateful.

I consulted many books, but the most relevant from which I drew information and have quoted are:

Tony Benn, *Free at Last!: Diaries 1991–2001* (Hutchinson, 2002)

Tom Bower, *Broken Vows: Tony Blair – The Tragedy of Power* (Faber & Faber, 2016)

David Hirsh, *Contemporary Left Antisemitism* (Routledge, 2017)

Andrew Hosken, *Ken: The Ups and Downs of Ken Livingstone* (Arcadia, 2008)

Seumas Milne, *The Revenge of History: The Battle for the Twenty-First Century* (Verso, 2012)

Charles Moore, *Thatcher: The Authorized Biography, Vol. II – Everything She Wants* (Penguin, 2015)

Rosa Prince, *Comrade Corbyn: A Very Unlikely Coup – How Jeremy Corbyn Stormed to the Labour Leadership* (Biteback, 2016; revised edn, 2018)

Dave Rich, *The Left's Jewish Problem: Jeremy Corbyn, Israel and Anti-Semitism* (Biteback, 2018)

Tim Shipman, *All Out War: The Full Story of Brexit* (William Collins, 2016)

Francis Wheen, *Strange Days Indeed: The Golden Age of Paranoia* (Fourth Estate, 2008)

Philip Ziegler, *Edward Heath: The Authorised Biography* (HarperPress, 2010)

Philip Ziegler, *Wilson: The Authorised Life* (Weidenfeld & Nicolson, 1993)

Index